The Way of Agape

by

Chuck & Nancy Missler

KHW

The King's *High* Way Ministries, Inc.

The Way of Agape

© Copyright 1994 by Nancy Missler

Twelfth Printing, April 2005

Published by The King's High Way Ministries, Inc.
P.O. Box 3111
Coeur d'Alene, ID 83816
www.kingshighway.org

ISBN 0-9752534-0-9

All Scripture quotations are from the King James Version of the Holy Bible.

Cover design by David Clemons, Coeur d'Alene, Idaho

PRINTED IN THE UNITED STATES OF AMERICA

"Thou shalt love the Lord thy God with all thy heart, and with all thy soul, and with all thy mind. This is the first and great commandment. And the second is like unto it, Thou shalt love thy neighbor as thyself."

Matthew 22:37-39

Table of Contents

"By this shall all men know that ye are My disciples, if ye have Love (*Agape*) one to another."

John 13:35

Section One

"Blessed be God, even the Father of our Lord Jesus Christ, the Father of mercies, and the God of all comfort; Who comforteth us in all our tribulation, that we may be able to comfort them which are in any trouble, by the comfort wherewith we ourselves are comforted of God."

2 Corinthians 1:3-4

Chapter 1: The Flight of the Phoenix

I probably should never have married.

No one deserves to be put through what my wife, Nan, has had to endure. Although I married the most fabulous gal in the world, I spent several decades taking it all for granted. I discovered early that I was gifted, and I somehow always seemed to be at the right place at the right time, so I have enjoyed a spectacular, rewarding career. That was the problem.

We have lived an incredibly adventurous life. We have made—and lost—many millions. We have "done" almost everything that life has to offer. It seemed to be a fabulous adventure, indeed.

However, my family was something I presumed upon, rather than invested in. We have lived in 25 homes in our 38 years of marriage. And, like so many lives—Christians included—we were beautiful on the outside, but a real mess on the inside. Our marriage was essentially on the rocks, a tragic and characteristic example of our times.

But the incredible lessons that God taught Nan saved our marriage. My wife's diligence to ferret out the Scriptural basis for the amazing discoveries she has made resulted in studies that have blessed millions of lives and marriages all over the world. This is really her story.

She will present the solution.

I was the major part of the problem. But let me go back to the beginning.

The Early Years

I was reared in southern California by German parents. In fact, I can remember their getting their citizenship papers during my pre-school years. I came late in their lives and grew up in a very supportive home.

I was always somewhat of a "nerd." My unusual aptitude for technical things was to impact my entire life. I was a radio ham at the age of nine (W6OHD) and I started flying airplanes during my teens. When other guys were "hopping up" cars in high school, I was building a digital computer in my garage. That was in the late 40s, *very* early in the computer game!

A double major (math-science) in high school set me up to pursue a Ph.D. in Electrical Engineering at Stanford when I received a congressional appointment to the United States Naval Academy at Annapolis. This was one of the best things that could have happened to me. Initially attracted by the glamour of it all, it broadened my horizons and gave me an appetite for adventure which I have never lost. I graduated with honors and took my commission in the Air Force. This was before the Air Force Academy existed: a small percentage of both West Point and Annapolis graduates could elect an Air Force commission, a highly desirable option in those days. Participating in flight training and then the missile program, I eventually was a branch chief of the Department of Guided Missiles when I left the service and entered an industrial career.

I became a systems engineer at TRW, then a senior analyst with a non-profit "think tank" doing a variety of deep projects for the intelligence community and the Department of Defense.

Along the way I earned a Masters Degree from UCLA in engineering, supplementing previous graduate work in applied mathematics, advanced statistics, and the information sciences.

The Management Challenge

A major management opportunity occurred when Ford Motor Company recruited me. Lee Iacocca was attempting to deepen and broaden the company's senior management and was seeking to add a generalist from a non-automotive technical background. At first I really wasn't interested and that turned out to be precisely the posture to get spoiled rotten. When a $20 billion multinational corporation decides to flex its muscles it usually turns out to be exciting. I was on private salary roll in Dearborn for six years in a variety of senior positions. These were the days (1963-1968) that Ford was a remarkably creative place to work: we introduced the Mustang and the Twin-I-Beam truck as products, and introduced to the industry advanced techniques—computer graphics, information networks, and numerically controlled machining. I also had the opportunity to establish the first international computer network.

The Dearborn years were highly rewarding in many ways, but I eventually left Ford to start my first company on my own. It was a computer network firm that was subsequently acquired by Automatic Data Processing (NYSE) to become its Network Services Division.

The Corporate Development Years

Returning to California, I found myself consulting, organizing corporate development "deals," serving on a number of boards of directors, and eventually specializing in rescuing troubled technology companies.

If a normal company gets into trouble, well-established "turnaround" specialists can come in, restructure the balance sheet, hire professionals, and move on. A high technology company, however, really has no balance sheet: its assets are mainly know-how, intellectual property, and people. The most important assets leave the company each evening! Rescuing a high technology company requires a different approach. As an engineer by training (and a promoter by temperament), I found that I seemed to be a "one-eyed man in the land of the blind." It was challenging, very rewarding, and great fun.

Over the past 25 years I have served on the boards of directors of over a dozen public companies and was the chairman and chief executive officer of six of them. I have taken half a dozen companies out of Chapter 11, and found that I thrived on the high risk, "improbable" situations.

A few fortunate successes in the early years established my credibility with major creditors—the critical credential in entering a troubled situation. Chase Manhattan Bank asked me to step into a laser memory company in Silicon Valley that was in Chapter 11 and we were able to achieve some surprising results. First Interstate Bank then invited me to take on Western Digital Corporation, also in Chapter 11, and viewed by the semiconductor industry as obsolete, undercapitalized, and hopeless. Western Digital was probably the most conspicuous challenge of all and yet is now a Fortune 500 company on the New York Stock Exchange.

But there was another dimension to our life that was to prove vastly more significant.

My Special "Hobby"

I had developed a love for the Bible even before the age of ten. I made my decision for Christ in my teen years. I then spent over 40 years deepening my studies of the Bible as my primary "hobby." Even at the Naval Academy, I participated in pre-reveille Bible studies and other Christian activities. For the past 20 years I have taught Bible studies at Calvary Chapel in Costa Mesa, California. The pressure of a substantial weekly audience kept me seriously in the Word of God, preparing and researching, without which the intense pressures of my business life would probably have made a casualty of my study time.

During those years, I took myself *very* seriously as an executive, but I never took myself seriously as a Bible teacher. The study of the Bible was simply something I just loved to do for its own sake. Little did I realize that the Lord had other plans.

My Day of Reckoning

A few years ago, as a result of a merger, I found myself as chairman and major shareholder of a small publicly-owned development company known as the Phoenix Group International.

When we took Western Digital out of Chapter 11, I had developed a special management award known as the "Phoenix Trophy." The phoenix was a legendary bird that emerged from its own ashes, and we felt this was an appropriate symbol to honor the key managers who had "resurrected" the company. When we reorganized this later venture dedicated to undertaking similar challenges, it again seemed to be the appropriate corporate symbol. (We should have researched the legend more thoroughly: the legendary phoenix was also *consumed in flames* every five centuries!)

Through some very unusual circumstances, we were granted the opportunity to establish a large joint venture ($8 billion!) with the Soviet Union to supply personal computers to their 143,000 schools.

Instead of simply proposing to supply them with products, we had submitted a detailed plan to assist them in developing their own capabilities. We were also willing to deal in "counter trade" since the Russians' access to hard currency was severely limited.

After we were awarded the relationship, the Russians pointed out at a press conference in New York that 16 companies from seven countries had been competing for this opportunity for the previous three years. If I had known that beforehand, I wouldn't have even tried to compete.

The announcement opened doors around the world. The deal was unusually complex since it dealt largely with counter trade: it required the three-way transfer of commodities instead of cash. We were in the process of organizing a major financing with both European and Asian participants. It all looked very exciting, albeit quite risky.

At home in Orange County, the local press did their best to disparage the deal. They even attempted to interfere with our negotiations.

In my characteristic enthusiasm, I put everything I had into the program, including guaranteeing bank loans to the corporation, etc. Like the apostle Peter, I was always long on action and short on caution. (My Jewish friends have explained to me what a guarantor is: that's "a schmuck with a pen.")

Well, we went down. Down big. We lost everything. Our "ultimate" home, everything. There were many reasons: the slanderous attack by the local press; a breach of trust by some of the officers; the ineffectual performance of "old friends"; an unfortunate choice of investment bankers, etc. But it was entirely my responsibility, and I got what I deserved. There are very few mistakes I've missed.

We ultimately had to put the Phoenix Group into Chapter Seven. Most of the invested capital was my own, but there were other investors who also lost significant investments.

Had I stayed in the "corporate development" field, I probably would have subsequently bounced back: that's the game. You're up; you're down; then you're up again. It's all part of a "deal-maker's" life, but the Lord had other plans.

Phase Two

In my "Biblical life," I have enjoyed wonderful sponsorship from Chuck Smith—my teacher, mentor, and close friend over these many years. His tutorship and his personal example have been among the most profound influences on my life. In my opinion, his philosophy of ministry is without equal. His emphasis on the study of the Word of God above all other things has made Calvary Chapel unique.

I have also enjoyed a close personal friendship with Hal Lindsey. Although he was chosen as *"Author of the Decade in Non-fiction"* by the New York Times, to me Hal was just a mischief-making buddy for over 20 years.

When Hal heard that I was "down," he immediately dropped everything and came alongside and, if I might indulge in an indelicate metaphor, planted his boot in my backside and suggested that perhaps the Lord was telling me to make my "hobby" my *profession*. He pointed out to me that with my apparent personal following (from the 20 years of teaching and the subsequent distribution of the resulting cassette tapes) I could easily make it as an independent author/speaker and could be doing full-time what I really enjoyed best. It was through his personal encouragement I decided to give it a serious try.

(I later discovered from Doug Wetmore, the head of the tape ministry of Firefighters for Christ, that I had almost seven million tapes scattered around the world.)

Koinonia House

Because I had organized "Koinonia House" as a small ministry many years earlier, it became my vehicle to develop a publishing ministry. The rest, as they say, is history.

We have focused our attention on the promotion of the serious study of the Bible through the creation, development, and distribution of materials intended to be provocative, stimulating, and helpful for Biblical study.

Through incredible worldwide encouragement, we now find ourselves in the most exciting adventure of all. We've never worked harder, never been poorer, but never been happier!

Lessons From the Valley of Despair

During our corporate years, I was totally consumed with my executive career. I was in an exciting, but demanding and competitive environment, frequently undertaking commitments that many knowledgeable experts felt just couldn't be done. That was part of the appeal, of course.

But the costs to my family were *severe.* My family—my beautiful wife and four wonderful kids—were the ones who paid the price. As a highly intensive, obsessively competitive and project oriented corporate "gladiator," I was totally insensitive to *their* needs. I looked to them for support rather than as the actual centroid of my life.

Unfortunately, that is also the common tragedy of most of my contemporaries in the executive suites of America.

The Ultimate Turnaround

Our marriage survived my abuse and neglect *through a miracle.* This miracle was accomplished through my incredible wife, Nancy. She unilaterally set an example and applied Scriptural principles in such a remarkable way that our marriage was set back on a proper track.

But that wasn't enough for her. As God moved in such a remarkable way in our personal lives, she steadfastly insisted on learning more and more of the *Biblical basis* for what was now beginning to turn our entire lives around.

(Remember, we were "practicing Christians" throughout these various escapades.)

From her research over a 15 year period, she developed a series of studies which have now been enjoyed all over the world through her personal appearances and through her well-known tape cassettes.

The Results

By discovering the real meaning of love—God's Love—and learning how to apply His ways in our day-to-day lives, God has wrought a miracle in our marriage, in our children, in our entire lives. The inevitable tensions are now dealt with on a Biblical basis and I am more in love than ever with this incredible woman. There's a predictable warmth and comfort in our home that was never there before.

God is not through with us yet! But what we have discovered has impacted so many lives that we felt we should try to summarize it in this book. Our prayer is that you will also find it edifying and helpful.

The amazing discoveries that God has revealed to us in our lives are really Nan's story. Let's let her tell it...

Chapter 2: Up in Flames

Eighteen years ago, Chuck and I had what seemed to most people a fairy tale life and a "perfect marriage."[1]

At this point, we had been married for about twenty years. Chuck was a successful business executive. We lived in a beautiful, sprawling, three-acre ranch house with pool, stables and guest quarters. We also had four gorgeous children, two boys and two girls. On the *outside* it looked like we had everything anyone could ever want.

But on the *inside* we were like so many others you see today; just existing—with no joy, love, meaning or real purpose in our lives. All six of us were incredibly unhappy, unfulfilled and empty inside.

We were what the Bible calls "whited sepulchres," which look beautiful on the outside but on the inside are "full of dead men's bones and everything unclean." Jesus charges, "outwardly [you] appear righteous" [and loving], but on the inside you are full of hypocrisy. (Matthew 23:27-28) That's exactly what Chuck and I had become.

What makes our story a little different from so many others you might hear is that we were Christians at this time. We were not backsliding Christians: We taught Bible studies in our home, went faithfully to church and prayed daily, but we had no idea what it meant to love God the way He wanted us to.

Both of us were teaching others that Christ was the answer to all their problems, and in our hearts we knew this to be true. Yet, in our lives behind closed doors, it wasn't true at all!

We often invited our neighbors to our Bible studies. We wanted them to share God's Love with us. However, our kids would ask sarcastically, "Why would our neighbors want what you have? You are no different from the people who don't even know God. In fact, some of those people are probably kinder and more loving to each other that you guys are." Oh, those words hurt...because they were true!

In the early 1980s, the <u>Los Angeles Times</u> reported: "Marriage is a quiet hell for about 50% of American couples. Four out of 12 end in divorce, and another six (that's ten out of 12) are loveless, utilitarian relationships to protect the children." Recent statistics now show that one out of every two marriages ends in divorce.

A "loveless relationship" is exactly what our marriage had become. We had what I like to call a professional marriage—a marriage where two people are *existing* together only for the purpose of convenience, show, security or, as the newspaper article stated, "to protect the children."

Marriage Trials

Let me back up and explain how we got to this point in our marriage.

I was reared by parents who always gave first priority to their marriage relationship. My dad was always there for my mom and her needs, no matter what they were. He was there for us kids, too, whenever we needed him. Dad and Mom always seemed to have a united front on all matters. I remember a very calm and undisturbed household with no internal tensions or outside pressures tearing it apart.

When I thought of marriage, then, Mom and Dad's was the kind I envisioned and hoped for. I didn't know any other kind existed. So it was a huge shock to find myself married to a dynamo, who placed ten times more importance on time spent in business and at work than he did with me or the kids. And it seemed the tighter I grabbed hold of him and tried to make him change to meet my needs, the more he pulled away from me and threw himself even deeper into his business.

At this time, he was chairman of the board and chief financial officer of a major computer company. He lived, ate, and breathed this company, thriving on the high stress and challenge of "growing" a big, dynamic corporation.

Chuck's typical workweek consisted of six eighteen-hour days; moreover he always brought home mountains of paperwork in the evenings and on the weekends. His secretary used to tell me he received between 40 and 50 important phone calls to return each day. It was an incredibly high pressure job, but Chuck loved it.

Chuck loved to travel. He was on the road—or more precisely, "in the sky"—an average of one-to-two weeks each month. You can imagine the result of this kind of lifestyle—he had very little time for home and family. When he was home, with all the tremendous pressures on him, he would be totally preoccupied with the phone, the computer, business reports, mail, and other pressing issues.

When I complained about his long hours at the office or his travel, he just responded, "Hey, that's what you married; that's what you're stuck with!" In other words, "Don't rock the boat! Don't try to change me!"

Personality Differences

Chuck has incredible verbal abilities. These abilities are great assets in the business world, but these same attributes are devastating if you are on the other end of an argument with him.

I used to have the best fights with the bathroom mirror *before or after* confronting Chuck. In the bathroom I could always say just the right things. But when actually talking with Chuck, it would all come out wrong; or he would use a word I didn't understand, and it would send me to the dictionary to find out what he'd just called me.

I'm not an explosive person. I have, in general, a rather placid temperament. I tend to shy away from confrontation. But when hurt or attacked verbally, I used to take everything inward and allow it to stay there, festering, and growing, because I didn't know what else to do with it. On the outside, then, I smiled and pretended everything was fine, but on the inside, without realizing it, deep roots of bitterness and resentment began to grow. Unknowingly, they began to motivate my actions.[2]

Financial "Roller Coaster"

In addition to our marital trials, we've also had tremendous financial trials. We have <u>never</u> in our 38 years of marriage (maybe with a few exceptions at the very beginning) had an eight-to-five job with a stable income. We have either been millionaires (I think we've been there twice!) or at the other end of the gamut: totally broke and paupers.

The last several years of our marriage have probably been the hardest of all financially. We have literally *lost everything*. Four years ago we lost our beautiful dream house in Big Bear Lake, California, our cars, and our medical and life insurance through bankruptcy when Chuck's company failed. Then, three years ago, our rented home was on the epicenter of a 6.7 earthquake and we lost many of our personal possessions. Financially and materially, it's been an incredible roller coaster ride. When we were first married, Chuck used to say to me, "I can't promise you our marriage will be easy, but I do promise it won't be dull." He has definitely kept that promise!

Problems With Our Children

As if our marital and financial problems weren't enough, we've also had tremendous problems with our children. One of the reasons for the problems is that we were always moving. We have moved 25 times in 37 years of marriage. The kids used to ask us after a move, "Shall we keep our bags packed?"

We have four beautiful children: Chip, who is now 36; Mark, 34; Lisa, 27; and Michelle, 21. In the midst of our trials, 18 years ago, the boys were just teenagers. As a result of our continual moving, they had their own set of problems. Adjusting every year or so to new friends and new schools was very traumatic.

Everything seemed to come to a head in 1975, the year we moved to the San Francisco area. The boys were in a high school that they absolutely loved. But because of the move they had to give it up, making it a very difficult year for them. Thus, they began to look elsewhere to find answers to their questions, trying desperately to fill the emptiness that they were experiencing inside.

In addition to the boys' problems, our last baby, Michelle was born allergic to the "entire" cow. If she drank any milk or ate meat, cheese, jello, whey, casein—anything from the cow—she would vomit uncontrollably and have diarrhea for days.

Also when Michelle was 18 months old, we discovered she was hyperactive. We then began an incredible period of about four years where we tried desperately to find a suitable diet that wouldn't hype her up. She was forbidden to eat anything containing artificial colorings, flavorings or preservatives. We even had to withdraw apples, peaches, grapes and other fruit from her diet because they, too, contained the natural chemicals that cause hyperactivity. This left us with a diet consisting of papayas, bananas, fish, lima beans, squash, spinach and rice cakes. Try cooking for a two year old with that diet!

If that weren't enough, at the age of two Michelle began to limp. One day she just started dragging her leg. The doctors told us she had a disease of the bone marrow and if we ever wanted her to walk again, we had to permanently keep her off her feet and in bed for an indefinite period of time. Have you ever tried to keep a two year old in bed for any length of time? Imagine trying to keep a hyperactive two year old in bed for any length of time!

Excruciatingly Painful Time

This time in my life was excruciatingly painful, with our marriage breaking up, our financial roller coaster ride, the boys' problems, our continual moving and Michelle's trauma.

Many times I would go to God and ask, "Where, Lord, is this Abundant Life I'm supposed to have as a Christian? You say in John 10:10 that You have come so that I might have *life* and that I might have it more *abundantly*. Oh God, where is that life? Where is the Love You promise us in Your Word? If You are the Answer, then why is my life so empty and so unfulfilled? Why, God, am I so miserable?"

Sometimes my feelings of unhappiness over our situation—or Chuck's comments—would consume me and almost suffocate me. I remember in 1975 locking myself in a darkened room and crying until I thought I would "die."

Have you ever felt that way? Have you ever kept on crying until you thought your heart was going to burst?

That's exactly how I felt. However, since I didn't know any other solution to my overwhelming hurts, I'd push all those emotions deep down in my heart, lock them up tightly, force a smile on my face, and come out to begin all over again. I thought that by burying my real feelings and putting on a smile, I'd get rid of the pain and no one would ever know the difference.

I'm convinced the world functions this way because *they have no other choice!* I'm certain that without Jesus in our lives to take away our hurts, we are all walking time bombs, ready to explode!

The truth is, when we bury our real feelings, we never really get rid of them; we only drive them down deeper and, even though we don't realize it at the time, those hurts eventually begin to motivate all our actions. This is exactly what happened to me.

I really wanted to love Chuck the way God wanted me to. I'm not a career-oriented person. Home and family have always been my highest priorities. All I've ever wanted out of life was to be a "good" wife and mother. But so often *those buried resentments and bitternesses* (that I had secretly tucked away), *Chuck's curt responses*, and the *continual stressful circumstances* would cause me to act just the opposite of how I wanted to act.

I know how Paul must have felt when he said in Romans 7:15, "I hate the things I do and I do the things I hate." That's exactly how I felt.

Example: Cold as Ice

Often Chuck would call from the office around 7 p.m., after I had already prepared a nice dinner, and say, "I'm sorry, Honey, but I have to work late tonight. I'll probably be home around 10 or 11 p.m."

Immediately the buried feelings of rejection and bitterness that I had never dealt with would be triggered and my composure would fall apart. I couldn't seem to control how I reacted. Those buried feelings were always right there—ready to explode.

Rather than act lovingly, as I really wanted to, my voice automatically became cold as ice. Even on the phone, Chuck could feel my attitude change. He would ask, "Is everything all right, Honey? Is anything wrong?"

"No," I'd respond icily, "I'm fine!" Then, I'd furiously bang the phone down. Anger and frustration and hurt would totally consume me. At that time, I didn't realize that my anger was just a symptom of a much deeper cause. Underneath my icy exterior lay unvented rejection and hurt that I had never properly dealt with before.

All evening long, then, rather than catch the negative thoughts as they came into my mind (and give them to God), I continually "mulled" them over and over. Constantly I entertained angry thoughts about what Chuck had done. And this was the atmosphere my poor Chuck came home to later that night. Looking back, it's a wonder he even bothered to come home at all. Proverbs 14:1 says, "Every wise woman buildeth her house: But, the foolish plucketh it down with her hands." That's exactly what I was doing, brick-by-brick.

I Hated Being a Phony

I knew the Bible was Truth. And over and over again in the Bible it says we are to love; we are to love God, and then we are to love others. Yet I didn't know how to do this without being a phony. To me, a phony is one who says one thing on the outside but feels another way on the inside. That's exactly what I felt I was being forced into doing.

Again, I would go to God and ask, "Will You please tell me *how* I am supposed to do this genuinely? When I fake love for Chuck, I feel like a hypocrite. And yet, when I don't fake it, there is no love at all to give. How am I supposed to love him genuinely, as You say in the Bible?"

God's Love Growing Cold

Matthew 24:12 is a perfect Scripture to explain what was happening to us, and to so many couples I see today. It says, in the end times, "because iniquity shall abound, the love of many shall wax cold."

The Greek word for "love" in this Scripture is *Agape*—God's Love. This passage is talking about people who have God's Love in their hearts (i.e., Christians). This Scripture is saying that in the end times (which is now), "because sin shall abound, the Love of Christians will grow cold." Romans 14:23 tells us that any choice we make that is "not of faith" is sin and will cause God's Spirit to be quenched. Thus, God's Love in our hearts will be blocked from coming forth into our lives.

At that time, I had no conception that God's Love was supernatural and totally different from my own human love. I didn't realize that God's Love could only flow through me if my heart and life were cleansed.

I thought God's Love was poured into my heart when I first accepted Christ, and that all I had to do was claim it and use it. I had no idea that *Agape was God Himself working through me.* And the only way He could do that was for me to give Him a cleansed and unclogged vessel to use.

A Hopeless Situation

So without God intervening and doing something pretty radical at this point in our lives—breaking the total deadlock (the wall, the barrier, the pride) in one of our hearts—the situation was a totally hopeless.

I felt like I had tried every way I knew of to change our marriage—books, marriage counselors, seminars and other classes. Yet nothing had worked. Neither Chuck nor I saw any other way out of our hurts and our problems but to escape and run away—divorce.

I ended up making arrangements to leave Chuck. I planned to take the kids back to my folks in Los Angeles. Two days before I was to leave, Chuck and I ended up in another heated argument. Right in the middle of the conversation, in response to something Chuck had said, I blurted out, "But don't you ever want to hear what God wants to say to you?" (I meant if he would just listen to God, God would show him how messed up his priorities were.)

Chuck's reply was something I will never forget. Four little words that are burned into my memory forever. He simply asked, "Won't you let Him!" (Meaning, *I* was the one in the way of his hearing God!)

Well, I was so completely stunned at his remark that I sat back, speechless. I had always felt that I was the one who was "spiritual." After all, I was the one continually in Bible studies and prayer groups. And I was the one who had all my friends praying for Chuck.

Chuck must have sensed that he struck a sensitive cord in me, because he began—for the first time—to tell me what he really desired in a wife (and I quote):

"Someone who is easy and comfortable to be with. Someone I can just be myself with and not on guard or defensive. Someone who makes the atmosphere one of love and acceptance, not one of tension and judgment. Someone I can turn to for constant companionship and support, a team mate. Someone who would love me for myself, not for what she wanted to make me into...."

Chuck went on to state that he had always desired a family and a home because he never really had one growing up. But, he said, with my constant bickering and griping, I had eroded that desire. Then I had turned around and blamed him for putting his business before his family.

Beam in My Own Eye

As I listened, God began to turn my attention and focus <u>away</u> from Chuck. And He began to shine His Holy Spirit spotlight directly on me, bringing to light all the sin I had buried and hidden for so long in my own heart. He brought up self-centered things that I never realized were there.

Matthew 7:3-5 puts it so appropriately: "Why beholdest thou the mote that is in thy brother's eye, but considereth not the beam that is in thine own eye? Thou hypocrite, first cast out the beam out of thine own eye; and then shalt thou see clearly to cast out the mote out of the brother's eye."

God began that night to show me all the things in my own heart that had quenched His Spirit and had become sin. He showed me my judgmental attitude, my self-pity, my spiritual pride, my self-righteousness, my unforgiveness, my resentment, my bitterness, and my anger—things I had stored up for years. These were things I had never given to God; thus they had automatically blocked God's Love in me.

God promised me that day that if I would give those things to Him and learn to really *love Him* the way He desired me to, He then would enable me to love Chuck the way I was supposed to. And I <u>could</u> be that wife Chuck was talking about.

The Real Problem

So the real problem was with me, not Chuck! The problem was my holding on to and burying hurts, negative thoughts and emotions (justified or not) and not recognizing that those things quenched God's Spirit in me and stopped His Love. It was "sin" because I kept those things, entertained them, and mulled them over rather than immediately giving them over to God.

Having the original negative thought is not sin. *It's what we choose to do with that thought that makes it sin or not.* We have three options: We can <u>vent</u> that negative thought; we can <u>bury</u> it; or we can <u>give</u> it <u>to God</u>.

If we can recognize the negative junk when it first comes in and immediately give it over to God, we have not sinned. We are still a cleansed vessel. However, if we choose to hold on to those negative things by either venting them or mulling them over and eventually burying them, they will become sin and cover our hearts.

God had been in my heart all along;[3] however, *I* was the one preventing Him from coming forth and manifesting His Life and His Love through me, because I insisted upon holding on to my own "justified" hurt feelings. These negative things then acted like a wall or a barrier over my heart.[4]

So the first thing I needed to learn was *how* to release and give these buried hurts and emotions over to God. In other words: 1) How to confess them as sin (i.e., how to acknowledge that I "owned" them and that they had separated me from Him);[5] 2) How to repent of them (i.e., how to change my mind about following them) and; 3) How to literally give them over to God. We will cover these steps in detail in Chapter 14.

True Meaning of Loving God

From the time I had first asked Jesus into my life to the time I finally learned what it meant to love God, had taken me twenty years. I learned that to love God the way He wants us to love Him is not an emotion or a feeling. *To love God means to lose self*, to relinquish self, to set self aside, and to be broken of self. In other words, we must give God all our thoughts, emotions, and desires that are contrary to His so that His Love and His Life can come forth from our hearts.

I'd never equated loving God with John 12:24. And yet this is exactly what it means to love Him: "Except a corn of wheat fall into the ground and die, it abideth alone [it will have none of God's Love]; but if it die [learns to yield itself], [then] it bringeth forth much fruit [God's Love to others]."

As God began to show me how—moment by moment—to love Him and how to give Him all my hurts and anything that blocked His Love in my heart, He did two very important things in me. Not only did He begin to remove all my negative emotions, but He also began to permeate my being with His supernatural Love for Chuck. Thus, I began to handle all my situations in a "much more excellent way" (1 Corinthians 12:31).

Example: Burnt Roast

Remember the incident I told you about earlier in this chapter when Chuck was late for dinner? About a year later, a similar situation occurred. Chuck called around 6 p.m. and said, "Hey, Honey, I have a free night. I'll be home around 7 p.m. Why don't you call the boys and invite them over for dinner and we'll have a great evening together."

"Terrific," I said. I quickly put in a leg of lamb, called the boys at their apartments and told them, "Come on over! Dad's coming home early and we'll have an evening together." We rarely had dinner together as a family because Chuck traveled so much.

Seven o'clock came and went, and no Chuck! 7:30, 8, 8:30, 9, and still no Chuck. Finally, at 9:30 p.m., he walked in the door—genuinely sorry. He had met some "important" businessmen as he was walking out of his office, and they had decided to go out to dinner to talk over some business matters. He was genuinely sorry, but he had just forgotten to call us.

Now, my *natural* emotional reaction was still the same as it had been the year before. Remember something very important: *Self life* (our own thoughts, emotions and desires that are contrary to God's) *does not improve with age*! No matter how long we have been Christians, our self life will be just as ugly today as it was the first day we believed.

My natural reaction was to tell Chuck off: My roast was burnt to a crisp; the boys and I had wasted a whole evening just waiting around doing nothing; and the girls had finally given up and gone to bed. By the world's standards, I would have certainly been justified to be angry and upset. But God had begun to show me a better way, a "more excellent way" to respond and to love.

All night long as I was waiting for Chuck, instead of being consumed in anger and frustration, I kept choosing, as best as I could, to give these things to God so I could stay an open and cleansed vessel for His Love. I neither buried my real feelings nor pretended they weren't there. I just kept recognizing them as they came up and verbally handing them over to God, thus allowing His Love, which was already in my heart, to come forth.

Let me tell you it's hard work, constantly choosing not to go by your own feelings. But how excited and thrilled I was when at 9:30 p.m. it was God's genuine, supernatural, unconditional Love that met Chuck at the door and not my normal human responses. I really felt no bitterness or anger or frustration over what had happened, because *God had literally taken them all away*. Chuck and I were able to sit down and talk freely and openly about what he had done.

[Note: There definitely is a time to take a stand and tell the other person how you are feeling. But we should only do this when we are *clean* vessels. Otherwise, we end up deeper in the pits than when we started. When we are cleansed vessels, the encounter will be done in God's Love. Then not only will the lover be freed from presumptions and expectations, but also the love recipient (the one being loved) will respond from his heart and not his defenses.[6]]

Chuck was so sweet and apologetic that night. I know he saw the new responses in me, and I know he felt the peaceful atmosphere. We played games with the guys until midnight and had a great time.

My Diary

There are volumes of examples of how God's Love began and continues to work in my life as I stay that open and cleansed vessel for Him to work through. I kept a diary over those first few years and here are a few of my favorite entries:

August, 1976 (three months after we had the "blowup" and God began to work so mightily in my life): "Chuck called today while away on a business trip and said,

'Honey, the only thing wrong with our new marriage relationship is that it's no fun to travel anymore!'"

How many times I had pleaded, cried, and begged Chuck not to travel so much. But nothing ever made a difference until *I* changed and allowed God's Love to become a part of my life.

September, 1976: "Chuck has begun to come home from the office at noontime now, just because he says he misses my company and wants to talk."

Chuck is a total workaholic. He would *never* take time off for anything. Also, he has always had a difficult time sharing personal things, until God's Love became a part of our relationship.

This last entry is the most precious of all...

December, 1976: "Chuck asked me today, 'If you were single again, would you marry me?' He just wanted to make sure I was happy with what I had."

Focus On Jesus

When I stay that open channel for God's Love, and I keep my eyes squarely focused on Jesus to meet my needs for love, then three important things happen:

1) I am able to stop strangleholding and suffocating Chuck to meet my desperate need for love.

2) I am able to stop trying to conform Chuck into my desired image for a husband. I am able to accept him as he is and genuinely love the "whole package."[7]

3) I am able to trust God to fix what He wants fixed in Chuck, in His timing and in His way.

There is so much freedom in this way of loving. I am no longer responsible for how Chuck thinks, what he says, or what he chooses to do. I am totally aware of those areas that need changing, and I will continue to pray earnestly about them and will share them with Chuck as God leads. But my responsibility is not to try to control and fix those areas, but only to be that conduit for God's Love and *love Chuck as he is* (the whole package). However, the minute I stop looking to the Lord to meet my needs and stop being an open channel for His Love, it never fails—I grab hold of Chuck, and once again, we both sink.

Loved Once Again

Of course, all this love and freedom has caused Chuck to "fall in love" with me all over again.[8] So now I'm not only getting God's supernatural Love (as I continually lay my will and life down to Him), but I'm also getting back from Chuck all the human, emotional love that I used to dream of.

I know without a doubt, if it hadn't been for God's intervening in our lives 18 years ago and showing us how to love with His Love, we would *not* be together today. God's Love has not only saved our marriage, it has turned it around to where it is a hundred times better than it ever was, even when we were first married.

Don't fall into Satan's trap, thinking that if God puts your marriage back together, it will be just the same as it always was. I guarantee you, if Jesus puts your marriage back together with His *Agape* Love in the middle, it won't ever be the same again.

Still in Love?

We were on a trip recently, and someone noticed how affectionate we were to each other. They commented "you must be newlyweds." We answered, "No, we've been married thirty-five years." "No," they said, "You can't be!" Their underlying thought was, "How could they be married for 35 years and still be in love? What a sad commentary on today's marriages.

Our kids, who saw us at our very worst 18 years ago, are now being reintroduced to the *real* God of Love. They constantly kid us about being in love and about being lovers. They jokingly remark, "Oh, they're going upstairs again!" "Don't you ever get tired of hugging and kissing?" Or, "Don't you two do it in my house!"

How wonderful it is for kids to see their parents totally in love, especially if they haven't always been. It is living proof that *Christ is the answer to every problem*—if we'll only let Him be!

The Way of Agape is such an incredibly freeing way to live. What others see on the outside of me is now exactly what's going on inside. There's no more hypocrisy or phoniness because God took and continues to take away the causes of my hypocrisy— my hurts, my bitternesses, my resentments (my sins).

Not Perfect

I still have negative thoughts and feelings, and I will until the day I meet Jesus face to face. But as I choose—moment by moment—to give these things over to the Lord and not dump them on Chuck, my kids, or my family, God's Love can continue to flow. Chuck and I are *not* perfect by any means. Many challenges still confront us daily. But as we stay open and yielded to God, His Love can freely work through us and continue to reconcile us.

To me, *maturity in Christ* is not knowing a bunch of Scriptures, going to church regularly, attending prayer meetings, leading Bible studies, writing books or being on T.V., but simply *knowing how, moment by moment, to love God.* Then we can go on and love others the way God intends. God's Love through us is the only thing that will bring our husbands, our children, our relatives, and our friends back to Him. It's His lovingkindness, in spite of the circumstances, that is going to draw them.[9]

Willing to Love

We need to be willing to love with God's Love, even if our circumstances and our situations never change. Our motivation is wrong if we are loving only to have our circumstances or the other person change. That is again conditional, human love and not God's Love.

A young woman in one of my *Agape* seminars illustrated this principle. She told me, "After I began to learn the *Way of Agape*, I never could figure out if my husband changed or if I just fell madly in love with him again."

Abundant Life

God desires us all to have His abundant Love-filled Life right where we are walking now. God's Life is: His supernatural Love, His supernatural Wisdom and His supernatural Power. John 10:10 declares, "I am come that they might have life, and that they might have it more abundantly."

God is not talking about heavenly life, but life right here on earth. Right now! *Abundant Life is simply experiencing God's Life through us.*[10] God wants us to have this kind of life, even in the midst of our trials and our circumstances. That's the miracle He's after. To me, this is far more dramatic and more of a testimony to others than all the signs and wonders in the world! *Joy, peace, and love come not with the absence of trials, but with the presence of God.*

The question we always come back to is: Are you willing? Are you willing to allow God to perform a miracle through you? Are you willing to lay down your will and your life so that God's Love can be released through you to others?[11] 1 John 3:16 teaches us, "Hereby perceive we the love of God, because He laid down His Life for us: and we ought to lay down our lives for the brethren." (1 John 3:16)

God's Promise

Eighteen years ago, God promised to make me into the wife that Chuck desired. I'll never forget the night a few years ago when God showed me He had fulfilled that promise. Chuck and I were sitting in his library. Chuck paused and looked at me. "You know," he said, "I've been thinking. I'm a professional executive. That's my job and my role. You know what you are?"

"No," I said. "What?"

Chuck responded, "You're a professional lover!" I was so excited I ran to the dictionary to see exactly what "professional" really meant. It said, "a learned profession." I thought that very appropriate, because I have learned to allow God to love through me. Now, I certainly don't do it perfectly, but I have learned His Way of Love.

The Secret

The secret is that *I* am not the one loving — it's God! He's the source of Love, and He's the One in the business of love-making. I'm the one, however, who gets all the benefits when I allow Him to love through me. Oh, how our worlds would change if we would all choose to be "professional lovers." First, *loving God with all our heart, will and soul;* then, *loving others as ourselves.* This is truly **God's Way of Agape.** Jesus said, "Thou shalt love the Lord thy God with all thy heart, and with all thy soul, and with all thy mind. This is the first and great commandment. And the second is like unto it, Thou shalt love thy neighbour as thyself. On these two commandments hang all the law and the prophets." (Matthew 22:37-40) "This [love] do, and thou shalt live." (Luke 10:28)

For almost 20 years, I was walking right smack in front of God, blocking His way. Now God has put me into *His Way of Love,* and let me tell you, it's a much more excellent way!

Endnotes:

1. You can read our entire life story in my book, <u>Why Should I Be the First to Change?</u>

2. Hebrews 12:15

3. Be sure to read "The More Excellent Way" in Section Seven.

4. See Psalm 119:70 and also Chapter 11, "Fat as Grease."

5. Be sure to see Chapter 11, "Nothing Shall Separate Us."

6. See Chapter 3, "Characteristics of God's Love."

7. See Chapter 16, "Don't Be Holy Spirit Naggers."

8. See Chapter 5, "Can Become a Blessing."

9. Jeremiah 31:3

10. See Chapter 7, "Do You Know God?"

11. Luke 10:25, 27-28 and Matthew 7:14

Scriptural References:

Chapter 2

"Except a corn of wheat fall into the ground and die, it abideth alone: but if it die, it bringeth forth much fruit." (John 12:24-25) "For we which live are alway[s] delivered unto death for Jesus' sake, that the life also of Jesus might be made manifest in our mortal flesh." (2 Corinthians 4:11)

Why Does God Allow Trials in Our Lives?
(Deuteronomy 8:2-3; Psalm 107:25-30; 119:69, 71, 75; Acts 14:22c; 1 Peter 4:19; Hosea 6:1; Job 33:29-30)
    A. Because He loves us and He wants us to be healed, to be whole and to have abundant life (Psalm 71:20; Job 5:17-18)
    B. Because He wants our attention:
        1. So we might *see* our true selves (Psalm 38:1-18)
        2. So we might *hear* His voice (Deuteronomy 4:1; 6:3-5; 8:2-3)
        3. So we might *choose* His way (Deuteronomy 8:2; 30:19-20; Psalm 119: 67; Judges 2:22; 1 Peter 4:1-2)
    C. Because He wants every hindrance removed that keeps us from being fully yielded (Psalm 51:7-9; James 1:13-15; 2 Corinthians 1:9b; 3:5; 4:7-12; Romans 5:3-5; John 15:2; Hebrews 12:1)
    D. Because He wants us to *love Him* (Job 13:15; Deuteronomy 13:3-4)

Whole Purpose of Being a Christian Is: (1 Timothy 1:5)
    A. To be *emptied of self life*, so we can be *filled with God's Life* (John 3:30; 12: 24a, b; 13:37b; Colossians 2:12; 1 Corinthians 15:31b, 36; 2 Corinthians 4: 8-12,16; Matthew 23:26; James 4:8-10; Luke 12:33; Mark 8:35). This is the *fullness of God* (Ephesians 3:19; 4:13).
    B. So others might see God's Life manifested and reflected in us, not our own self life (Exodus 9:16; Philippians 1:21; Galatians 1:16a; 2:20; 4:19; Colossians 3:4a; John 1:16; 3:30a; 10:10; 12:24; 1 Corinthians 10:31; 2 Corinthians 4:7, 11b; Ephesians 5:2, 18b). We are to *be in this world, as He is* (1 John 4:17; John 12:26a). We are to walk as He walked (1 John 2:6; 3:16). "Laying our lives down"
    C. To be a genuine witness (Luke 11:33; 1 John 4:12; John 1:7a; Matthew 5: 16)

God's Way of *Agape* Is:
(Matthew 22:37-40; 16:24-25; John 12:24-25; 2 Corinthians 4:10-12)
    A. Learning first that *God loves us* (Jeremiah 31:3; Isaiah 49:16; John 3:16; Hebrews 13:5b; 1 John 4:10)
        1. Learning what His Love is (1 Corinthians 13:1-8)
        2. Learning that He has poured this kind of Love in our hearts (Romans 5: 5; 8:35-39)

B. Learning what it means to *love God* in return with all our heart, will, and soul (Matthew 22:37; Deuteronomy 6:4-6; 10:12; 11:22; 30:20; John 14:21a; 1 John 5:3)
C. Learning what it means to *love our neighbor as ourselves* (Matthew 22:39; 1 John 2:8-11; 3:16; 4:21; John 13:34)

READ: Deuteronomy 30:15-20. "He is our life."

Section Two

Introduction: God's Way of Love

As I began to share some of the miracles that God had done in our marriage, people began to ask me what the Scriptural secrets were.

I found it very difficult, however, to adequately explain what God had done Scripturally. I could share the "experience" with them as I've done with you, but I couldn't explain to them Biblically *why* it had happened the way it did.

Each of our experiences is different, and sharing our experiences by themselves—without putting the Word of God (God's principles) alongside—won't affect or change another person's life. *Only the Word of God will radically alter and change another's life.*

So I began to pray and ask God to show me Scripturally what He had done in my life. I wanted to share from His Word so other people's lives would be touched and changed. I prayed this prayer for three years, and *The Way of Agape* (God's Way of Love) was His answer to that prayer.

I have been teaching *The Way of Agape* since 1978 (about 150 seminars), all over the United States, in Australia, Scotland, and England. Classes are also being held in Thailand, New Zealand, Israel, and Africa.

Along with this textbook, there is a *Way of Agape Personal Application Workbook, Leader's Guide* and an eight-tape *Way of Agape* audio series. Together they can be used for personal Bible studies, small group studies, Church ministries or counseling situations.

At the end of each chapter in this book you will find endnotes containing supplemental Scriptural notes, plus outlines of the principles presented in the chapter and the references for each.

Many real-life examples have been included in this book, although the names have been changed to avoid embarrassment. Also, for the sake of simplicity, whenever I speak of "he" (him, himself), I also naturally mean "she" (her, herself).

The *key* that changed my life was, and continues to be, the implementation of three truths:

1) Learning **what God's Love is** and how it differs from human love. Learning that most of us, even as Christians, are still functioning only on human love; this is why so many of us have become confused and disheartened. God's Love is not dependent upon our feelings, our circumstances, or the other

person's responses, as is human love—it's unconditional. Also, learning that ***God loves us*** with this same kind of unconditional Love, which is not based on what we do for Him, but simply on who we are in Him.

2)   Learning what it means ***to love God with all our heart, will, and soul*** and learning the differences between each of these terms. Learning what quenches God's Love in our hearts and how practically to yield these conscious and subconscious things over to Him. We need to be cleansed and open vessels, so God's Love from our hearts can flow freely through us to others.

3)   Learning what it means ***to love our neighbors as ourselves*** and how to put their will and desires above our own. The only way we can do this is for us to love God first, to totally give ourselves over to Him. Then He, in turn, enables us to love others before or instead of ourselves.

God's Will for us is to learn to love: to learn to love Him and then to learn to love others. Romans 13:10 declares, "*Agape* [God's Love] is the fulfilling [completion] of the law." In other words, the whole Bible is summed up in the word Love. (Matthew 22:40)

The Way of Agape is a new way of loving. It's a way of loving that is totally opposite from the way the world teaches, and is probably completely opposite from the way you have been used to, even as a Christian.

In this book, we are not going to learn techniques or methods so that we can love like God. *We can't learn to do what only God can do.* Only God is Love, and we can't learn to be what only God is. What we will be learning, however, is how to totally yield ourselves to God—how to choose to set aside our own thoughts, emotions, and desires that are contrary to God's—so He, then, can love His Love through us.

I'm not a theologian. I'm not a professional, nor do I pretend to be. I am just a sister in the Lord, who has found a way that works. My only desire in writing this book is simply to share that way with you and, by so doing, to glorify God.

Therefore, I pray that you will make Acts 17:11 a very real part of reading this book. It's my husband's favorite Scripture: "They received the word with all readiness of mind, and [then they] searched the Scriptures daily, [to prove] whether those things were so."

This message is not just for women, nor is it just for married people. *Wherever there is a relationship, you need God's Way of Agape!* It really doesn't matter if we have been Christians seven months, seven years, or 77 years. It doesn't matter how many Scriptures we know, how many prayers we say, how many Bible studies we lead (or how many books we write), it's still a moment-by-moment choice to love God and to lay our lives down to Him so His Love can be manifested through us.

We can't change the circumstances we are in. We can't change our past, and we can't make everything turn out the way we want. But we certainly can: 1) Keep our eyes squarely focused on Jesus; 2) Yield ourselves totally to Him; and 3) Allow His Love to flood our souls and overflow into all of our experiences today.

The meaning to life lies in our relationships—first, our relationship with God, and then our relationship with others. By loving God first with all our heart, will, and soul, He will then enable us to love others as ourselves. (Matthew 22:37)

1 John 4:17 states that the way God's Love is made perfect, completed, or finished is that *we might become in this world as He is...**and that is Love.***

Truly, this is the King's ***High*** Way. (Numbers 21:22; Jeremiah 31:21)

* * *

Chapter 3: What Is God's Love?

Love With No Strings Attached

I once read an article in the *Los Angeles Times* that made a very big impression on me. It told the story of a nine-year-old girl flying from England to the United States to have a kidney transplant. The girl's parents had raised all they could toward the operation, but had managed to raise only $7,000, far short of the $30,000 total cost.

The people on the flight from England to the United States somehow heard of the little girl's plight. Unconditionally, they began to give of themselves all they could; men gave watches, cash, and checks. One man wrote a check for $10,000. Women gave rings and any other jewelry they had. The people on that plane raised an amazing $23,000! That, plus the $7,000 the parents had raised made the exact amount needed.

The beautiful thing about this story was that the little girl's nationality, religion, or social status didn't matter to the people on that plane. They didn't say, "Well, let's see here, I will lend you this money, but you must pay me back." They just gave all they could give of themselves with no strings attached.

When I think about this story, I think of God's Love, because God's Love does exactly the same thing. It's an unconditional giving of yourself for another with no strings attached. God's Love is a Love that keeps on loving even when the object of that Love ceases to please or even tries to stop that Love from coming. This is the kind of Love we will learn about in the next several chapters.

What Is God's Love?

What is God's Love? The Bible tells us that God's Love is a Person. 1 John 4:7-8 notes, "Beloved, let us love one another; for love is of God, and everyone that loveth is born of God, and knoweth God. He that loveth not knoweth not God; for *God is Love.*" (emphasis added)

God's Love is a supernatural Love poured into our hearts the moment we invite Him in to take control of our lives.[1] It's God Himself who comes into our hearts at that moment, and *He is that Love*!

This personal Love is what makes Christianity so totally different from all the other religions in the world. Christianity is the only religion where God Himself (who is Love) comes to dwell within each one of us.

A precious story exemplifies this truth. About 15 years ago I read Arthur Katz's book, *Ben Israel*. Mr. Katz, a brilliant Jewish philosopher and teacher at the University of California at Berkeley, decided to go on his own quest to find God. He literally traveled all over the world to find Him.

While riding on a train in Germany, Mr. Katz happened to sit next to a young Christian girl who had only recently become a believer. They began to talk about God. A few minutes into the discussion, Mr. Katz sarcastically asked the young woman, "What makes you think your Jesus is any different from all the other religions in the world?" The girl simply and lovingly looked at him and said, "Because Jesus is God. He is Love and He lives in my heart."

This response was not what Mr. Katz had expected, and caught him totally off guard. He could not refute her from his intellect. For months, those simple words echoed in his mind... "Because Jesus is God and He lives in my heart."

Finally, Mr. Katz found himself in Jerusalem, Israel. A Jewish Christian befriended him and shared his own testimony. After having much love and compassion bestowed upon him by this Israeli, the Holy Spirit broke down the walls of Mr. Katz's heart and he accepted Christ as his own personal Messiah. The God of the Universe, who is Love just as that young Christian girl had testified, came to live in Arthur's heart.

Definition of God's Love

To define God's Love, let's read how God Himself describes His Love in 1 Corinthians 13:4-8:

"[God's] Love suffereth long, and is kind; [His] Love envieth not; [His] Love vaunteth not itself, is not puffed up, Doth not behave itself unseemly, seeketh not her own, is not easily provoked, thinketh no evil; Rejoiceth not in iniquity, but rejoiceth in the truth; Beareth all things, believeth all things, hopeth all things, endureth all things. [God's] *Love never faileth.*" (emphasis added)

Listen to these verses again in a more modern translation to get the full impact of God's definition of Love:

"God's Love is very patient and kind, never jealous or envious, never boastful or proud, never haughty or selfish or rude. God's Love does not demand its own way. It is not irritable or touchy. It does not hold grudges and will hardly even notice when others do it wrong. It is never glad about injustice, but rejoices whenever truth wins out. If you love someone [with God's Love] you will be loyal to him no matter what the cost. You will always believe in him, always expect the best of him, and always stand your ground in defending him. God's Love never fails." (Living Bible, emphasis added)

God's Love can do these things because it is not a human love. Please hear this—loudly and clearly. This is where we so often become confused. *God's Love is not a human love*! It's a supernatural Love! God's Love is a supernatural Love because it's not dependent or based upon human understanding, human desires, or human emotions. It's also not based upon the other person's responses, or upon the circumstances we are in.

God's Love is a Love that is dependent only upon God. He is always faithful, always trustworthy, and always reliable. No matter how we feel or what we think, no matter how another person responds, and no matter what circumstances we are in, God always has Love for that other person, even when we don't.

In the Greek language, God's Love is called *Agape*. *Agape* represents something greater than what most of us can even imagine because *Agape* is God, and no one can really fully comprehend God.[2]

The Greek word *Agape* was coined exclusively for its specific use in the New Testament. Every time it's used in Scripture it means, without exception, God's pure and divine Love. Besides the Bible, there is no other usage of the word *Agape* in literature. (There is one exception—a counterfeit.[3])

Therefore, since there is no precedent upon which to define *Agape*, the true meaning, nature, and purpose of God's Love is not easily understood. This is why there is so much confusion in this area and why the enemy of our souls rejoices. Let's be educated, then, and learn exactly what God's Love is, and how to love and be loved as He desires.

Characteristics of God's Love

Agape is the only unconditional, non-reciprocal, freeing, other-centered Love there is.

God's Love is *unconditional* because it loves no matter what. In spite of what the other person does or how he responds, God's Love keeps on coming. Even though the other person tries to stop it from coming, God's Love still flows to him unceasingly. (God's Love is a paradox because it can be both unconditional and conditional at the same time.[4])

God's Love is a *one-sided* Love because it doesn't have to be returned to be kept alive. In other words, it's not "I'll love you, if you will love me;" it's "I'll love you no matter what!" God's Love is an initiating and unilateral Love—that is, it's the first to reach out.

God's Love is a *freeing* Love because it not only frees the person loving from his own expectations and presumptions, but it also frees the one being loved by making no demands upon him and allowing him to respond from his real feelings and not from his defenses. In other words, it's a Love that not only lets us be who we really are, but it also frees the one we are loving to be himself. All our relationships will be affected when we love like this.

Lastly, God's Love is an *other-centered* Love because it always puts the other person's interests above and before its own. C.S. Lewis calls *Agape* the only "giving-gift Love" there is.

Example: A Father's Confrontation

Years ago, we knew a pastor and his wife who discovered their 19-year-old daughter was being promiscuous with her boyfriend. The mom was absolutely crushed and horrified, but even worse, she was afraid to tell her husband for fear of what he would do. The pastor had a total intolerance for that sort of thing.

After a while, the mom realized she couldn't handle the situation by herself and knew she had to tell her husband. Wisely, however, she went to the Lord first. She confessed to God how afraid she was to tell her husband the true story, but she told God that she was willing to trust Him no matter what He wanted her to do. Then she relinquished her life to God so He could work through her.

She called her husband at church and told him everything. Just as she had imagined, he blew up, determined to come home right then and confront their daughter, forbid her to see the boy again, take away her car, and kick her out of the house.

Fortunately, the mom had been learning about God's Love and discovering that only when we take a stand in God's Love will any troubled situation have a chance to be righted. She knew that if we react out of our own emotions and hurts, we'll usually make the situation ten times worse.

Believing that God had the perfect solution, the mother prayed again and asked God to soften her husband's heart so she could share her real feelings with him. This was a frightening thing for her to do, because her husband always intimidated her and rarely asked her opinion.

God answered her prayer, however, and she was able to convince her husband that they mustn't confront their daughter in anger, but take a stand in God's Love.[5] As they prayed together, the pastor repented of his own critical attitude and asked forgiveness. Together, they gave all their disappointment, anger, frustration, and bitterness over to God and both of them became open, cleansed vessels so God could pour forth His real *Agape* Love through them.

That night the mom and dad did take a stand in God's Love with their daughter. First they shared their own hurt in finding out what she had been doing; then they shared how grieved God must be, since He loved her more than they did. The parents continually kept the emphasis on themselves and on God, without accusing or pointing fingers at their daughter.

The daughter immediately felt God's Love pouring forth through her parents, convicting and convincing her that what she was doing was wrong. Because it was God's Love, she was free to react from her heart and not from her own emotional defenses. She became totally broken, repenting not only to her parents but also to God, asking His forgiveness. In the end, the entire family was reunited in God's Love.

The daughter later shared that, before the meeting, she was prepared to move out because she knew what her dad's reaction would be. But, when she saw his genuine Love and concern that night, she said it "blew her away!" She said it was like the very presence of God in that room tearing down all the walls and barriers and exposing her own sin.

God's Love Exposes Sin

Notice in the above story that *Agape* not only prompted *contrary to normal "actions"* on the part of the pastor, but it also caused *contrary to normal "responses"* on the part of the daughter.

God's Love is the light that pierces through the darkness and exposes the truth. That light will expose the sin of the one being loved and either cause him to draw closer to God or sometimes that light can cause him to flee and hide.

Don't be discouraged if, after you have loved someone with God's Love, he temporarily runs. It's a very powerful thing to stand naked in front of a Holy God, totally exposed by His light. Many people cannot bear this and will often run. In many cases, however, if the one loving continues in God's Way of *Agape* the end result is that the relationship will be reconciled.[6]

Also, don't make the mistake of comparing what God has done or is doing in one person's life with what He is doing in another's life. Often, the responses of two parties can be totally opposite, and yet the end result will be the same. Remember, God works in each of our lives differently. So don't box God in. Let Him be free to initiate, expose, and prompt a response in the way only He knows is best. Keep reminding yourself that you are doing the perfect will of God; you are loving as God desires. God promises you that no matter how the other person responds, or how the situation looks to you, ***His Love will never fail!*** (1 Corinthians 13:8)

Chesed Love

At this point I would like to emphasize something very important. In the Old Testament God's Love was called ***chesed***. Chesed Love has two distinct sides to it:

One side is a longsuffering and merciful Love; the other side is a strict, firm, and disciplinary Love.[7]

Therefore, God's Love can manifest itself either mercifully in our lives when appropriate, or it can manifest itself in strictness and firmness as the occasion demands (like the pastor with his daughter). Both ways are facets of God's Love. As we seek God's Wisdom and His discernment (i.e., the Mind of Christ) for each occasion, God will let us know which type of Love to use for our own particular situation. (See Chapter 16, "It's Not Sloppy *Agape*" and "No Doormat Feelings.")

Agape Involves a Choice

In order for us to love others as God desires, we must make a choice—the choice to allow Him to use us as an open vessel through which He can pour His Love. *Agape* Love is not a human emotion or a human feeling but *God Himself loving through us*. God is the One doing the loving, not us. All He requires from us is the choice to allow Him to love His Love through us.

Agape is not a natural love, but a supernatural Love. We can't produce this kind of Love in our own strength and ability. To love with God's Love is a matter of our will; it's a volitional choice. It's not: "I will love this person if it kills me" (with human love it probably will). But it's: "I choose to set my self (all my thoughts, emotions and desires that are contrary to God's) aside and allow God to love this person through me. I willingly give God my life to do this." (Remember John 12:24)

Therefore when we pray, "Lord, I need more love for this person," what we are really saying is, "Lord, I need to set more of my self aside, so that more of Your Love can come forth." Only our willpower is involved in loving with God's Love, not our emotions, our thoughts, or our desires. This is totally opposite from our natural, emotional way of loving, which is always dependent upon how we feel, what we think, and what we desire.

Agape Is Not Automatic

Naturally, even as Christians, we are still full of self, especially in trials. Our fears, hurts, and justified feelings that we keep and continually mull over in our minds cover and quench God's Love in our hearts. These negative things then control and direct what we think, what we say, and how we act.[8]

Some of the hurts, unforgivenesses, bitternesses, and resentments that we choose to keep are fully justified by the world's standards. But by God's standards, these negative emotions quench God's Spirit and they become sin because we nurture them and entertain them.[9]

[Note: Having the original negative thought is a natural and normal part of being human. This, in itself, is not sin and does not separate us from God. But when we nurture, entertain, and continually mull over these negative thoughts and emotions, they do become sin and they do separate us from God.[10]

Lest I confuse you, let me explain exactly what I mean when I say *"separated from God."* If we are believers, we always have God's Love and His Life in our hearts. Romans 8:28 states that "nothing separates us from His Love," and 1 Corinthians 13: 8 tells us "His Love never stops coming." However, if God's Spirit in our hearts is quenched because of sin (any choice we have made that is not of faith), then that Love of God will not be able to flow out into our lives (our souls). Technically, yes, we still have God's Love in our hearts, but practically, until we deal with our sin, we will not experience His Love out in our lives. Thus, Isaiah 59:2, "Your iniquities have separated between you and your God, and your sins have hid His face from you, that he will not hear," is also true.]

We have, at this point, chosen to hang on to the negative things that we are thinking and feeling, rather than give them over to God. These negative thoughts and feelings not only clog and block God's Love in our hearts, but they also ultimately control and direct all of our actions.

If, however, we can choose to yield our *selves*[11] and become those open vessels that God desires, He will be able to love His *Agape* Love through us. And then the supernatural Love of 1 Corinthians 13 will be genuinely manifested.

Can you imagine what our marriages, our families, and our churches would be like if more of them were built on this kind of unconditional Love? Christians would make such a huge impact on the world. Scripture tells us that the world will know we are Christians not by our words, our signs, our doctrines, our knowledge of Scripture, our spiritual gifts, or our church attendance, but in being open vessels showing forth God's Love."[12] In other words, we prove we are Christians when we love with God's Love.

A Gift of Love

In the original King James Version of the Bible, God's Love is translated *charity,* which is an Old English term meaning "unconditional love in action." The significance of the word charity, as we said before, is that it was a *gift of love with no strings attached,* such as the love displayed in the airplane story at the beginning of this chapter.

God's Love is exactly that. It is a Love that loves the poor, the needy, the maimed, and the ugly. It's a Love that originates in the heart of God and keeps on coming, even when the object of that Love refuses to reciprocate or tries to stop that Love from coming.

Unconditional Acceptance

God's Love includes "unconditional acceptance." People will be drawn to us because of the freedom we give them to be themselves! We, too, will find a freedom to be who we really are when we love with God's Love. We are able to do this not because we're perfect, but because we've already given all our own negative thoughts, anger, bitterness, unforgiveness, and hurts over to God. Thus we are cleansed vessels, without the need for masks or facades.

2 Corinthians 3:17 states, "Where the Spirit of the Lord is (Love), there is liberty [freedom]." This is so true.

Someone recently told me, "This is the first time in 25 years that I am beginning to like who I really am, and what God is doing in me. I am finally free to be who I really am, and you know what? It's not bad at all."

Unconditional Forgiveness

God's Love is the only thing that will enable us to unconditionally forgive and forget what others have done to us. We can't do this naturally. *Our negative thoughts and emotions just won't go away on their own*. It's only by God's Love that the wounds we have received from others can be totally eliminated from our lives. As we choose unconditionally to forgive that other person,[13] God pours His Love into our souls and our wounds and hurts are soothed, healed and removed. Only when those arrows are removed can we genuinely forgive what others have done to us.[14] Then, in God's timing, He will align our feelings with our choices and we'll begin to "feel" that forgiveness.

Example: Justified Wrongs

Let me tell you a beautiful example of how it is possible to forgive and love with God's Love even in the toughest of trials. If we can just choose to lay our wills and our lives down to God, He can enable us (in His strength) to unconditionally forgive that other person.

I have a friend named Bill.[15] Many years ago, Bill called and wanted to speak to Chuck. However, since Chuck wasn't home that day, the two of us began to share. He told me about his life, his family and how he came to know the Lord.

After that initial one-hour call, Bill began to call me every three or four weeks to bring me up to date on his walk with God and on his family. He loved the Lord and was truly seeking His abundant Life.

When his wife, Marie, became pregnant you would have thought Bill had found a million dollars. He was so excited! The morning his daughter Kristen was born was the most important day of his life! He called me from the hospital and talked for almost an hour describing his precious new gift from God.

I have never seen a dad so excited about his baby's birth. Kristen became "his life," and from then on, all the phone calls revolved around her—her growth (to the inch), her development, her eating habits, and so on. She was the light of his life.

A year or so later, Bill called and said he and his wife were having marital problems, and he asked if I would please send Marie the *Agape* tapes. I immediately sent them.

A few months after that he called again. This time, however, he sounded absolutely devastated. Marie had suddenly left him and had given him temporary custody of Kristen. "Having Kristen is all that's keeping me going," he said. He sounded very angry and bitter—emotions I had never heard from Bill before.

When I asked him how he was handling it, Bill said he had such overwhelming resentment and bitterness towards Marie that he couldn't think of anything else but getting back at her. Mentally, he said, he was "keeping a long list of all the wrongs she had done to him and the baby." He said he was consumed with hatred for her.

I tried to share with him some principles from *The Way of Agape*, but he was in no mood to hear. So I just listened to him.

I didn't hear from Bill for a couple months after that. But when he finally did call, he sounded like a new man. I could not believe it was the same bitter and resentful person I had talked to just two months previously. I listened as Bill began to tell me some of the incredible things that had happened to him.

Marie had evidently conspired with her brother and some of her friends. They had kidnapped Kristen and had taken her to another state. The police couldn't find a clue as to their whereabouts; the searching went on for months.

At this point, Bill was destroyed. He was absolutely consumed with hatred, bitterness, and thoughts of revenge. He justified his own hatred and anger because, by the world's standards, he had real cause to despise Marie.

In the meantime, when Bill went to church seeking counsel and help, his friends constantly asked him, "Is Marie ever going to come home?" "Is there any hope for reconciliation?" He couldn't believe they would ask him such things. Mentally, he said, he would bring out his long list of justified wrongs Marie had done to him and think to himself, "There is no way in the world I'd ever take her back after what she has done to me!" Revenge was all he could think about.

One night, feeling such complete loneliness and despair, he spotted the *Agape* tapes sitting on the shelf in the kitchen. Evidently, Marie, had never even touched them. Bill was driven in desperation to pick them up and to listen.

One of the first things he heard was 1 Corinthians 13:5: "*Agape* Love never keeps track of injustices done to it (*it doesn't keep lists*); God's Love thinks no evil; is not easily angered; always protects, always trusts, always hopes and always perseveres."

As he listened, God began to pierce his own heart and expose his own self-centeredness and his own sin. (His experience was similar to the night back in 1975 when God shined His spotlight on my own self-centered heart.) Bill had never realized how his bitterness, hatred, resentment, and unforgiveness had covered his own heart and had prevented God's Love from coming forth.

He saw that he had been blocking God out of his life in the very moments he needed Him the most! Crying for hours—totally broken and repentant—he confessed that he had been entertaining those negative thoughts and mulling them over and over in his mind. He confessed those things were sin and he asked God to purge them from him and make him an open vessel.

Bill said he felt a freedom that night that he'd never had in all his life! It was as though God had taken a 1,000-pound weight off his shoulders. God answered his prayer and he began to experience the supernatural ability to pray for Marie and to genuinely forgive her.

Slowly, God began to instill in Bill a new supernatural Love (God's Love) for Marie. God also took the veil away from Bill's eyes, and Bill began to see and understand the reasons why Marie had acted the way she had. [Note: When we become cleansed vessels, we not only receive God's Love, we also receive God's thoughts (i.e. the Mind of Christ). Then we are able to see things more clearly from God's perspective.]

By this time, the police had discovered a lead as to where Marie and the baby were. Bill anxiously traced it down and through a series of events (which I know God directed), he found Marie and they were reunited.

I wish I could tell you that they lived happily ever after. Some of God's miracle stories do end that way, but others don't. Marie and Bill tried to work out their problems for over a year, but she finally decided that she didn't want to be married and obligated with a family. So she chose to leave Kristen and divorce Bill.

Kristen stayed with her dad, who had learned the *Way of Agape* and who was now free from any bitterness, resentment, hatred, and so on. He had learned how to love and forgive Marie unconditionally, in spite of her reactions and in spite of the circumstances. And, because he was a "free" man, he was then able to pursue God's best for his life.

Three years later, God brought Bill another beautiful Christian girl who, like Bill, wanted a family. They were married two summers ago. His new wife continues to write me about all the beautiful things God is doing in their relationship.

Ultimate Question

Let me ask you the ultimate question. Do you have this kind of unconditional, forgiving Love in your life? On your own power and ability, can you love like this: "Never keeping records of wrongs, never noticing when others do you wrong, not easily angered, never self-seeking, loving no matter what the cost?"

There's no way on earth I can even fathom a Love like this, let alone produce it on my own. Yet, throughout those difficult years of my own marriage, I was told over and over again that I was to love like 1 Corinthians 13. So I would set out trying, striving, and trumping up all I could to love like 1 Corinthians 13. And as I have shared in my own story, I failed miserably.

Only God can love like 1 Corinthians 13, because only God is *Agape* Love. All God desires from you and me is an open and pure vessel so *He* can love like 1 Corinthians 13 through us. This one truth has changed my entire Christian experience. I can now say that, yes, God does—when I allow Him to—love like 1 Corinthians 13 through me, and it's the most exhilarating, most meaningful and most fulfilling experience of my life. Being an open channel for God's Love is where I desire to stay, because I know when I am filled with His Love, I am filled with God.

God's Love Never Fails

I want to interject something critically important here. 1 Corinthians 13 declares, "God's Love never fails." What happened with Bill and Marie? Did God's Love fail? We must remember when we hear stories of God's miraculous dealings that the most important thing God desires in each of us, and one of the reasons He allows the trials and the testings in our lives, is so we might be *conformed into His Image of Love.*

Sometimes through these trials, both parties are transformed and the marriage is miraculously saved, as ours was. But often, because of unbelief or just plain unwillingness in one of the partners—like Marie—God's "perfect" Will is prevented. If you look closely, however, at the partner who was willing to go all the way with God, like Bill did, that person will have been transformed into God's Image in spite of the failure of the marriage. Look at Bill. He was freed from bitterness and resentment, he was freed from Marie's reactions, and he was freed from the situation. Truly, ***God's Love never fails*** in the one who chooses to allow it to flow.

Fifteen years ago, I had a group of women who were experiencing marital difficulties get together once a month for fellowship, encouragement, Bible study, and prayer.

At the end of one year, as the women looked at their circumstances, they all became a little discouraged: very few of their situations had really changed much. Then they took a good, long, hard look at themselves, and they realized that although their situations hadn't changed, they had! The miracle God had performed that year was in them! They were all being conformed into His Image and beginning to experience His supernatural Love![16]

We need to be willing to love with God's Love even if our circumstances and our situations never change! We need to learn to love even if we are not loved in return. I believe our motivation is wrong if we are loving only to be loved in return, or to make the circumstances improve, or to have the other person change. That again is human, conditional love and not God's Love at all.

Are You Willing to Love?

My question to each of you is: "Are you willing to love as Bill did?"

Can you tear up your long list of justified hurts and wrongs? Can you unconditionally forgive that person who has hurt you over and over again? Can you lay aside all the things that other person has done and said and, for the hundredth time, choose to give yourself totally over to God? Are you willing to open yourself up again and again, so God can reach that other person through you?

Remember, there's no way in the world that you or I can love as Bill did. What happened to Bill was completely supernatural and contrary to our normal human reactions and behavior. It's totally opposite to our own emotional way of loving. Only God can love like this through us. And it's only as we yield our selves—all our negative thoughts, emotions and desires that are contrary to God's—and become open vessels that God can love like this through us.

John 12:24 asserts, "Verily, verily, I say unto you, Except a grain of wheat fall into the ground and die, it abideth alone; but if it die, it bringeth forth much fruit [God's Love]."

The secret, the *key*, the truth that changed Bill's life, that changed my life, and that can change your life is *learning how to get rid of negative thoughts and emotions by giving them to God and becoming an open and cleansed vessel*. Then God's Love can fill you to overflowing and His Wisdom and Power can lead and guide you in every way, His Way!

Be a Hosea

Hosea in the Old Testament is such a wonderful example of one who loved God. Hosea loved God so much that he chose to become an open vessel that God could use to reach his adulterous wife, Gomer, and by that Love, reconcile her to himself.

I don't believe Hosea on his own power and ability could have loved Gomer the way he did. Yet, because of his faithfulness to love God first, yielding his will and life totally to Him, God enabled him to love Gomer unconditionally.

When we allow God to love others through us, as did Hosea (and Bill), it's God they see in us and not ourselves.

The question is: "***Are you willing to be a Hosea***?"

1 John 3:16a states, "Hereby perceive we the Love of God, because He laid down His life for us: and *we ought to lay down our lives for the brethren*." (emphasis added)

Jesus is our example. He is the Creator of the universe and the most powerful Being in the world. Yet Jesus chose of His own free will to lay His Life down for us, so *Agape* Love could be poured forth through Him to us. He was the mediator, the channel and the vessel of God's Love to us. He died so God's Love could be released to us. His whole purpose and ministry in life was to willingly lay down His life so that we might receive the Father's Love.

Are you willing to lay down your life so that God's Love can be released through you to others?

"No man hath seen God at any time. [But] If we love one another, God dwelleth in us, and His Love is perfected [allowed to flow] in us." (1 John 4:12)

Endnotes:

1. Romans 5:5
2. Romans 11:33-34
3. The only other usage of the word *Agape* appears in literature as a perfect *counterfeit* to the Trinity of the Bible.

   Agape was another name for the Egyptian goddess, Isis, whose center of worship was Rome. Isis, her husband Osiris (known as the word *logos*), and their son Hermes were classically called *the trinity* throughout history. It is said that Isis' supernatural and divine powers superseded that of all the other deities combined.

   Isis was said to have resurrected her husband, Osiris, and to have brought him back to life. After this incident, Isis became known as the *giver of life*. People believed she held in her hands the power of life and death.

   Isis was also said to be the "*I am*" in the beam of the sun and a direct emanation from god. The truth, of course, is: The God of the Bible is the only true *I AM* (Exodus 3:

14-15) and that is His Name forever. He is the only true God (Jeremiah 10:10). Jesus Christ, God's Son, is the only true radiance and true reflection of God (Hebrews 1:3). Jesus is God's Life personified.

The Isis counterfeit proves all the more that Satan is behind all the confusion over God's Love. These false gods never had God's Life. They never had His Love. They never knew Jesus. Therefore, Isis was an imitator of Agape in name only.

"In this the children of God are manifest, and the children of the devil: whosoever doeth not righteousness is not of God, neither he that loveth not his brother." (1 John 3:10)

4.   If we are believers and have Jesus' *Agape* Love in our hearts, when we sin that Love in our hearts will become quenched (blocked, stopped up). Scripture tells us that God's Love will always continue to flow into our hearts. However, because of sin, that *Agape* Love will be blocked from flowing out into our lives (souls). (1 Corinthians 13: 8: Romans 8:38-39; Isaiah 59:2)

5.   See Chapter 12, "Classic Example: Did You Tell Him Off?"

6.   Colossians 3:14 and 1 Corinthians 13:8, "God's Love Never Fails...."

7.   See Strong's Exhaustive Concordance, #2617 in the Dictionary of the Hebrew Bible.

8.   See Chapter 13, "We Think Before We Feel" and Chapter 14, "Take Every Thought Captive."

9.   Romans 14:23c says, "Whatsoever is not of faith is sin" and separates us from God (Isaiah 59:2; Psalm 119:70).

10. See Chapter 11, "Nothing Shall Separate Us."

11. See Chapter 14, "Eight Steps to Survival."

12. John 13:35

13. 2 Corinthians 2:10-11

14. See Chapter 4, "What Unites Us?"

15. I finally met Bill in 1993 at our conference in Vail, Colorado. It was wonderful to finally put a face with his voice. It had been 15 years since we first met by phone.

16. 2 Corinthians 3:18

Scriptural References:

Chapter 3

God's Love Is Called *Agape* in the Greek language
   A. *Agape* is defined in 1 Corinthians 13:1-8 (Galatians 5:22-23)
      1. *Agape* is not an emotion or a feeling, but *God Himself loving through us* (1 John 4:8b, 12)
      2. *Agape* is a supernatural Love
         a. *Agape* is not a human love (1 Corinthians 13:4-8)
         b. *Agape* is poured into our hearts only when we accept Christ into our lives (Romans 5:5; John 3:3)
      3. We cannot produce this kind of supernatural Love on our own (Luke 6:27-37). Only *God is Agape* (1 John 4:16; John 15:5)
      4. What is required of us is the *choice* to allow God to love His Love through us (John 12:24-25; 1 John 3:16; 1 Corinthians 15:36; Psalm 119:88; 2 Corinthians 4:7-12)
         a. We must choose to *yield ourselves* completely to God
         b. We must become an *open and cleansed vessel*
         c. We must remember that God is the one loving, not us
   B. *Agape* is totally opposite to our own human self-centered way of loving (Luke 6:27-37; Galatians 5:22-24; 1 Corinthians 13:4-8)
      1. *Agape* is not dependent upon human understanding, or how the other person responds, or on our circumstances (1 Corinthians 13:4-8; Psalm 103:17)
      2. *Agape* prompts a supernatural response (1 John 4:19)
      3. *Agape* exposes and brings to light sin (1 John 2:10; Ephesians 5:13; Example in John 8:3-12)
      4. *Agape* is unconditional acceptance
      5. *Agape* includes unconditional forgiveness (Mark 11:25-26; Hebrews 10:17)

Characteristics of *Agape* Love
   A. *Agape* is the only unconditional, non-reciprocal, freeing, and other-centered Love there is (Jeremiah 31:3; Song of Solomon 8:7a; 1 Corinthians 13:4-8; Luke 6:27-38)
      1. *Agape* is a *gift of Love* with no strings attached—it's unconditional— it loves no matter what (1 Corinthians 13:4-8; Isaiah 54:10; Hebrews 13:5; Romans 8:35-39)
      2. *Agape* is a *one-sided Love*—it doesn't have to be returned to be kept alive (Luke 6:27-37)
      3. *Agape* is a *freeing Love*—it frees the lover from expectations and pre-sumptions and it frees the one being loved to respond from his heart (2 Corinthians 3:17)
      4. *Agape* is *other-centered Love*—it always puts the other's interests above its own

B.   *Agape* is the "lily among the thorns" (Song of Solomon 2:2)

More Attributes of God's Love (See Supplemental Notes)
  A.   *Agape* Love is electing, initiating, identifying, and faithful Love
       (Deuteronomy 7:6-8)
       1.   *Electing Love* means the lover selects its object to love (Ephesians
            1:4-5; John 15:16)
       2.   *Initiating Love* means the lover is the first one to act—it's a one-way
            love (1 John 4:9-10,19; Jeremiah 31:3; John 3:16; Hosea 2:19)
       3.   *Identifying Love* puts itself in the other's place (Hebrews 2:17-18;
            Isaiah 63:9; Galatians 2:20; Hosea 2:19)
       4.   *Faithful Love* is a love that always performs its word (Hosea 2:20;
            Deuteronomy 7:9)
  B.   God is Love (1 John 4:8)

Chesed Love
  A.   God's Love (*chesed* in the Old Testament) had two facets:
       1.   God's *longsuffering and merciful Love* (Genesis 24:12; 2 Samuel 7:15;
            1 Chronicles 19:2; 2 Chronicles 6:14; Psalm 103:4,8,11,17; 2 Peter
            3:15a)
       2.   God's *strict, disciplinary Love* (Job 37:13; Proverbs 14:34b; 25:10;
            Leviticus 20:17)
  B.   *Agape* can be both merciful and strict (Hebrews 12:5-11; Revelation 3:19;
       Hosea 2:19)
       1.   God's mercy and His truth always work together (Psalm 89:14)
       2.   God is grieved when we disobey Him (Jeremiah 4:18-19,21; 7:23-24;
            2 Samuel 7:14-15)
       3.   We have a choice to obey or not (Deuteronomy 11:27)

Taking a Stand in God's Love
  A.   Follow these guidelines
       1.   Will it edify the person and ultimately bring him closer to God?
       2.   Would Jesus take a stand over this?
       3.   Is this God's timing? (Proverbs 25:11)
       4.   What is my motive? (Romans 15:1)
  B.   Love with God's Wisdom

God's Love Never Fails
  A.   God's Love *never stops coming* (1 Corinthians 13:8; Psalm 89:33; 90:33;
       103:17; Jeremiah 31:3)
       1.   Jesus is the mediator (the vessel) of God's Love to us (1 John 3:16a)
       2.   We must be willing to love as He did, even if our circumstances never
            change (Acts 20:24)
  B.   Are you willing to be a Hosea? (Hosea 1-3; 1 John 4:9-10)

Chapter 4: Why Is God's Love So Important?

God Is Love

Why is *Agape* so important? Why do we make such a big issue about *Agape* Love? What's so special about it? There is only one answer to these questions. 1 John 4:8 declares, *"God is Agape."* This is why Love is so special, and this is the reason we are commanded to seek *Agape* with all of our being.

Let's explore six more reasons why God's Love is so important to experience for ourselves and then to pass on to others.

Meaning and Purpose of Our Lives

1) Having God's Love in our lives is **the whole meaning and purpose of our Christian walk**. I believe God has called us as Christians for two primary reasons: *To love Him*, and then *to love others*. I don't believe we were called to be "Christians" just to be happy and content within ourselves, but to be vessels and channels of God's Love—experiencing His Love firsthand, and then passing that Love on to others.

1 Timothy 1:5 teaches that *Agape* is the goal of our instruction and the fulfillment of all of God's Word in us! In other words, the whole Bible is summed up in our personally knowing and passing on God's Love![1]

1 Corinthians 13:1-3 says, "Though I speak with the tongues of men and of angels, and have not [*Agape*], I am become as a sounding brass, or a tinkling cymbal. And though I have the gift of prophecy, and understand all mysteries and all knowledge; and though I have all faith, so that I could remove mountains, and have not [*Agape*], *I am nothing*. And though I bestow all my goods to feed the poor, and though I give my body to be burned, and have not [*Agape*], it profiteth me nothing." (emphasis added)

God declares here that without His Love, all the intellectual knowledge in the world, all the supernatural understanding in the world, and all the faith in the world will profit and benefit us nothing. Without His Love, God says, we will still be empty, lonely, and without meaning or purpose to our lives. Without His Love, God avows, "We are nothing." Love is the reason God created us in the first place. And, I believe, *if we don't learn to love and be loved in the way God intends, we truly will have wasted our lives.*

Many people recognize this fact too late. After working hard their entire lives to reach their aspired goals (to be happy, to have their own business, to have financial independence, etc.), many realize that in the process they have lost the true meaning of their lives, which is love and love relationships. Materially, some of these people have attained everything that they could ever want, yet they still feel empty and unfulfilled.[2]

When Chuck was in the corporate world, I had many opportunities to talk to successful business executives—many of whom said they'd give anything to be able to live their lives over again. If they had a second chance, they said, they would be careful *not* to miss the most important thing in their life—the people they loved and those who loved them.[3]

A newspaper article written many years ago told the story of a very wealthy and famous man whose name you would recognize. Throughout his life, he thought kids and family were just a nuisance and a deterrent to what success was all about. He thus determined to amass a fortune for himself and to make his name known. He did both. But in the process, he lost all his relationships. In the end, when he was too old to work, he sat night after night, alone in his huge, empty mansion, filled with priceless—yet worthless—possessions. He had missed the very reason he was created—to be loved and to love.

Edgar Jackson has written an excellent book called *Understanding Loneliness*. He shares that psychologists have now exchanged the word *identity* for the word *love*. Love is our true identity. Without love we are lost, in spite of all the fortune, power, prestige, and education we amass. Love must be the supreme and central issue of our lives or we will die psychologically, socially, spiritually, and even physically.

Christianity is unique in that it is a religion of Love. Christianity has the answers that everyone is so desperate for—***Jesus is that Love***. God has called us as believers to be His co-workers, His co-laborers, and His partners in spreading His gospel of Love to others. Our lives as Christians, then, are not just something to be enjoyed or to derive happiness from, but an opportunity to be an open vessel for God's Love. God has called us specifically for this very purpose!

1 John 3:14 warns, "He that loveth not...abideth in death." This simply means, *if we are not loving, we are dying.* We're dying because we are separated from the true meaning of our lives, which is Love.

How Will They Know We Are Christians?

2) Another reason God's Love is so important in our lives is because God's Love is the only way **others will know and see that we are, indeed, Christians.**

"By this shall all men know that ye are My disciples, *if ye have love one to another*." (John 13:35, emphasis added)

As we look around us—at our churches, our families, our friends, and our kids—many of us are dying from a lack of love. Many of us are caught up in the do's and don'ts of Scripture, the prophecies, the gifts, the healings, the miracles, the faith, the signs and wonders, etc., but *where is God's Love?* Scripture says, "They will know we are Christians by our Love." Where's God's Love? How can we be Spirit filled and yet not Love filled? To me they're the very same thing!

God's Love, the glue that ties us all together, is missing.

1 John 2:4 avows, "He that saith 'I know Him,' [I am a Christian], and keepeth not His commandments, [to love one another] is a liar, and the truth is not in him."

God's Love doesn't just fall out of heaven. His Love comes through us. *We are extensions of God's Love* to one another. God just needs a willing body—arms and legs—to pour His Love through.

Larry Crabb has written a book called *Inside Out* in which he shares that Christians can spend years in the Bible developing a real love for the truth; but, he says, if they come away without knowing God in a deeper and more real way and without His Love for people, then they will have wasted their time. The whole purpose of Bible study is to make us more loving, not more scholarly.

David Needham (*Birthright*) confirms this same thought: "...the big task is not the finding of the truth, but the living of it!"[4] To me this statement says it all!

It's only Jesus' Love through us—in our actions—that will bring our families, our husbands, our children, our neighbors, and our bosses to the feet of Jesus. Since God is Love, the only way these people will know that we are indeed Christians is by the *real* Love that comes from us.

1 Peter 4:8 urges us, "Above all things have fervent Love among yourselves; for Love shall cover the multitude of sins." This simply means that if love is true *Agape* Love then it will stop the sin right there. In other words, if we hear something negative (some sin) about a brother, we will take it to the Lord first, pray about it, and, if need be, go to that brother to find out the truth. True *Agape* Love will not pass that sin on to another through gossip, but rather, will stop it when it's first heard.

A non-believer told me recently, "I don't want to go to church anymore because the people there are just a bunch of phonies. I work with 'so and so' (a church goer) and you should see what he does during the rest of the week! How can he call himself a Christian?"

That non-Christians know the "real thing" when they see it is fascinating to me. They can spot the phonies a mile away. I find this interesting, since we Christians are often fooled by our so-called "brothers and sisters." So often God must combat and unravel not just unbelief in a person, but also the damage other "so-called" Christians have done. It's only God's genuine Love through us that can truly touch these skeptical people and bring them to Jesus. Our flowery and empty words *about* Jesus are not enough. Our actions must match our words in order for it to be truth. In other words, we simply must "live His Love."

1 John 3:10 asserts, "Whosoever doeth not righteousness [right actions] is not of God, neither he that loveth *not* his brother." (emphasis added) This means that if we are not genuinely loving others with God's Love, we are showing the world that we're really not God's children at all.

Proof of Abiding in God

3) Loving with God's Love **proves we are abiding in God.**

John 15 is a wonderful chapter—totally devoted to what it means to abide in God. It says abiding in God simply means staying in His Love, remaining in His Presence, continually presenting our will and life to Him, as open channels, so that He can pass His Love on to others through us.

A dear friend of ours, a Greek scholar who has been studying *The Way of Agape*, pointed out to me recently that the word *to bear* in John 15:2 could be translated "*to carry fruit from one location to another*" in other words, to be an open channel, passing Love from the Father to others.

He also suggests that the phrase "abide in Me" or "remain in Me" could also be translated "*rest in My Love*." Then God's promise in verse 7 makes much more sense. If we continue to "rest in His Love" (i.e., continue to be an open channel for it), then we can ask whatever we will, consistent with bearing fruit, and He will do it.

Here is my friend's translation of John 15:1-7:

"15:1: I (Jesus) am the true vine and my Father is the vine keeper. 2: He takes away each of My (Jesus') branches that don't carry fruit, and He cleanses each (one) that is carrying fruit so that it may carry even more.

"3: You are already clean through the teaching that I have spoken to you. 4: Rest in my Love, and I will be with you. Just as the branch cannot carry fruit by itself (unless it remains on the vine), so neither can you, unless you rest in My Love.

"5: I am the vine; you are the branches. Whoever rests in My Love and lets My Love rest within him can carry lots of fruit, because without Me you cannot accomplish anything. 6: If anyone fails to rest in My Love, he shall be cast out like a branch and shall become withered, and they shall gather them and cast them into the fire, and the fire shall burn.

"7: If you rest in My Love, and my sayings take root within you, ask whatever you want to happen, and it shall come about for your benefit. 8: My Father is glorified by doing this, so that you can carry lots of fruit and can demonstrate that you have become my disciples."

As we noted before, the proof that we are Christians comes not through our knowledge of Scripture, from our spiritual gifts, nor by our church attendance, but only by how much of God's Love we are sharing.

John 15:14 states that if we are obedient and do what God commands (remain in His Love and carry fruit) then we will be His friends. Abraham is a good example of one who rested in and remained in God's Love. Thus, Abraham is remembered in Scripture as a "friend of God" and one who "walked with God." Abraham had the intimate relationship with God that we all desire. Staying in, remaining in, and resting in God's Love is the only way to achieve that union.

A beautiful Scripture that exemplifies this relationship is Proverbs 22:11: "He that loveth [totally gives himself over to] pureness of heart...the King shall be his friend."

Again, the *key* is having that pure heart. Why? Because God's Love can then flow freely and purely from our hearts out into our lives as open channels. This is what it means to "stay in" God's Love, and this is what makes us His friends. Having God's Love in our lives then is the proof that we belong to and are abiding in God.

Filled With the "Fulness of God"

4) Loving with God's Love shows we are **filled with the "fulness of God."**

What is the "fulness of God?" It is experiencing God's Life, His supernatural Love, Wisdom and Power in and through us, in place of our own. It is God's Character, His Image and His Fulness that we are passing on.

Ephesians 3:19 urges us "to know the Love of Christ, which passeth knowledge, that ye might be filled with all the fulness of God."

Stephen, in Acts 6-7, is a wonderful example of being filled with the "fulness of God." Even when the elders and the high priests persecuted Steven and charged him falsely before the Sanhedrin, they could still see that he was "full of faith and power." (6:8) Thus, they "were not able to resist the wisdom by which he spoke." They "saw his face as it had been the face of an angel." (Acts 6:10,15) Then in Acts 7:60, as they were stoning him, Stephen—still full of the Love of God—said, "Lord, lay not this sin to their charge." Steven, at that moment, was so "full of the Holy Spirit" (verse 55) that he could unconditionally love and forgive them even as they were killing him.

Being "filled with God" is the most thrilling and the most exhilarating experience imaginable. We are called for this very purpose. Experiencing His Wisdom, Love, and Power through us becomes the whole meaning and purpose for our existence.[5]

As Paul explains in 2 Corinthians 4:7,10-12, "But we have this treasure in earthen vessels, that the excellency of the power may be of God, and not of us... Always bearing about in the body the dying of the Lord Jesus, that the life also of Jesus might be made manifest in our body. For we which live are always delivered unto death for Jesus' sake, that the life also of Jesus might be made manifest in our mortal flesh. So then death worketh in us, but life in you."

What Unites Us?

5) God's Love is **the perfect "bond of union," not only between God and me, but also between others and myself.**

God's Love not only initiates a relationship and maintains that relationship, but His Love also continually reconciles that relationship. God's Love is the only power that can enable us to unconditionally forgive and forget what others have done to us. Only God, by His unconditional *Agape* Love, can cleanse, heal, and remove our hurts and wounds so that we can genuinely forgive and forget what others have done to us. When God cleanses and heals us, our wounds are not just buried and pushed down—continuing to unconsciously motivate all our actions—they are literally removed from us.

I heard a Christian radio psychologist once expound, "You just forgive and forget what others have done to you and go on as if nothing ever happened."

Have you ever tried to do that in your own power? It's a total impossibility! How can we, on our own, get rid of all the hurts and wounds we have unjustly sustained by others, in order to forgive them? We can't! There is absolutely no way on earth we can unconditionally forgive another person and go on in that relationship as if nothing had ever happened unless, of course, we bury our real feelings, build walls over our hearts, become totally desensitized, and then go on, hardened and unfeeling.

I believe many people live this way because they don't realize they have another option.[6] They don't realize that by having Jesus in their hearts, He will totally heal and completely remove their wounds and hurts if they will simply confess and acknowledge those hurts and choose to give them to Him.

As God promises in Psalm 103:12, "As far as the east is from the west, So far hath He removed our transgressions [our sins] from us."

Only God's Love can cleanse us, heal us, and enable us to forgive others. Only His Love will reconcile us. Only His Love will wipe away our divisions and our discords. And only His Love will unite us again as one!

John 17:22-23a records, "And the glory which Thou gavest Me I have given them; that they may be one, even as We are one: I in them and Thou in Me, that they may be made perfect [complete] in one."

God's Love is the bond of completeness or wholeness. God's Love through us is the finished product. Colossians 3:14 declares that "above all these things we are to put on *Agape*, which is the bond of perfectness." (Perfectness simply means completeness, or perfect union with Christ.) God's Love is the completion, the perfection, and the finished product God longs for in each of us.[7] If we obey Him, by loving Him first, His Love will then be made complete and perfect in us.[8]

As God's Love is allowed to grow in each of our lives, it will overshadow everything else. God's Love is the mark of becoming a man and producing the finished product (1 Corinthians 13:11). As we said in the beginning of this chapter, God's Love is superior to everything else in our lives.

What Proves We Love God?

6) Finally, having God's Love in our lives is **proof that we love Him.** If we choose continually to lay down our wills and our lives to Jesus in order for Him to love others through us, that Love is going to be the proof and the evidence that we do, indeed, love God.

John 14:21 asserts, "He that hath My commandments, and keepeth them, he it is that loveth Me."

God's Love through us is the proof we have reached the goal of our instruction[9] and the fulfillment of God's purpose in our lives. It is proof we have set aside, relinquished, and totally given ourselves over to Him in obedience. It's proof we are those open channels, carrying fruit from one place to another. Others are going to know that we belong to God just by hearing our words and seeing our actions. God's Love filling our hearts and lives proves that we not only love God, but we have "passed out of death into life." (1 John 3:10,14)

God's Love in our lives is to be preeminent, unsurpassed and superior to everything else in its importance to us. We must learn how to receive it, how to stay filled with it, and how to pass it on. Then and only then can we genuinely reflect God in all that we think, say, and do.

1 John 4:17 promises, "Herein is our Love made perfect [complete], that we may have boldness in the day of judgment: *because as He is, so are we in this world*." (emphasis added)

Endnotes:

1. Romans 13:10; Matthew 22:40

2. See Chapter 2 and Chapter 6, "Two Basic Needs."

3. Prime Time by Howard Barks is a great book on this subject.

4. See Chapter 8, "What Is Truth?"

5. See Chapter 7, "Do You Know God?"

6. When we choose to accept Jesus as our Savior and our Lord, we then receive His super-natural Life. God's Life within us is what enables us to forgive and <u>forget</u> what others have done to us. Jesus is the only one who can literally take that hurt and totally remove it from us. (Psalm 103:12)

7. John 17:22, 26

8. 1 John 2:5

9. 1 Timothy 1:5

Scriptural References:

Chapter 4

Why Is God's Love So Important?

A. *God is Love.* This is why Love is so important (1 John 4:8)
   1. God's Love protects us from the enemy (Isaiah 59:19; Song of Solomon 2:4a)
   2. God's Love casts out all fear (1 John 4:18; 2 Timothy 1:7; Romans 8:15)
   3. God's Love covers sin (Proverbs 10:12b; 1 Peter 4:8). This means God's Love stops the sin right there.

B. *God's Love is the goal and purpose for our lives* as Christians (1 Timothy 1:5; 1 John 3:14; 4:16; John 13:35; Ephesians 1:4; 2 Corinthians 5:14)
   1. God's Love should be the central issue of our lives (1 Corinthians 13:1-3; Psalm 63:3a; 1 Peter 4:8; 1 John 3:14)
   2. God's Love is the fulfillment of the law (Galatians 5:14; Matthew 22:40; Romans 13:8,10)

C. God's Love is the only genuine way others will see that we are Christians (John 13:35; 1 John 3:10; 4:12)

D. God's Love is proof that we are abiding in God (John 15:4-10; 1 John 2:4-5; 1 John 3:14; 4:7,12,16)—and we are His friends (John 15:14)

E. When God's Love flows through us, we are filled with the fulness of God (Ephesians 3:19; Acts 6:8,10; 7:55)

F. God's Love is the perfect "bond of union" between others and ourselves (John 17:22,26; 1 Corinthians 13:11; Colossians 3:14; Psalm 103:11-12; 1 John 4:12). It's the "mark of maturity" (1 Corinthians 13:10; Colossians 3:14; 1 John 2:5; 3:14; 4:7,17-18)

G. Having God's Love is proof that we are loving Him (John 14:21; 1 John 3:14)

Chapter 5: God's Love vs. Natural Love

Natural love is the total opposite of God's Love. It's critical that we understand this. Human love is contrary to everything that 1 Corinthians 13:4-8 describes. In fact, we can read that Scripture putting "not" in front of each sentence and it fits human, natural love. (i.e., human love does *not* suffer long, it is *not* kind, etc.)

Human love is based upon our feelings, our circumstances and others' responses, whereas God's Love is dependent only upon God. Therefore, no matter how we feel, what we think, or what our circumstances are, God will always have Love for that other person.

Everyone has human love—we're born with it. Human love is the most beautiful flower the world has to offer, but it's a poisonous flower—like a thorn—because it often causes heartaches, divorces, broken homes, and wrecked families.

Not everyone, however, has God's Love. God's Love is a gift we receive only when we ask Jesus Christ into our hearts. His Love then, is the only Love that will cover a multitude of sins[1] and will unconditionally and unilaterally keep on loving no matter what the object of that Love is doing.

The Song of Solomon 2:2 uses the image, "As the lily among thorns, so is my Love." I believe the lily is God's Love, whereas the thorns are the human loves.

Human Love

Left to operate on their own, without the tempering power of God's *Agape* Love, all human loves are conditional, two-sided, bondage and self-centered loves.

Human love is *conditional* because it always depends upon three things: what we think, feel, and desire; what our circumstances are; and how the other person responds to us.

Human love is *two-sided* because it always bargains, "I'll love you if you love me. But if you stop loving me, then I will stop loving you." (Interesting: I read recently, "hate occurs when we don't get human love returned.")

Human love is a *bondage* love because we become totally wrapped up with our own presumptions and expectations of the other person. Then the other person is not free to respond from his heart, but is often pushed into self-defensiveness.

Lastly, human love is a *self-centered* love because no matter how selfless it looks on the outside, we will always be loving that other person hoping to get in return the love, the admiration, or the notoriety we so desperately need.

A few years ago as Chuck and I were flying to Australia, I showed him my conclusions about human love and asked him how he felt about it. At first he didn't agree with me at all, and he said he could prove me wrong. He began going through all the examples he could think of that might be "unconditional, freeing, and other-centered" human love.

He thought of heroes in the world wars who gave their lives for others; he thought of martyrs who died in place of others; and he thought of close friends of his in the armed forces. But after pondering and studying each example more closely, he, too, came to the conclusion that, yes, if we really could see into each of those hearts, *all human loves do have ulterior motives*: notoriety, glory, power or fame

As C.S. Lewis explains, human love is always a need love, with self-centered motives. But God's Love, he states, is always a gift of Love with no strings attached.

Three Natural Loves

There are three human or natural loves. Let's briefly go over each one of these and see how they differ from God's Love. We do this not as an academic exercise, but so that we can recognize these different types of love in our own lives.

Storge Love

The first natural love we'll explore is ***storge*** love. *Storge* is the Greek word for our natural, emotional, "feeling love." It's simply our "affection love" for one another. It's an instinctive love like the love of a parent for a child, or of a husband for his family. *Storge* actually means "to cover over" or "to protect."

However, *storge* love, like all the other natural or human loves, is a conditional love because it must be reciprocated or returned in order for it to be kept alive. Therefore, *storge* love can often become a suffocating or strangleholding kind of love, especially if the one being loved chooses not to return it. Then, there develops in the "lover" a desperate need to control that other person and to get their love at any cost.

We often see this in mothers whose whole lives have revolved around their children. When the children grow up and leave home, these moms often fall apart because they have no life of their own. Their needs have always been met by their kids and not by God. Because of the overwhelming and unbearable vacuum left in their own lives, these moms develop a desperate need to somehow grasp and retain the love of their children.

Example: Mama's Boy

Gary was the only child of a very domineering mother. He married once, but after ten years he was divorced because of the negative influence of his mom. (Genesis 2:24 includes the concept of "leaving" as well as "cleaving.")

After the divorce, he moved in with his mom and has lived at home ever since. For eight years now, Gary has been going steady with a woman who really adores him. The last time I saw him, I asked if he was ever going to get married again. His response was, "Well, Nan, when mom doesn't need me anymore, then I'll marry." Gary is now 59 years old! This to me is a perfect example of *storge* love on both sides.

Storge love can also become a possessive love or a clutching love rather than a freeing love. Sometimes we experience *storge* love in a dying marriage, where one spouse has an overwhelming need to protect and hang on to the marriage at all costs. It's not for the love of the partner that the spouse is hanging on, but rather a self-centered fear of losing the protection, the comfort and the status of being married.

I know quite a few women who have chosen to stay in their horrible, marital situations because of this very thing. Rather than let go and allow God to work in their husbands' lives, they suffocate their husbands with *storge* love (suffocating, covering, hovering love). Usually the men end up leaving anyway.

Jealousy often plays a big role in *storge* love. Fear of losing control of someone you love to another person can entirely motivate one's behavior. It's again not an unconditional love for their spouse that motivates them, but a self-centered, emotional love. Then, of course, their spouse becomes open prey for the enemy because of his own bitterness, hate, and resentment.

Storge love, like all the other natural loves, is a self-centered need love and without God's intervention, it will seek and desire only its own good, not the good of the other person. If, however, God's Love can become the foundation of that relationship, then *storge* love can become the blessing God intended it to be all along.

Eros Love

The next natural, human love is **eros** love. *Eros* is the Greek word for our natural, sexual love based on physical attraction. I like to call this kind of love our "falling in love" love. *Eros* love is a passionate, erotic love that has an intoxicating effect on us. When we're engulfed in *eros* love, we feel like we're on a high!

One of the reasons we are so captivated by *eros* love is that it momentarily lifts us above ourselves, like an escape. In this temporary ecstasy, we are transported beyond our problems, beyond our unhappiness, and beyond our loneliness, as we allow another person to momentarily fill that emptiness, that void deep within us. This is why I believe *eros* love is so rampant in our chaotic world today.

Eros love can also distort a person's self-reflection and self-examination. In other words, when we are engulfed in *eros* love, our rationality is often blurred, and we can easily become totally deluded!

Example: Enslaved

Shawn is a Christian friend of ours who had been married for nearly 25 years, when his wife found out he'd spent a number of those years secretly having an affair. She confronted him with the truth—that he was living in sin. But, all Shawn could say was, "Oh no, you're wrong! God has shown me I am right in His Will. I've never really been happy with you or loved you, and God wants me to be happy."

This is a perfect example of how *eros* love can delude us and lead us right into deep deception and trouble. If we're captivated by this kind of love outside of marriage where God intends it to be, it can lead us into Satan's trap. The truth is that God cares more about our walking in His Will than He does our *momentary* happiness. If we will choose to walk according to His Will, we will be guaranteed a *long-lasting* joy.

When we are consumed or engulfed in *eros* love, our own willpower (our own volition) is often negated and overshadowed by our strong physical desires. Our emotions then overrule our reason, take control of our actions, and we end up spiraling downward.

A Scriptural example of this engulfment is David with Bathsheba. In most everything else, David used such strong willpower. In fact God called him "a man after [His] own heart" (Acts 13:22) because he was willing to do all of God's Will. But something happened to David's willpower when he saw Bathsheba. His emotions simply overtook him and he didn't recognize it (or perhaps he didn't want to recognize it). He then ended up "spiritually" spiraling downward with his emotions completely in control.

This is why I believe God continuously warns us against the passions and the desires of the flesh. Because when *eros* love is controlling us, we'll be carried on by the tide of emotion and there will be no room to choose God's Will. So, if left alone without God's intervention, *eros* will always be a conditional love that only desires the good and the satisfaction of itself and not the other person.

In Love With Our Mates

In the right context, however, *eros* love is a fabulous love. In our Christian marriages, *eros* love is desperately needed. Wives, we need to enthrall, intoxicate, and captivate our men so they don't need to look elsewhere for this kind of excitement.

We need to give our men the kind of "high" that only we as wives can give them, because then it's done in the sight of God and is blessed beyond description. We are then able to experience that oneness—not only spiritually but also physically—that God intended for us all along. I believe we need not only to love (*agapao*) our husbands, but we also need to be "in love" (*eros*) with our husbands.

After 38 years of marriage, Chuck always holds me in his arms after we make love, and together we thank God for what He has restored to us. We praise Him for allowing us to experience the ecstasy and rapture of being brought right to the throne of God—as one. Because God's *Agape* Love is the foundation of our marriage, we are able to put *eros* love in its proper and wonderful place.

Eros love is a desperately important area of Christian marriages. Don't ignore or neglect it. If counseling or help is needed in the sexual area of your marriage, please seek it. If the problem is mental or emotional and perhaps just the "desire" is missing in your relationship, God can and will change your feelings as you learn to become an open vessel through which He can pour His Love. If, however, the problem is physical, then do pray and, by all means, seek medical help as the Lord leads. This is a critical area of marriage, and it cannot be overlooked.

Eros love, like the other human loves, however, can only be restored and rebuilt on the solid foundation of God's Love.

Phileo Love

The third kind of natural, human love is ***phileo*** love. *Phileo* love is the Greek word for anything that we are strongly attached to. The Bible has much to say about *phileo* love—personal attachment love. For example, John 12:25 which warns, "He that loveth (*phileo*) his life shall lose it." It's true. If we are more attached to our own life (our own thoughts, emotions and desires), than God's Life through us, we will lose our lives. (Just like the man we spoke of last chapter who amassed a fortune, but in the process lost everyone he loved and that loved him.) If we don't learn to love and be loved in the way God intends, we will have wasted our lives here on earth.

Phileo love is based on a similarity of outlook and interest. It's a mutual attraction love, a friendship love, a companionship love, or a sharing of common interests.[2] We *phileo* someone because we're bound together doing the same thing.[3] *Phileo* love is having something in common, being compatible, being able to think alike, seeing eye to eye. Many marriages are built on this type of love.

Example: Friendship Not Enough

Geri, one of my good friends in college, got married at the same time Chuck and I did. She was adamant, however, that because she and her husband were best friends; they didn't need to have the "typical marriage" relationship. They didn't need kids or a home to be tied down to. They wanted to be free to write, travel, teach and so on.

Ten years later, after extensive traveling and a "mobile" home, they changed their minds and decided that children and a home were, after all, desirable. When they found out they couldn't have babies, many problems ensued and they quickly found out that their "friendship love" was not enough to hold the marriage together. The husband eventually found someone else with whom he "had more in common" and my friend's marriage broke up.

[Note something interesting here: *Phileo* love comes as a result of an intimate relationship. This is important because with *phileo* love, the relationship and the friendship need to come first, and then the love follows. Whereas, with God's Love, if you remember, the Love comes first (it's initiating Love), and then the relationship follows.[4]]

Seeks Only the Good of Itself

Human love, whether it's *storge, phileo* or *eros*, if left alone without God's intervention, seeks only the good of itself and not the other person. Human love is always based on certain reciprocal expectations and certain underlying agreements between two parties. "I'll love you, if you will love me. But if you stop loving me, then I'll stop loving you!"

I think reciprocity is one of the reasons why so many Christian marriages are falling apart today. We are confusing human love with God's Love. And because of this fact, many of us have become discouraged, overwhelmed, and ready to give up.

Yes, God's *Agape* Love is in our hearts, but often it has become buried under a ton of hurts and resentments. Thus, God's Love is not able to flow—it's quenched, blocked and covered over. Therefore, the love that we are functioning on is purely human love and not God's Love at all. Human love, as we said before, is based upon what we think, feel and want, upon what the other party does, and upon our circumstances. And, I believe, if we look closely enough, this is the type of love that we will find in our marriages, even though we are Christians.

Can Become a Blessing

All three of these natural loves can be good or bad, depending upon the foundation on which they're based. If these human loves are based on self, our own emotions, thoughts and desires which are usually contrary to God's, then these natural loves are always going to be conditional and reciprocal (two-sided), trying to fulfill their own needs. If, however, these human or natural loves can be built upon God's unconditional *Agape* Love as a foundation, then they can become the blessings that God intended them to be all along.[5]

So, we don't want to negate the importance of these human loves, but we must always make sure they are built on God's Love as a foundation. Then if the human loves fail—and they will, because they're natural and human loves—God's Love will still be there—working to revive them and to reconcile us.

I must be honest with you. I still function much of the time on human love, based on self. Just like you, it's been a habit for me for 50 years to depend upon how

I feel, how the other person responds, and what my circumstances are. The difference now, however, is that I can discern those times when I am functioning on human love (based on self). And, most important of all, I now know how to get back to being that open and cleansed vessel, so that God's Love can once again begin to flow.[6]

So human love, whether we're Christians or not, will always let us down, continually failing. It will fail us because we will continue to get hurt; that other person will continue to respond in a way that's displeasing to us; and we will continue to find ourselves in circumstances totally out of our control. However, if we can make those faith choices to cleanse our hearts and do what God wants, God's Love will always be there to heal us and reconcile us back to that other person. God then will align our feelings to match the faith choices we have made, and once again we will *feel* that love.

"A More Excellent Way"

I received a letter a while back that gave a perfect analogy of God's Love contrasted to human love. The letter spoke of our need to continually be filled with God's never-ending Love. It also spoke of human love, which is always in constant short supply because it's dependent upon our own thoughts and feelings, the other's responses, and our circumstances. The following is an excerpt from the letter:

"Out here in Lakeview where I live, there are farms with *irrigation channels* that flood and irrigate the fields. Irrigation channels are channels for the flood waters to flow through. The flood waters are stored somewhere far away from the field and when the channels are open, the flood waters just pour through them. The flood waters are essential because they bring life and growth to the fields.

"There are also *plain ditches* on the farm where I live that often have water in them because of the rain. These plain ditches, however, can become stagnant pools of water filled with debris; thus, these ditches cannot be used for irrigation.

"Water in the farmer's plain ditches is like human love in man. It is in short supply and useful only to the ditch that it is in. Not only is there too little water in it, but it often becomes stagnant and polluted. Often these ditches are blocked with other foreign matter or with rocks and weeds. When a neighbor needs water, he certainly won't benefit much from the water in these ditches.

"The irrigation channels, however, are different and very much like God's Love. The farmer who wants to share his water with his neighbor (as we do with God's Love), needs only to open his irrigation channel and let the flood water pour through. The farmer cannot take credit for the water as it came from a source far away. But as the farmer is willing, and leaves his irrigation channel open, the neighbor can get all the flood water he needs."

Only Solid Foundation

God's supernatural Love is the only solid foundation upon which *storge, eros* and *phileo* love can be built, and, if need be, the only foundation upon which they can be rebuilt and allowed to grow.

I believe even if all the human loves have died in a marriage, if just one party is willing to initiate God's Love, there is still a possibility of restoring that marriage. Mine was! If, however, all the human loves have already died in a marriage, and God's Love is also missing because it's quenched or blocked in both their hearts, then that marriage is probably doomed to failure.[7]

This is one of the reasons why I believe so many Christian marriages are falling apart today. God's Love has become buried under a ton of rubble and debris in both spouse's hearts and neither one is willing to be *first to change* and become that open, cleansed vessel. Remember Matthew 24:12, "Because iniquity [sin] shall abound, the [*Agape*—God's Love] of many will grow cold."

This is exactly what is happening in our Christian world today. We have chosen to hold on to our own "justified" hurts and rights, rather than to unconditionally love God and give all these things to Him. No wonder Satan is rejoicing!

I believe, therefore, it's critical to know the difference between God's Love and human love—to know when we are functioning on God's Love and when we are not. And when we are not, to be honest with ourselves and recognize that we have, at that moment, quenched God's Spirit and blocked His Love in our hearts—which is sin.[8]

Most importantly, then, we need to know what to do about that sin: We need to know how to confess it; how to turn around from following whatever is the cause of that sin; and then, how to give that sin over to God and go His Way.[9]

I Thought I Was Loving Chuck

During our marital difficulties, I thought I was loving Chuck unconditionally with God's Love. After all, I had been a Christian for 20 years! In truth, I didn't even know the meaning of the word *Love*. I was submitting to Chuck and trying many "ways" to save our marriage, but only out of *storge* and *phileo* love, not God's Love at all. God's Love was buried under a ton of debris in my own heart and certainly had "grown cold" in my life.

By loving Chuck, I was hoping to get in return the love I so desperately needed; that's human love, based on self, trying to fulfill its own needs. It was conditional, self-centered, natural love and not God's Love at all. I wasn't experiencing God's Love for myself. Therefore, I was trying to find the love and security that I needed in Chuck. I was looking horizontally, not vertically to have all my needs to be met. And it was only when my eyes were focused back on Jesus—the only one who can meet my needs for love and security—that I could finally begin to love Chuck in the way God intended from the very beginning.

I believe many Christians are confusing these natural loves with God's Love—just as I did. They are looking to their spouses, families, friends and relatives to meet their need for love, rather than to God alone. This is where many of us are getting off the track, becoming totally confused and ready to give up because it's not working.

Without His Love We Are Nothing

The three natural loves we have been studying here are loves that we desperately need from each other in order to get along in this world. But God's supernatural Love is a Love we must have in order to survive at all. God's Love is the only Love that can make us whole and give us our identity, meaning, and purpose in this life.

1 Corinthians 13:1-3 declares, "Though I speak with the tongues of men and of angels, and have not [God's] Love in my life, I am become as sounding brass, or a tinkling cymbal. And though I have the gift of prophecy, and understand all mysteries and all knowledge; and though I have all faith, so that I could remove mountains, and have not [God's] Love, *I am nothing*. And though I bestow all my goods to feed the poor, and though I give my body to be burned, and have not [God's] Love, it profiteth me nothing." (emphasis added)

"If I have not [God's] Love, I am nothing." (1 Corinthians 13:2, emphasis added)

Endnotes:

1. 1 Peter 4:8

2. David and Jonathan are good examples of *phileo* love.

3. Being bound together in God's Love and loving others is what makes us God's friends (*phileo*).

4. See Chapter 4, "Abiding in God."

5. See Chapter 16, "When God Restores a Marriage."

6. See Chapter 14, "Inner Court Ritual."

7. See Chapter 16, "When God Restores a Marriage." See also 1 Thessalonians 5:19.

8. See Chapter 11, "What Is Sin?"

9. See Chapter 14, "Inner Court Ritual."

Scriptural References:

Chapter 5

Human Love
  A. How does human love differ from God's Love?
  1. God's Love and human love are totally opposite
      a. God's Love is supernatural (1 John 4:8)
      b. We receive it in our hearts, only as a result of being born again (Romans 5:5)
      c. God's Love is a gift of Love
  2. *Everyone has human love.* Only those who have asked Christ into their lives have God's Love in their hearts
  3. Human love is always a need love. God's Love is a gift of Love
  4. Human love is always dependent upon *how we feel, how the other person responds*, and *what our circumstances are.* God's Love is de pendent only upon God
  B. Four characteristics of human love:
  1. Human love is *conditional*
  2. Human love is *two-sided*
  3. Human love is a *bondage* love
  4. Human love is a *self-centered* love

What Are the Natural, Human Loves?
  A. *Storge* love
  1. Natural, *emotional*, feeling love
  2. Instinctive love (mother's love for her child)
  3. Covers over and protects
  4. Possessive, clutching love
  5. Without God's intervention, is a conditional, self-centered, need love that desires the good of itself and not the other person
  B. *Eros* love
  1. Natural, *sexual* love
  2. Based on mutual physical attraction
  3. An erotic love that gives a high, and transports one above his problems
  4. Is dangerous, because it overrules our reason and prevents rationality. It engulfs our own will, and we are "carried on by the tide" of emotion
  5. In Christian marriages, erotic love is desperately needed
  6. Without God's intervention, is a conditional, self-centered love that desires the good of itself and not the other person
  C. *Phileo* love
  1. Natural, *friendship* love—strongly attached to something (John 12:25)
  2. Result of an intimate relationship (whereas with God's Love, the Love comes first and then the relationship follows) (John 15:13-15)

3. Based on similarity of outlook, common interest, seeing "eye to eye"
4. A mutual attraction love (2 Timothy 3:1-5)
5. Without God's intervention, is a conditional, self-centered love, based on reciprocal expectations from each party

Human Loves Can Be Good or Bad

A. All three of these human, natural loves can be good or bad depending upon their basis (God or self)
B. If these loves are based on self (own thoughts, emotions, and desires), they will be conditional and reciprocal loves
C. If these loves can be based on God's *Agape* Love, then these human loves can become the blessing God intended

Why Is This So Critical to Understand?

A. In the end times, "God's Love will grow cold" (Matthew 24:12)
B. Why will God's Love grow cold? One of the reasons is that we don't know the difference between God's Love and human love
C. We need to know when we are functioning on God's Love and when we are not
D. When we are not, we need to know what to do about it.
   1. How to confess it as sin (we have "missed the mark")
   2. How to turn around from following our emotions and our will, and go God's way
   3. How to give our sin to God
   4. How to get into God's Word and replace the lies with the truth

"If I have not [God's] Love, *I am nothing.*" (1 Corinthians 13:2, emphasis added)

Section Three

Chapter 6: True Identity and Security

Two Basic Needs

God created man and woman to have *two basic needs*: the need to be loved and the need to love. Furthermore, both of these needs can only be satisfied by God and His unconditional *Agape* Love.

Only by our knowing without a doubt that God loves us can our need *to be loved* be fulfilled. We must know that God's Love will never "leave us or forsake us" (Hebrews 13:5), no matter what we do or don't do. It's critical that we know He loves us like this, not just in our heads but also in our every day lives.

Knowing God loves us is the only foundation that will give us our *identity* and our *security* in this life. (Remember in Chapter 5 we said that in some circles, love and identity have become synonymous.) Our security and identity do not come from the conditional loves of others, from our accomplishments, or from our circumstances, but only from knowing that God loves us personally and unconditionally.

Isaiah 43:3-4 declares, "I am the Lord...[You are] precious in my sight...and I have loved thee."

God's Love is the only basis and the only foundation upon which we can build our lives. 1 Corinthians 3:11 tells us that there's no other foundation we can lay but that which is laid in Christ Jesus.

Our need *to love* (which we will discuss in Chapter 8) is just as strong as our need to be loved. Only by loving as God desires will our lives be given the *meaning* and *purpose* that we are all seeking.

So many of us have spent our entire lives trying to fulfill these two basic needs in every other conceivable way, rather than the way God intended and designed them to be fulfilled. We have sought for our husbands, our wives, our children, our families and our friends to meet our needs for identity and security. And then we have looked to our careers, our accomplishments, our prestige, and our wealth to meet our needs for meaning and purpose.

These two needs can never be satisfied completely by other people, things, or accomplishments. Momentarily, on the outside, our desires might be touched; but inwardly, lastingly, these needs will never be completely met.

Philippians 4:19 states, "My God shall supply *all* your need[s]." (emphasis added)

Example: Who Am I?

Kitty Dukakis is the wife of Michael Dukakis, who was a presidential candidate in 1988. During the campaign, Kitty had identity, security, fulfillment, and meaning to her life. Everyone loved her because she was the wife of the potential President of the United States. She was going to be the First Lady of the country. Her whole life was mapped out for her. She was an immediate "success."

But in one day, when her husband lost the election, it was all taken away from her and she again asked the questions, "Who am I? What's my purpose in life?" Outwardly, she had fame and fortune but inwardly her deepest needs were still not satisfied. We have all read in recent years of her dependence on drugs and alcohol, and her struggles to find herself. She has shared openly about looking to these various substances for her security and "self worth."

God must be the total provision for our two basic needs—our need to be loved and our need to love—whether we are married (happily or unhappily), divorced, widowed or single.[1] Then, whatever we get from our mates, our families, our circumstances, our accomplishments, or our careers is an added blessing. And we won't be shaken to the core if these people or things are taken away from us.

[It's interesting to note that the Armed Services have become alarmed that among officers of flag rank, Admirals and Generals, there is a high rate of divorce *after* retirement. One of the contributing factors appears to be a "lack of identity" for the wife. The husband usually has ways to stay involved with the service through Pentagon advisory committees, etc., but the wife's identity is shattered when she no longer is "the Admiral's wife."]

Psalm 73:25 tells us there should be "none upon earth that [we] desire besides Thee."

Personal Example: Shattered

I'd like to share a personal example of the importance of our identity and our security being only in Jesus Christ and not in our accomplishments or what we "do" for Him. Twelve years ago, after I had been teaching *The Way of Agape* for about four years, I unintentionally disobeyed God in a very visible way. God had allowed something in my life that I didn't understand at the time, and I ended up making some very poor choices.

Through a series of hurtful events, God took me out of the ministry for a while and put me in the "back woods." He set me, the ministry, the teaching, and the book I so longed to write aside for about four years. This is a very painful experience, especially after one has been used by God in a mighty way. Needless to say, I was shattered.

Along with my ministry collapsing, my identity also collapsed because it was built solely upon what I was doing for the Lord, i.e., the ministry, and not simply on His unconditional Love for me.

1 Kings 13

One day during this time, God gave me 1 Kings 13 as an answer to one of my prayers. This chapter is about a man of God who unintentionally disobeys God just as I had done. God sends a lying prophet to this man of God, who convinces him to go against what God had originally told him to do. The man of God obeys the lying prophet, thinking it was God speaking. Then God sends a lion and kills the man of God for disobeying Him. It is a bizarre chapter, but it fit my own circumstances perfectly.

I felt sure God was saying to me that "since you disobeyed Me—unintentionally or not—I am going to set you and the ministry aside." I was absolutely devastated and crushed by the whole experience because, like that man of God in 1 Kings 13, I had thought God *was* in the things I had chosen to do.

I can remember crying convulsively in my living room as I realized, "I've blown it with God. I'm not going to be used by Him anymore. I'm not special. I'm not loved anymore."

I lost all hope for the future, because my hope had always been based in God's Love for me. As a result, I let go of God's hand. I determined to build thick walls around myself and retreat to the safety of trusting in myself. I decided I would close off my heart to God and set about "going my own way." I had this "mind set" for about seven months. Then one day I passed by a mirror and I happened to see myself. What I saw was absolutely shocking. There was no "life" in my face at all—it looked as if I had cut my lifeline and I was dying. It shook me to the core and made me realize that what I was doing was living, but without a "source" of life. I had cut Him off.

That same afternoon, a dear friend called and asked me, "Nan, how long are you going to run from God?" That did it! The next day, totally by faith with no feelings whatsoever, I chose to obey, trust, and follow Jesus once again. God had never left me—I was the one who had walked away from Him. My own choices had caused and created the situation in the first place, and yet for seven months, I had blamed God.

Throughout the entire seven months that I had closed my heart off to God, He never left my side. Interesting, the part in 1 Kings 13 that I had missed, was that the lion "stood by" and "guarded" the man of God's carcass and never left him. Even though I was the one who had moved away from God, God still remained loving and faithful to me. All I had to do was reach up, take His hand, and unconditionally trust Him once again.

God had allowed these things to happen because, in His infinite Love for me, He needed to teach me some very important lessons. My identity and my security had become totally wrapped up in—and inseparable with—the *Way of Agape* teaching and counseling ministry. God had seen this misplaced security in my life, and in His Love for me He needed to take the ministry away for a while. He is a jealous God and He will have nothing before Him in our hearts; not even our families, our husbands, our wives, our children, our careers—or even our ministries![2]

Often the above things can become more important to us than God. And, as Psalm 73:25 tells us, there should be none upon earth that we desire more than God. If God has become second in our hearts, then we will never quite be able to give Him our total lives because "something" will always be standing in the way.

My ministry had subtly become more important to me than God. So, in His Love for me, God needed to correct that wrong priority in my life. And He lovingly did so through a situation that I, myself, had created.

God Loves Us Unconditionally

God used this circumstance to show me experientially that I am loved, special in His eyes, and of inestimable worth, just because of who I am in Him, just because I am His child. Period! Not because of what I do, or what I teach, or what I write. I am loved and special in God's eyes no matter what I do or don't do for Him. I am loved and special just because I'm His kid. And He is going to continue to love me regardless if I ever teach, write, counsel, or minister again. Regardless of how many mistakes, failures, or errors I make, God loves me unconditionally and never-endingly.

So whether I am home, ministering and loving my husband and children, or whether I am out speaking to thousands and traveling all over the world teaching, God loves me—regardless! What freedom this brings me—the freedom just to be me. What hope this gives me. God loves me unconditionally, with no strings attached, just as I am.

We are God's own children, His beloved, His prized possessions, His *poema*, His new creations. We are holy, accepted, complete, alive, forgiven, freed, reconciled, called, chosen, victorious, strong, and conquering. What an incredible identity we have. So many of us forget these things, and we try to add to what God has already done by trying to "work our way to heaven." What for? It's already been done for us! We can't add to the finished work of Christ on the Cross!

Our security and our identity need to be built solely upon God's Love for us, not on what we do for Him. Our confidence needs to be in Him and in how much He loves us, and not in our accomplishments for Him.

God's Love Never Fails

We must know that God's Love will never stop coming, no matter what we do or don't do. 1 Corinthians 13:8 says it all, "[God's] Love never fails." Do you understand what this really means? It means that His love is unending; it just keeps on coming and coming, no matter what the object of that Love is doing. Now if there is sin in our lives, His Love in our hearts will be blocked and quenched from flowing out into our lives, and our fellowship with Him will be broken. But His Love will never stop flowing into our hearts.

Romans 8:38-39 tells us that nothing shall separate us from the Love of God: "For I am persuaded, that neither death, nor life, nor angels, nor principalities, nor powers, nor things present, nor things to come, nor height, nor depth, nor any other creature, shall be able to separate us from the Love of God, which is in Christ Jesus our Lord."

We must know and understand that nothing, absolutely nothing, can ever separate us from the Love of the Father in our hearts. Even our waywardness, our unfaithfulness, our doubts, and our disobedience won't stop God's Love from coming. His Love is everlasting and it just comes and comes; nothing can alter it or stop it.

Example: Humiliation and Ridicule

A wonderful, dear old friend of ours, who happens to be a minister, sinned very publicly some years ago. He was humiliated and ridiculed by all of his friends. Totally guilt-ridden, he began to run from God. In the process he lost everything he ever had: his wife, his children, his family, his home, his ministry. He hit bottom, and out of desperation became a used car salesman. I'm not saying that a used car salesman is at the bottom, but for a renowned minister to end up there, it was.

The Holy Spirit, however, would not leave him alone, nor would He stop loving him and trying to woo him back. The minister received what he called a "prophecy" from a woman whom he respected and loved. The prophecy told him how God was going to restore to him everything he had ever lost and more if he would just choose to turn around and once again trust God.

The neat part of this story is that, at that time, the minister did not believe that the gifts of the Spirit were for today, but somehow he knew in his heart that this prophecy was true and that it was specifically for him. First the minister went to God and with much remorse he confessed and repented of everything he had done. Claiming the promise of 1 John 1:9, "If we confess our sins, He is faithful and just to forgive us our sins, and to cleanse us from all unrighteousness," the minister asked God for His forgiveness.

Then he began to read his Bible once again, and began to choose by faith to believe that God did still loved him, even though he felt nothing. Finally, he took a public stand, confessed, and repented of all he had done.

Over the years, we watched as God did, indeed, restore everything this precious minister had ever lost—his marriage, his children, his ministry. Just like Job, this man became more blessed than he ever was to begin with. We must know that God's Love never fails. It never stops coming to us, no matter what we do or what we don't do. Song of Solomon 8:7 assures us, "Many waters cannot quench love, neither can the floods drown it."

Even when we blow it badly, and we fail and we don't stay an open and cleansed vessel, we must know that God will continue to love us no matter what. I love Psalm 37:23-24: "The steps of a good man are ordered by the Lord; and He delighteth in his way. Though he fall, he shall not be utterly cast down; For the Lord upholdeth him with His hand." [3]

Someone wrote me a cute story that exemplifies these verses perfectly:

"One night my friend went roller skating at a Christian family skate night. She loved to stand on the side and watch the children skate. One particular little girl caught her eye.

This little girl was holding tightly onto her mother's hand as they went very slowly around and around the rink. At times, they didn't even seem like they were moving. The little girl fell frequently, but never cried. She would just get back on her feet, with her mother's help, and off they would go again.

The mother noticed my friend watching them. And as they skated by the next time, the mother said to my friend, "It's rather like the Father with us, don't you think?"

That is so true. How patient, how longsuffering, how forgiving, how kind our Father is with us, even when we slip and fall. All we have to do is reach up to His waiting hand, take hold, and know He still loves us.

God's Unconditional Forgiveness

We must also remember that *a part of God's Love is His unconditional forgiveness.* Again, we just need to reach up, as did the little girl, and take hold of that forgiving Love.

Two women at one seminar several years ago came up to me and said they had been backslidden for years because they believed that what they had done against the Lord was beyond forgiveness. In their eyes, their sins were too horrible ever to forgive; and, of course, Satan was right there telling them that it was so.

When I told the story in class about our minister friend, the Holy Spirit pierced these women's hearts. They saw how doubt and unbelief kept them from experiencing God's unconditional Love and forgiveness all these years. They came up afterwards and cried as they realized the magnitude of God's Love for them.

"Failures"—a Blessing or a Curse?

One of the reasons I believe we don't fully realize the extent of God's Love for each of us personally is that we don't really see and understand that God uses our failures, our mistakes, and our errors as a means of drawing us closer to Him. God's view of failure is that He expects it; He forgives it; and then, He uses it.

I know He has done this in my life. Both *studies—The Way of Agape* and *Be Ye Transformed*—evolved as a direct result of wrong choices in my life. But look at the fruit God has brought out of them! He does work all things together for good to those who love and totally give themselves over to Him. (Romans 8:28)

Insecure in God's Love

If our identity and our security are in God and in His unconditional Love for us, then it becomes permissible to fail because who we are, our true identity, is still intact. We know we are still loved by the Father, so we can pick up the pieces and begin all over again.

However, if are *not* secure in the fact that God loves us and His Love is *not* the only basis for our identity and security, then when we fail and have problems, rather than act on the truth and go on, we think as the world thinks: "I've failed. No one will love me now. I have to cover up that failure and earn their love again."

At that point, it becomes almost impossible to accept ourselves the way we really are. We either justify our failures and make excuses for them, or we try to hide and cover them up. Even if we do the latter, the memory of that failure will still linger in our minds if it's not properly dealt with and given over to God. That failure then becomes the instigation and the motivation for all we do—"I am going to prove myself"—rather than being motivated simply by God's Love.

Secure in God's Love

We need to be so secure in God's Love that we'll let Him use our failures as a way of binding us even closer to Him. The end result of seeing God use our mistakes "for good" is that we will realize His Love to an even deeper degree than we did before. God's unconditional forgiveness in my life only proves to me all the more that He loves me.

Luke 7:47 notes, "To whom little is forgiven, the same loveth little." Well, I believe the opposite is also true, "To whom much is forgiven, the same loveth much." In other words, because God forgives us much, we are able to experience His Love to an even greater degree.

That inner identity and security that we all are seeking can only come from personally knowing that God loves us. And the fulfillment and meaning in our lives can only come from loving God, and, through Him, loving others. This is *God's Way of Love* (His *Way of Agape*): 1) *knowing that God loves us* personally; 2) *loving Him in return*; and 3) *loving others through Him*.

"Blessed be the God and Father of our Lord Jesus Christ, Who hath blessed us with all spiritual blessings in heavenly places in Christ: According as He hath chosen us in Him before the foundation of the world, that we should be holy and without blame before Him in love: Having predestined us unto the adoption of children by Jesus Christ to Himself, according to the good pleasure of His will, To the praise of the glory of His grace, wherein He hath made us accepted in the Beloved: In Whom we have redemption through His blood, the forgiveness of sins, according to the riches of His grace." (Ephesians 1:3-7)

Endnotes:

1. Colossians 2:10

2. Psalm 73:25

3. Jeremiah 31:3-4

Scriptural References:

Chapter 6

Man Has Two Basic Needs:
- A. Need *TO BE LOVED...*
    1. Which can be fulfilled only by God's Love (Jeremiah 31:3; 1 Corinthians 13:2c; 1 John 4:16)
    2. Which brings us our only true *identity* and *security* in life (Isaiah 43:4; 54:10; Galatians 2:20; 1 Corinthians 13:4-8; Romans 8:28; Hebrews 13:5c)
        - a. Love and identity are synonymous
        - b. God's Love is our only true foundation (1 Corinthians 3:11)
- B. Need *TO LOVE...*
    1. Which can be fulfilled only by God's Love (1 John 3:14; 4:11-12,17)
    2. Which brings *meaning* and *purpose* to our lives (1 Timothy 1:5; Philippians 1:21)

These Two Needs Can Never Be Met by Others, Things, or Accomplishments (Philippians 4:19; 1 Corinthians 3:11)
- A. We must not look to anything else but God to supply these needs (Psalm 73:25)
- B. We are loved and special to God, not because of what we do, but because of who we are in Him (Isaiah 49:16; Hebrews 13:5)
    1. We are loved just the way we are (Song of Solomon 8:7a)
    2. We are loved regardless of our mistakes and failures (Romans 8:35; Psalm 37:23-24; 1 Corinthians 13:8)
    3. And we can love regardless of how we feel, what we are going through at the time, and regardless of how the other person responds

God's Love Will Never Stop Coming
- A. His Love will never stop flowing into our hearts (Song of Solomon 8:7; Romans 8:38-39)
- B. His Love will never stop flowing no matter what we do or don't do (Psalm 103:11; Isaiah 54:10; 1 Corinthians 13:8; Hebrews 13:5; Psalm 37:23)
- C. When we sin, we quench God's Love from flowing out into our lives (our souls) (Matthew 24:12; Ephesians 4:29-32)
- D. If we confess and repent of our sin, then once again His Love will flow from our hearts into our lives (1 John 1:9; Proverbs 28:13)

Love Includes Unconditional Forgiveness
- A. God uses our failures as a means of drawing us closer to Him (Psalm 119:67; Romans 8:28)

B. Knowing God's forgiveness in my life proves God loves me (Luke 7:47)
C. If God's Love is our only security, when we fail we will still know God loves us and we can go on (Romans 8:38-39; Psalm 37:23-24; Ephesians 1:3-7)
D. If God's Love is not our only security, then we feel we must not fail because no one will love us and we'll be unable to go on

Chapter 7: Knowing God Loves Us

Living "Experiential" Knowledge

Let me ask you a question. Do you have firsthand "experiential knowledge" that God loves you? I don't mean "intellectual knowledge" or "head knowledge." I mean the moment by moment intimacy that only a loving Father and child can have. As Christians, no matter what our circumstances, we all need to live in the security of His Love. If we have His Love, then we can do anything; without His Love, we are nothing.

Before we can go any further in God's Way of *Agape*, we need to know without a doubt that we are loved by the Father; that He has laid down His Life expressly to give us His Love through Jesus Christ; and that He has called and elected us to be His vessels of Love. If we know and have a living experience of these things, then we will have the confidence and the trust to lay our wills and our lives down to Him and love Him in return.

1 John 3:16 states, "Hereby perceive (know) we the love of God, because He laid down His life for us."

How Do We Know God Loves Us?

When I first began teaching *The Way of Agape*, I focused in on the two great commandments.

"Thou shalt love the Lord thy God with all thy heart, and with all thy soul, and with all thy mind...and thou shalt love thy neighbour as thyself." (Matthew 22:37-39)

After several years of hearing the reactions of the women in those first classes, however, I realized there is no way we can learn to love God or others until we *first* know and experience that God loves us. Knowing that God loves us is the *foundation* of our faith. Without first being able to experience His Love and acceptance for ourselves, we're not going to be able to move forward in our Christian walk.

In other words, we can't lay down our lives to someone and love Him, if we don't really think He loves us. This principle is true no matter how long we have been Christians, no matter how many people we have led to the Lord, no matter how many Scriptures we know, nor the number of Bible studies we have led. If we don't know that God loves us personally, we'll be unable to grow simply because we don't trust Him.

Do You Know He Loves You?

If we know that God loves us personally, then: 1) we'll have the confidence and the trust to continually lay down our wills and our lives to Him and love Him in return; and, 2) we'll have that daily experience of knowing His Love, not only for ourselves, but also for others.

But if we doubt God's Love for us personally, then: 1) we won't have the confidence or the trust to lay down our wills and our lives to Him and love Him in return; and, 2) we'll limit our ability to intimately experience His Love, both for ourselves and for others.[1]

This doesn't mean that God is not in our hearts, loving us. He is! It just means we won't have that daily, living experience (personal, touching, loving intimacy) of encountering and seeing God's handprint and His Love at every turn. I think this is one of the reasons why so many of us are not experiencing God's abundant Life after being Christians forever. It all goes back to the fact that we really don't know God loves us.

Example: "I Want Out!"

Sandy is a young Christian girl in her late twenties whom I met at a retreat in Northern California. She has had a very hard life and a very troubled background: drugs, alcohol, homosexuality, abuse and so forth.

When Sandy came up to the retreat in the mountains, she had told God, "This is it. I can't go on anymore. You have to show me that You really love me." She had become so despondent and so disillusioned with her life, her friends, her church and her family, that she decided if God didn't really love her, she wanted "out." Sandy begged God to show her that weekend that He really cared. She told Him that if she didn't see or hear anything, then she was going to take matters into her own hands.

Saturday afternoon, day two of the retreat, Sandy walked the grounds of the camp, contemplating how she was going to end her life because she had neither seen nor felt anything from God so far.

That evening we had communion. By this time, Sandy was totally despondent. Out of desperation, she told God she was going to refuse to take the communion cup until He somehow showed her that He loved her. Now, in general it's not a good idea to give God an "ultimatum" like this. It's not Scriptural to do this. But God knew Sandy's heart and the desperate state that she was in.

After everyone had taken communion and left the auditorium, Sandy moved from her seat in the audience up to the communion table. She quietly knelt down in front of the table, folded her arms on it and put her head down. She was determined to stay there until somehow she felt God's Love.

After she had knelt there for almost an hour, the doors in the back of the auditorium opened and someone came in. Sandy couldn't see who it was because of the shape of the room. This person quietly moved over to the fireplace, knelt down, and began to sing in the Spirit.[2] The fireplace was still out of view from Sandy, but she said later that this woman "sang like an angel."

Sandy kept her head on the communion table for at least a half hour. The woman continued to sing. Finally, Sandy could stand it no longer, and came around the corner towards the fireplace to see who it was. The young girl singing seemed startled at first, but then in an authoritative voice she told Sandy: "Sit down, God has sent me to you." Absolutely shocked, Sandy sat down and they began to share.

The Lord had laid Sandy heavily upon this young girl's heart all weekend, but because of Sandy's intimidating countenance, the girl had kept her distance. In fact, she was a little frightened of Sandy. After the Saturday night session, the young girl had gone to bed. She was almost asleep, when God prompted her to get up and to minister to "someone who needed Him in the main sanctuary." Never dreaming it was Sandy, the young girl rolled over and tried to ignore the Holy Spirit's voice, but as no peace would return, she finally got up, put on her robe and obeyed.

When she arrived in the auditorium, no one was there. But the Lord made her stay, wait and sing. When Sandy finally did appear, the girl said at first she was scared to death. But again, she gave her fear to God and He told her what to say. The two women shared all night long. They cried together, they hugged and they laughed. God had, in His unfathomable way shown Sandy the extent of His Love for her. And He used this precious young girl, "His angel," to do so.

The next morning, both girls got up in front of the entire woman's group and shared what had happened. There wasn't a dry eye in the entire auditorium.

No Fear in God's Love

I think Sandy is typical of so many of us. In our haste to be "like Jesus," we have forgotten the first basic step, which is to really know the extent and the depth of God's Love for us personally.

If we really knew how much God loves us, there would never be any reason for us to fear what He might allow into our lives. We would have the confidence and the trust to continually abandon our lives into His care because we would know that He loves us, and that He is faithful and trustworthy to take care of us no matter what.

Isaiah 43:2-4 states, "When thou passest through the waters [trouble], I will be with thee; and through the rivers, they shall not overflow thee: when thou walkest through the fire, thou shalt not be burned: neither shall the flame kindle upon thee. For I am the Lord thy God...Thou wast precious in My sight... and *I have loved thee.*" (emphasis added)

And Isaiah 49:16: "Behold, I have graven thee upon the palms of My hands; thy walls [our souls] are continually before Me."

God's Love Is Our Foundation

Knowing that God loves us personally is the bottom line. It is the only foundation, the only building pad our whole spiritual house can be built upon. We can't lay down our lives to someone if we don't think he really loves us.

Therefore, we can't go further in God's *Way of Agape* until we know without a doubt that God loves us and He won't ever let us down.

Example: Discovering God's Love

Let me share another beautiful example of someone who learned not only how much God loved her, but also went on to experiencing His Love in and through her.

Linda was brought up in a church that taught that God was not a God of Love, but One to be feared, a God of Righteousness, Justice and Judgment. The truth is, of course, that God is a God not only of Righteousness, Justice, and Judgment, but also of Love, Mercy, and Compassion.

When Linda's personal life began to fall apart, she desperately wanted to throw herself upon God for His consolation and His compassion. She could find no help or solace, however, in a God of Justice and Holiness. The thought that God was only One to be feared made her feel so alone and so insecure.

Finally, one of her friends who went to another church began to show her from Scripture that God is a God not only of Holiness, Justice, and Righteousness, but also a God of Love, Compassion, Forgiveness, and Mercy. He told her that God loved her and would unconditionally forgive her for all her transgressions, no matter what they were. He told her that God desired not only to heal her with His Love, but also to fill her with that Love so she could pass it on to others.

Linda could hardly believe what she was hearing; it was too wonderful to comprehend. She had never understood that God loved her like that.

For the first few weeks after that conversation, she tried to believe in a loving God who would unconditionally forgive her. Each time she chose to believe, however, the old nagging doubts would come rushing back in; and the overwhelming fear of condemnation would consume her. Thus, God's Love—which was in her heart all along—was again quenched and blocked from coming forth.

Out of pure desperation and as a matter of life and death, Linda ended up writing down all of God's promises of Love in the Bible. The one thing she did know was that the Bible was Truth. On 3x5 index cards, she wrote out God's promises of how much He loved her, and she carried these cards around with her everywhere—in her pocket, in her purse and in her car.[3]

When the doubts, unbelief, and Satan's taunts came in, she whipped out those cards, and she would read out loud what God said about His unconditional Love and forgiveness. She would confess that her own doubts and unbelief were not of God, repent of them, and give them to God. Then she would choose to believe what God had said in His Word, even though she didn't feel it.

It took three years for God to align her feelings with what she had chosen to believe—in other words, for her to *feel* His Love. The reason it took so long for her to feel His Love was that she had been programmed for so many years the opposite way that God was a God of wrath.

It seems that the length of time it takes for our feelings to align with our choices depends upon the time and the depth that that *thing* we are giving over to God" has had a hold on us.[4] In Linda's case, it had been years.

Linda persevered by faith and not feelings, and finally, in God's timing, she began to have living experience that God did, indeed, love her. Upon this foundation then, she was able to continue in the *Way of Agape*, by learning to lay her will and life down to God and love Him.

Linda is a perfect example of a Christian who believed in God, but didn't have that living experience of God's Love in her personal life. Therefore, she was not able to move forward in her Christian walk.

Can't Move Forward

So it doesn't matter how long you have been a Christian, how many people you have led to the Lord, how many Scriptures you have memorized, or how many Bible studies you have taught. If you don't know God loves you personally, you're not going to be able to grow.

If you have difficulty really believing and intimately experiencing that God loves you as Linda did, then see the *Knowing God Loves Me* Supplement at the end of this book. Make up 3x5 cards, like Linda did, with all the Scriptures you can find on how much God loves you. Keep these cards with you at all times—in your car, in your purse, on the mirror in the bathroom, etc. Then, when doubt and unbelief come over you, whip out those cards, confess your doubts and fears, give them to God, and then choose by faith—not by feelings—to believe what God promises. God will, in His timing, align your feelings with those choices.

Prove It to Me

Okay, you might say to me, "Nancy, prove to me that God loves me personally. I don't feel it. I don't see it. I don't hear Him. So how can I believe it's true? What proof do I have?"

As one person said to me recently, "Nancy, God's Love is a gift only some receive, not all of us are that lucky." Well, God's Word says differently. Thus, we *are* all that lucky, and, with the Holy Spirit's help, I can prove it!

I would like to focus on four major reasons we can know that God loves us personally:

1) One of the major reasons we can know God loves us individually and personally is because *He says so in His Word.* Listen:

- Jeremiah 31:3: "The Lord hath appeared of old unto me, saying, 'Yea, I have loved thee with an everlasting love: therefore with lovingkindness I have drawn thee.'"

- Isaiah 43:4-5: "Since thou wast precious in my sight, thou hast been honourable, and I have loved thee...Fear not: for I am with thee."

- John 15:9b: "As the Father has loved Me, so have I loved you."

- And 1 John 3:1: "Behold what manner of love the Father hath bestowed upon us,[5] that we should be called the sons of God."

These are just a few Scriptures; there are many more that say declare how much God loves us personally. (Be sure to see the Knowing God Loves Me Scriptures in the Supplemental Notes.) Since God's Word is truth, we need to trust and believe what He promises.

2) Not only does God state in His Word that He loves us personally, but *He also has proven His Love for us by sending His Son* to die for us.

Jesus did come and that He did die for all of our sins on that cross 2,000 years ago. Scripture tells us that Jesus loved us so much that He came expressly to take away our personal sins past, present and future and to reconcile us to Himself.

Listen to 1 John 4:9-10: "Herein is love, not that we loved God, but that He loved us, and sent His Son to be the propitiation for our sins."

Propitiation simply means substitute offering. In other words, Jesus came and died in our place for our personal sins, so that we could be freed from sin's penalty, which is death. He died so that we could be saved. To me, *this is ultimate Love!*

John 15:13 avows, "Greater love hath no man than this, that a man lay down his life for his friends."

All we have to do is reach up and receive that incredible gift. That Love is ours for the asking.

3) Not only does the Bible say God loves us personally, and that He has proven His Love by dying on the cross for us 2,000 years ago, but the Bible also states that if we choose to believe and accept Jesus' pardon, His provision for our sins, *then we'll receive His Spirit (Himself) into our hearts.*[6]

God's Spirit is like the guarantee or the down payment, a pledge or a voucher, that confirms God's Love for us and assures us that His promises are true. Romans 8:16 informs us that, "The Spirit Itself beareth witness with our spirit, that we are the children of God."

It's the Spirit of God who continually acknowledges and validates in our hearts that God loves us.

4) God loves us so much that He has not only told us so in His Word, sent His Son to die for us, and given us His Spirit to confirm His Love, but He also loves us so much that *He has given us His abundant Life* here and now. Abundant life is simply experiencing His Life through us.

Remember John 10:10 which states, "I [Jesus] am come that they might have life, and that they might have it more abundantly." God's abundant life is His supernatural *Love*, His supernatural *Wisdom,* and His supernatural *Power* to perform these things in and through our lives.[7]

By "abundant life," I'm not only talking about the eternal Life that we will one day receive when we die and go to Heaven, I'm talking about the abundant life—His supernatural Life—that we can experience right here on earth.

Experiencing His Life in place of our own is what will convince us more than anything else that God is real, and that yes, He does love us. When we experience His Love for a person we know we can't love in our own ability, we know that God must love us; when we experience His supernatural Power getting us through circumstances we know in our own strength we couldn't manage, we know that He cares; and when we experience His supernatural Wisdom shedding light in an area we know we didn't understand before, we realize that God is intimately concerned about every detail of our lives. And He really does love us!

Personal Example: No Way Am I Going!

I've been traveling and teaching for about 15 years now. As I am getting older, my body is beginning to go through many changes. At certain times of the month I am incredibly weak, so I'm supposed to stay home in bed. During these times, there is no possible way I can travel because of embarrassing emergencies that can arise.

Several years ago, I was asked to speak in Northern California. When I accepted the invitation months before, I felt great. But when the actual weekend came, it was that time of the month, and I said to the Lord, "There is no way I can go now! I can't run to catch planes. I can't lift my bags. The bottom line is I am afraid to go for fear of what will happen." I even asked the Lord at this point whether I should stop traveling and teaching so much because of this problem.

However, since I do practice what I preach, I took these thoughts captive and gave my fear and doubt over to God. I told Him, "If You want me to go on this trip, I'll just trust You with my physical problems and know that You will do Your work through me—regardless." So I went.

The first thing God did was to confirm His Love for me over and over again in His Word. I kept getting James 1:12 and others like it, "Blessed is the man that endureth temptation [trials]: for when he is tried, he shall receive the crown of life." Then He confirmed His Love for me by literally taking away my fears, my doubts and my anxieties, as I repeatedly gave them over to Him. He did as He promises in Psalm 103:12, taking them "as far as the east is from the west."

He also reconfirmed His Love for me by the witness of His Spirit. The women at the retreat knew nothing of my physical condition and fears. Yet when they prayed for me, the Spirit had them pray precisely what my own prayers had been.

However, as I taught that weekend, the thing that convinced me of God's Love more than anything else, was that He allowed me to experience His abundant Life. I was so weak in my own strength that He completely filled me with His supernatural Love, Wisdom, and Power, and He anointed the teachings more than ever before.

As 2 Corinthians 12:10 puts it, "...for when I am weak, then am I strong." When we are yielded, open, cleansed vessels, then He can be strong and pour forth His Life through us!

The neatest part of the whole story was that when I got home, a FAX was waiting for me, inviting me to go to Scotland and speak for a week—all expenses paid. This, to me, was the answer to whether I should quit teaching or not. The whole incident proved to me again that God loves me personally, and I don't need to fear what He will allow in my life. He does hear my every prayer, and He is concerned about my every need.

God Loves Me

I pray this book will help each of us begin to grasp and experience in a deeper and more meaningful way how much God loves us. Reading that God loves us in His Word and even understanding that He died for our sins, can still be merely an intellectual pursuit. But receiving God's own Spirit and beginning to experience His Life in and through us, is something we can never deny as being ultimate, personal Love.

Ephesians 3:17-19 urges us, "That Christ may dwell in your hearts by faith, that ye, being rooted and grounded in love, May be able to comprehend with all the saints what is the breadth, and length, and depth and height; And to know the love of Christ, which passeth knowledge, that ye might be filled with all the fulness of God."

So, God's Love is not a gift that only some receive, but a gift that we all receive when we are born anew by His Spirit. Therefore, if you have asked Jesus into your heart as your Savior and Lord, then not only Jesus is in your heart, but His Love is there also. John 17:26 validates this: "And I have declared...that the Love wherewith Thou [Father] hast loved Me [Jesus] may be in them, and I in them."

How Does God Communicate His Love?

Okay, you might say, so God loves us. "How, Nancy, does He communicate that Love to us? How can we begin to experience His Love in our lives? How could Sandy and Linda have known earlier that God loved them personally?"

1) God cannot be boxed in; He will manifest Himself to each of us in many different ways. But one of the sure ways He communicates His Love to us is in our daily *reading of His Word*. This is where it all starts. This is how God talks to us, and this is how we hear His Voice.

We must choose—again by faith, not feelings—to believe what God's Word says about His Love, and then we must step out in faith, knowing that in God's timing He will align our feelings to match what we have chosen. It all begins, however, with constantly reading and believing God's Word.

2) God also communicates His Love to us *through our Christian brothers and sisters*. We are extensions of God's Love to each other—we are His arms and His legs. This is what He is asking each of us, moment by moment, "Are you willing to allow Him to love others through you?"

It's so very important that when someone asks us to pray for them that we not only remember to pray for them, but also be willing to do anything else that God lays upon our hearts: either call them, write them, visit them, take them a gift or even make a personal sacrifice for them. Each time we let God use us in some personal way, it's a touch from Him saying to that other person, "I love you."

3) Another way God communicates His Love to us is through *situations and circumstances*. There's nothing quite so comforting as knowing that God's hand has personally orchestrated our circumstances. It's a constant reminder that He does, indeed, love us.

Personal Example: Lost Everything

After we lost our dream home in Big Bear Lake, California, because of bankruptcy, we moved into a rented home. This rented home turned out to be on the epicenter of 1992's big 6.7 earthquake. Because of this traumatic experience and after much prayer and counsel, we decided to move to Idaho.

We moved all of our belongings into the garage of a house that had been purchased for us here in Idaho. However, we found out two days later that the escrow was falling apart, and once again we would have to move. Now this made four moves in one year! At this point we were all living in one motel room—four birds, four dogs, a hampster, a cat, Chuck, Lisa and me.

If you had asked me at this point if I'd seen God's Love and His hand in these things, I'm sure I would have honestly said, "No way! I know He's up there somewhere, but I sure don't see or feel Him." However, I kept on making those faith choices and kept on walking.

Finally, one of our dear friends decided she was going to find us a place to live. She went to one of the most beautiful subdivisions in our town, picked a brand new house that she knew had been on the market for two years, and convinced the salesman to at least ask the owner if he would rent it. She also gave the salesperson several of our ministry products to give to the owner.

Because houses in Idaho were still selling like hotcakes, why would this owner even consider renting a brand new one? But the owner evidently stayed up all night reading our material and felt convinced we were to have this beautiful new house.

Bear in mind, the house originally purchased for us was a farmhouse and probably 40 years old. This home that we would rent, was brand new, decorated in my favorite color scheme, had the right number of bedrooms, plus a study large enough for Chuck and all of his books. It was perfect for us.

We signed the lease papers that very day. The next day, would you believe, the owner received two cash sale offers. The house had been listed for sale for two years and he had no offers at all. Then, all in one weekend, he signed the rental papers for us and got two cash offers. He was very sweet when he told us about the other two offers. "I'm not sorry I rented it to you," he said. "This house was meant for you."

This to me is a small, but very significant, example of how God does communicate His Love to us through our circumstances. You can't convince me that this situation wasn't orchestrated and manipulated from Heaven. I know better.

Do You "Know" God?

I believe most Christians don't really know God. They know *about* Him and they know Scriptures, but they're not intimately acquainted with His character and His daily "loving" touch upon their lives.

To know God means to have living experience of Him. The Greek word for this kind of knowledge is ***oida*** which comes from the root word ***eidon*** meaning "to see" and "to experience." To know God means to experience His Life through us.

1 John 5:13 promises, "These things have I written unto you that believe on the name of the Son of God; that ye may know [have living experience] that ye have eternal life." And, 1 Corinthians 2:12 declares, "Now we have received, not the spirit of the world, but the spirit which is of God; that we might know [have living experience of] the things that are freely given to us of God."

Experiencing God's Love in our life is one of the major ways that we can know Him. And when we really know Him and how much He loves us, we'll never fear the circumstances that He allows into our lives. We'll know that everything is "Father-filtered" and will be used for His purposes. Remember Job 13:15 which avows, "Though He slay me, yet will I trust in Him." How could Job say that, with all the things God was allowing in his life? He could say that because he knew without a doubt that God loved Him.[8]

Beautiful Example: All Your Hairs are Numbered

A beautiful example of one who knew that God loved her and therefore could say, "Though you slay me, yet will I trust you," was Diana Bandtlow. Diana was a precious sister of mine in the Lord and one of the most incredible witnesses of God's Life manifested that I have ever seen. That's saying a lot because I have been a Christian for over 38 years.

Diana was only two years old in the Lord when she was diagnosed with leukemia and given six months to live. But no matter what the circumstances were and no matter how much pain she was in, she continually chose to trust God and lay her life down to Him because *she knew He loved her.* And she knew He wouldn't allow anything into her life that wasn't "Father-filtered" or that wouldn't eventually bring Him glory.

She was invited to teach a Bible study those last six months of her life. If it had been you or I, we probably would have spent those precious months at home with our families. Diana had a husband who adored her and two beautiful, little children, Hillary, 3, and Stephanie, 1. But not Diana. She prayed about it and felt strongly that God wanted her out there sharing with her friends exactly what He was doing in her life. What incredible faith and trust!

The Bible study grew to about 50 people, because we all saw in Diana an intimacy with God that none of us had. I had been a Christian about 15 years at that point, and yet I had never met anyone like Diana. She loved God and it was apparent to all of us that she knew God loved her, and her life and walk reflected that knowledge.

Diana's leukemia was diagnosed in June, and by November she was permanently confined to the hospital. At Thanksgiving, I wanted desperately to give her something to show her how much I loved her and how much she had ministered to my life.

That particular weekend, my three-month-old daughter Michelle was ill, and I needed to run to the pharmacy to pick up her medication. I thought it would also be a good time to get something for Diana. In the car I prayed and asked God to point out something He had in mind for Diana, that perfect love gift to communicate His Love to her. I got the prescription, and on the way out of the pharmacy I noticed a cute bird's nest, all done in fall colors with two little sparrows in it. I just knew it was for Diana. I quickly bought it and raced home.

On the way home, I looked down at the little bird's nest in my lap and began to wonder about the appropriateness of this gift. I asked God, "Is this really what You had in mind for Diana? A bird's nest?" The Scripture that immediately came to me was Matthew 10:29-31, "Are not two sparrows sold for a farthing? And one of them shall not fall on the ground without your Father. But the very hairs of your head are all numbered. Fear ye not therefore, ye are of more value than many sparrows."

Well, I was excited because it fit so perfectly. I wrote it on a card, put it with the nest, and asked Chuck when he got home to deliver it to the hospital for me.

About a half an hour later, Diana called and said, "Oh Nancy, I love the bird's nest! I know it's from God because He always tells me not to fear! But," she said, "what you don't know, and what no one else knows—except for God—is that I am losing all my hair. And God tells me right here that *He loves me so much that 'all the hairs on my head are numbered' to Him.*"

That's our faithful and loving Father who is interested and concerned about every detail of our lives. He personally communicates His Love to each of us, prompting us to say in response, "Lord, I know You love me so much that though You slay me, yet will I trust You."

My precious friend Diana went home to be with the Lord on Christmas day, 1974. She had touched more lives in her short life here on earth than many Christians I know who have lived long and healthy lives.

Hope For the Future

Experiencing God's Love is the only thing that will give us a consistent hope for the future, hope which leads us to faith and belief and the ability to trust God in everything, even though we can't see or understand where He is leading us.

God's Love helps us endure, persevere, and hang on through the trials and the pain and suffering. Hope in God's Love is what will give us the faith to look beyond the near term, beyond the current situation, beyond the horrendous problems, and look to Christ for our final victory, just as Diana did. If we know without a doubt that we are loved by the Father, then there is always hope for the future!

1 Corinthians 13:13 states, "And now abideth faith, hope, charity [God's Love], these three; but *the greatest of these is charity* [Love]." (emphasis added)

Endnotes:

1.   Doubt causes our hearts to be covered, insensitive to His leading, and blocks His Love from coming forth. See Chapter 11, "What Is Sin?"

2.   She "sang in the spirit" like 1 Corinthians 14:15 says we can.

3.   See *Knowing God Loves Me* Scriptures in the Supplemental Notes.

4.   See Chapter 12, "A Holding Pattern."

5.   Psalm 18:6-7,9,16-17,19

6.   1 John 4:13

7.   John 3:16

8.   Job 11:18a

Scriptural References:

Chapter 7

Why Is It So Important to Know God Loves Us?
   A. Two essential reasons:
      1. *Knowing God loves us* is the first step to living God's Way of *Agape*. It is the foundation to our whole Christian walk (Malachi 1:2a; Isaiah 43:1-4; Matthew 10:29-31; Romans 8:29-30; John 3:16; 1 John 4:10; Luke 12:7)
      2. We must know God loves us before we can have the confidence to lay down our wills and our lives for Him (i.e., love Him) (Jeremiah 29:13; 2 Timothy 1:12b: 1 John 3:1; 4:19)
   B. If we knew how much God loves us, we would never fear what God would allow in our lives (Isaiah 43:2-4; 2 Timothy 1:7; 1 John 4:18)
   C. We would always be secure in our identity of who we really are (Isaiah 49:16)

How Can We Know *Experientially* that God Loves Us?
   A. He says so in His Word (Jeremiah 31:3; Isaiah 43:4; 49:16; 54:10; Psalm 18:4-6,9,16-17,19; 103:11,17; John 3:16; 13:1; 15:9b, 16; 17:26; 1 John 3:1)
   B. He sent His Son to die in our place, so we might be free from sin's penalty (John 3:16b; 15:13; Romans 5:8; 1 John 3:16a; 4:9-10)
      1. He died so we could be saved
      2. This is *ultimate Love* (John 15:13; Ephesians 3:17-19)
   C. He has given us His Spirit in our hearts as proof of His Love (Romans 5:5c; 8:16; Ephesians 1:4; 1 John 4:13; 1 Corinthians 6:17; Galatians 4:6)
   D. He has given us His abundant Life (His Love, His Wisdom and Power) here and now (Romans 5:5b; James 1:12; John 3:16c; 10:10; 17:3,26; Ephesians 3:17; John 17:26)

How Does God Communicate His Love to Us?
   A. Through our daily reading of His Word (Psalm 119:113-114, 116, 133,147,154)
   B. Through our Christian brothers and sisters—*we are extensions of God's Love to each other* (1 John 3:16)
   C. Through our situations and circumstances

Do You Know (Have Living Experience of) God?
   A. Most of us know about God, but we really don't have living experience of Him in our day-to-day lives.
      1. To "know" in the Greek is oida. It means to have living experience of (1 John 5:13,20; 1 Corinthians 2:11-12)
      2. *Oida* comes from the root *eidon* which means "to see" or "to experience" (John 12:21)

B. Experiencing His Love in our lives will bring us this knowledge (Ephesians 3:17-19)
C. Experiencing His Love will give us the hope we need for the future (Jeremiah 29:11; Psalms 18:19; 34:19; 86:5-7; Hebrews 6:19)
D. Experiencing His Love will give us the ability to endure present trials (Job 13:15; Psalms 27:5,13-14; Isaiah 43:2-4; Romans 5:3-5; 2 Corinthians 4:17; 1 Peter 5:10)

Section Four

Chapter 8: What Does It Mean to Love God?

Now that we understand what God's Love is and that God loves us with that same unconditional Love, we can move forward and learn what it means to love God the way He desires.

As we discussed in Chapter 6, God created man with two basic needs: the need *to be loved* and the need *to love.* Our need to be loved, we shared, can only be fulfilled by our knowing that God loves us. This is what gives us our security and identity in this life. Our need to love can be fulfilled only by our learning to love God and others in the way that He desires. This knowledge is what will give our lives the meaning and purpose that we are all searching for.

Since God gave us His highest form of sacrificial Love—*Himself*—He desires our response to Him be the very same. He desires that we give Him back all we have to give, which is *ourselves.*

The Bible states, "We love Him, [only] because He first loved us." (1 John 4: 19)

Loving God

What exactly does loving God mean? Does it mean to love Him with our human "emotional" love (*storge*)? Does it mean to love Him with our "friendship" love (*phileo*)? What kind of love is God talking about here?

2 John 6 declares, "And this is love, that we walk after [in obedience to] His commandments."[1] And John 14:15 says, "If you love Me, keep My commandments."

In other words, the way God wants us to love Him is for us to obey His commands. Okay, which commands does He mean? There are hundreds of them in the Bible. Galatians 5:14, Matthew 22:40 and Romans 13:10 tell us that the whole Bible, all of God's commands, is literally summed up in only two commandments. And they are:

> "Thou shalt love (*agapao*) the Lord thy God with all thy heart, with all thy soul, and with all thy mind. This is the first and great commandment. And the second is like unto it, Thou shalt love (*agapao*) your neighbour as thyself." (Matthew 22:37-39)

If we walk in obedience to these two commandments, then God says we will be loving Him as He desires. These two commandments are inseparable and must go in the order they were given. In other words, we can't love others as ourselves until we have first loved God with all our heart, mind and soul. We must first learn to love God—become that open and cleansed vessel—so then God can love others through us.

Agapao Defined

The Greek word for love used in both of these great commandments is the verb **agapao**. To *agapao* something means *to totally give ourselves over to something*; to be totally consumed with it; totally committed to it. What we *agapao* is what we put first in our lives. All our intentions and abilities are focused and consumed with this one thing. In other words, it's a commitment or a binding of ourselves to something, so that we become "one" with it.

This *commitment love (agapao)* can either be to God, or to man, or to things of the world. So be careful not to get this <u>verb</u> *agapao* mixed up with the <u>noun</u> *Agape* (which we studied in Chapter 3), because they mean two totally different things.

Agape, we said, is God's pure unconditional Love and it's always used as such in the Bible. There is never a negative usage of *Agape* in the Scriptures. In fact, the word *Agape* was actually coined for its usage in Scripture, whereas *agapao* (what we are studying here) is what we give ourselves over to. And we can give ourselves over to something that is good (like God or others), or we can give ourselves over to something that is bad (like things of the world—money, materialism, pleasure or sex).

Look at the following Scriptures and see what the people in the Bible "gave themselves over to" (the Greek word in each of these Scriptures is *agapao*):

- John 3:19, "men loved [*agapao*] darkness rather than light, because their deeds were evil."

- John 12:43, "For they loved [*agapao*] the praise of men more than the praise of God."

- Luke 11:43, "Woe unto you, Pharisees! for ye love [*agapao*] the uppermost seats in the synagogues."

- 2 Timothy 4:10, "For Demas hath forsaken me, having loved [*agapao*] this present world."

- 1 John 2:15, "Love [*agapao*] not the world, neither the things that are in the world."

- And lastly, Luke 6:32, "for sinners also love [*agapao*] those that love them."

Some current examples of things we *agapao*—and bind ourselves to—are careers, houses, money, pleasure and *self*.

We could almost call this "commitment" love a fourth kind of natural love. 1) *Storge* is our emotional love; 2) *Eros* is our sexual love; 3) *Phileo* is our friendship love; and now, 4) *Agapao* is our commitment love.

When we *agapao* something, we are submitting our wills and our lives to it. In other words, what we *agapao* is the ultimate commitment of our selves; it's what we put first in our lives.

Do You Love God?

If I asked you, "Do you love [*agapao*] God?" most of you would automatically say, "Yes, of course I do!" But if you are really honest with yourself, how often do you seek to put His Will and His Desires above your own? How often are you consumed with what He desires for your life and not what you want out of life?

Can you honestly say that you desire God's Will above your own happiness?

This question puts it right into perspective, doesn't it? People everywhere are seeking happiness and contentment as their ultimate goal. Is this your goal? Or is it to set yourself aside and please God?

There was a woman in my last seminar who really took offense at my statement that we should desire God's Will above our own happiness. She asked, "Nancy, surely you mean our perception of happiness?" I said, "No, I really believe there are many times that we must choose to do God's Will over what we *know* will bring us happiness." There have been many times in my own life where I've had to make choices I knew would not bring me momentary happiness. However, I also knew that nothing would compare with the long-lasting joy I would experience as a result of choosing God's Way over my own.

Example: A Miracle

There was a woman not too long ago who knew that God wanted her to stay in her marriage, regardless of the horrible circumstances. Her husband no longer loved her and he had told her so. He had tired of her, and wanted her out of his life. He was doing everything he could to make her life miserable because he wanted her to be the one to file for divorce.

Certainly she would have been much happier out of the house and away from her tormentor. Yet, she knew that God had not given her permission to leave. And she was more concerned about doing God's *perfect* Will than her own momentary happiness.

I happened to see this lady recently at a party, and she had incredibly wonderful news. God had totally changed her husband's heart, and he was now doing everything he could to love her and make things up to her. God eventually restored their marriage; they began to experience not only *Agape* Love for each other, but also a restoration of all the human loves. I believe the "miracle" was due to the fact that my friend was *more* concerned about doing God's Will than what she knew would bring her momentary happiness.

To Love God Is to Lose Self

To love God is not an emotional feeling. To love God, the way He desires us to love Him, means to lose self (all our thoughts, emotions, and desires that are contrary to His). It means to relinquish and set aside our life, so that His can come forth from our hearts.

2 Corinthians 4:10-11 says, "Always bearing about in the body the dying of the Lord Jesus, that the life also of Jesus might be made manifest in our body. For we who live are always delivered unto death for Jesus' sake, that the life also of Jesus might be made manifest in our mortal flesh."

Because of our ignorance of the different types of natural, human loves, Christians often get our feeling love (*storge*) confused and mixed up with this commitment love (*agapao*). And because most of us have great emotional love for God, we think we are loving Him as He desires when, in fact, we are not even close.

Ever since I was a little girl, I have loved God. But my love for Him always seemed to fluctuate depending upon how I felt and what my circumstances were. I see now that my early love for God was really an emotional love (*storge*) and not the commitment love (*agapao*) that God desired.

The more I grow in learning to love (*agapao*) God His Way, the more I see the meaninglessness of having only affection love for Him. Affection love (*storge*) comes and goes, depending upon how we feel, what we think, and what our circumstances are. One day we're "up" and feeling *close* to God; the next day, because we are "down," we feel *far* away from Him.

God confirms this in Isaiah 29:13: "This people draw near Me with their mouths, and with their lips do honour Me, but [they] have removed their heart far from me, and their fear [love] toward Me is taught by the precept of men."

And also Luke 6:46, "Why call ye Me, Lord, Lord, and do not the things which I say?"

To Love God Defined

Let's explore in detail what it really means to love God in the way He desires.

In Scripture, to love (*agapao*) God means three specific things. I compiled these from Jesus Christ's three responses to Satan on the mountain of temptation in Matthew 4:1-10, where Satan tries to tempt Jesus not "to give Himself totally over to God," but to himself.

To love (*agapao*) God means:

1) To choose continually to <u>obey God's Word</u> (His Will) in our lives and not our own thoughts, emotions, and desires that are prompting us to go the opposite way.

2) To choose continually to <u>trust God's Power</u> (His Ability) to perform His Will in our lives, and not our own natural ability and power.

3) And lastly, to love God means to choose continually to <u>worship and serve Him</u> only by following, cleaving and so binding ourselves with Him that we become one.

A Scripture that sums up all three steps of loving God is Matthew 16:24:[2] "If any man will come after Me, let him *deny himself* [choose to obey God's Will and not our own thoughts], and *take up his cross* [trust God to perform through us, not in our own ability], and *follow Me* [worship and serve God only]."[3] (emphasis added)

Example: "Me, Wash His Feet?"

Let me tell you how my precious friend Melissa learned what it meant to love God. When this incident occurred, Melissa and her husband, Walt, had four small children under the age of seven.

Melissa had become extremely exhausted caring for all the needs of her small children. She had begun to pray that Walt would be more sensitive to her needs and help her out more with the kids when he got home in the afternoons. He was a medical technician and went to work around 6 a.m., but got home between 2 p.m. and 3 p.m. Melissa had prayed this prayer for some time, but had no visible results.

One evening Walt came home early only to find the house a total mess. He had to step over dirty laundry, broken toys, and what was left of lunch in order to find his way upstairs to where Melissa and the kids were. She had all four children in the bathtub, washing their hair. Walt stuck his head in the door and asked, "What on earth is going on? Why is the house such a mess?"

Since Melissa had been entertaining and mulling over thoughts of "Why can't Walt help me more?" and "I just can't take this anymore!" she immediately reacted out of those frustrations and shouted, "Well, if you would only help me more with these kids, I'd have more time to clean your house!" Obviously, it was not a response out of God's Love, but a response triggered by her own built-up frustration and resentment.

Poor Walt was terribly hurt. He immediately became defensive and said something else about her messy house. She retaliated with another jab. More words were exchanged, and then Walt slammed the bathroom door and started downstairs, mumbling something like "Boy, it's great to be home."

Melissa finished putting the kids to bed, shushing their inquisitive little questions of, "Is Daddy mad at us?" and "Why did Daddy slam the door, Mommy?"

After tucking the kids in bed, Melissa went downstairs. Not wanting to be in the same room with Walt (ever felt that way?), she went to the opposite end of the house, got out her Bible and began to pour out her true feelings to God. She started to cry and told God how tired, how lonely, and how unhappy she was, feeling as if Walt didn't even care about her anymore. He seemed, at times, so distant and insensitive.

After weeping quietly for a long time she told God, "But, I do really love You and I want to obey You and do what is right. What would you have me to do?" God, in His still small voice, directed her to Matthew 16:24, the passage we just read. "If any man comes after Me, let him deny himself, pick up his cross, and follow Me." Melissa sat there for a long time, contemplating how on earth this verse applied to her situation. Again God, in His still, small voice said, "If you will Love me first, I'll enable you to love your husband."

Melissa immediately replied, "But Lord, I do love You. How else am I supposed to show You? What else am I supposed to do?" With that, God impressed upon her mind, *"If you really love Me, then get a basin of water and go and wash your husband's feet."*

Well, you can imagine her reaction! If that were you, what kind of reaction would you have? Her reaction was the very same. "Are you kidding? After what he has done to me, *he* should be the one to wash *my* feet!"

God was silent. Finally Melissa began to understand, for the first time, what it really meant to love God: To deny yourself, pick up your cross and follow Him. In other words, do what Jesus would do. God was asking her not only to deny what she wanted, but He was also asking her to get up and do something she absolutely didn't want to do, which was to wash Walt's feet. God was asking her to do what Jesus would do in her situation.

Melissa had been studying about *Agape* Love and she knew if she didn't obey God and do what He was asking, she would quench His Spirit and His Love would then be covered in her heart. She couldn't stand that.

So she made that difficult faith choice (denied herself), got up, went into the kitchen, got a bowl of water and towel (picked up her cross), and went into her husband's study. Walt was lying on the couch, reading. She knelt quietly beside him and began to untie his shoes, crying softly as she did. At first, she said she didn't feel a thing for it was totally a *faith* choice. But, she said, by the time she began to take off his shoes and socks, it had become pure genuine love (doing exactly what Jesus would have done). God had aligned her feelings to match her faith choices.

Walt was flabbergasted when he saw Melissa walk into the room with that bowl of water. He was sure it was going to be thrown over his head! But when he saw her tears and felt her genuine Love, he reached down and drew her up to himself. And they were reconciled—both emotionally and spiritually.

After holding and embracing each other and truly realizing how much they really loved each other, Melissa was able to share with Walt her deepest needs. Because she was at this point a cleansed vessel, he could hear her from his "heart" and not his defenses. This became a special time in their marriage where they both became more sensitive to each other's needs: he began to help her more around the house and with the kids, and she tried to prepare a loving atmosphere when he came home at night.

Key Discovery

To love God the way He desires is definitely not an emotional feeling; *to love God literally means to lose self*—all of our own thoughts, emotions, and desires that are contrary to God's. It's John 12:24: "Except a corn of wheat fall into the ground and die, it abideth alone [no fruit]: but if it die, it bringeth forth much fruit [God's Love]."

We won't really learn to love God in our private worship times. It's only when we lay our lives down for someone else that loving God is truly realized. Of course, when we "lose ourselves" to God, we'll be "filled with His Love" and then enabled to go on and love others in the way He intends.

When I say "losing self," I don't mean losing who we really are and becoming some sort of a mindless robot. I mean setting aside all our thoughts, emotions, and desires that are contrary to God's and becoming a cleansed and open vessel. God's Life in our hearts is then freed to come forth and fill our souls. At this point Jesus is not just in our lives; *He is our very life itself!*

Let's take a few minutes and review each of the three steps of loving God, so we can begin to bind ourselves to Him (*agapao*) the way He desires.

Obey God's Word

What specifically does it mean to choose to *obey God's Word* (His Will) rather than our own thoughts, emotions, and desires that prompt us to go in the opposite direction? To obey God's Word means to choose continually to set aside and relinquish what we think, what we want, and what pleases us, and choose instead to do whatever God has asked us to do.

This is the <u>denying of ourselves</u> of Matthew 16:24. To deny ourselves does not necessarily mean denying "outward" things (i.e., houses, cars, fashionable clothing, etc.). That sort of denial, I think, is actually a lot easier! Rather, denying ourselves means "inward" things (i.e., our own "justified" thoughts, emotions, and desires that are contrary to God's). This step, to me, is much harder.

To deny also doesn't mean to push down and bury our real feelings. Nor does it mean to negate the existence of our true emotions or pretend that they don't exist. No, to deny ourselves means to bar ourselves from *following* our own feelings and emotions; in other words, prevent ourselves from being influenced by these negative things.

Interestingly, the definition "barring ourselves from following something," comes from the Greek root meaning of the word *to suffer*. When we bar ourselves from doing what we want, what we feel and what we desire, we often do suffer.[4]

To deny ourselves, then, does not mean to deny the existence of our negative thoughts, emotions, and desires. We are human and we'll always have these negative emotions until we see Jesus. We need to look at these things and call them what they are so that we'll know exactly what to give over to the Lord. But then we need to "bar ourselves" from following them and, instead, give them over to God.

Melissa chose to deny herself, not by burying her real feelings or pretending that they didn't exist, but by choosing not to give in to them, and not to be motivated by them. Melissa "barred herself" from following them. She chose instead to give them over to God and to be motivated by her commitment love (*agapao*) for God.

Obedience is simply our love response to God. By our choosing to obey God's Word and His Will rather than our own desires (no matter how we feel, no matter how that other person is responding, and no matter what our circumstances are), we are answering God with "I love You." Loving God is simply giving God free reign of our wills and our lives.

Hebrews 5:8 declares that Jesus learned obedience by the things which He suffered.

Obedience Is the Only Answer

I have learned the hard way that obedience is the *only* answer. I've learned to choose to obey God even when I don't feel like it, even when I don't want to, and even when I don't think it will work. I have tried all the other ways and *obedience* is the only way that truly works.

I've learned that even when it's the last thing on earth that I want to do, I must obey, because then and only then is God free to begin to work out the circumstances in my life according to His Will. Until I choose to obey, those circumstances are still *my* responsibility. But once I choose to obey and relinquish myself, those circumstances then become God's responsibility.

Romans 8:28 takes on a whole new light here. "And we know that all things work together for good to them that love (*agapao*) God." (To those who totally give themselves over to Him, not to those who only *phileo* or *storge* Him. If we have only affection love (*storge*) for God, don't expect Him to orchestrate our circumstances. We have tied His hands.

Example: Raw Eggs

Many years ago, Chuck and I had an evening planned at the Music Center in Los Angeles with some very important business friends who were non-believers. Because we lived in Orange County and it was at least an hour to Los Angeles, we had to pick up these friends by five o'clock in order to make dinner on time.

As it happened, that day was my carpool day for Michelle. I figured if I got all the girls home by 3:30 p.m., I'd still have plenty of time to get dressed and pick up our friends by five. That afternoon, however, one of the little girls in the carpool smashed her finger in the car door as she was getting in. We had to rush her back into school, soak her finger, call her mother and do some T.L.C. (tender loving care). I lost half an hour there.

When Michelle and I finally got home, I noticed a horrible smell coming from the back of the car. It turned out to be a whole carton of spilled and spoiled milk that one of the little girls had forgotten. Since this was the car I was using that evening, I needed to do an extra special job of cleaning up the mess so it wouldn't stink. I lost another 15 minutes here. (I think the "Lysol" smell from cleaning was probably worse than the original spoiled milk smell!)

When I finished cleaning the car, I rushed into the house to make a soufflé. I was hosting a luncheon the next day for twelve women, and I needed to make some last-minute preparations. The soufflé needs to be made a day in advance so it can sit in the refrigerator overnight.

I have one special pan that I use for a soufflé—none of my other pans work. That day, for some reason, I couldn't seem to find it. After spending ten anxious minutes opening and shutting all the cupboards in my kitchen trying to find my pan, I remembered we had lent our house to some people over Christmas. I thought perhaps by mistake they had taken it home. I called, and after several minutes of chit chat the wife verified that "yes," she had my pan. She said she could return it "tomorrow." "No, thank you," I said, "that's too late. I need it now. Thank you anyway."

By now it was 4:15 p.m. I wasn't dressed, the soufflé wasn't made, the kids weren't fed, and I was beginning to get a little panicked. I took out another pan, threw in all the ingredients and tried to stir. But the bowl was too small and I couldn't mix it properly. In desperation, I threw the whole mixture (a quart of milk, a dozen eggs, mustard, Worcestershire sauce, etc.) into my new Cuisinart, not realizing that liquids can't go above the two-inch tube in the center or they will overflow. Well, that's exactly what happened!

Twelve raw eggs and one quart of milk began to ooze out all over the counter, down the sides of the cabinets, into the drawers, down my legs, into my shoes, and onto the floor. It was now 4:30 p.m. By this time I was totally out of control! I began to scream, kick, and yell. Have you ever been there? Can you identify?

God gently tapped me on the shoulder and asked, "Nancy, do you love Me? Will you choose right now to obey Me? Do you love Me that much?" God wanted me to choose, at that very moment, to relinquish my anger, my frustration, and my anxiety to Him, and not allow my wild emotions to direct my actions anymore.

Do you know how hard that is, in the middle of a "fit," to stop, turn around, and choose to act in a calm manner? It's impossible; it's totally supernatural!

But I have learned over all these years that I have been a Christian that no other way works. I literally have tried *every* other way and none of them work. So out loud, almost crying, right there in the middle of the egg yolks, I made that commitment to God that I would obey Him. Now I certainly didn't feel like it; it was totally a faith choice, a non-feeling choice. I consciously relinquished my anger, my frustrations, and all of my wild feelings. I confessed that they were obviously not of faith and were therefore sin. And I asked Him to purge them from me.

In other words, I denied my self. I barred myself from following my wild feelings by not giving in to them, but by giving them to God and doing what He was asking me to do! Then I asked God to help me get ready on time, to pick up our friends by five, and even to be a genuine representation of Him that evening.

God is so faithful. He did "work all things together for good" because I chose to *agapao* Him, instead of giving in to my own feelings and emotions. I ran upstairs and was able to find a perfect outfit to wear. I jumped in the shower and did what I could with my wild hair. I was only 15 minutes late picking those people up that night, and yet we were right on time for the dinner and the show in Los Angeles.

The best part of the whole evening was experiencing God's Love, not only for me personally, but flowing through me to our friends that night. Can you imagine what kind of a Godly representative I would have been had I not made that choice to obey and love God?

Obeying God's Will—instead of our own emotions and desires—is the first step towards loving God the way He desires.

Trust God to Perform His Will

This leads us to the second step of loving (*agapao*) God, which is *trusting God to perform His Will* in our lives and not our own strength and power to do so. This step must go alongside of obeying God's Will.

What good is it if God tells us what His Will is, but then we go out and perform that Will on our own power and strength? Scripture tells us, "If any man speak, let him speak as the oracles of God; if any man minister, let him do it as of the ability which God giveth: [why?] that God in all things may be glorified..." (1 Peter 4:11)

Trusting God is relying upon Him and His Ability to accomplish His Will in our lives, no matter how we feel, what we think, or what the circumstances are. This is the daily picking up of our crosses (Matthew 16:24) and doing what He has asked—whether we feel like it or not! This second step is probably the hardest part of loving God because we must do in action what God has asked, regardless of how we feel and what we think.

Remember Melissa. She didn't "feel" like getting up and getting that bowl of water and washcloth, and yet by faith she chose to do it anyway. And by the time she actually began to wash her husband's feet, she experienced genuineness. 2 Corinthians 8:11 talks about a readiness not only to will, but also a readiness to perform.

Trust God to "Align" Our Feelings

Trusting God to perform His will through us is difficult because we often *feel* one way, and yet by faith we must choose to *act* in another way. For example, it's much easier for the wife of an alcoholic to choose to obey God in the privacy of her own prayer closet than it is for her to go home and trust God to give her the Love and compassion that she needs for her verbally abusive husband.

We must not only trust God to perform through us what He has promised, but we must also trust Him to make us *genuine* by aligning our feelings with what we have chosen. God is the only One who can do this and we must trust His faithfulness.

Habakkuk 2:4 states, "The just shall live by his faith." In other words, we live the life that pleases Christ by trusting God's faithfulness to perform that life in and through us.

God binds Himself to His Word and He is always faithful to do it. Jeremiah 1:12 promises, "Thou hast well seen: for I will hasten My Word to perform it."

What Is Truth?

A definition of Truth that I really like is: Truth is where the word and the deed match and become one. Jesus Himself is the Truth. He is the Word that became the Deed. As John 1:14 puts it, "The Word was made flesh, and dwelt among us."

Truth can also be translated to mean *faithful*. God promises us certain things in the Bible and He is always faithful, reliable, and trustworthy to perform them. We need to be faithful to God as well. If we promise God something in our prayer closet, we need to be faithful to lay our lives and our actions alongside. How often we choose God's Will in our prayer closets, but because we don't *feel* Him when we begin to perform what He has asked us to do, we don't think He has really heard us. Once again, doubt and unbelief covers our hearts.

Galatians 2:20 states, "I am crucified with Christ: nevertheless I live; yet not I, but Christ liveth in me: [it's His Life now in me] and the life which I now live in the flesh I live by the faith [or the faithfulness] of the Son of God, Who loved me, and gave Himself for me."

Trusting God is cleaving to Him with unreserved confidence, being fully persuaded that what He has told us to do He will perform in our life actions, whether we feel it, or see it or not! One of my favorite Scriptures is: "Commit thy way unto the Lord; trust also in Him, and He shall bring it to pass." (Psalm 37:5)

Example: I Almost Drowned

Several years ago, Chuck and I went to Australia on a business trip. We decided to celebrate our anniversary early by going to the Great Barrier Reef to do some scuba diving. Chuck has always loved to dive, and one of his greatest desires was to someday dive at the Great Barrier Reef. This was a perfect opportunity.

I, however, had not made a dive in ten years. Ten years previously, I had taken a one-week scuba "crash course" so I could get certified and go diving with Chuck in the Virgin Islands. We had a great time, but I hadn't had the opportunity to dive since then. So I had not thought about diving—or even tried out the equipment—in ten years! I was so busy traveling and writing before this trip that I didn't even have time to reread the diving manual.

Arriving at Hayman Island on the Great Barrier Reef very late in the afternoon, we immediately asked if there were any "refresher courses" offered before the big dive the next morning. They said no. Then we asked if there was a possibility of an afternoon boat trip the next day so I could take the morning practice course. Again, the answer was no.

They also told us if we wanted to go on the planned trip to the Reef early the next morning, we needed to take a quick "check out" dive right then. They needed to see if we were proficient. (Oh boy, just what I was afraid of!) Well, Chuck passed with flying colors.

I jumped into the water ready to do my very best. The instructor made me sit on the bottom of the pool, take off my breathing apparatus and my mask, and put them both back on. Well, after ten years, I had forgotten exactly how to do this properly. I couldn't remember how to "clear" my mask underwater. I could only clear the water down to just above my nose. After one minute of holding my breath, I finally had to breathe in. Tons of water went into my lungs. Instinctively, I shot to the top. (A cardinal rule in diving is that you never shoot to the top. You can easily kill yourself by holding your breath while going up—causing an embolism. A change in depth of only three feet can prove fatal.)

The instructor followed me to the top, calmed me down, and said everything would be okay and to try again. He then led me back underwater to try out the "buddy breathing" technique. At the bottom of the pool, he took a deep breath and then handed me his breathing apparatus. Again, I had forgotten you don't just breathe in when you put the apparatus in your mouth. You must first blow out through the regulator to get rid of the water that has come in as it was passed to you. I took a deep breath, expecting to get air, but got a mouthful of water instead. Once again, I instinctively shot to the top.

The instructor was very nice, and surprisingly said I could go on the trip the next morning, but he said he was a "little nervous" for me. He was nervous? At this point I was panic stricken! I had almost killed myself twice in only eight feet of water; what would I do the next morning in 100 feet of water?

All night long, fear absolutely gripped me! I'm not normally prone to be fearful. But that night I was paralyzed! I made up my mind, there was no way I was going on that boat trip the next morning. The problem was, however, it was Chuck's birthday, and he had his heart set on diving at the Barrier Reef, and he had told me that he wouldn't go without me. What on earth was I supposed to do?

I didn't sleep half the night. I just laid there awake. By faith (because I certainly didn't feel it), I kept giving God my fear and panic, telling Him that I was willing to trust Him with whatever He wanted me to do. I acknowledged it was His body and His life (He owns me), and I committed to rely on Him totally. I finally fell asleep and when I woke the next morning, I knew in my heart that God would not fail me.

Chuck and I didn't talk much about the diving trip at breakfast, because I'm sure he sensed my fear and that I might say, "I'm not going."

After breakfast we took a walk and "coincidently" ran across a gal whom we had befriended on the boat coming to the Island the day before. She mentioned that she was taking a scuba diving refresher course that morning and then was going on an afternoon boat trip to the Reef. She asked us if we would like to accompany her and her husband. Well, we were floored because of the response we had gotten from the diving people the night before that there was no morning refresher course and no afternoon boat trip.

I knew immediately it had to be the Lord! He knew how badly I needed that refresher course and He had arranged one just for me!

I took the diving course with my new friend and we went on that afternoon boat trip. I made several dives with my precious husband and we had an absolute ball, taking loads of pictures and even seeing several sharks.

This is just one small example, but these "little hassles" are where we women (and men, too) live. If God can be trusted in these tiny tests, how much more can He be trusted in the big ones. Trusting God is simply relying upon Him and His ability to accomplish His Will in our lives, no matter how we feel, what we think, or what our circumstances are.

God wants us—with the big as well as the little opportunities—to not only choose to obey His Will, but also to trust Him to perform that Will in our lives. We can't serve God with our words only; we must also put alongside of those words our life actions.

Romans 4:20-21 declares, "He [Abraham] staggered not at the promise of God through unbelief; but was strong in faith, giving glory to God; And being fully persuaded that, what He had promised, He was able also to perform."

Worship and Serve God Only

This leads us to the third and final step of what it means to love (*agapao*) God, which is *to worship and serve God only*.

Worshipping God (Greek word **proskyneo**) is something we do internally. It means to prostrate and bow before God, laying aside our selves (our lives), in order that God's Self (His Life) can be manifested.

Serving God (Greek word **latreia**) is something we do externally. It means to present our body as a living sacrifice and our members as instruments of righteousness, in order that God—and not ourselves—be glorified. (Romans 12:1)

Worshipping and serving God are the same thing as <u>following God</u>. Remember Matthew 16:24, "If any man will come after Me, let him deny himself [obey God and not self], and take up his cross [trust God and not self], and follow Me." Following God literally means to cleave unto something (to adhere to it like glue) so that we become one with it.

Do you recall the rich young ruler in Matthew 19:16-22, who came to Jesus and asked Him how to obtain eternal life? Jesus answered him and said, "If you want life, "keep the commandments." The rich young ruler replied by naming the various commandments he was keeping. He then asked Jesus, "What lack I yet?" Jesus answered him by saying, "Go and sell that thou hast, and give to the poor... and come and follow Me."

[Notice, by the way, the First and Second Commandments were just about the only commandments the rich young ruler was not keeping].

Jesus' answer is, of course, applicable to all of us. He is asking us to forfeit all rights to ourselves. This means relinquishing the totality of our life and body to Jesus. He is also asking us to come and follow Him. In other words, will we actually do what He would do in each of our difficult situations? God encourages each of us to "sell (trade) what we have"—our own thoughts, emotions, and desires that are contrary to God's—in order to "buy" God's Life (His supernatural Love, Wisdom, and Power). He then exhorts us to "give all we have" (His Life in us) to the "poor and needy." Then, and only then, will we be following in His footsteps.

Luke 14:26 states, "If any man come to Me, and hate not [is not willing to set aside] his father, and mother, and wife, and children, and brethren, and sisters, yea, and *his own life* also, he cannot be My disciple. And whosoever doth not bear his cross and come after Me, cannot be My disciple." (emphasis added)

Following God is *not* merely walking in the same direction as Jesus. There are many, many Christians today who are doing just that, slowly meandering behind Him. This is not God's definition of "following Him" or "loving Him." "Following God" means cleaving unto Him, binding ourselves with Him, so that *we actually become one with Him;* one heart, one will, and one soul.

Cleaving to God is analogous to those little two-inch dolls that open their arms and legs when we squeeze them in the back and grab on to whatever is in front of them. I think of following God in the very same way. It's almost as if we are clinging to God, binding ourselves so closely to Him, that *"wherever He is, we will be also."* Remember John 12:26, "If any man serve Me, let him follow Me; and where I am, there shall also My servant be." We will be there because we'll be tightly wrapped around His leg and hanging on "for dear life!"

Being one with God is being willing, as Mark 8:31 and Luke 9:22 indicate, not only to *suffer* as Jesus did and be *rejected* as He was, but also to be willing *to die* as He did. It's being continually willing to lay down our life and our body, so Jesus can love others through us. Peter tells us: "Forasmuch, then, as Christ hath suffered for us in the flesh, arm yourselves likewise with the same mind [attitude]; for he that hath suffered [barred himself from sin] in the flesh hath ceased from sin." (1 Peter 4:1)

Jesus is our example. He loved (*agapao*) God the Father so much that He was willing to be crucified in order to do His Will. Philippians 2:5-9 explains, "Christ Jesus: Who, being in the form of God, thought it not robbery to be equal with God: But made Himself of no reputation, and took upon Him the form of a servant, and was made in the likeness of men: And being found in fashion as a man, He humbled Himself, and became *obedient unto death*, even the death of the cross. Wherefore God also hath highly exalted Him and given Him a name which is above every name." (emphasis added)

Do you love God that much? Are you willing to lay down your will and your life, to die to your self, so that he might live His Life through you? You may respond, "That's Jesus' role, not mine!" You might be interested to note what Peter and Paul had to say on this subject. "For even hereunto were ye called, because Christ also suffered for us, leaving us an example, that ye should follow His steps." (1 Peter 2:21)

And also Ephesians 5:1-2 states, "Be ye therefore *followers of God*, as dear children: And walk in love, as Christ also hath loved us, and hath given Himself for us an offering and a sacrifice to God for a sweet smelling savour." (emphasis added)

Paul reiterates this in 1 Corinthians 15:31, "I die daily."

Example: There Was Not a "Me" There

I have a dear Christian friend named Sue. After a painful divorce, Sue decided to move to the East Coast. Her estranged husband Jim, who was Jewish, continued to live in Southern California with his new girlfriend, Joy.

A year or so after the divorce, Sue had to come back to California on a business trip. She could hardly wait to see all of her old friends again. She found out that there was a party being planned and she was so looking forward to seeing "the old gang," most of whom were Jewish.

After she arrived in California, someone called Sue and told her that her ex-husband Jim and his girlfriend were also going to be at the party. Feeling extremely angry and upset, Sue thought to herself, "How dare they invite Jim and his girlfriend. There is just no way in the world I am going to that party now."

For one entire week Sue argued with God, knowing that God would have her obey Him (by giving Him her hurts, resentments, and bitternesses); trust Him (by allowing Him to perform His Will through her); and then follow Him (by doing whatever Jesus would have done in this situation).

Sue knew in her heart that God wanted to pour out His Love on these precious Jewish people who didn't *know* Him. She knew God wanted to use her at that party. However, sometimes we just can't give ourselves over to God right away. Sometimes it just feels good to feel sorry for ourselves and to wade in the muck and mire of self pity for awhile. Do you know what I mean? Do you ever feel this way?

God is so wonderful, though. He loves us even through these difficult times— even when we are being brats. He patiently waits by us, never leaving us or forsaking us, until we just can't stand the "pig sty" any longer; and we finally give in and choose to do it His Way.

That's just what happened with Sue. After an entire week of wrestling with God, He convinced her that it *was* His Will that she attend the party and carry His Love.

After finally reconciling herself to the Lord's desires, Sue told God, "Okay, I'm willing to go to that party; I'm willing to give you my hurts and my past memories and become an open vessel; but it's impossible for me to love them. You're going to have to do that for me." That's all God needed.

When Sue arrived at the party house, the first person she met at the door was Jim's girlfriend, Joy. Sue said later, "It was absolutely wild. My body stayed outside the door when it opened, but something deep within me stepped inside, reached out to Joy and in total genuineness said, "I am so glad to meet you. I really have heard so many nice things about you" (which was true).

Joy and Sue sat on the couch talking comfortably for about an hour and a half. Jim must have sensed Sue's openness and genuine concern because later he, too, asked Sue if they could go into another room and talk privately. Sensing her genuine compassion, Jim felt free to share from his heart many intimate things about their marriage.

Later, when Sue was relating this story to me over the phone, I stopped her and asked, "But Sue, how did you feel when Jim began to share all those painful things?" Sue's immediate answer was: "Nancy, it was incredible, *there was not a 'me' (self) there.*"

Sue was so completely one with God at that moment that it was God's Character and God's Life (His Love and His Thoughts) flowing through her and not her own. 1 John 4:17 declares, "*... as He is, so are we [to be] in this world.*" (emphasis added)

Sometimes it may only be for one moment that we are an open vessel and God's Love can pour forth. That's okay; tomorrow, it will be five minutes, the next day, perhaps ten.

He Is Our Life

This complete surrender is the union, the oneness, and the marriage relationship God desires for every one of us: *One heart, one will, and one life.* He wants us to become so "at one" with Him, that what others see and hear through us is His Love and His Wisdom and His Power. In other words, it's His character coming forth from us and not our own.

Loving God is not an emotional feeling, nor is it an emotional high; rather, loving God is losing self to the point where we can say, "there was not a 'me' (self) there," only God! At this point, *Jesus is not just in our lives; **He is our Life.***

Do you love God so much that you are willing not only to choose to obey His Word, but also to lay down your life and your body and trust His Spirit to perform His Word through you?

In John 21:15-17, Peter is asked three times by Jesus, "Do you love Me?" The first two times Jesus uses the word, *agapao*, "are you able to totally give yourself over to me?" Will you "bind yourself to Me?" "Will you become *one* with Me?" Peter, however, could only answer back, "Lord I have friendship love (*phileo*) for you." (At least Peter was being honest.)

The final time Jesus asks Peter, "Do you have love for Me?" This time He comes down to Peter's level and uses the word *phileo*. "Peter, do you at least have friendship love for Me?" Peter was grieved because he knew that Jesus knew, at that particular time, Peter wasn't able to totally relinquish himself to Him (*agapao*).

Jesus is asking you the same questions: Do you love (*agapao*) Me? Will you totally give yourself over to Me? Will you bind yourself with Me? Will you become One with Me?"

Can you answer Him, "Yes, Lord, I *agapao* You?"

If your answer is, "Yes, I *agapao* You," then your life is going to be full of God's supernatural Love, Wisdom, and Power. Jesus' declaration is precise and direct: "He that hath My commandments, and keepeth them, he it is that loveth Me; and he that loveth Me shall be loved of My Father, and I will love him, and will manifest Myself to him." (John 14:21)

If, however, your answer is like Peter's, "I can only *phileo* you now," then you will be exactly like that rich young ruler in Matthew 19, who "went away sorrowfully."

"Strait is the gate, and narrow is the way, which leadeth unto life, and few there be that find it." (Matthew 7:14)

Will you be one who does?

Endnotes:

1. 1 John 5:3 and John 14:21

2. Matthew 19:21

3. Luke 9:23 says, "take up his cross <u>daily</u>."

4. When we endure, refuse or bar ourselves from following (Greek word, *anechomai*) any lust, sin or evil affection (Greek word, *epithumia*), it causes us suffering (Greek words, *pathema, pathos* and *pascho*).

Scriptural References:

Chapter 8

What Is Our Response to God's Unconditional *Agape* Love?
A. Our response should be to love Him (*agapao*) (1 John 4:19)
B. What exactly does this mean? How do we love Him?
    1. By keeping His Commands (John 14:15; 1 John 5:3; 2 John 6)
    2. Which Commands?
        a. The whole Bible is summed up in only two Commands (Romans 13: 10; Galatians 5:14; Matthew 22:40)
        b. *"Thou shalt love the Lord thy God with all thy heart, with all thy soul, and with all thy mind. This is the first and Great Commandment. And the second is like unto it, thou shalt love thy neighbour as thyself."* (Matthew 22:37-39, emphasis added)
C. If we walk in obedience to these two Commandments, we will be loving God as He desires
    1. These two Commandments are inseparable and must go in the order they were given
    2. In other words, we can't love others until we have first learned to love (*agapao*) God

To Love (*Agapao*) Means:
A. To *agapao* something means to totally give yourself over to it; to be totally consumed with it; it's what you put first in your life; it's a *commitment love* or a binding of oneself to something so that you become one with it. (Deuteronomy 11:22; 30;20; Joshua 22:5; Luke 9:23)
B. This commitment love can be to something good or to something bad
    1. Something good: love God with all your heart, mind, and soul (Matthew 22:37; Deuteronomy 6:5) and love others as yourself (Matthew 22:39)
    2. Something bad: love self, things, or pleasures of the world (John 3:19; 12:43; Luke 6:32; 11:43; 2 Timothy 4:10; 1 John 2:15)
C. *Agapao* is a fourth kind of natural, human love—our commitment love.
D. We often mistake our emotional, feeling love (*storge*) for this commitment love (*agapao*)

To Love (*Agapao*) God Means: to Lose Self
(Matthew 4:1-10; 16:24; 2 Corinthians 4:10-11; John 12:24-25; Luke 14:26,33; Mark 8:31)
A. To choose continually to *obey God's Will* and not our own desires (Matthew 4:4; 16:24a; 26:39; Deuteronomy 6:17; Psalm 40:8; Luke 22:42; John 5:30; 14:15,23; James 1:21-22; 1 John 2:5)
    1. This is the *denying of ourselves* (denying our own thoughts, emotions, and desires, and choosing instead to obey God's Will (Matthew 16:24a; Luke 9:23a; Philippians 2:8; Matthew 22:37-39)
        a. This doesn't mean outward things (Colossians 2:18,23), but inward things, which are often harder to give up

      b.   This doesn't mean to push down and bury our real feelings, but to bar ourselves from following them and choosing instead to follow God's Will (Galatians 6:17; 2 Corinthians 4:10; 1 Peter 2:19-20; 3: 14; 4:1-2,19)

      c.   Denying ourselves comes from the Greek word that means to suffer. When we "bar ourselves" from following what we want, feel, and desire, we often do suffer (Hebrews 5:8)

  2. This is being obedient unto death (Philippians 2:5-9; Matthew 22:37-39; Mark 10:21b; 2 Corinthians 4:10-12)

  3. Obedience is our answer to God's question, "Do you love Me?" It's our answer to hearing God's Word (His Will), no matter what we think, feel, or want. (Luke 5:5c; James 1:22-25; 1 John 2:5; Romans 6:17; John 14: 21)

  4. Loving God is wanting His Will more than our own happiness (Psalm 40:8; 1 Peter 4:1)

      a.   Knowing that if we don't obey, we will "perish" (Deuteronomy 8:19; 30:16-18)

      b.   We will only be joyful in doing His Will (Romans 14:17; 15:13; 1 John 1:4; John 15:11; Psalm 16:11)

D. To choose continually to *trust God's Spirit to perform* God's will in our lives (Matthew 4:7; Deuteronomy 6:16; 8:17; Exodus 17:7; Psalm 18:32; 37:5b; 1 Thessalonians 5:24; 2 Corinthians 1:9) "For it is God Which worketh in you both to will and to do, of His good pleasure. (Philippians 2:13, emphasis added). Also see (Romans 7:18; 2 Corinthians 8:11)

  1. This is the *picking up of our crosses* (Matthew 16:24b; Luke 9:23), re-lying only upon God to accomplish His will in our lives (no matter the circumstances)

      a.   Bearing our own cross (Luke 14:27; Matthew 10:38)

      b.   Knowing we will suffer and be rejected (Mark 8:31)

  2. This is trusting God with unreserved confidence that He will do what He has promised (Jeremiah 1:12; Psalm 57:2; Ezekiel 12:25; Hebrews 11: 11,27; 1 Peter 4:11)

      a.   Doing it without feeling it (Galatians 2:20)

      b.   Walking by faith, not sight (Romans 4:21)

      c.   Knowing God is trustworthy (Psalm 52:8-9)

      d.   Knowing God is faithful (Deuteronomy 7:9; Hebrews 10:23)

      e.   Knowing God will align our feelings with our choice (Habakkuk 2:4)

  3. We can't just serve God with our words, we must put our actions alongside (2 Timothy 3:5)

      a.   This is called faithfulness or truth (truth is where the word matches and becomes one with the deed) (Matthew 3:16-17; John 6:63; Romans 1:16)

      b.   Jesus is the Truth (John 1:1, 14a). He is always faithful to perform His Word (Jeremiah 1:12; 23:20; Deuteronomy 7:9; Isaiah 34:16; Ezekiel 12:25)

      c.   We live by God's faithfulness to do what He says (Habakkuk 2:4b; Galatians 2:20; 1 Thessalonians 5:24)

       d.   "Without faith it is impossible to please Him." (Hebrews 11:6)

C. To choose continually to *worship and serve God only* (Matthew 4:10)

    1. We must be willing not only to obey His Word and trust His Spirit to perform, but we must also be willing to lay down our lives and bodies, moment by moment, so He can work out His plans and purposes through us (Luke 14:26; John 12:25)

       a. *Worshipping* (*proskyneo*) God means: prostrating, bowing to, and laying aside our own self (own life), so that God's Self (His Life) can come forth (Psalm 95:6; Matthew 10:39; 26:39; John 4:23-24)

       b. *Serving* (*latreia*) God means: presenting our bodies "as living sacrifices," so God's works can be shown forth (Romans 12:1; 6:13) and He can be glorified, not ourselves.

    2. Worshipping and serving God means *following God* (Matthew 16:24c), which means to bind ourselves with Him so that we become one: one heart, one will, and one life (Jeremiah 32:38-39; Deuteronomy 11:22; Ephesians 5:1-2; John 14:23; 17:24-26)

       a. So that "where I [Jesus] am, there shall also My servant be." (John 12:26; 17:24; 1 John 4:17)

       b. Jesus was one with the Father (John 14:9)

    3. Following God means not only suffering and being rejected as He was, but also being crucified and raised as He was (Luke 5:11b, 28; 9:22; 14:26-27; Matthew 19:27; Galatians 2:20; 5:24; Colossians 2:12; 3:3; Mark 8:31; 1 Corinthians 4:9-16; 2 Corinthians 4:11; 1 Peter 4:1-2; 5:9-10)

       a. This is the "dying of Jesus" (2 Corinthians 4:10a)

       b. So that the "life of Jesus" might be made manifest (2 Corinthians 4:10b)

    4. Worshipping and serving God is the union and the oneness that God desires for every one of us (that full marriage relationship); "...*for me to live is Christ*." (Philippians 1:21; Deuteronomy 30:20; Hosea 2:19-20; Galatians 2:20; Colossians 3:4; 2 Corinthians 11:2)

       a. Loving God means losing self (John 12:24-25; 14:21a, 23)

       b. Selling what we have (self life) and buying God's Life (Luke 14:26; Matthew 19:16-22)

    5. Jesus is our example. He loved God so much that He was willing to be crucified in obedience to him (1 Peter 2:21). Do you love God that much? Are you willing to die so that His Life (His Love) can be poured forth through you to others? (John 12:24; 21:15-17; 13:38a; 1 John 4:8; Matthew 10:37-39; Luke 14:26-27; Acts 21:13)

"God is love; and he that dwelleth in love dwelleth in God, and God in him." (1 John 4:16) "Strait is the gate, and narrow is the way, which leadeth unto life, and *few there be that find it*." (Matthew 7:14 emphasis added) **Will you be one who does?**

Chapter 9: Satan's Three Temptations

Satan tries everything he can think of to keep us from loving (*agapao*) God: from giving ourselves totally over to God; from relinquishing ourselves to Him; from putting Him first in our lives; and from becoming one with Him.

We have seen in the last chapter that to love God means: to obey Him, to trust Him, and to worship and serve Him only. Satan will go to any length to keep us from doing this. He doesn't want us to *obey God's Word*, but to submit and give in to our own feelings, thoughts, and desires. He doesn't want us to *trust God to perform His Word in our lives*, but to trust in our own ability and power to perform. And, lastly, Satan doesn't want us to *worship and serve God only*; he wants us to be in complete bondage to his own tricks and schemes.

In Matthew 4:3-11, God gives us a perfect example of what it means to love God. Here we have a specific example of Satan's tempting Jesus *not* to totally give Himself over to God. I believe we can learn a great deal from Jesus' answers to Satan. I think we can pattern our own faith answers after Christ's example and put to silence our adversary when he tempts us to go our own way over God's.

Obey God's Word (His Will)

In the first temptation (Matthew 4:1-4), Satan tries to tempt Jesus not to obey God but to follow His "own" personal desires and will. "Come on, you are hungry, command these stones be made bread" (i.e., "Do what you desire").

Jesus, however (because He loved God), rebuked Satan and said, "Man shall not live by bread alone, but by every word that proceedeth out of the mouth of God." In other words, there is no other way a man can live except by choosing to continually obey God's voice—God's Will—and not his own human desires.

This also should be our continual response to Satan's temptations.

When Satan comes along and says (like he did to the lady with the alcoholic husband in Chapter 8),[1] "Come on, give it up! Your husband will never get better. He's a habitual drunkard. He's hurt you so much. He doesn't deserve to be loved. You don't need this. Leave him." We should say to this temptation (like Jesus did), "No, I am going to choose to deny my self (what I want, what I feel, and what I desire) and choose to obey God. I am going to continue to love my husband with God's Love because that is what God has told me to do."

Trust God's Power to Perform His Will

In the second temptation (Matthew 4:5-8), Satan tries to tempt Jesus not to trust God, but instead, to trust in His own power and ability to make things happen. Satan taunts Jesus, "Cast yourself down, God's angels will catch you." (i.e., "put God's Word to the test.")

Because He loved God, however, Jesus replied, "Thou shalt not tempt [or put to the test] the Lord thy God." In other words, man should not tempt or test God by trying to perform in his own power and his own way, what he thinks God's Will is. Man should trust in God's ability and God's timing for His perfect Will to be done.

This kind of trust should be our continual response to Satan's temptations. When Satan comes along and says (like he did with me after I almost drowned during my scuba test in Chapter 8),[2] "You almost killed yourself twice in that water. There's no way you should go on that dive tomorrow! You have a right to be afraid. You don't have to go!" We should say to this temptation (like Jesus did), "No, I am going to choose to trust God to work His Will out in my life in the way He knows is best. I am going to give my fear to God and give Him my body to perform His Will through."

Follow God

In the last temptation (Matthew 4:8-10), Satan tries to tempt Jesus not to worship and serve God only. "All these things, the kingdoms of the world and the glory of them, will I give thee if you will put me (Satan) first in your life."

Because He loved God, Jesus responded, "Thou shalt worship the Lord, thy God, and Him only shalt thou serve." In other words, Jesus is saying here that man should not follow or bind himself with anyone or anything else, but God Himself. We have only one Master, one Lord, and one God in our lives. Man is to be consumed only with Him and put Him first in everything.

This should be our continual response to Satan's temptations. When Satan comes along and whispers (as he did with Sue in Chapter 8),[3] "How dare they invite Jim with his girlfriend; there's no way in the world you should go to that party now!" We should say to him (as Jesus did), "No, I worship and serve God only. I am going to follow and bind myself only to Him, even if I don't understand how He is going to work it out. I'm going to put Him first in my life by giving Him my hurts and my anger, and then trusting Him to perform His Life through me."

Personal Example: Satan's Schemes

Several years ago, Satan prompted—and God allowed—a situation to happen in my life that included all three of these temptations. At this particular time, we lived right on the edge of the water in Newport Beach, California. The sea wall holding back the ocean was only ten feet from the front of our house. The wall itself was at least 30 years old and in desperate need of repair.

The night before I was to give a very important lecture on what it means "to love God," a violent storm hit. All night long, huge waves pounded against the sea wall, cracking and crashing so that the very foundation of our house shook. I tried to stay awake as long as I could, thinking the rain, the wind, and the huge waves would finally pass and I would be able to go to sleep. But the waves just continued. They battered that old sea wall for hours. Every time a wave would hit, our whole house rumbled. Finally, I was so tired I went to bed. But every time another wave would hit, fear and panic would consume me.

Will You Obey Me?

I kept remembering the class I was to teach the next day. I decided I'd better put into practice the very thing I would be teaching. So all night long, I kept choosing to obey God by giving Him my fear and terror, rather than giving in and being consumed by them. God finally aligned my feelings with my choices, and I was able to sleep.

The next morning, as I was getting ready to leave the house, a hurricane hit. The radio and T.V. warned everyone to stay home and board up their houses. My own thoughts and emotions were screaming the very same thing, "Stay home and protect the house yourself."

Will You Trust Me?

I knew, however, that the lesson I was to teach that particular morning was the most important of all. And I knew God wanted me there. I had prayed weeks before if I was to teach the class, and God had confirmed that I was. Once again, I had to choose to obey God, give Him my panic, and trust Him to take care of the house while I was gone.

Finally, I became totally aware of who was tempting me not to love God, when on my way to the class—traveling 50 miles per hour down the Coast Highway—my entire gearshift came apart in my hands. It literally tore itself away from the floorboard!

Will You Become One With Me?

This was such a blatant attack from the enemy, I couldn't miss it. I quickly chose to abandon myself to God and His protection. At this point, I became bent on teaching that class—if it was the last thing I ever did. I chose to follow God and do whatever He wanted me to do, no matter what.

Luckily the brakes and the steering wheel still worked, so I was able to turn off the engine, glide over to the side of the road and stop.

When we totally abandon ourselves to God and His care, we set ourselves up for real miracles. And that's just what happened. Would you believe an "unoccupied" taxi that had "coincidently" been following me immediately pulled over and stopped behind me. Listen, in Los Angeles this never happens.

The driver, it turned out, was a believer and loved God. He picked me up and we fellowshipped in the Lord all the way to the class meeting. To this day, I really believe that driver was an "angel in disguise," sent by the Lord.

Satan Wants Our Faith

Satan is after our faith itself because our faith is built upon the faithfulness of God. If Satan can cause doubt and unbelief in the faithfulness of God, he has won, because then we won't choose to obey, trust, or follow God (love Him) in every aspect of our lives.[4] It takes faith to love God, to totally lay our wills and our lives down before Him. And Satan will do everything in his power to keep us from making those choices.

1 John 5:4 promises, "For whatsoever is born of God overcometh the world; and this is the victory that overcometh the world, even our faith."

Our faith choice to love (obey, trust, worship, and serve God only) is the victory that is going to allow all things to be "born of God" and, therefore, "overcome the world."

Remember *to love God is to lose self.* Revelation 12:11 says we have victory over the enemy by "the blood of the Lamb, and by the word of their testimony; and [because] they loved not their lives unto death." The one thing so many Christians are *not* doing today is laying down their lives unto death (i.e., loving God); therefore, many of them are not having the victory that they so very much desire.

Jesus didn't succumb to Satan's three temptations. Jesus loved God and chose continually to obey, trust, and follow Him in everything.

Do you love God? Tell Jesus your answer.

Matthew 16:24: "If any man will come after me, let him deny himself, and take up his cross, and follow me."

Endnotes:

1. See Chapter 8, "Trust God to Align Our Feelings."

2. See Chapter 8, "Example: I Almost Drowned."

3. See Chapter 8, "Example: There Was Not a 'Me' There."

4. See Chapter 11, "Often the Unexpected."

Scriptural References:

Chapter 9

Satan Does Not Want Us to Love God (Matthew 4:1-11)
- A. Satan does not want us to *obey God's Word* (His Will), but to obey our own personal desires (Matthew 4:1-4)
  1. Our answer to Satan should be, "No, I am going to choose to *deny myself* (how I feel, what I think, and what I want) and choose to obey God (Matthew 16:24a; Luke 9:23)
  2. "Man shall not live by bread alone, but by every word that proceedeth out of the mouth of God." (Matthew 4:4; Deuteronomy 8:3)
- B. Satan does not want us to *trust God to perform* His Will in our lives, but to rely upon our own power and ability to do what we want (Matthew 4:5-8)
  1. Our answer to Satan should be, "No, I am going to choose to trust God *(pick up my cross)* to work His Will out in my life the way He knows is best." (Matthew 16:24b; Philippians 2:13)
  2. "Thou shalt not tempt the Lord thy God." (Matthew 4:7; Deuteronomy 8:17-18)
- C. Satan does not want us to *worship and serve* (follow) God only, but to bind ourselves and give ourselves over to anything else (Matthew 4:8-10)
  1. Our answer to Satan should be, "No, I am going to *follow* and bind myself to God only." (Matthew 16:24c; Deuteronomy 11:22)
  2. "Thou shalt worship the Lord, thy God, and Him only shalt thou serve." (Matthew 4:10; Deuteronomy 11:16)
- D. Satan is after our faith itself, because our faith is built on the faithfulness of God. We live by "His faith." (Galatians 2:16.20; Ephesians 3:12) This is the "victory that overcomes" (1 John 5:4)

God Allows These Temptations Because:
- A. They force us to choose God's way or our own (Deuteronomy 30:19)
- B. God tests us to see what is in our hearts. He wants to see if we will live by His Word or not (Deuteronomy 8:2)
- C. God tests us to see if we really love Him or not (Deuteronomy 13:3-4)

"Blessed is the man that endureth temptation: for when he is tried, he shall receive the crown of life, which the Lord hath promised to them that love [*agapao*] Him." (James 1:12)

Section Five

Chapter 10: "Ye Are the Temple of God"

We saw in Chapter 8 that the greatest and most important commandment in the whole Bible is Matthew 22:37, "Thou shalt love [*agapao*] the Lord, thy God, with all thy *heart*, and with all thy *soul*, and with all thy *mind*." (emphasis added) Jesus goes on to declare in Luke 10:28 that if we love God in this way we shall "live" and have that abundant Life He promises.

We also studied that to love (*agapao*) God means to totally give ourselves over to Him. It means not only to *obey* Him and *trust* Him, but also to *follow* Him.[1] God wants us to follow Him so closely that we become "one" with Him.

In this chapter, we want to explore exactly what it means to love God with all our heart, with all our mind, and with all our soul. In other words, we want to learn *how* to become "one" with Him in each of these areas.

[Note: The Greek word for "mind" in the First Commandment is ***dianoia***. Properly translated, *dianoia* means "willpower" (or volition) and not mind at all. The proper Greek word for mind is ***nous***. *Nous* refers to our "whole process of thinking," something totally different than our will or our willpower.[2] From now on, whenever I refer to the First Commandment, I will always call *dianoia* "will or willpower" (rather than mind) in order to avoid further confusion.][3]

I believe, then, this commandment should read: Love God with all our heart, with all our soul, and with all our willpower (*dianoia*).

As we proceed in this chapter, be sure to follow the charts carefully. If you can perceive what I am saying and the Lord opens your understanding, you will be able to apply these principles to your life in a much more meaningful way.

Research

Fifteen years ago when I began exploring the concepts of spirit, heart, will, and soul, I was told, "Don't bother to study and research these things because all these words really mean the very same thing." That response bothered me because I believe God is very precise in His instructions to us. Chuck and I both believe every word, every sentence, and even every period in the Bible means something very explicit. God is not a God of confusion.

[The rabbis in Israel have a quaint viewpoint. They say that they really won't understand the Scriptures until the Messiah comes. But when He comes, He will not only interpret the passages, He will interpret each word, He'll interpret the letters, He will even interpret the spaces between the letters! When we first heard that, we dismissed it simply as a colorful exaggeration—until we re-read Matthew 5:17 and

18: "Think not that I am come to destroy the Law, or the Prophets: I am not come to destroy, but to fulfill. For verily I say unto you, till heaven and earth pass, one jot or one tittle shall in no wise pass from the Law, till all be fulfilled." Now a "jot" or a "tittle" is a Hebrew equivalent to our "crossing a 't'" or "dotting an 'i'." It seems the rabbinical view may be closer to the truth than we first imagined!]

So, if God instructs, "Love Me with all your heart," He means something very specific; and if He says, "Love Me with all your willpower," He means something totally different; and if He says, "Love Me with all your soul," He again means something special and unique. Otherwise, I believe God would have simply said, "Love Me totally," or "wholly" or "completely," since there are places in the Bible where He does just that.

I'm convinced that God is a God of extreme detail and precision. There is something very specific and distinct meant by each of these terms *heart, willpower,* and *soul.* Therefore, we need to understand exactly what these concepts mean so we can love God and become one with Him in each of these areas.

We Are the Temple of God

In order to explore these terms in more detail, we are going to compare the floorplan of the Temple of God to the "interior" architecture of man—spirit, heart, soul, and body. If you recall, in Hosea 12:10 God tells us that He often uses similitudes, analogies, or "word pictures" in order to help us understand His Word better. (Interesting, the root meaning of the word *similitude* is "because we are dumb.")

One of these analogies or word pictures is 1 Corinthians 3:16 which declares, "Know ye not that ye are the temple of God, and that the Spirit of God dwelleth in you?"

Again, Paul makes clear in 2 Corinthians 6:16, "For ye are the temple of the living God; as God hath said, I will dwell in them, and walk in them; and I will be their God, and they shall be My People."[4]

Paul is making an analogy, a comparison or a similitude here in these two Scriptures by saying, "Our body [itself] is a temple" and that temple is now the dwelling place of the Holy Spirit. Jesus even refers to His own Body as a temple in Mark 14:58.

[Note: Also, be sure to see Chuck's "An Engineer's View" in Section Seven at the end of this book. He has a very provocative way of introducing this material.]

The Temple of Solomon

In the Old Testament, the Shekinah Glory (which was the visible sign of God's presence) used to dwell in the physical Temple of Solomon in Jerusalem. Now, however, Scripture tells us that God's presence or His Spirit dwells in "temples made without hands,"[5] namely, us!

Paul is saying in the above Scriptures that there is a correlation between Solomon's Temple in Jerusalem, which used to be the dwelling place of God's Spirit, and our bodies that are now the dwelling place of God. If so, he is saying that Solomon's Temple in Jerusalem, in some mystical way, is a model, a blueprint, or a type of a "believer indwelt by the Holy Spirit."

The reason I refer to Solomon's Temple is because it was special. In contrast to Herod's, Nehemiah's and Ezekiel's temple, Solomon's was the only Temple where all the detailed plans—not only of the construction of the Temple, but also of all the furniture of the Temple—were given to David by the Spirit of God (see 1 Chronicles 28:11-12,19). No other Temple could boast of this. It was also the only Temple in which God's Spirit dwelt permanently[6] until the Temple was actually destroyed. Lastly, Solomon's Temple was special because it was the only Temple in which the Ark of the Covenant rested. None of the other Temples contained the Ark.[7]

Thus, in order for us to understand ourselves better, we are going to compare our bodies (as the Temple of God now) to the actual layout and structure of Solomon's Temple way back in the Old Testament. And, by doing so, we will gain a better understanding of exactly what our spirit is, what our heart is, what our willpower is, what our soul is, and what our body is.

The Temple as a model of man is not a new idea. Charles Scofield (of Scofield Bible fame) wrote a book back in 1915 called *New Life in Christ* in which the same ideas are expressed.

CHART 1: The Elevation View

F   Chart 1

Chart 1 is the front or elevation view of Solomon's Temple. Let's begin with the main sanctuary. You can see how it rested on a raised platform. The Temple consisted of the Holy of Holies (A) in the rear; the Holy Place in the middle (B); and the Porch (C), with its two pillars in the front (D), facing the Inner and Outer Courts (F).

Note the side wings on either side of the main sanctuary (E). These were secret, hidden, wooden chambers that were supposed to be used for storing the priests' worship items used in the Holy Place and also for storing the historical records of Israel. (We will see in a moment, however, what was really stored there.)

The Temple structure faced east, overlooking the Inner and Outer Courts, which were on even lower levels than the main sanctuary.

CHART 2: The Floor Plan View (next page)

Looking down upon the actual floor plan of the Temple, we can see that the main sanctuary was again made up of the Holy of Holies (A) in the rear, the Holy Place (B) in the middle, and the Porch (C) in the front.

[Note: The Porch not only included the golden vestibule between the Holy Place and the Inner Court (C), but it also included the two bronze pillars on either side of the Porch (D).]

The sanctuary itself rested on a raised platform (G). Surrounding the sanctuary were the secret hidden chambers (E), where the priests were supposed to store the worship items for the Holy Place and some of Israel's treasures and trophies to remind them of all that God had done for them. However, it was here that the priests actually stored their own personal idolatrous worship items, thinking that since they were out of sight, no one would see; no one would know. (Be sure to read Ezekiel 8:6-12.)[8]

Stepping down seven steps from the Porch, one would find the Inner Court (H), and on an even lower level, the Outer Court (I).

The Temple of God

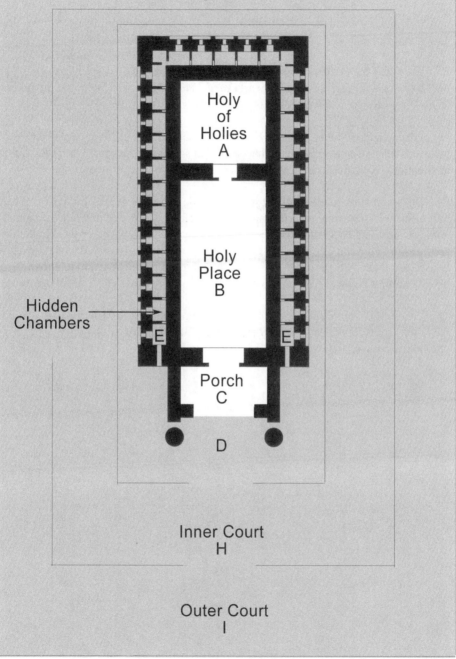

Chart 2

"Blueprint" of a Believer

CHART 3: The Spiritual View (next page)

Let's study the Temple (**Chart 3**) now as a model or a blueprint of the New Testament Believer (i.e., one who has the Holy Spirit dwelling within).

I believe the Holy of Holies is analogous to a believer's new spirit (***pneuma***) (1); the Holy Place represents his new heart (***kardia***) (2); the Porch (including the pillars) is analogous to his new willpower or volition (***dianoia***) (3).

The secret, hidden, wooden chambers around the main sanctuary represent a believer's subconscious (***cheder***)—that part of our soul where we store our hurts, doubts, and fears thinking because they are hidden, *no one will see, no one will know* (6).

It's interesting to observe that just as God designed the secret, hidden chambers to hold Israel's historical records and treasures, He purposed for our subconscious to hold pleasant and special memories of all of God's actions in our lives. He wanted continually to remind us of His presence. But just as the priests abused God's "treasure house" for their own personal idolatrous worship items, so our "hidden chambers" have become a Rogue's Gallery—a black gallery of our bitter and painful memories.

The Inner Court represents the conscious part of a man's soul (***psyche***) (4); and the Outer Court represents his body (***soma***) (5). In other words, the *flesh* is all of the grey area on the charts.

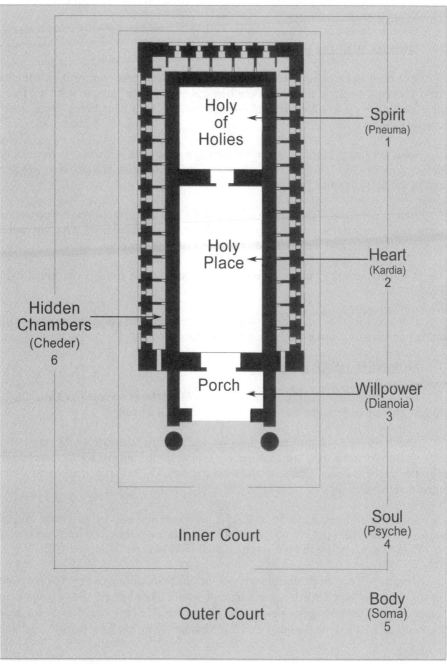

Chart 3

See **CHART 4** (next page)

We need to understand, first of all, what the terms *spirit, heart, willpower, soul,* and *body* really mean. So, in **Chart 4** we'll give the "overall picture" as to what each of these areas are. Then in succeeding chapters, we'll explore in detail what it means to love God with each of these.

(1) **OUR NEW SPIRIT** (*pneuma*)

As a born-again believer (one who has asked Jesus to take control of his life), the Spirit who now dwells at the core of our being is not our "old" human spirit anymore, but a totally *new spirit* given to us at our new birth. That's what being "born again" actually means.[9]

John 3:3 states, "Except a man be born again, he cannot see [know intimately] the kingdom of God." And, "That which is born of the flesh is flesh; that which is born of the Spirit is spirit." (John 3:6)

Being "born again" means receiving a totally *new life source* or *power source*. It is now God Himself (the Father, Son, and Holy Spirit) dwelling in us. God has united our spirit with His, and we have become one spirit with Him.

1 Corinthians 6:17 notes, "He that is joined unto the Lord is one spirit [with Him]."

God's Spirit is the new energy (or power) source that is going to create new life within our hearts. (It's like the "generator" of a building.)

(2) **OUR NEW HEART** (*kardia*)

Our heart is the actual place where God's Life (His Love and His Thoughts) is created, started, or brought into "new" existence by God's Spirit.

The Hebrew word for create is ***bara*** which means to create something out of nothing, to make alive, or to bring into new existence something that wasn't there before. In Psalm 51:10 it says, "Create in me a clean heart, O God" (i.e., make something brand new, something that wasn't there before).

God also says in Ezekiel 36:26-27, "A new heart also will I give [create in] you, and a new spirit will I put within you; and I will take away the stony heart [old heart] out of your flesh, and I will give you a heart of flesh [a new, living heart]."[10]

This new "heart of flesh," then, is not the old heart simply changed or renewed, but it's a totally "new" heart, something that wasn't there before. So, when we are born again, we not only get a new spirit (1), but we also receive a brand-new heart (2). In other words, God replaces our "old" human heart life (our human, "natural"

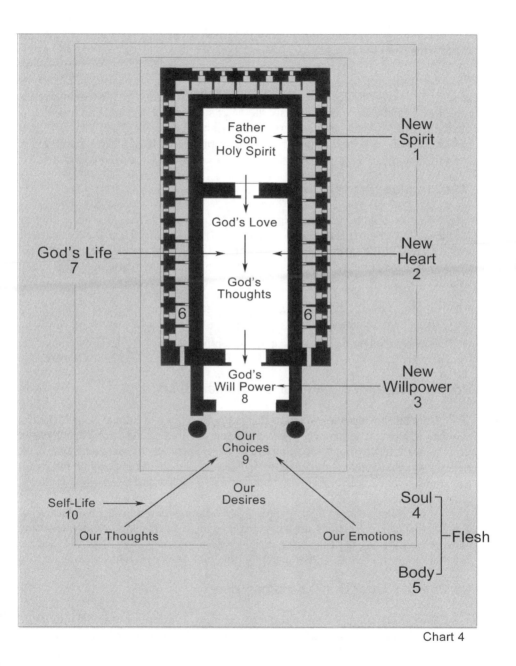

Chart 4

love and our human, "natural" thoughts) with His brand-new heart life (7): God's supernatural Love (*Agape*), His supernatural Thoughts (*Logos*),[11] and His supernatural Power (*Dunamis*).

This "new" heart that God gives us is "*Christ in [us]*, the hope of glory"; it's the very "nature" of God Himself. (Colossians 1:27, emphasis added)

We speak of our heart as being the center core or the foundation of our whole person. This is why it's such a critical area for us to understand. In many commentaries and books about the makeup of man, the heart seems to be a confusing area that is often overlooked. And yet, there are more Scriptures about our heart than any other part of our body. Because of the number of Scriptures about our heart, I believe God has validated this as a desperately important area, and one we must not overlook.

"Old" Human Heart Is Corrupt

Scripture tells us that our old, human heart *before* being born again (before receiving God's Spirit) is evil and corrupt from birth. This old heart will always be self-centered, proud, and going its own way. It will never, on its own, seek God. Genesis 8:21 tells us why: "For the imagination [purposes] of man's [old] heart is evil from his youth."

Even in the New Testament, wherever the evilness of the heart is mentioned, it is always the old, human heart they are speaking of. It is always *before* the Spirit of God comes to dwell within the person permanently.[12] Mark 7:21 declares, "out of the [old, human] heart of men, proceed evil thoughts, adulteries, fornications, murders."

No One Can Understand Our Old Human Heart

Jeremiah 17:9 goes on to tell us that not only is our old, human heart "deceitful above all things, and desperately [incurably] wicked,"[13] but no one can even understand it! This means that without God's Spirit interceding (without our being born again), we will not be able to understand our hearts. We won't be able to understand the things we naturally think, feel, and choose to do.

This explains why so many people, after spending thousands upon thousands of dollars in psychiatric sessions, are still not finding the answers they so desperately want and often getting worse. The reason is right here in Jeremiah 17:9, "The [old] heart is deceitful above all things, and desperately (incurably) wicked: who can know it?"

No One Can Cure Our Old Human Heart

Even if we could understand the corruptness of our old hearts, this Scripture goes on to tell us the worst part of all—no one knows how to cure it.

It's incurable! In other words, without God's intervention in our hearts, there's no hope for any change because there's no cure—there's no remedy![14]

We know of one young girl's family who has spent thousands upon thousands of dollars trying to cure her of drug abuse. Heather has been in psychiatric hospitals, care units, drug rehab hospitals, etc. Nothing has helped. Some of these hospitals have cost her family over $5000 a week. Her family was so desperate, they took her to every psychiatrist, every therapist, and every counselor they could find. Nothing, however, ever touched or changed this girl's life—until she met Jesus.

When the Spirit of God came inside Heather's heart, she not only received a new power source (a new Spirit), but she also received "new life" itself (a new heart). She now has God's "supernatural" Power within her, giving her the capability for real and lasting change. She no longer has to rely upon natural human ability for change which, as we all know, will always let us down.

God is telling us here in these Scriptures that our nature, before His Spirit intervenes, is basically corrupt and evil. We are not basically good, as so many want to think and believe. This is why we are in such desperate need to be born again, not only to receive a new Spirit, but also to receive a new heart. Then, God's new Life can begin to come forth through us.

2 Corinthians 5:17 verifies this. "If any man be in Christ, he is a new creature: old things are passed away; behold, all things are become new." We now have a brand-new energy source (new spirit) and a brand-new heart (filled with God's supernatural Love and Wisdom).

Example: Prisoner in Sydney

Let me share a wonderful story about the new nature God gives us when we are born again.

Several years ago, as I was ministering in Australia, a woman came up and told me a true story about some friends of hers. The husband had always been very jealous of his wife. One time, he lost control of himself, exploded over some incident, and literally tried to kill his wife. He was put in jail, but he escaped, and while his wife was recuperating in the hospital, he once again tried to kill her. In a fit of rage, he tried to rip her large wedding ring off her finger and in the process, bent the ring completely out of shape.

Again he was caught, only this time, he was placed in a maximum security prison. During the years he was there, someone shared Christ with him. He accepted God into his heart, became born again, and received God's new life.

At that particular time, someone sent him our *Agape* tapes. (Can you imagine, from a Newport Beach, California housewife to a prisoner in Sydney, Australia? Certainly God's Ways are not our ways!) Through the tapes, God revealed to this man that he *was* a new creation in Christ, and that he now had God's supernatural Love within him to give out. The man's life was transformed, and he became devoted to the Word and to showing forth Christ's life.

Some months later, he was released from jail and decided to look up his ex-wife. After a period of time, in which I'm sure she was very leery of him, he led her to Christ. They were eventually remarried, and she now wears that broken, bent-out-of-shape wedding ring around her neck as a symbol of the miracle that God performed in their lives.

"If any man be in Christ, he is a new creature: old things are passed away; behold, ALL things have become new [brand-new Love, brand-new Thoughts, and brand-new Power]."

God's Life in Our Hearts

Our old heart, then, which Scripture tells us is evil (incurable and unknowable) from birth, is totally replaced by a brand-new heart when we are born again by God's Spirit. So the Life that is now in our hearts is totally pure, totally incorruptible, and completely holy because it is now God's Life and not our own.[15] This again is "Christ in [us], the hope of glory." (Colossians 1:27) This is also what "being circumcised of heart" means (Colossians 2:11)[16] and what the "new wineskins" refer to in Luke 5:37-38.[17]

When I first taught the *Way of Agape* years ago, I thought our hearts were still basically evil (even after we became born again) and that our hearts were transformed only by our making the right choices moment by moment. I was wrong! It's not our hearts that need to be transformed anymore, that was done at our new birth. It's our lives, our souls, that are in such desperate need of transformation. The only life that now exists in our hearts if we are born again is God's incorruptible Life (His Love and His Thoughts). We just need to learn *how* to let it out.

A girl at one of my recent seminars told me, "This is the most liberating message I have heard in years." She had heard the first *Agape* Series back in 1982 and confessed that the "divided heart" message I had spoken of then had always been a stumbling block for her. She said that she felt defeated before she even started, knowing that no matter how hard she tried, her heart would always be evil. This new insight—that when we are born again we receive a brand-new heart (God's heart)—was just what she had been waiting for. "God's Life is already in me," she gleefully said, "I just need to learn how to let it out!"

1 Peter 3:4 states, "But let it be the hidden man of the heart [God's Life in us] in that which is not corruptible."

The new heart, the "hidden man of the heart," is now the center core and true essence of our being. Upon this foundation everything else is going to be built, and all continuing activity will depend. So this message will not work unless we have a new spirit and a new heart—Christ in us, our hope of glory. Then we will have the power and capability for real and lasting change.

(3)   **OUR NEW WILLPOWER** (*dianoia*) (Review **Chart 4**, page 149)

The most critical area of all, is the new willpower that we receive as a result of being born again. The Greek word *dianoia* means our will and the power to perform it. Our willpower is the "key" to our whole Christian walk[18] because what we choose, moment by moment, determines whose life will be lived in our souls: God's or our own.

Our willpower is what enables us to put God's Life from our hearts out into our lives (souls). You can see the strategic importance of our willpower by looking at **Chart 4**, page 149. Our willpower is the passageway, the doorway or the gateway for God's Life in our hearts to flow out into our lives. This passageway or doorway can be "opened" so God's Life can flow freely, or it can be "closed" and God's Life quenched and blocked.

Interestingly, *dia* means channel and *noya* means of the mind. Our willpower is exactly that. It's the channel or conduit for God's Spirit to flow from our hearts out into our lives.

Notice on the Chart, our new willpower has two distinct parts. First, we have *God's supernatural Will and Power*, given to us as a part of our new birth (8).[19] This is where God counsels us as to what His Will (***thelo***) is, and where He gives us the supernatural Power (***dunamis***) to perform that Will in our lives.[20] What an incredible gift of the Holy Spirit this is!

The second part of our willpower, however, is something I wish God had left out of my own makeup. This is *our own free choice* (***exousia***) (9)—the freedom to choose to follow what God has shown me and trust in His Power to perform it in my life (i.e., make a faith choice); or, the freedom to choose to do what I think, feel, and desire, and then trust in my own ability and power to perform that choice in my life.

Validated by the Temple Model (Review Chart 3, page 147)

The Temple model illustrates our comparison. Just as there are two parts to our supernatural willpower, there are also two parts to the porch of Solomon's Temple.

The *Golden Vestibule* (C) represents God's supernatural Will and Power, given to us at our new birth. And the *Bronze Pillars* (D) represent the second part of our willpower—our free choice.

The Bronze Pillars were named Jachin and Boaz. Most commentaries will tell you that these were free-standing pillars, not structural. Why were they there? What function did they serve? And why on earth did these pillars have names?

Jachin means "in His Counsel" and *Boaz* means "by His Strength." I believe the pillars represent choices made *in His Counsel* because He will show us what His Will is, and *by His Strength* because He will give us His power to perform these choices in our lives.

God's Will or Our Own

We constantly have two choices facing us. We can make a *"faith choice"* and follow what God desires us to do, by saying "not my will, but thine." (Matthew 26:39) Or we can make an *"emotional choice,"* where we choose to follow what *we* think, what *we* desire, and what *we* want over God's Will. Here's a perfect example:

Example: It's Worth a Million Dollars

One summer about 10 or 15 years ago, I was teaching the *Way of Agape* and a friend of mine, Tammy, volunteered to watch Michelle for me. One day Tammy decided to take the kids to the beach. My Michelle is very fair, and Tammy forgot to bring sunscreen. When I picked up Michelle that night, she was "burnt to a crisp."

The following afternoon she seemed better, so I decided to take her grocery shopping with me. She acted fine until my cart was completely filled with food. She then began to lean over the front of the grocery cart, moaning and groaning about her sunburn. I needed the groceries desperately, so I decided to gamble and see if I could check out quickly. As you know, whenever you are in a hurry it always ends up taking forever.

When we got up to the check-out stand and there were at least five people in every line. Michelle was still leaning over the front of the cart, crying softly. People began to stare. I'm sure some of them thought I was beating her because you couldn't see the sunburn. Terribly flustered and embarrassed, I felt like leaving the groceries and running out of the store, but I really needed the milk and butter that were at the bottom of the cart.

Finally getting through the line and out of the store, we flew home. As I was driving, I was thinking to myself, "I can't wait to get home, put Michelle to bed, wash my filthy hair, get comfortable, put my feet up, and read all evening." I was totally bushed!

When we pulled up to our street corner, however, we found it had been dug up for repairs and a detour sign posted. That detour was two miles out of my way! Michelle was still whining in the back seat of the car. By the time I got home, I was absolutely frazzled.

Finally, we pulled into our driveway. As I was carrying the first grocery bags down the steps, with Michelle on my arm, I could hear the phone ringing. I dropped the bags, fumbled for my keys, and finally reached the phone on the ninth ring. It was

Chuck's secretary and she seemed frantic. "Nancy, where have you been? We almost sent the police after you!"

With that, Chuck got on the phone and said, "Honey, don't say a word, just quickly get dressed in your fanciest outfit. We are being driven by a chauffeur up to Scandia, a fancy restaurant in Los Angeles, and it could be worth a million dollars to the company. But you need to be here by 5 p.m. sharp!" With that, he hung up! I looked at the clock. It was now twenty minutes to five!

CHOICE POINT: Faith choice or an emotional choice? Which way am I going to choose? Am I going to scream, stamp my feet, call him back and say, "I'm sorry, but there's just no way I can do it: I'm a mess, Michelle's a mess, groceries are still in the car, dinner's not made, etc.?" Or, am I going to make a "faith choice" and choose what I know to be God's Will and trust Him to get me ready and there on time? Now, I had been praying that God would make me a more supportive wife for Chuck in his business. Now, that's an easy commitment to make in the prayer closet. It is quite another thing, however, to trust God to do it in my life. God was giving me a perfect opportunity to see what I would choose.

Lisa had come home by now and had heard the commotion. I took Michelle and Lisa by the hands and said, "We really need to pray for Mommy." In that prayer, I told God it was impossible to do what Chuck had just asked. Nevertheless, I told God I was willing to do whatever He wanted me to.

With that, little Michelle said, "Mommy, don't worry about me, I'll just go lie down and rest." Michelle has never—before or since—lain down of her own free will! Lisa then chimed in, "Mom, don't worry about the food. I'll bring in the groceries and fix dinner for the two of us." Lisa had never, up until that time, offered to make dinner for the two of them. This was a first! It was a miracle!

I was left free to concentrate on me. I flew upstairs, took a one-minute shower, did what I could with my wild hair, got dressed, and would you believe I made it to Chuck's office by five past five, rush-hour traffic and all.

We didn't get the contract, but Chuck sure noticed and appreciated my support-iveness. And I again experienced God's faithfulness to perform His Life through me, in spite of how I felt.

Our Choices Are Critical

Our new, supernatural willpower is not only God's *authority* to enable us to choose His Will over our own negative thoughts, emotions, and desires (self life), but it's also His *power* to carry out and perform His Will in our lives.

"For it is God Which worketh in you both *to will* and *to do,* of His good pleasure."
(Philippians 2:13, emphasis added)

Again, our supernatural willpower is critical because what we choose, moment
by moment, determines the direction of our lives, and also whose life will be lived in
our souls—either God's or our own!

(4)   **OUR SOUL** (*psyche*) (Review **Chart 4**, page 149)

Our souls are made up of our conscious thoughts, emotions and desires. This
is our "self life" that we have so often referred to. (There is a hidden, subconscious
part of our soul—those secret chambers (6)—but we'll talk more about them in just a
moment.) Together, our soul and body are known as *"the flesh."*

For the sake of simplicity, think of our souls as the "visible" part of our lives.
It's the *outward expression or manifestation* of our lives. In other words, our souls
are what we see, feel, and hear coming forth from one another.

What's confusing is that "life" exists both in our hearts and in our souls. What
is the difference? The difference is that life is originally created, started, and brought
into new existence (*bara*) in our hearts,[21] and then that life is outwardly expressed,
manifested, or shown forth in our souls. In other words, life is created in our hearts,
but we don't consciously experience that life until it reaches our souls.

Therefore, you could say that "heart life" is invisible life. You can't see it—only
God can, whereas, "soul life" is mainly visible life (you can sense it, feel it, see it and
hear it coming from each other). Does that help clarify the difference a little?

An Analogy

The best analogy I can think of to show the difference between heart life and
soul life is with plants in a garden. Our *heart life* is like the root life of those plants.
We can't see it—it's underground—but nevertheless, it's essential to the health and
growth of the plants above.

Our *soul life* is like the beautiful flowers, or the weeds, that grow above the
ground. The flowers, or weeds, are the direct result of the health of the root life. We
can visibly see the flowers; we can smell them, feel them, touch them, and enjoy them.
Jeremiah 31:12 even says, "[Our] soul shall be as a watered garden."

I think of the soul as a neutral area that is either going to be filled with God's
Life from our hearts, flowers—if we have chosen to be open and cleansed vessels, or
self life, our own thoughts, emotions, and desires that are contrary to God's, weeds—if
we have quenched God's Life by making wrong choices.

Let's see exactly how this works.

(Turn to the next page and review Chart 5.)

Ideally, you can see in **Chart 5** (on the facing page), that our souls (4) *should be* the expression or the manifestation, or the showing forth, of God's Life (7) from our hearts, if we have made those faith choices. In other words, His *Agape* Love (11) in our hearts becomes our Love (12) in our souls, His Wisdom (13) in our hearts becomes our thoughts (14) in our souls, and His Will (8) becomes our will (16) in our lives.

God's Life coming forth through us is what it means to be "spirit filled" (17) or filled with "the fulness of God." This is also called "single-mindedness," or more precisely, *single souled* because only one life is being lived here—God's (7)![22] This person is an "open vessel," loving (*agapao*) God.

Notice: this temple now looks like a *flashlight*. This is what Luke 11:33 means when it says, "No man, when he hath lighted a lamp (candle), putteth it in a secret place, neither under a bushel, but *on a lampstand, that they who come in may see the light*." (emphasis added)]

So, in a believer, our soul can either show forth God's Life (7) from our hearts (if we have chosen to be open and pure channels, by making faith choices) or:

(Turn to the next page and review **Chart 6**.)

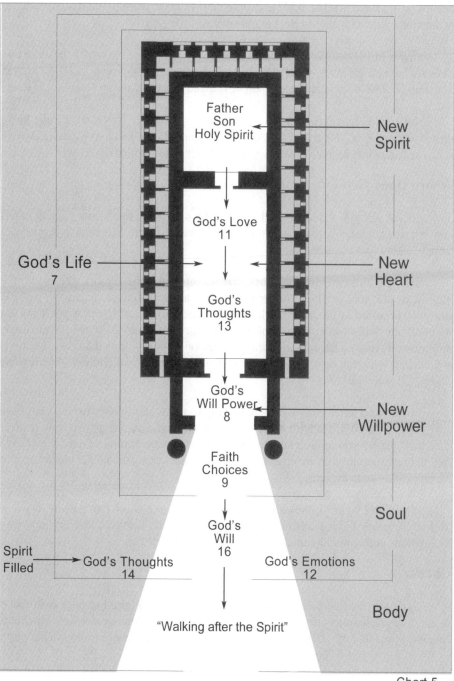

New
Spirit

God's Love
11

God's Life ——→
7

New
Heart

God's
Thoughts
13

God's
Will Power
8

New
Willpower

Faith
Choices
9

Soul

God's
Will
16

Spirit
Filled ——→ God's Thoughts
14

God's Emotions
12

Body

"Walking after the Spirit"

Father
Son
Holy Spirit

Chart 5

As you can see in **Chart 6**, God's Life (7) can become quenched or blocked (18) when we make *emotional choices* (9) to follow our own thoughts, emotions, and desires (19) instead of what God has prompted (8). Thus, the soul life that is produced is not God's Life as it should be, but our own self life (10).

This is called *double-mindedness* or more precisely, *double souled*, because two lives are being lived here—God's (7), still in our hearts, and our own "self life" (10) in our souls.[23] This person is not an open vessel and he is not loving (*agapao*) God.

Notice: the light in this temple is blocked or quenched. This is what Luke 11:33 means when it says, "No man [should], when he hath lighted a lamp (candle), *putteth it in a secret place, neither under a bushel....*" (emphasis added)]

Where Does *Self Life* Come From?

Let me ask you a question. If we have God's Life in our hearts (7) and this is now our true nature, where does this *self life* (10) come from? Where does it originate from? Where is it triggered from?

Self life comes from the hurts, the resentments, the doubts, the pride, the bitterness, etc. that we have never properly dealt with before, and have instead, stuffed and buried in those secret, hidden chambers (6). Self life is triggered when we choose to follow what those "buried" things are telling us to do over what God is prompting us to do. Those buried things work on our conscious thoughts, emotions and desires, which in turn, cause us to make wrong, emotional choices. (Look at the arrows (21) on **Chart 6**.)

I received a letter with a very interesting analogy. Someone wrote: "I envision my "self life" to compare with those deep underground rock vaults that hold nuclear waste. At the bottom of the granite rock vaults is a concentration of deadly elements (possibly plutonium) that are cracking the vaults and leaking the poisonous waste into the river and ocean systems."

Interesting letter. I think she is right, as long as we allow that poisonous waste (things from our hidden chambers) to leak out, it will continue to crack our very foundations and contaminate all we come in contact with.

Cheder

Experts tell us that everything we think, say, and do (good or bad) is stored in secret, hidden chambers deep within us for future use. Scripture calls these chambers *cheder* in the Hebrew. Often, we call them our subconscious or our innermost part.

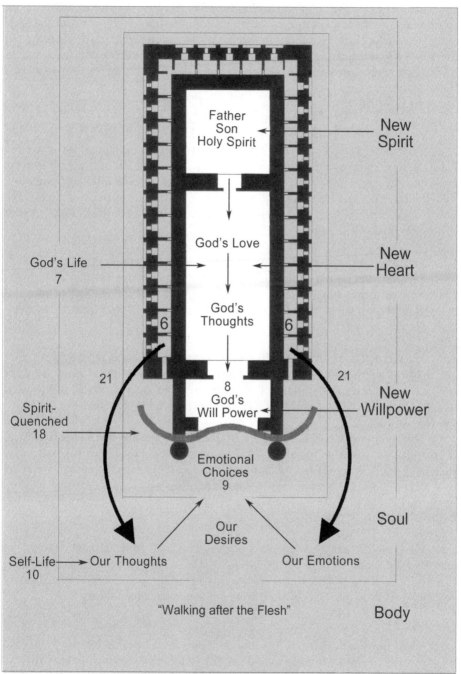

Chart 6

Self life is triggered by the negative things we have stored there; things we've never given over to God. Self life is "residual life," which means part of the original has remained even after another part has been taken away. When we became born again we received a new spirit, a new heart, and a new willpower, but our soul and body (gray area on the charts) remained the same. It was not changed; it was not renewed; nor was it regenerated. Self life is "habitual life," which means it acts according to habit, not out of learned responses.

Temple Comparison

To visibly show you how this works, go back again to **Chart 3**, page 147. Notice that in the Temple, the Holy of Holies (A) (which is our new spirit), the Holy Place (B) (which is our new heart), and the Porch (C) (which is our new willpower) are rooms that are white—which signifies that these rooms had solid gold walls and solid gold furniture. What does gold symbolize? It symbolizes purity and holiness. In believers, it symbolizes God's new imparted nature that each of us has as a result of our new birth.

Notice, however, that the Pillars (D) (our free choice), the Inner Court (H) (our soul), and the Outer Court (I) (our body) are all gray—which signifies that these rooms had bronze structures and furnishings. Bronze is symbolic of something that must still be judged. It means that sin is still present in these areas. Bronze means something that's not yet regenerated.

The secret hidden chambers (E) are also gray on the Charts, but they were actually made of wood, which symbolizes humanity. The root of the Hebrew word for wood means "something to be burned up"; interesting, because that's exactly what God would have us do with most of the "junk" we have stored in this area.

The Temple model (**Chart 6**, page 161) supports our view that, at our new birth, we are given a *new* supernatural spirit (1), a *new* supernatural heart (2), and a *new* supernatural willpower (3), but the gray area—our soul (4) (including our subconscious (6)), and our body (5)—is not yet renewed or regenerated.

Sanctification Process

This renewal is the *sanctification* process we are all going through now and the area that God is concentrating on in each of us. He is trying to teach us how to choose to set aside our own self life (our own thoughts, emotions, and desires that are usually contrary to His) so that His new Life from our hearts can come forth.

2 Corinthians 4:10-11 says, "Always bearing about in the body the dying of the Lord Jesus, that the life also of Jesus might be made manifest in our body. For we which live are always delivered unto death for Jesus' sake, that the life also of Jesus might be made manifest in our mortal flesh."

Listen to what A.J. Gordon in *Ministry of the Spirit* says about our sanctification: "Our sanctification moves from within outward. It begins with the spirit, which is the holy of holies; the Spirit of God acting first on the spirit of man in renewing grace, then upon the soul till at last it reaches the outer court of the body at the resurrection and translation. When the body is glorified, then only will sanctification be consummated, for then only will the whole man—spirit, soul and body—have come under the Spirit's perfecting power."

"Off With the Old—On With the New"

Our old heart is the "old man" that Paul tells us in Romans 6:6 is "crucified" and destroyed when we become born again. Paul says this old man "is corrupt according to the deceitful lusts." (Ephesians 4:22) Another translation says it's corrupt "according to the desires of the evil one."

So the "old man," then, is our old, unconverted self; it's the "old me," strong in deeds of sin. But, praise God, Paul tells us again in Colossians 3:9 that we have *"put off" that old man* at our new birth. The "putting off" of the old man, however, is twofold: positionally at our conversion and experientially in the gradual process of sanctification.

The new heart that God gives us as a result of our new birth is now "Christ in us."[24] Scripture tells us that if we have been baptized into Christ, we have *"put on" Christ*. The putting on of Christ is also twofold: positionally it begins in our hearts at our new birth, as you can see in **Chart 4**, page 149; experientially, however, putting on Christ in our lives (our souls) is a moment by moment process (see **Charts 5** and **6**). This is the process of sanctification that we will be in until we see Jesus.

Ephesians 4:24 exhorts us to "put on the new man, which after God is created in righteousness and true holiness." And Colossians 3:10 confirms this: "Put on the new man, which is renewed in knowledge after the image of Him that created him." Paul is referring to Christ's Life in our hearts, which we are to daily (moment by moment) "put on" in our lives. *This is the "new man,"* the new me. (Review 2 Corinthians 4: 10-11.)

(5)   **OUR BODY** (*soma*)

Review **Chart 6**, page 161

Our body (5) is compared to the Outer Court of Solomon's Temple, which was on an even lower level than the Inner Court. The Outer Court was constantly exposed to many "outside" influences, just as we are through our bodies.

King Solomon's own palace was adjacent to and opened up into the Outer Court. There he housed his 700 wives (yes, 700 wives)! In the Outer Court he also had his harem buildings, where it is said that he kept 300 concubines. Talk about outside influences!

1 Kings 11:1-6 tells us that it was these foreign wives (and playmates) and their ungodly influence that turned Solomon's heart away from following the Lord. He wasn't careful to only love the Lord, as his father, David, had done. And thus, the Bible says his heart "was not perfect with the Lord" anymore.[25]

In Jesus' day, the Outer Court was the place where the money changers and the dove sellers were allowed. Even Satan himself tempted Jesus from the pinnacle of the Outer Court. Just think of all the outside influences in our own lives (television, movies, magazines, advertisements, etc.) that continually try to draw us away from wholeheartedly and single-mindedly following God.

1 John 2:16 tells us, "For all that is in the world, the lust of the flesh, and the lust of the eyes, and the pride of life, is not of the Father, but of the world."

Our Vehicle of Expression

Our bodies are the "vehicles" (or the carriers) for the expression or manifestation of our lives. In other words, we need a soul in order to express life, and we need a body in order to express life through. Thus, our souls and our bodies[26] cannot be separated.

If we choose to *walk after the Spirit* by making faith choices (see **Chart 5**, page 159, (20)), our bodies will be filled with and manifest God's Life (7) from our hearts (i.e., the "new man"). If, however, we choose to *walk after the flesh* by making emotional choices (see **Chart 6**, page 161, (22)), our bodies will manifest and reflect our own self life (l0) (i.e., our "old man").

We can therefore be Christians all our lives, yet because we continue to make *emotional choices*, no one will ever know that we are. God's Life in us will be quenched, and no one will ever see the difference between our life and that of our neighbors who don't even know God.

This is exactly what a hypocrite is: one whose words and actions don't match. We say we are Christians, and yet our lives show something totally different. We know that Jesus is the answer, but our lives don't prove it. I believe this is why the Christian body is having such a difficult time these days. So many of us are living two lives. We're double-minded. We *say* one thing, yet *do* something else.

Power of Sin

One of the reasons we are so prone to making those wrong, emotional choices that quench God's Life in us (Review **Chart 6**) is that our souls (4) and our bodies (5) (i.e., the *flesh*) are still dominated and controlled by the "power of sin" (23). The power of sin is the energy force that Paul tells us dwells in our unregenerate bodies. (Romans 7:20-21, 23) Sin's whole intent and purpose is to cause us to veer off course and to miss the mark, the mark being total conformation to the Image of Christ.

Satan uses the power of sin as his tool. And it's his hold on us through our self life that keeps us constantly making these wrong choices. No one can take us out of the keeping power of God once we are born again[27], but we can, by our continual choice, quench God's power in us and open ourselves up to the power of sin. And we do this every time we make an emotional choice to follow our self-life.

When we make this choice, you can see on **Chart 6** that Satan (through the power of sin) not only has access to our conscious thoughts, emotions, and desires (19), but he also has total access to our subconscious life (6), all our hidden doubts, fears, insecurities and so forth. Satan, through the power of sin, has access to our flesh, all the gray area on the chart (that's his "playground"). And this is how he tries continually to influence our choices. It's our constant choices that he is after. Satan wins when we forget to "take every thought captive,"[28] begin to mull those things over in our minds, and eventually, bury our hurts, rather than give them to God.

Proverbs 5:22 is provocative in this light. "His own iniquities shall take the wicked himself, and he shall be holden [held] with the *cords of his sins*." (emphasis added)

In other words, our unconfessed sins, our unresolved hurts and anger, and our unvented thoughts (whatever has separated us from God) form a chain that will bind us. "Whatever is not of faith," or whatever we have not dealt with, is what the enemy uses to his full advantage to keep us his captive and to "revenge God." Satan wants to get back at God, by using our emotional choices to thwart His plans and purposes. Therefore, it's not so much that our own natural thoughts, emotions, and desires themselves are warring against us, but that the power of sin is using them for that very purpose.

Remember that neither Satan nor the power of sin have access to our new spirit, our new heart, or our new willpower. These areas are inviolate. Interestingly, in the Temple of Solomon, the Holy of Holies, the Holy Place, and the Vestibule of the Porch were all rooms that also were inviolate. In other words, there were no doors from the outside into these rooms. There was only one entrance to the entire Temple sanctuary and that was the main front door. The side walls of the Temple Sanctuary (between it and the hidden chambers) were literally two feet thick and, again, there were no doors from the hidden chambers into the Sanctuary.

This picture of the Temple's structure really helps me, because I believe Scripture teaches us that a believer cannot be "demon-possessed." Our hearts cannot belong to God and to Satan at the same time. We will either have a "new heart" (Christ in us," our hope of glory), or an "old heart" ("evil from birth" and obviously, open to the enemy's attacks). However, we can open up areas of our soul and our body (i.e., the flesh), by our moment-to-moment choices, to the power of sin and thus, the enemy's involvement.

The War

Thus, the *war* that goes on within us between the "Power of God" (24) and the power of sin (23) is not in our hearts, but in our souls (4) and bodies (5) i.e., the flesh. (Galatians 5:17)

Romans 7.23 validates this when it says, "But I see another law in my members [body], warring against the law of my mind [Law of the Spirit] and bringing me into captivity to the law of sin [power of sin] in my members."

Recognizing this conflict and bringing our soul and our body (the flesh) into captivity ("putting off the old man") so that God's Life can come forth is what the sanctification process is all about.

Paul tells us in Romans 6:6-7 that since our old, evil heart life (our old man) has been exterminated and done away with at our new birth, the power of sin's hold on the flesh has already been destroyed; we have been (if we choose to be) freed from sin. So Christ in our heart is now the overcoming power to constantly free us from this war. In other words, if we choose to love God (obey, trust, and follow Him), then we can in His Strength overcome whatever the "flesh" is urging us to do and be filled with His Spirit (i.e., "putting on the new man").

Galatians 2:20 states, "I am crucified with Christ: nevertheless I live; yet not I, but Christ liveth in me: and the life which I now live in the flesh I live by the faith of the Son of God, Who loved me and gave Himself for me."

God Wants Us to Be "Spirit Filled"

Just as Solomon's Temple in 1 Kings 8:10-11 and 2 Chronicles 5:13-14 was filled from the inside out with God's Spirit as He came forth from the Holy of Holies and filled the Temple, this is exactly God's purpose for us. Daily we are to allow God's Spirit to issue forth from the Holy of Holies of our hearts and fill our souls and our bodies with His Life and His Glory (review **Chart 5**, page 159).

"He that believeth on Me, as the Scripture hath said, out of his belly shall flow rivers of living water." (John 7:38)

This is not a one-time event. It's a moment-by-moment choice to be filled with His Spirit. "Be ye not unwise, but understanding what the will of the Lord is. [That ye] be [*being*] filled with the Spirit [all day long, every day]." (Ephesians 5:17-18)

And 1 Corinthians 6:20 declares, "For ye are bought with a price: therefore glorify [be filled with, reflect, manifest, and shine forth] God in your body."

However, the only way we are going to be filled with, shine forth, or manifest God's Life in our bodies is for us to learn to love (*agapao*) Him. We must learn to totally give ourselves over to God with all our heart, with all our will, and with all our soul. In other words, we must so bind ourselves with Him in each of these areas that we become one—one Heart, one Will, and one Life! In the following chapters we will explore just how we do this.

Endnotes:

1.   Matthew 16:24

2.   Be sure to see the Be Ye Transformed tape series.

3.   See Chapter 12 for more details on our willpower.

4.   This statement that we "are the Temple of God" occurs seven times in the New Testament: 1 Corinthians 3:9-16; 6:19; 2 Corinthians 6:16; Ephesians 2:20, 21; Hebrew 3: 6; 1 Peter 2:5; 4:17.

5.   Acts 17:24

6.   1 Kings 9:3

7.   For a complete background, see briefing package, The Mystery of the Lost Ark, from Koinonia House.

8.   We will explore these "hidden chambers" in more detail in Chapter 13, "Strongholds of the Enemy" and Chapter 14, "Mandatory Steps."

9.   1 Peter 1:3,23

10. Ezekiel 11:19

11. See Romans 5:5 and Luke 8:12 (Hebrews 8:10). This is the supernatural Life of God. God is Love (*Agape*) (1 John 4:8,16). The Word (*Logos*) is God (John 1:1,14; 5:7)

12. John 20:22

13. Ecclesiastes 9:3

14. Romans 3:11-12

15. Ecclesiastes 3:11 ("world" here can be translated *eternity*)

16. Philippians 3:3 and Galatians 6:15

17. Mark 2:21 and Matthew 9:17

18. See Chapter 12 for more details.

19. Hebrews 8:10; 10:16 (check the Greek)

20. Philippians 2:13

21. Proverbs 4:23

22. John 4:11, 14

23. James 3:10-11

24. Colossians 1:27

25. 1 Kings 11:4

26. 2 Corinthians 4:16

27. Colossians 1;13-14; Mark 13:22; John 10:27-29; 1 John 5:18

28. See Chapter 14, "Take Every Thought Captive."

Scriptural References:

Chapter 10

What Does It Mean to Love God With All Our Heart, Will, and Soul?
(Matthew 22:37)
- A. What is our heart, willpower, and soul?
  1. God is very specific in the use of these terms in the Bible
  2. They are not at all the same thing, otherwise God would have said Love me wholly (or completely)" (1 Timothy 4:15)
  3. There is something specific meant by each of these terms, and we need to understand what they mean, so we can love God as He desires
- B. God often uses similitudes (word pictures) to help us understand His Word better (Hosea 12:10)
  1. An example is 1 Corinthians 3:16. Paul is saying here that our bodies are a temple (also in 1 Corinthians 6:19-20; 2 Corinthians 6:16) and this temple is now the dwelling place of God's Spirit (Acts 17:24)
  2. Jesus even calls His own body a temple (John 2:19-20; Mark 14:58)
  3. God wants to fill us (as the temple of God) with His Spirit (His glory), just as He did Solomon's Temple in 1 Kings 8:10-11 (Ezekiel 10:4; 2 Chronicles 5:13; Ephesians 5:17-18; John 4:14)
  4. By so doing, God wants us to reflect and glorify Him (1 Corinthians 6:20)
- C. Solomon's Temple is a model or a blueprint of a New Testament believer (heart, will, and soul) indwelt by the Holy Spirit
  1. Solomon's Temple was special:
     a. It was the only Temple where all the detailed plans of construction and furniture were given to David by the Spirit (1 Chronicles 22:6-15; 28:11-12,19)
     b. It was the only Temple in which God's Spirit dwelt permanently (1 Kings 8:13; 9:3; 2 Kings 21:7; 2 Samuel 7:13), as He does with us (John 14:16-17)
     c. It was the only Temple where the Ark of the Covenant dwelt
  2. By our gaining an understanding of the structure of the Temple, we will gain a better understanding of ourselves: heart, will, and soul

We Are the Temple of God (see *Be Ye Transformed* Series for more detailed Scriptures) See **Chart 1 & 2**
- A. Comparison of Solomon's Temple to born again believers:
  1. Holy of Holies = believer's *new* Spirit
  2. Holy Place = believer's *new* heart
  3. Porch = believer's *new* willpower
  4. Inner Court = believer's soul
  5. Secret, hidden chambers = believer's subconscious
  6. Outer Court = believer's body
- B. The temple of our bodies in detail: See **Chart 3 & 4**

1. Our *new Spirit* (pneuma)
    a. Totally new spirit—that's what being born-again really means (1 Peter 1:3,23; John 3:3; Ezekiel 11:19; 36:26; 2 Corinthians 5:7)
    b. It's God Himself (Father, Son, and Holy Spirit) dwelling in us (John 14:23). We have become one spirit with Him (1 Corinthians 6:17; Galatians 4:6; Romans 8:11)
    c. It means receiving a totally *new energy source* or power source
    d. God's Spirit in us is the new energy source that will create new life in our hearts (Ezekiel 36:27-28; Job 33:4)
2. Our *new Heart* (*kardia*) (Ezekiel 11:19; 18:31b; Jeremiah 24:7; 32:39; Deuteronomy 30:6; Romans 2:28-29)
    a. Our heart is the place where God's Life is started and begun by God's Spirit (Ezekiel 36:25-27; Psalm 51:10)
        .   This is totally new heart life—eternal life (Ecclesiastes 3:11b; 2 Corinthians 4:6; 1 John 5:12)
        .   This is God's Life in us (1 John 4:8, 16: John 1:1,14; 1 John 1: 1; 5:7)—"Christ in [us], the hope of glory" (Colossians 1:27; 1 John 5:11; 2 Timothy 1:7; 1 Peter 3:4)
    b. Our new heart consists of *God's supernatural Love* and *His supernatural thoughts* (Romans 5:5; 8:39; Luke 8:12; John 17:26; 4:24; Hebrews 8:10; Galatians 4:6; Ephesians 3:16-19, 2 Corinthians 4:6; 1 John 1:5; 4:8)
    c. Our heart is the center core and foundation of our whole person
    d. Our old heart:
        .   Our old heart is the "old man" of Romans 6:6 that is crucified when we become born-again (Colossians 3:9)
        .   It no longer has any power over us. "He that is dead is freed from sin" (Romans 6:7,14,18)
        .   Our old heart is evil and corrupt from birth (Genesis 8:21), because our old human spirit is unregenerated
        .   It's self-centered (Isaiah 47:10)
        .   It can't be changed or understood (Jeremiah 17:9; Ecclesiastes 9:3; Matthew 15:19-20; Mark 7:21)
        .   Old heart is incurable (Jeremiah 17:9)
        .   Old heart is proud and arrogant (Isaiah 14:13-14; Ezekiel 28:2; Jeremiah 13:9-10; 48:29; 49:16; Deuteronomy 8:14,17)
        .   Old heart will never on its own seek God (Romans 3:11-12; Philippians 2:21)
        .   Old heart will never want to know God (Romans 1:21-22)
    e. This is why we desperately need to be born-again (John 3:3,5-6; 1 Peter 1:3) and receive a new spirit and a new heart (Jeremiah 24:7; 32:39; Ezekiel 11:19-20; 36:26-27; Galatians 4:6; Hebrews 8:10)
    f. The Life that is now in our hearts is totally pure, completely incorruptible and holy because it is God's Life (1 Peter 3:4; 2 Corinthians 5:17) and His divine nature (2 Peter 1:4)
        .   "Christ in us" (Colossians 1:27)
        .   "Hidden man of the heart" (1 Peter 3:4)
        .   "Mystery hid from all ages" (Colossians 1:26-27)

    g.   The only Life that is in our hearts (if we are born again) is God's Life; we just need to let it out

    h.   So, it is not our hearts that need transforming anymore, it's our lives (our souls) (Romans 12:2; 1 Corinthians 6:20)

3.   Our *new Willpower (dianoia)*

    a.   Our new willpower is the most critical area of all

       .   It is the key to our whole Christian walk

       .   It *determines the direction or the course of our lives* (Deuteronomy 30:19-20)

       .   It determines whose life will be lived in our soul: God's or our own.

    b.   Our new willpower has two parts to it:

       .   *God's supernatural Will and Power*, given to us as a part of our new birth (Hebrews 8:10; 10:16; Jeremiah 31:33) where God counsels us as to what His will is, and then gives us the supernatural power to perform that Will in our lives (Philippians 2:13; Romans 9:17; 1 Corinthians 2:4; 2 Corinthians 6:7)

       .   *Our own free choice* to follow what God has shown us and rely upon Him to perform it in our lives, or to choose to do what we want and rely upon our own ability to perform it

    c.   The Temple floorplan illustrates the believer's supernatural willpower

       .   The golden vestibule represents the super-natural authority and power of God to make faith choices (Philippians 2:13; Zechariah 4:6) "Not my will, but thine" (Matthew 26:39)

       .   The pillars (Jachin & Boaz) represent our free choice: to follow God's Will or our own (Deuteronomy 30:17-19)

4.   Our *soul (psyche)*

    a.   Our souls are made up of our mostly conscious thoughts, emotions, and desires (we will discuss the hidden, subconscious part of our soul later)

    b.   Our soul is the "outward" expression (or manifestation) of our life—it's our character shown forth through our bodies. It's the life we see, hear, and feel coming from each other

    c.   If "life" exists in both our hearts and souls, what is the difference?

       .   Life is originally created, started, and begun in our hearts (Proverbs 4:23)

       .   It is subconscious life—root life

       .   Only God can see the life in our hearts (Jeremiah 17:10; 12:3; 1 Chronicles 28:9; 1 Samuel 16:7d; Psalm 17:3; Proverb 21:2b; Luke 16:15b)

       .   Life then is outwardly expressed or shown forth in our souls (Isaiah 58:10-11; Proverbs 14:30a; Matthew 12:35)

       .   It's conscious life—it's visible (Jeremiah 31:12; 1 Samuel 16:7c)

       .   Our souls should be "like a watered garden" (Jeremiah 31:12)

d. Our souls are like a neutral area that will either be filled with God's Life from our hearts (flowers), or filled with self life (weeds). See **Chart 5**, page 159.

.   Ideally, our souls should be filled with God's Life if we have chosen to be open vessels His Love becomes our love in our soul, His Wisdom, our wisdom, and His Power, our power

.   This is called being "Spirit filled" (John 4:14). One life is being lived

.   This is also called "single-mindedness"

.   However, if we make emotional choices and we quench God's Life, our soul will be filled with self life. See **Chart 6**, page 161

.   God's Life is blocked from coming forth

.   The soul life that is produced is our own thoughts, emotions, and desires, not God's

.   This is called "double-mindedness." Two lives are being lived

e. Where does this "self life" come from?

.   Self life comes from the hurts, doubts, resentments, bitternesses, etc. that we have never given over to God, but have stuffed and buried in secret hidden chambers (*cheder*) in our souls

.   Self life is triggered when we choose to follow these things rather than what God is prompting us to do (Proverbs 5:22; John 8:34)

f. *Cheder* (our innermost part) (1 Kings 6:5-10)

.   Analogous to the hidden, inner chambers of the temple (1 Kings 6:5-10) used for secretly storing the priests' idolatrous worship items (Ezekiel 8:6-12)

.   Represents the place in our souls where we hide, bury, and store our hurts, wounds, guilt, and fears (Proverbs 18:8; 26:22; Ezekiel 14:3-5)

.   Called "chambers of death" (Proverbs 7:27); source of evil (terror) (Job 37:9 *cheder* is here translated "south")

.   Power of sin, that resides in the flesh, has full access to these chambers (James 1:14-15; Romans 7:17-24); "cords of sin" (Proverbs 5:22); "strongholds of the enemy" (Nehemiah 4:10; Psalm 11:3; 2 Corinthians 2:10-11)

.   God wants these hidden areas exposed so we will be free of the power of sin's hold on us (Proverbs 20:27,30; Deuteronomy 7:20; Numbers 33:55)

.   God desires these chambers to be cleansed, sanctified, and filled with His Spirit (2 Chronicles 29:15-16; Psalm 51:6)

.   Only by intimate knowledge of God can all these chambers be filled with "pleasant riches" (Proverbs 24:4)

    g. Our souls are in the process of being redeemed (2 Corinthians 4:16c)
- We are learning to set aside our self life, so that God's Life can come forth (Romans 6:6,7,11-13; Colossians 2:11; 1 Corinthians 5:7-8; Acts 20:24)
- This is called "putting off the old man" (Ephesians 4:22)
- Christ's Life in our hearts is what we are daily to "put on" (Colossians 3:10; Ephesians 4:24)

5. Our *body* (*soma*)
- a. Our body is the vehicle or the carrier for the expression of our life (Philippians 1:20; 1 Corinthians 6:19-20)
- b. Our souls and bodies cannot be separated; otherwise there is death
- c. Our bodies are unregenerate
  - Unregenerate body and soul = the *flesh*
  - Sometimes called "the body of sin"
- d. We will either be "walking after the Spirit" manifesting God's Life (Galatians 5:22-25), or we will be "walking after the flesh" showing forth self life (Galatians 5:17-25)
- e. One of the reasons we continue to make wrong choices is that our souls and bodies are still dominated by the *power of sin* (Romans 7:20-21, 23)
  - Power of sin is an energy force whose purpose is to cause us to "veer off course" and "miss the mark" (Philippians 3:14)
  - No one can take us out of the keeping power of God once we are born again (Colossians 1:13-14; Mark 13:22; John 10:27-29; 1 John 5:18)
  - However, any choice we make that is "not of faith" Satan uses to keep us captive and "revenge God"
  - This is the reason we are not sinless, even though we have God's Life in our hearts
  - It is Satan's hold on us, through our self life, that keeps us making wrong choices (Proverbs 5:22; Romans 7:17; John 8:34; Joel 1:10,12)

The War
A. Since our old heart (old man) no longer exists (Romans 6:6) the power of sin's hold on the flesh has been destroyed and we have been freed from sin (Romans 6:7-14,22), i.e., the flesh (Romans 6:11-13,16; Luke 11:17)

B. Christ's Life in my new heart is now the overcoming power to free me from this war (Romans 6:2,6-7; 8:9,13)

C. Therefore, the war that goes on within us between the power of God and the power of sin is waged in our soul and body, not in our heart (Romans 7:21-23; 6:13,16; 8:5-6; Galatians 5:17)

God Wants Us Spirit filled
A. Just as Solomon's Temple was Spirit filled, this is God's will for us also (1 Kings 8:10-11; 2 Chronicles 5:13-14; Ephesians 5:17-18; 1 Corinthians 6:20; Ezekiel 10:4; John 7:38)

B. Only way we can be Spirit filled (filled with God) is to love Him, become one with Him: one heart, one will, and one soul (John 12:24-25; 2 Corinthians 4: 10-11; Luke 9:23)

Chapter 11: Loving God With All Our Heart

Nature of Our Hearts

The Bible tells us over and over again that our "heart life" is the center core of our whole being; it's the essential nature and the true essence of our whole person. Our heart is the place where our thoughts, emotions, and desires are originally created, started, and begun. If we are a believer, then our heart life is going to be God's Life: His supernatural Love and Thoughts ("Christ in us").

Proverbs 4:23 warns, "Keep thy heart with all diligence; for out of it are the issues [all the sources] of life."

Our heart is the foundation block or the underlying support upon which everything else is built. In other words, all continuing activity depends on the "life" that resides in our heart.

Proverbs 14:30 declares, "A sound heart [inside] is the life of the flesh [outside]."

What Does It Mean to Love God With All Our Heart?

We love (*agapao*) God with all our heart when we make our initial choice to give our hearts to Him and become born again! We choose at that time to bind our hearts with His and become one heart with Him. At this new birth, God takes away our old, stony heart (human love and thoughts) and gives us a brand-new heart.[1] Therefore, the only life that now exists in our hearts is God's Life; His supernatural Love and Wisdom.

1 John 5:12 says, "He that hath the Son hath life [God's Life is now in this person's heart]. "He that hath *not* the Son of God hath not life." (emphasis added)

Not only do we love God with all our heart at our new birth, but we also love (*agapao*) God with all our heart every time we allow His life in our heart to be the *motivation*, the prompting, or the instigation for all we choose to do and not our own "self life." In other words, continually "doing the will of God from [our] heart"[2] and allowing "the Love of Christ to constrain (or control) us." (Ephesians 6:6; 2 Corinthians 5:14)[3]

Fountain of Living Water

God's Life in our hearts is often spoken of in the Bible as a "fountain of living water"[4] that wells up within us, gushes forth, and fills us to overflowing.

See **Chart 5**, page 159, (17).[5] As John 7:38 explains, "He that believeth on Me, as the Scripture hath said, out of his belly (heart) shall flow rivers of living water."

However, when we make wrong, emotional choices our hearts become covered over and that "fountain of living water" blocked so that His Life is unable to come forth. See **Chart 6**, page 161, (18).[6] At this point God's Love in our hearts is not the one controlling or motivating our actions, but our own self life (our hurts, bitterness, memories, fears, insecurities and so on, from the hidden chambers). This grieves God because it's not at all what He intended.

James 3:11 questions, "Doth a fountain send forth at the same place sweet water and bitter?" And verse 10, "My brethren, these things ought not so to be." In other words, God's Life (the sweet water) and self life (the bitter water) should not be coming forth from the same place. This is not at all what God planned.[7]

God desires His Life (His Love) in our hearts to be the sole motivation for all our choices so that His Life and *only* His Life comes forth from our souls.

"Fat as Grease"

Psalm 119:70 tells us that when we make choices that quench God's Life, our hearts become "fat as grease." When we say no to God's promptings and leadings, our hearts become covered over with a layer of grease or fat, just like Psalm 119 says. This grease not only clogs, chokes out, and quenches any communication or personal leading from God, but also causes us to become insensitive and unfeeling towards others. This, then, is where the "pure fountain water" gets blocked off and then comes out bitter.

Did you know when you put grease or fat on a physical burn, you not only make that area insensitive and resistant to healing, but you also cause a scar to be formed? Sin is just like that grease—it not only makes us insensitive and resistant to God's leading in our hearts, but it also leaves a scar on our lives. We always reap the consequences of our wrong choices.

Example: Could I Borrow Some Money?

Joanne is a Christian hairdresser and very much a perfectionist. She has never been able to stand any untidiness or messiness in her salon.

Years ago, she had a friend named Susie, a Christian who worked in the booth next to hers. Susie was a single mom, who out of necessity (when her babysitter did not show up) brought her two little kids to work with her. Of course, the kids often brought crackers and cookies, and before long the whole place would become a total disaster.

Joanne tried to put up with this situation for a while. She smiled and pretended everything was fine, even taking care of Susie's kids sometimes. But after months of this inconvenience, the constant mess really got to her, and she unknowingly allowed deep roots of bitterness to grow.

Like many of us, Joanne didn't realize that when we don't deal with our real negative thoughts and emotions right away[8], they are programmed down in our sub-conscious, and then those buried things eventually become the motivation for our actions and not God's Love.

One day while out shopping, Joanne ran into Susie who was trying to buy some lingerie. Susie's estranged husband was coming over the next night for a visit, and she hoped there might be a chance for a reconciliation. When Susie went to pay for the lingerie, the cashier for some reason, wouldn't take her credit card and she didn't have enough cash. Susie turned to Joanne and asked, "Please, could I borrow some money? I'll pay you back at work in the morning."

Before Joanne could even think, she responded with, "No, I'm really sorry, but..." and then she made up some feeble excuse for why she couldn't loan Susie the money. Joanne actually had plenty of money in her purse, but because her heart was so covered and clogged by undealt-with resentment and bitterness, she automatically reacted out of that *grease*, rather than God's Love.

Susie responded, "Oh, I understand. I was just hoping to make tomorrow night special. It's okay." And then she left.

Joanne was so grieved as she could easily have lent Susie the money. Guilt ridden and ashamed of herself, she had to go to the ladies' room to regain her composure. In the bathroom, she wept, asking the Lord to forgive her. He exposed the bitterness and resentment that she was still harboring in her heart. Joanne thanked God for revealing the truth. (Remember, we have to "see" our sin before we can give it over to Him.) Joanne then chose to confess and repent of her sin and to give it all over to God, knowing He would forgive her and cleanse her.

When she left the bathroom and went back into the store, she saw Susie's pile of lingerie, still sitting there on the counter. Prompted by God, she bought the lingerie as a gift for Susie. When Joanne went to work the next morning, she told Susie the whole story, asked her forgiveness and then gave her the "love gift" out of her heart. Once again "the sweet fountain water" of God's Life in Joanne's heart was able to flow.

When we daily wash our hearts with that cool, fresh, running water of the Word by confessing, repenting, and giving our sins to God, our sins will not only be washed away, but no scars will be left!

What Is Sin?

One of the reasons we don't fully realize the extent of God's Love towards us is that we don't see our own sin. We don't see and understand the subtle things that quench His Spirit in us.

Isaiah 59:2 states, "Your iniquities have separated between you and your God, and your sins have hid His face from you, that He will not hear."

Sin is anything that causes us to be separated from God. Anything that is not of faith, the Bible tells us, is sin. (Romans 14:23)

When I used to think of sin, I thought of Galatians 5:19-21 which lists the works of the flesh and I could say, "Hey, I'm really okay. I don't do those things!" Then I came across a little book called *The Calvary Road* by Roy Hession, and it changed my life. In this little book is a list of subtle things that cover our hearts and separate us from God just as much as the big ones of Galatians. Let me recall just a few:

> "*Self-pity, self-defensiveness, oversensitivity, criticalness, resentfulness, worry, grumbling, bossiness, self-complacency, self energy, self-seeking, self-indulgence, self-consciousness.*"

If anyone reading this book doesn't experience and deal with any of these things, you may close this book now. You have no need of this teaching.

The above list describes sins that separate us from God (just like Isaiah 59:2 says) and cover our hearts with grease (just as Psalm 119:70 states). This separation forms a barrier or a blockage that prohibits His Love not only from being experienced in our lives (our souls), but also from being passed on to others. (See **Chart 6**, page 161, (18)).

Nothing Shall Separate Us

If we are believers, we always will have God's Life and His Love in our hearts. Romans 8:35-39 tells us that "nothing separates us from God's Love," and 1 Corinthians 13:8 tells us that "His Love never stops coming."[9] However, if our hearts are clogged or covered over by "grease" (sin), then we'll not have "living experience" of God's Love in our lives. Nor, will we be an open channel so that God's Love can flow through us to others.

Please note that the original, negative thoughts themselves are not sin. These thoughts are a normal and natural part of our being human. The sin (the separation from God) comes when we choose to follow what these ungodly thoughts are telling us to do. We sin (grease over) when we choose to mull over, entertain, and eventually do what these thoughts are prompting, rather than do what God is telling us—relinquish and yield these things to Him and do His Will.

What Is Pride?

Following what we think, feel, and desire (self) over what God is telling us to do is called *pride.* Remember, there was someone else in Scripture who continually put "self" above God. Five times in Isaiah 14:13-14, Satan (Lucifer) states, "I will..." And in his last statement he declares, "I will be like the Most High."

That's exactly what we are saying when we choose to follow what our own thoughts and desires are telling us over what God is prompting. We are making ourselves out to be "like God," and that's prideful.

Pride is simply *not loving God* (*agapao*) but loving ourselves. It's totally giving ourselves over to what we want, think, and desire. Pride comes from disobeying, not trusting, or relinquishing ourselves to God. Pride is putting ourselves first, not God. Proverbs 8:13 tells us that God hates pride. The reason He hates pride is that pride immediately quenches and prevents His Life and His Love in our hearts from being manifested out in our lives. When we pridefully choose our own way over God's Way, we immediately block His Love in our hearts and we thwart His purposes. The prideful and the arrogant are those who go their own way because their hearts are callous and unfeeling—"fat as grease." (Psalm 119:69-70)

Pride and unbelief are the two sins that continually prevent God's workings. Because, more than anything else, they affect every choice that we make. If we can recognize our pride and unbelief, and if we can choose to confess and repent of them, then once again God's Love can flow from our hearts.

"For as the heaven is high above the earth, So great is His mercy [Love] towards them that fear Him. As far as the east is from the west, So far hath He removed our transgressions [our sins] from us." (Psalm 103:11-12)

There is no experience quite so wonderful and exhilarating as having our sins forgiven and washed clean by God's unfathomable *Agape* Love.[10]

Read Psalm 51 when you can.

Four Types of Hearts

Luke 8:11-15 teaches us that there are four different types of hearts: the unregenerate heart, the hardened heart, the clogged heart, and the pure heart.

The first two types of hearts, refer to unbelievers. The *unregenerate heart* refers to a person who is definitely not a believer because it says the seed of the Word of God has fallen, not in this person's heart but "by the wayside." The *hardened heart* refers to a person who hears and receives the Word of God with joy but, because he has no root in himself (he is as hard as a rock, thus no seed can be implanted), "in time of temptation [he] falls away."

The last two hearts are the two hearts we've been talking about in this chapter: a *sin-covered heart*, with none of God's Love flowing, and a *willing heart*, ready and willing to do all God's Will.

Both of these hearts are believers. The "clogged or choked heart" is the one who allows the "cares and riches and pleasures of this life" to choke out (grease over) God's Life in him. Therefore, "he brings no fruit to perfection [completion]." In other words, he never experiences God's Life (His Love) for himself, nor is he able to pass it on to others. (See **Chart 6**, page 161.)

The "pure heart," however, is one who not only receives the seed of God's Word in his heart, but he has also chosen to keep it and to obey God's commands. This person loves God with all his heart, will, and soul. Therefore this person, because he is an open vessel, brings forth much fruit. This is the one loving God with all his heart because he is doing the Will of God from his heart. (See **Chart 5**, page 159.)

How Do We Know God's Will?

How does God reveal His Will to this willing-hearted person? The answer is, of course, by reading His Word. Reading the Bible is how we'll know what God's Thoughts are on any subject. This is how He talks to us and how He daily shows us what His Will is. This means that we must be in the Word every day (not just opening the Bible and haphazardly reading some passages, but having some sort of consistent reading plan).

I keep a daily journal to help me log my conversations with the Lord. When I have questions for Him, I write them out. I ask God only one question at a time, so that when He does answer I know exactly which question He is answering. Then as I read my daily reading, I expect God to answer me and He always does, in His time and in His way.

"Thy word is a lamp unto my feet, and a light unto my path." (Psalm 119:105)

Example: Do Not Turn the Punishment Away

Here is a classic example of how God can answer our prayers specifically from Scripture: About seven or eight years ago, my Michelle was going to have her twelfth birthday party. Everyone had already been invited and the place for the party had already been planned. Even the food and the cake had been ordered and paid for. However, Michelle's attitude towards me that week had been horrible.

After praying about it, I told her that if her bad attitude kept up, I would have to cancel her party. Her "snotty" behavior not only continued but got even worse. I sought the Lord with all my heart and asked Him, "What am I supposed to do here? Canceling her party will be so humiliating and so public. Is that what I am supposed to do?"

That very morning, in my daily Bible reading plan, I was in Amos 1. Now, how many times a year are we in Amos 1 for a devotional! Not very often. Five times in Amos 1 it says, "Do not turn the punishment away." Coincidence? I don't think so! I canceled her party and after she went "ballistic" on me, she calmed down and admitted that she had acted horribly and deserved what she got.

God's Counsel

God will gently and specifically counsel us as to what His Will is for our lives. He is the great counselor,[11] so His counsel to us will be very specific—if we are seeking and listening. We might find His answer right away (like I did with Michelle), or it may take a day or even a week or more to hear Him. But if we persevere, I promise you that God will answer and show us His way.

When we find something in the Scriptures that looks like it might pertain to our situation, we should write it down and put a question mark beside it. When God confirms the same thing at least two more times in His Word, through counsel of intimate friends or through circumstances, then we can know assuredly it's from Him. We can also know He will give us the power we need to perform that Will in our lives.

It's through God's Word that He speaks to us. Don't just trust in "voices" and "urgings" you hear or feel. I have been so deceived by voices that I thought were of God. When we get an answer from the Word and His Spirit confirms it in the above ways, only then can we be pretty confident that it is truly God's Voice.

When in a Hurry

If you have to move quickly and you just don't have the time or the liberty to wait for God's answer and His Will, then: 1) Pray and acknowledge God is in control of your life; 2) Tell Him that you are not sure of what His Will is yet, but that you have to move; 3) Tell Him what you are about to do; and then, 4) Ask Him to block what you are about to do if it is not His Will.

I assure you, God is great at slamming doors!

Often the Unexpected

Something God has impressed upon my heart lately which I believe to be of the utmost importance to us all, is that we should not "constrain" or box God in, by personalizing His individual promises from His Word only according to our own preconceived notions. In other words, we should not limit God's promises to our own interpretation of His Word.

Even though these are God's words and His promises and are in themselves certain and true, their actualization in our lives does not always come about exactly as we understand them. And sometimes, it even seems as though we have been deceived because these revelations turn out contrary to our expectations.

We see examples of this kind of confusion in Scripture. God's prophecies in the Old and New Testament did not always turn out the way the people expected because they understood them in their own human understanding, whereas God intended them for a much larger spiritual purpose. For example:

In Genesis 15:7, God told Abraham "I am the Lord that brought thee out of Ur of the Chaldees, to *give thee this land to inherit it*." Abraham believed God and in Genesis 15:8, he asks God "Lord God, whereby shall I know that I shall inherit it?" God then revealed to Abraham that actually he would not inherit or possess the land, but his offspring, some 400 years later, would. Abraham was misled in his own interpretation of God's promise and had he acted accordingly, he would have erred and, those who saw Abraham die without having received the promise from God would also have been baffled.

Another example is Jacob. On his journey to Egypt to see his son Joseph, God appears to him and tells him, "... fear not to go down into Egypt; for I will there make of thee a great nation: I will go down with thee into Egypt; and *I will also surely bring thee up again*." (Genesis 46:1-4, emphasis added) These words were not fulfilled according to how we would understand them because Jacob died in Egypt. (Genesis 49:33) However, the prophecy was fulfilled in the way God meant it, in that Jacob's offspring were guided and delivered from Egypt years later.

Here is one last example from the New Testament. Remember Christ's two disciples on the Emmaus road? The time was just after Christ's death and these two, in a very defeated state, were walking and talking together, when Jesus Himself drew near. (Luke 24:13-21) They supposed Jesus to be a stranger in Jerusalem and they said to Him, "... *we trusted that it had been He [Jesus] which should have redeemed Israel.*" They had believed and hoped that Christ would, at that very time, set up a temporal reign. But, since Christ had just been crucified, they felt their promise had been wrong and they were discouraged. Yet, as we know, the promise *will* be fulfilled upon Jesus' Second Coming.

We must not consider God's promises only from our own limited perspective, for God's language is far above and beyond the ordinary meaning we might understand. We must give Him room to fulfill that promise in whatever way He desires. If we are bound to a literal and personal interpretation, we might become misled and perplexed, as Christ's disciples were. We must always allow God to accomplish His promises in our lives in His own way and in His own timing.

Isaiah 55:9 declares, "For as the heavens are higher than the earth, so are My ways higher than your ways...."

I have learned this from first hand experience. I believe it's important for all of us to understand, so that if God's promises do not turn out as we expected, we will not become bewildered and begin to disregard and distrust God's Word.

The Motivation of Our Lives

God wants the motivation of our lives to be the "new" heart He has placed within us. He wants His supernatural Life—is Love and His Thoughts—in our heart to determine all of our choices.

Only God knows our heart. Only He knows the real motives behind our choices. And only He knows if we are truly loving Him with all our heart like we are supposed to. Often, "that which is highly esteemed among men is an abomination in the sight of the Lord." (Luke 16:15) This is true because God can discern what man cannot.

God wants us to stop filling the "hidden chambers" with hurts, resentments, criticisms, bitterness, and other weaknesses of the flesh. Moment by moment, He wants us to "take every thought captive" (2 Corinthians 10:5) and not let the negative thoughts and emotions accumulate. God wants the motivation of our lives to be the new heart that He has placed within us. He wants His supernatural Love and His supernatural Thoughts[12] to constrain us, to control us, and to determine all our choices.

1 Peter 4:2 instructs us that we "no longer should live the rest of [our] time in the flesh to the lusts of men, *but to the will of God*." (emphasis added)

Loving God with all our heart not only means asking Him into our life, thus receiving His eternal, supernatural Life and becoming one heart with Him, but loving God with all our heart *also* means allowing His Life, His Love, Wisdom, and Power in our heart, to be the motivation for all we choose to do.

In Galatians 2:20, Paul declares, "I am crucified with Christ: nevertheless I live; yet not I, but Christ liveth in me [I am one heart with Him now]; and the life which I now live in the flesh, I live by the faith [faithfulness] of the Son of God [to perform His Life through me]."

Endnotes:

1. Jeremiah 2:13; 17:13

2. Ezekiel 11:19-20 and Romans 6:17, "obeyed from the heart"

3. Romans 5:5

4. Jeremiah 17:13

5. John 4:11-14

6. Psalm 119:70

7. Psalm 17:10

8. 2 Corinthians 10:5

9. 1 Corinthians 13:8

10. Hebrews 12.11

11. Isaiah 9:6

12. Ephesians 6:5-6 and Colossians 3:22

Scriptural References:

Chapter 11

How Do We Become "One Heart" With God?
A. Technically, we love God with all our heart when we make the initial choice of giving our heart to Him and becoming born-again (John 3:3-5)
1. Becoming *one heart* with Him (Ezekiel 11:19; 36:26; Jeremiah 32:39; Psalm 86:11b; 1 John 5:12)
2. Receiving His Life as our own: His Love, His Thoughts, and His Power (Ecclesiastes 3:11)
B. Loving God with all our heart also means allowing God's Life in our heart to be the *motivation* for all we do (and not our self life) (Ephesians 6:6; Matthew 12:34-35; Romans 6:16-17; 2 Corinthians 5:14a)
C. The nature of our hearts:
1. Our heart is the *center core* of our whole being (Proverbs 4:23; 14:30a)
2. Our heart is the *foundation* upon which our whole spiritual house is built (Matthew 7:24-25)
3. God wants His Life from our hearts to be manifested out into our souls (Ephesians 5:17-18; John 7:38)
4. God wants His Life from our hearts to be as a *fountain of living water* that gushes forth and continually fills us to overflowing (John 4:11,14; 7:38)
5. In order for this to happen, our self life must be constantly yielded and set aside (Romans 6:6,11-13; Colossians 2:11; 1 Corinthians 5:7-8; Acts 20:24)
6. When we refuse to do this, our hearts become covered with grease (Psalm 119:70; Isaiah 6:10; Matthew 13:15) and God's Life is quenched (Mark 4:19; Luke 8:14; Hebrews 3:13). This is the "thorny heart" of Luke 8: 7,14; 21:34-36. This is sin
    a. Any choice we make that separates us from God is sin (Isaiah 59:2; Romans 14:23b; 1 John 5:17a)
    b. Sin is not only "all the works of the flesh" (Galatians 5:19), but any corrupt communication that is not edifying (Ephesians 4:29-32)
    c. Common sins we don't recognize as sin are: self-pity, self-energy, self-complacency, self-seeking, self-defense, self-consciousness, over-sensitiveness, criticalness, worry, anxiety and irritability (Galatians 5:19-21; Ephesians 4:31; Hebrews 12:15; Colossians 3:5-6)
    d. God's Love never stops flowing to our hearts (Romans 8:35), but if we sin, we will not experience His Love in our souls (our lives)

  e. Our negative thoughts themselves are not sin. It's what we choose to do with those thoughts that make them sin or not (2 Samuel 11:2-4)

  f. Following what we want over what God is telling us to do is *pride* (Psalm 119:69-70)
   . It's putting ourselves above God (Isaiah 14:13-14; 47.8)
   . It's not loving God first, but ourselves
   . God hates pride (Proverbs 8:13) because it quenches His Life, blocks His Love and thwarts His purposes (Proverbs 15:13b; 17:22b)

  g. When our hearts are "covered" with grease (sin) we become insensitive to God's leading (Job 18:7; Psalm 106:13; Ephesians 4:19; Hebrews 3:13)

  h. The "whole lump" is then contaminated (1 Corinthians 5:6-7; Mark 7:21-23)

  i. God will not hear our prayers (Lamentations 4:44; Isaiah 1:15)

  j. Works of the "flesh" then result (Galatians 5:19-21; Colossians 3:5-6; Ephesians 4:31; Hebrews 12:15)

 7. This is where the pure water from God's fountain gets clogged and comes out bitter (James 3:10-11)

 8. This grieves God because it's not what He intended (James 3:10-11; Ephesians 4:30-32; 1 John 3:6-9, 5:18)

 9. This ought not to be (James 3:10) because then the seed remains unfruitful (Mark 9:19)

Four Different Types of Hearts

 A. Parable of the Sower (Luke 8:11-15; Matthew 13:18-23; Mark 4:3-21)
The *sower* is the Lord. The *seed* is the Word of God. The *root* is the Word implanted in our hearts. The *soil* is the condition of our hearts.

 B. Biblically there are four types of hearts:

  1. *Unregenerate heart*: Seed falls *by the way* (out of the heart, no soil at all) (Luke 8:12)
   a. Hears the Word in an unbelieving heart
   b. Not able to understand it
   c. Satan comes along and snatches seed away

  2. *Hardened heart*: Seed falls into *stony places* (no depth of soil, hardened) (Luke 8:13; Zechariah 7:12; Mark 3:5b; 6:52; Romans 2:5; Luke 24:25)
   a. Hears the Word in a shallow and surfacy heart
   b. Accepts, receives with gladness and believes for awhile ("tastes the Word")
   c. Seed, however, is not allowed to root and grow
   d. Trials come along and seed is scorched, withers and dies

  3. *Covered heart*: Seed falls into *thorns* (clogged heart—unproductive soil) (Luke 8:7,14)
   a. Hears the Word in a choked-out, busy, and troubled heart (Luke 10:41-42; 21:34)

       b.   Double-mindedness, cares of the world and pleasures of this life cause God's seed in heart to be quenched and stifled

       c.   These lives then become unfruitful and barren (Mark 4:19; Hebrews 6:8a; Luke 21:34-36)

   4.   *Perfect heart*: Seed falls in *good ground* (receptive and cleansed heart, willing to do all God's Will) (Luke 8:15,21; 1 Chronicles 29:19a)

       a.   Hears the Word in a clean, open, and willing heart

       b.   Single-minded and allowing God's Life to flow

       c.   "Eating the Word," not just tasting it

       d.   These lives bear much fruit (Proverbs 12:12b)

 C. "No man, when he hath lighted a candle, covereth it with a vessel, or putteth it under a bed; but setteth it on a candlestick, that they which enter in may see the light." (Luke 8:16)

How Do We Know What God's Will Is?

 A. How does this "willing-hearted" person know God's Will?

   1.   God's Will is found in His Word (Psalms 32:8;119:9, 105, 130, 169)

   2.   God's comprehensive Will is to love Him and then to love others (Matthew 22:37-39)

   3.   The way we know what God's Will is, is to be in His Word daily (Proverbs 8:34-35)

       a.   Have a daily reading plan

       b.   Write out your questions to Him (one at a time) (James 1:5-6)

       c.   God will answer through Scripture (Psalm 119:42b)

       d.   It may take awhile to hear His answer, but wait and expect Him to answer and He will (Ephesians 5:17)

       e.   Then, God will confirm His Word with other Scriptures, circumstances, and other counsel

   4.   If you have to move quickly:

       a.   Pray and acknowledge God is in control

       b.   Tell Him you are not sure what His Will is, but you have to move

       c.   Tell Him what you are about to do

       d.   Ask Him to block it, if it is not His Will

 B. If we have a cleansed, willing heart, it's God's responsibility to show us what His Will is

 C. Sometimes God's Will is not what we expect (Genesis 15:7-8; 46:1-4; 49:33; Luke 24:13-21; Isaiah 55:9)

The Motivation of Our Lives

 A. God wants the true motivation of our lives to be the new heart Life that He has placed within us

 B. He wants His Life in our hearts to determine all our choices

 C. Only God knows our true motivations (Luke 16:15), because only He can see our hearts

D. This is why it is so critical to "take every thought captive" (2 Corinthians 10:5) and get rid of the negative things so that we can be motivated by God's Life (Ephesians 6:5; Colossians 3:22; Galatians 2:20)

E. We "no longer should live the rest of [our] time in the flesh to the lusts of men but to the will of God." (1 Peter 4:2)

Loving God with all our heart is not only our initial choice of becoming *one* heart with Him (Psalm 86:11b; Ezekiel 11:19; 36:26), but also it's allowing His Life in our hearts (Colossians 1:27; 1 Peter 3:4; 2 Corinthians 5:17-18) to be the motivation for all we do. (Proverbs 14:30; 16:23; Romans 6:17; 2 Corinthians 5:14a; Matthew 12:34-35)

Chapter 12: Loving God With All Our Willpower

Matthew 22:37 commands us to "Love the Lord, thy God, with all thy heart, and with all thy soul, and with all thy mind [*dianoia*]."

Dianoia

As discussed in Chapter 10, the Greek word for *mind* in this First Commandment is *dianoia*. *Dianoia*, more properly translated, means willpower, or volition, and not mind at all. The proper Greek word for mind is **nous**, which means our whole conceptual process. Our mind (*nous*) is what takes the thoughts of our hearts and produces them as actions in our lives. Our mind includes not only the conception of an idea, but also its fulfillment in action. (See the *Be Ye Transformed* tape series on the Mind of Christ for more details.)

In order to avoid further confusion, from now on whenever I refer to the First Commandment I will always call *dianoia* our "willpower" and not our mind. In other words, we are to love God with all our heart, with all our willpower, and with all our soul.

"To love" (*agapao*), as mentioned earlier, means to bind ourselves so closely with something that we become one with it. We love God with all our heart in our "born-again" experience, where we do become one heart with Him. Let's explore now what it means to love God with all our willpower; how do we become one will with Him?

The *Shema*

Remember the **Shema** in Deuteronomy 6:4-5 where God commands the Old Testament saints to: "Love the Lord thy God with all thine heart, and with all thine soul, and with all thine strength?"[1] Notice that God did not ask these saints to "love Him with all their willpower." Yet when Jesus quotes this same *Shema* in Matthew 22:37 He declares, "Thou shalt love the Lord, thy God, with all thy heart, and with all thy soul, [and then He adds] *with all thy willpower [dianoia]*." Loving God with all our willpower is never mentioned in the Old Testament.[2] Why?

Jesus exhorts us New Testament believers to "love Him with all our supernatural willpower" because we *now* have something that the Old Testament believers did not have—the indwelling power of the Holy Spirit.[3]

We have the authority and the power of the indwelling Spirit to enable us to live in complete obedience to God's Will. The Old Testament saints had the Spirit of God leading them, guiding them and coming alongside them, but He never "indwelt" them as He does us. The Spirit of God is the one that gives us the power and the authority to become one will with God.

Key to Our Christian Walk

Scripture tells us that when we are "born again" we not only receive a new spirit and a new heart, but we also receive a new supernatural willpower (*dianoia*)[4]. This new willpower gives us the authority and the power to set our self aside and choose God's Will, even when we don't want to, don't feel like it, or don't think it will work. This is why our new willpower is the *key* to our whole Christian walk—it's what enables us to put God's Life from our hearts into our lives, regardless of how we feel, what we think or what we desire.

We have a constant choice as to whom we yield our members. Will we yield them to God and His Will, or will we yield them to "self" to do our own will? It's our willpower—moment by moment—that determines whose life will be lived in our souls—either God's or our own. (See **Charts 5** and **6,** pages 159 and 161.)

Romans 6:12-13 instructs, "Let not sin therefore reign in your mortal body, that ye should obey it in the lusts thereof. Neither yield ye your members as instruments of unrighteousness unto sin: but yield yourselves unto God, as those that are alive from the dead, and your members as instruments of righteousness unto God."

Verse 16 declares, "Know ye not, that to whom ye yield yourselves servants to obey, his servants ye are to whom ye obey; whether of sin unto death, or of obedience unto righteousness?" And verse 19, "... for as ye have yielded your members servants to uncleanness and to iniquity unto iniquity; even so now yield your members servants to righteousness unto holiness."

God has all the Love, all the Wisdom, and all the Power we need. The choice, however, to be a cleansed vessel through which He can work these things, is always ours.

Contrary Choices (See **Chart 4**, page 149)

As we discussed in Chapter 10, our willpower has two parts: 1) We have *God's supernatural Will and Power*, where God counsels us as to what His Will is, and then gives us the supernatural Power to perform that Will in our lives; and 2) We have *our own free choice*, where we have the authority to choose what God has shown us and depend upon His ability and power to perform it in our lives, or we can go by our own desires and trust in our own ability to perform those desires.

Supernatural willpower is the authority and power of God to make a *contrary choice*. What's a contrary choice? It's *a choice that goes against what we naturally think, feel, and desire*. That's why I call it a "contrary choice." A contrary choice is simply a faith choice or a non-feeling choice. It's a choice to walk by faith and not by sight.

We are so programmed to "feel" everything we choose. And when we don't "feel" our choices, we don't think they're genuine. However, in God's Kingdom this does not have to be the case. Born-again believers are the only ones who possess a supernatural ability to go against "self." And the reason is, *we are the only ones who possess a supernatural power within us to perform something different than what we naturally think, feel, and desire.*

Certainly, non-believers have a choice to decide what they want to do. But, none of them has the authority to choose to go against how they feel, what they think, and what they desire because they don't possess a supernatural power within them to perform anything different than what they think, feel, and want. Therefore, they don't really have any other choice but to follow what their self life is telling them to do (i.e., "go with the flow").

However, Christians don't have to be carried on by the "tide of emotion" like non-believers, because we have God's authority, not only to choose what He desires—regardless of how we feel—but we also have His power to perform that will in our lives—regardless of how we feel.

"Not My Will, but Thine"

As Christians we can be honest with God and confess, "I don't want to love this person anymore. I don't want to forgive this person. I hate this person right now. I don't feel Your Presence. I am doubtful that You are leading me to do this. I don't understand what You are doing. I am fearful of what is going to happen. But, I don't want to follow what these thoughts and emotions are telling me. I want to follow what You want me to do. So, by faith, I give these negative thoughts to You for I know I have Your authority to say, like Jesus did in Matthew 26:39, 'Not my will [not my natural feelings and desires], but Thine.'" Then I can know, by faith, that I am a cleansed vessel and that God has been freed to perform His Will in and through me.

Our new supernatural willpower is simply God's authority to choose His Will over our own thoughts, emotions, and desires (our self life), no matter how we feel, what we think, or what we desire. To me, this is the most incredible gift of all. I don't have to "feel" my choices; I just have to be willing to make those choices. God then does the rest.

Example: I Love You More Than the Carpeting

About five years ago, we had our "dream house" remodeled. We actually moved out of the house and gutted it. There was only one bedroom, one bathroom, and a back porch left to live in during the remodeling.

The remodeling job was supposed to take only about six months. The contractor had promised that it would be finished by October 31. But, like many remodeling jobs, it wasn't actually finished until the middle of December. I was planning on having ten people stay with us for Christmas, beginning December 22. It was going to be a pretty big job to move all the furniture back into the house, put up the Christmas tree and all the decorations, and prepare the rooms for the guests in such a short period of time.

Finally, on December 19, the house was finished. The workers said they would help me move the furniture back into the rooms because Chuck was away working. I had become very close friends with the builder, the head contractor, and all the helpers. After all, we had "lived together" for eight months. I especially liked Red, the head contractor. We had long conversations about God. None of the workers knew God personally, so I had many opportunities to witness, not only with words, but with my life.

That last day, however, everyone's tempers were very short. The men were all eager to wrap everything up and get home for Christmas. In our haste, many things began to go wrong:

First, I had stored all my furniture in a storeroom off the garage and had placed all my precious valuables (crystal, china, pictures, etc.) on top of the furniture, because I knew I would be the one moving it all back in the house. When all four guys began to move the furniture, they were moving everything so quickly I couldn't get the precious valuables off the furniture fast enough. I asked them to stop and give me five minutes so I could move all the breakables into the closest bedroom. I quickly laid all my pictures, crystal, china, and other valuables all over the bedroom floor because there wasn't time nor room to put them neatly on the closet shelves.

Then I went back and continued to move the furniture with the men. When we finished moving everything, I went back to the bedroom to pick up the breakables. As I opened the door, I found two painters inside with an extra long aluminum ladder. I found out they had gone in and out of that room several times to paint the outside patio. In order to get to the patio, they had stepped in and around all my precious things all over the floor. When they told me what they had done, I nearly died. Talk about "bulls in a china shop!" Combat boots, aluminum ladders and crystal don't go together!

Next, the wallpaper man came to hang the last two strips of wallpaper in my kitchen. Going back to where he had stored the leftover wallpaper the night before, he found that the "gutter" people (drain pipe people) had come in, thought it was trash, and had walked all over the stored wallpaper. Needless to say, I was furious. This now meant I had to re-order two more rolls of wallpaper; and, of course, my kitchen would not be finished for Christmas!

Lastly, Red, my favorite contractor, decided to spray the living room fireplace with black paint (without putting anything down for protection)! We had just laid brand-new white berber carpeting in the living room the night before, and I had spent two hours that morning dusting and waxing my white upholstered furniture that had been stored for eight months. As I came into the living room, having just heard about my wallpaper being ruined, I saw a cloud of "black mist" settling down all over my white upholstery and carpet. I ran to the coffee table, put my hand over its surface, and held it up. It was solid black!

How would you have responded at this point? Would you have screamed and yelled and told them all to get out and that they were all idiots? I sure felt like it! By worldly standards I would have been justified. What they had done was stupid and careless! But, if I had done that, the witness I had so carefully tried to "live" the past eight months would have been destroyed. In that split second (in my mind) I turned to God and I told Him how angry and upset I was. But I also told Him that I didn't want to act out of my anger and ruin what He had done in their hearts. So I gave Him my wild feelings and negative thoughts, and I asked Him for His Counsel as to how I should respond.

I looked at Red and the Holy Spirit prompted me to say, "Red, I am really upset and angry now because there is black paint spray all over my living room carpet and furniture. I know this job could have been done three days ago when there was no furniture or carpeting in here. But I want you to know something, *I love you more than the furniture and the carpeting!*" And, with that, I just turned around and quietly began to clean up the mess.

When we really do give our circumstances to God, He comes up with the most creative and ingenious solutions! I never would have thought of that response myself. And I'm so glad God helped me hold my tongue because all the other guys, who had been standing around watching the whole scene, began shaking their heads at Red and calling him names. I didn't need to say a thing because they called him much better names than I ever could have come up with!

Again, we don't have to "feel" our choices, we just have to be willing to make them. God does the rest! It's only our "contrary choices" that will allow us to experience God's Life through us, in spite of everything that is going on.

Everyone always wants to know what happened to my white carpeting and upholstery in that house? Well, they were both a little gray for the remainder of our stay there. But, as you recall, this is the house that we eventually lost through bankruptcy.

God's Authority and Power

Our new, supernatural willpower is not only God's authority to choose His Will over our own negative thoughts, emotions, and desires (self life), it's also His power and ability to carry out and perform that will in our lives.

Philippians 2:13 declares, "For it is God Which worketh in you both to will and to do."[5]

I'm convinced that our supernatural willpower holds the "*keys to the Kingdom.*" If you remember Matthew 16:19, Jesus promises, "I will give unto thee the keys of the kingdom of heaven: and whatsoever thou shalt *bind* on earth shall be bound in heaven: and whatsoever thou shalt *loose* on earth shall be loosed in heaven."[6] (emphasis added)

We always associate this Scripture with the enemy (binding and loosing him by the Holy Spirit). But, in the personal sense, to bind literally means to "prohibit or forbid self" and to loose means to "permit or to allow self."

Check this out for yourself, but to me this Scripture is saying that we possess the authority and the power (by God's supernatural willpower within us) to choose to either "forbid self" (choosing to relinquish, surrender, and set self aside) and walk after the Spirit, or we have the authority and the power to "allow self" (choosing to let self reign) and walk after the flesh.

Exousia

We have the delegated authority and power of God to "relinquish ourselves" and do as God wants, or we can "hold on to ourselves" and do what we please. The Greek word for this "free choice" decision is *exousia*. *Exousia* means "it is permitted." In other words, we have the authority or the word of the person in charge, and we also have the power and the ability of the person in charge to make this kind of a choice.

Jesus states in John 10:17-18, "Therefore doth My Father love Me, because I lay down My life, that I might take it again. No man taketh it from Me, but I lay it down of Myself. I have power [*exousia*] to lay it down, and I have power to take it again."

If we are Christians, this means we have the authority and the Word of God, who is the Person in charge of us. We also have the ability and the Power of God, who is again the Person in charge of us. So God is the one who enables us and gives us the authority to override our own negative thoughts, feelings, and desires [i.e., to "forbid self"], and to say, like Jesus did, "Not my will [my own emotional desires], but Thine." (Matthew 26:39)

[Note: Take another look at **Chart 4**, page 149, and see how the Bronze Pillars, which represent our free choice (9), are on an even higher level than the Inner Court (which is our soul (4): our conscious thoughts, emotions, and desires). To me, this symbolizes that we do have God's supernatural authority and power to override anything our souls are telling us to do and to forbid that self.]

Our Free Choice

Born again believers, because of the power of the indwelling Spirit of God, are the *only* ones who have this free choice decision. We have the authority and power of God to follow His Will regardless of what we naturally think, feel, or want to do. Again, nonbelievers have a choice to decide what they want to do. However, none of them has the authority to choose to go against how they feel or what they think because they don't possess a supernatural power within them to perform anything different than what they feel and think. Therefore, they really don't have a free choice! They really don't have any other choice but to "allow self" and to follow what their own thoughts, emotions, and desires are telling them.[7]

These people, even though they might desperately want to change and not follow their own emotions and desires, can't make those "contrary choices" because they don't possess the supernatural power within them to do so. Romans 7:18 tells us "to will is present within [each of us]," but "how to perform that which is good" is not.

In other words, we all—believers and nonbelievers alike—can choose. We all can make contrary choices. But only Christians have the supernatural power and ability within them to be able to carry out and perform those contrary choices in their lives!

God Changes Our Feelings

What is so exciting about choosing God's Will over our own desires is that He changes our feelings and our thoughts to match the faith choices we have made. In other words, in His timing God aligns our feelings with our choices.

So we are *not* responsible to change our negative feelings and thoughts. There is no way we can do that! We are only responsible to put in charge the Person who *can* change our feelings, and that's God. And we do that by loving (*agapao*) God and by being willing to make contrary choices. God then is the One who will align our feelings with our choices and make us genuine.

Mark 9:24 validates this, "Lord, I believe; [now] help Thou mine unbelief." In another words, "Lord, I choose to believe by faith what You promise [contrary choice], now I trust You to make my feelings align with that choice."

Example: Rats, Spiders and Insects

My friend Leona is a good example of one who learned to make contrary choices. Leona is a missionary in Bangkok, Thailand. The first year she was there was absolute misery for her. She was allergic to much of the new food and she would get violently ill every time she ate any of it. She also hated the hot, sticky, and muggy weather, the huge spiders and insects, and the abundance of rats and crawling vermin that infested most of the buildings.

In addition to these problems, Leona didn't know the Thai language, so she was extremely lonely. Moreover, she had no permanent church home, so there was no one for her to turn to for spiritual help except, of course, the Lord. Over and over again by faith and not feelings, she made those "contrary choices." Continually, she chose to give God her own self-centered thoughts and emotions about her new environment, rather than be consumed by them. As a result, He eventually aligned her feelings with what she had so faithfully chosen. (I think it took nine months.)

Now, it's so special to hear her say, when she is visiting the United States, "I can't wait to get home to Thailand. I miss my friends, the food and yes, even the weather."

Contrary choices really do work! Someone recently called it "the habit of choice." And I think that's very appropriate!

Our responsibility is only to make those faith choices; God then is the one who will change our thoughts and emotions and make us genuine.

A Holding Pattern

Sometimes there is a period of days or weeks where we must walk by faith, without feeling it. I call this my "holding pattern." It's that period of time before my feelings are aligned with my choices. It's the same thing as if we were shot with an arrow. We can remove the arrow right away (by our choices), but the process of healing (to where we actually "feel" healed) takes time. It seems the amount of time the healing process takes depends upon how deep the wound is. The deeper the hurt, the longer the process takes for us to "feel" that victory.

Example: The Other Woman

I have a dear friend, Rose, who found out that her husband, Daryl, was having an affair with a nurse at his office. When the nurse became pregnant, Daryl decided to leave Rose and marry the nurse.

Obviously, Rose was consumed with hatred, bitterness, and resentment towards both of them, totally justified by worldly standards. God, however, wouldn't let Rose wade in her own "pity party" very long. Since Daryl was allowed by the courts to come over once a week to see the children, Rose was forced to continually deal with her own negative thoughts and feelings. Daryl was not a Christian and Rose wanted more than anything else for him to come to the Lord. So it was imperative that she not act out of her own hurts, but totally out of God's Love.

Rose continually had to choose to give her real feelings to God and unconditionally forgive Daryl and the "other woman." Repeatedly, she asked God to give her His Love for both of them. She certainly didn't feel like making any of these choices; nevertheless, she knew that God would be faithful to His promises. So she continued, by faith, to choose His Will.

Several years went by, and Rose never had to see or meet her ex-husband's new wife. Five years ago, however, Daryl's oldest son by a previous marriage decided to get married. The boy had always felt especially close to Rose so he called her and asked if he could have the wedding reception at her house.

Rose, too, had always loved her step son. So after much prayer and seeking God, she said yes, she would be delighted to have the reception at her home. This meant, of course, that not only Daryl would be coming, but also his new wife.

All of Rose's friends and relatives told her she was crazy to have the reception at her house. By worldly standards, they were right. However, Rose was convinced God wanted her to host it. She told her relatives she was going to trust God to give her the love and the compassion that she would need when she finally came face to face with Daryl and his new wife.

The day eventually came. When the doorbell rang, there stood Daryl and his wife. Much to Rose's own amazement, she reached out in genuine Love, put her arms around the woman and genuinely welcomed her in. Rose said later that the incredible part about the whole thing was that she meant it with all her heart. She said, "Nancy, it was a miracle. I didn't experience any of my old hatred or bitterness for this woman. All I felt for her was God's Love and His forgiveness."

In actuality, Rose was instantly and completely freed the moment she made those original faith choices some years previously, but it took several years for her to be able to genuinely "feel" what she had chosen (i.e., that total forgiveness).

Total or Partial Forgiveness

A precious sister wrote me not too long ago and asked, "Is there such a thing as giving only part of the problem to God?"

A hurtful situation had occurred in her life over and over again. She had chosen to forgive this person many times. But even after forgiving him, she said her hurt feelings were still there, and the situation continued to make her sad.

Later, when a similar incident occurred, she said it was so much harder to come around again to forgive this person. She said, "I must not be forgiving him with my whole being." In other words, she felt she was only giving him partial forgiveness, not total forgiveness, because she continued to feel bitterness and resentment towards him.

I believe this is an issue that we all wrestle with and not one unique to my friend. I wrote back to her that only God can change our feelings. I agreed with her that when we have a hurtful situation that occurs over and over again, it is difficult to forgive, knowing the same thing will probably happen all over again.

However, our only responsibility is to love God—to stay that open and cleansed vessel that He can use.[8] Then, He will enable us to love those difficult people in our lives. I know that if we do our part—love God and unconditionally forgive 70 times seven—God then will be faithful to do His part: once again giving us His Love and His Forgiveness and enabling us to respond correctly. At the same time, God will teach us how to walk in love "wisely," perhaps avoiding the pitfalls that keep getting us into the same hurtful situation.

Hal Lindsey once told me, "Just because we still think about that hurtful situation and the person involved doesn't mean we haven't forgiven him." Thinking about a past situation and being totally consumed with it are two different things. This advice has really helped me with various circumstances in my own life.

Our only responsibility is to be willing to make contrary choices (faith choices) to forgive that person and to love God. *God is the One who is responsible for changing our feelings* (taking the hurts completely away) and eventually enabling us to feel total forgiveness and the healing of that situation.

Healing Is a Process

Again, this whole business of being transformed into God's Image is a process, and that process takes time. It's a process that is made up of a million choices. Our "victory" in Christ is not just making one choice and thinking we're healed but making many, many choices. *It seems the deeper the hurt, the longer the process takes for God to align our feelings with the choice we have made* and for us to "feel" that victory. Actually God takes the things we give Him the moment we release them to Him, but often our feelings don't align with that choice for a while.[9]

It's God's prerogative when He allows us to "feel" the victory. He often allows a lapse in time to strengthen our faith and to see if we will walk "without feeling" anything. Of course, Satan wants to use this time lapse to confuse us, discourage us, and to whisper in our ear, "God is not faithful and it doesn't work for you." Satan wants us to take those negative thoughts back in, mull them over, and bury them once again.

After a painful circumstance, the first day is sometimes emotionally stable because we are fresh, and we know to choose God's way over our own. When night comes, however, we often take those hurtful thoughts and feelings back in by mulling them over and over and reliving the incident in our heads. "She said...," "He said...," "I should have said...," etc. The next day that hurt has become anger, and then a whole other set of choices are required. And on it goes...until we finally refuse to entertain those ungodly thoughts altogether and God ultimately aligns our feelings with our choices.

In my book, *Why Should I Be the First to Change?*, I called these moment to moment choices, our "M & M's." Listen to a letter a gal wrote me recently about our constant M & M choices: "I guess you could say my life was like making fudge. I had all the ingredients in the pan, turned the burner on high, and then walked away expecting it to cook on its own. I was too busy to stir constantly. So my good intentions were always burned. My daughter and I now call each other frequently (between Arizona and California) and do our 'M & M checks' to make sure each of us is checking the fudge moment by moment and stirring it constantly."

God Has Two Kinds of Will

God basically has two kinds of Will. In the Greek, they are ***thelo***, which means His instinctive, emotional desires (that which He takes pleasure in); and ***boule***, which means His planned purposes (the resolve of His Mind). Of course for God, both these kinds of Will are "perfect."

Since we are created in the Image of God, we, too, have two kinds of will. In the Greek, they are ***thelema*** which means our own natural, emotional desires from our soul (things we take pleasure in), and ***boulomai*** which means our "disciplined willing," or our choices free of any emotion (where we depend totally upon God's supernatural Will and Power within us).

In other words, we have two choices. We can either make an *emotional choice* (*thelema*) and be carried away on the tide of emotion by our own uncontrolled feelings, negative thoughts, and self-centered desires (just like an unbeliever); or we can make a *faith choice* (*boulomai*), where we make a disciplined choice (contrary choice) free of any emotion, to follow what God is prompting us to do and then rely upon His Strength to perform it in our lives.

We must remember that our emotional choices, because they are felt and experienced, are much stronger in intensity than our faith choices. These are the kind of choices we "want" to follow and we "want" to do. However, we must remind ourselves that our emotional choices will continue to keep us right in the grip of Satan's power of sin and in total bondage to our flesh.

In contrast, our faith choices—even though they are much harder to make because there is usually a tremendous amount of adverse or opposing emotion that goes along with making them—are the only ones that unleash all of God's Power to come to our aid. Faith choices are the only choices that will set us free from ourselves, free from our circumstances, and free from others' responses.

Our Faith Choices (See Chart 5, page 159)

When we make a contrary choice (or a faith choice) to follow God's Will—no matter what—**Chart 5** is what we look like. This is what walking "after the Spirit" means. We have made the appropriate faith choices (9), no matter how we feel, what we think, or what we desire, to allow God's Life from our hearts (7) to be manifested in our souls (4). God's Love (11) in our hearts has become our love (12) in our souls,

His Thoughts (13) in our hearts have become our thoughts (14), and His Will (8), our will (16). At this point, we are Spirit filled (17) and it's Christ's Image (God's Character) that we are portraying to the world and not our own.

Freed From the Power of Sin

Notice we are, at this moment, freed from the power of sin. We are freed from sin because our self life has been set aside, prohibited, and given over to God. Therefore, note on **Chart 5** that Satan has no control over us at that moment because there are no holes (no vulnerabilities) left for him to get his hands on.[10]

Romans 6:7 makes clear, "For he that is dead [he who has crucified the self life or forbidden the self] is freed from sin."

Our uncontrolled thoughts are reined in, our wild emotions are controlled and set aside, and our self-centered desires have been yielded.[11] For the time being, God has brought up all He wants to show us from our hidden chambers, and we have responded by dealing with it. God's Life from our hearts can now freely come forth and fill our souls. Obviously, there will be many more things in the hidden chambers that God will want to deal with at a future time.

Faith Choices Need to Be a Habit

Be aware as we begin this new inner adventure with God that it will take a while for this new way of thinking and choosing to become established. We must learn to make a habit of making faith choices, just as it has been a habit all our lives to make emotional choices. For years we haven't even thought about the choices we've made; we've just reacted and done what we've felt like. So realize it's going to take some time to re-establish new habit patterns.

Our old habit patterns and conditioned responses are so automatic by now that they are very comfortable to make. After all, we have been thinking and choosing this way for years. These new "supernatural responses" are going to be foreign and unfamiliar. So don't expect an easy or a quick transition.[12] Be sure to persevere, however. Don't let the enemy dissuade you. God is faithful and He promises to set us free, if we do our part.

We must learn to think first. We don't want to just "react" anymore. We need to think and then respond the way God would have us to do. I promise you, after repeated use, this new way of thinking and choosing *will* become first nature.

A friend called a few weeks ago. She has been drowning in physical pain for almost a year, with very little relief. She said, "Nancy, I am hurting so badly I don't even want to make the right choice."

I identified with her and said, "I know what you mean, I've been there myself! But, dear friend, you *don't* have to "want to" make the right choice, but just "be willing to" make the right choice. It will still be genuine. 'Not wanting to' is the same thing as 'not feeling like' making the right choice. God never said we had to want to or feel like making that choice; He just said we must be willing to make that choice."

[Note: People often ask me, "If I really didn't mean the choice I made, is it still genuine to God? Is it real to Him?" What they are really asking is, because they didn't feel that choice, will it still count to God? Again, I believe "meaning it" is the same as "feeling it." They didn't feel it; therefore, they thought they didn't mean it. God's answer to all of this is, "*it's by faith and not feelings.*"

Isaiah 1:19 promises, "If ye be *willing and obedient*, ye shall eat of the good of the land" (emphasis added). It doesn't say here, "if you feel willing," it just says *be willing!* Our faith choice is saying, "I don't want to, I don't feel like it, I don't understand it; nevertheless, I am willing!"

Classic Example: Did You Tell Him Off?

One Christmas we rented a house at Lake Tahoe for two weeks. Our intention was to be totally alone—just our family. What a dream. We would be together for two whole weeks, playing games and reading. I could even work on my upcoming speech for a new class I was teaching. I couldn't wait! My own mom and dad were visiting my brother in San Francisco, and we could have easily invited them down to Tahoe for a few days. But Chuck had said no, this was to be our own special vacation—just our family—with no outside intrusions.

One fabulous week went by. Our family never seemed closer. There was no T.V. and no outside influences to disturb our unity. We all read, talked, lay around and did our own thing. It was absolutely wonderful!

Then one morning, out of the blue, Chuck announces to all of us, "I hope you don't mind, but I have invited a business associate and his wife up here to join us for a few days." Well, you could have knocked me over dead. Chuck is the one who had made such a big deal about having no outside interferences! If I had known he would allow company, I would have had my own folks over!

"How long are these business people going to stay?" I asked. "Well, as long as they want, I guess," he responded. He had actually left the invitation open ended! At that moment, in the flesh I could have killed him! I was so angry!

Here we weren't supposed to have anything or anyone disturb our privacy, and now we're not only having an outsider over (someone I had never even met), but they were staying for who knows how long! I just couldn't believe Chuck would do something like that. I needn't tell you how I wrestled with anger and bitterness towards him. Wouldn't you have reacted the same way?

Later, when I was sharing this story in one of my seminars, someone stood up right in the middle of the story and asked, "Well, Nancy, did you tell Chuck off right then and there?"

I said to this precious sister, "You know, it's our natural human tendency to immediately tell the other person how we feel, but that's not always what God would have us do. No, I didn't tell Chuck off right then, and there were two good reasons why I didn't. 1) Chuck had already extended an invitation to this couple, so it was already a fact that they were coming, and I couldn't do anything about it by throwing a tantrum; and 2) I wasn't a clean vessel. I was full of my own wild emotions and uncontrolled thoughts. I had to first deal with my own anger and resentment before I could take a stand in God's Love with Chuck."

[Remember: We said in Chapter 5 that if we confront that other person in our emotional state of mind, we will force him to respond from his defenses and not his heart. His "walls" will go up and nothing at all will be accomplished. This certainly would have been true with Chuck. He would have just said something like, "Tough luck, Baby, that's the way it's going to be."]

Later, when I was clean (after I had confessed and given all my feelings to God) and my emotions were back in place, I did tell Chuck in Love how disappointed I was that he had gone against what he had promised for our vacation. I know he heard because all the kids went to him and shared the very same thing.

So, there's definitely a time when we can share how we really feel, but we must make sure it's done in God's Love and His Character and in His timing and not our own. Otherwise, we'll end up deeper in the pits than when we started.

Anyway, I had to choose, over and over again, every time the negative thoughts swept over me, to give them to God before they would consume and bury me.

The day after Christmas, we heard from the couple that they were on their way. In order to prepare for their arrival we had to rearrange the children's rooms so the guests could have a room of their own, make a special trip to the grocery store and clean the house particularly well. So much energy and fuss goes into having company, especially when they are business acquaintances and you don't really know them. These were all things I wouldn't normally have to do on a vacation.

I will never forget the day they arrived! Our girls were watching for them out the window and all of a sudden they yelled, "Mom, here they are! And Mom, *they have brought all of their kids*!" At that moment, if Chuck had been close enough, I would have murdered him! This now made 12 people to feed three times a day, clean up after, and entertain on "my" vacation!

I can't tell you the number of times I went to the Lord, frustrated and crying, saying, "You know I came up here to work on my speech for the next *Way of Agape* seminar, and now I can't!" And you know what the Lord would always answer? "I want you to work on the material for your next seminar, but I want you to "live" it first! I am giving you a perfect living opportunity to glorify Me and be full of My Life to these people." I told God I'd much rather "write" about it than "live" it!

I had to make a continual choice as to which way I would go. I could make an emotional choice (allow self) and follow what my anger, resentment, and bitterness (self life) kept telling me to do, which was to tell Chuck off, put on a smiling "front" for the guests, and get rid of them as soon as possible so I could work on my *Agape* studies! (Ha Ha!) <u>Or</u>, I could make a faith choice (forbid self) and follow what God was telling me to do, which was to give Him my hurts and anger, and know that He would give me the Love and the patience and the strength I needed to genuinely love Chuck and these new people.

Don't let me kid you—it wasn't easy! Making choices you don't feel, and es-pecially ones you don't want to make, is extremely difficult. On top of that, going out and "doing" what God has told you to do, especially before He has aligned your feelings with those choices, is even more difficult. But as I kept choosing over and over again to follow God and to go His Way, He was faithful to His promises. He took away my anger and resentment, and He filled me with His Love, not only for Chuck, but also for these people.

The business associate and his wife turned out to be a delightful Jewish couple, full of fun. They taught us some Hebrew and answered many of our questions about the Old Testament. We really had a marvelous four days with them. It was in this unexpected special time that God sparked the idea for the study *Be Ye Transformed* on God's Mind.

Can you imagine the impression I would have made on these people if I had not chosen to love (*agapao*) and follow God? I would have been full of my own hurts and bitterness, with a smile plastered over my face, pretending to be happy and glad they were there, a "phony-baloney Christian." You know they would have felt it.

"... ye are like unto whited sepulchres, which indeed appear beautiful outward, but are within full of dead men's bones, and of all uncleanness." (Matthew 23:27)

Faith choices or contrary choices are the only ones that unleash all of God's Power to come to our aid, and they are the only ones that can free us from ourselves.

"At Thy Word, I Will"

It will continually be our choice which way we will go. We should try to please God by saying, "I am willing to do what You ask me, simply because I know You love me and I know that You are faithful to keep Your Promises." (It's okay to say under your breath, "I don't see how You are going to do this, but nevertheless I'm willing to choose to follow You!")

Luke 5:5 is a great Scripture for this. After Peter has spent all night setting his own nets and not catching a thing, Jesus comes along and says to him, "Set your nets." Peter was probably thinking, "I've tried that all night long and it hasn't worked," but nevertheless, he willingly and obediently replies to Jesus: "*At Thy word, I will.*"

That needs to be our response also. "I don't want to, I don't feel like it, and I don't think it will work; nevertheless, "at Thy word, I will"! This response is the only thing that releases the power of the Holy Spirit and the situation into God's hands.

Our Emotional Choices (See Chart 6, page 161)

When we make emotional choices to follow what we want, think, and desire, **Chart 6** is what we will look like. This is what "walking after the flesh" means. We are at this moment allowing the *power of sin* (23) to control us rather than the *Power of God* (24). In other words, we have chosen to follow our own thoughts, emotions, and desires (our self life) (10), over what God is prompting us to do (8). God's Spirit has been quenched (18), and His eternal Life (7) cannot flow into our souls. Ephesians 4:30 states, "Grieve not the holy Spirit of God, whereby ye are sealed unto the day of redemption."

Notice, here on **Chart 6**, we still have a new spirit (1), a new heart (2) and a new willpower (3), but because we have emotionally chosen (9) to follow our own thoughts and emotions (self life) (10) instead of God's voice, we have quenched His Life within.

Wide-Open Prey For the Enemy

We are, at that moment, pleasing self and not God, which then opens us up to the arrows of the enemy. We are vulnerable and wide-open prey because our emotions are uncontrolled, our thoughts wild, and our desires totally self-centered. We have obviously given the enemy many holes to attack and many handles to grab hold of. On top of this, many things from our hidden chambers (6) (that we haven't given over to God) are also popping up, again giving Satan a perfect inroad for his strongholds (his cords of sin).[13]

Our self life, at this point, has taken over. We walk saying we are Christians and, yet, are manifesting our *own* thoughts, emotions, and desires and not God's Life at all. This not only grieves God, but it also gives a false witness to others.

We obviously don't need to give examples of this kind of choice, because every one of us is very familiar with this way of reacting. The result of this choice, however, is that we become a double-minded or a "twice souled" Christian—a Christian who is living two lives. God's supernatural Life is still in our hearts, but the life that is coming forth from our soul is "self life," our own thoughts and emotions, and not God's Life at all.

This double-mindedness is what a carnal Christian fights continuously. He still has God's Spirit energizing God's new supernatural Life in his heart, but he has chosen to hang onto his own self-centered thoughts, emotions, and desires, thereby quenching God's Life in him and showing forth his own "self life" (the old man) instead.

Whose Life Will Be Lived in Your Soul?

Again, our choices are critical because they decide whose life will be lived in our souls. Faith choices allow God's Life to flow from our hearts out into our lives; emotional choices quench God's Life. Jeremiah 21:8 explains this, "Behold, I set before you [continually] the way of life [faith choices], and the way of death [emotional choices]."[14] Which one are you going to choose, power of life or death?

It all comes down to our choice: Are you willing to set aside what you think, what you want, and what you feel to do what God wants? Or, will you yield to your own self-centered thoughts, emotions, and desires?

Our Choice Is Where Sin Begins

A woman in one of my seminars said to me, "I see and recognize the choices I have to make, but I keep blowing it." In other words, she was aware of her choices, but she wasn't able to let God perform those choices through her. I told her, "Hey Pat, don't be discouraged; you're doing great! At least you are recognizing your choices! Two weeks ago, you weren't even aware you had a choice to make. First, you must learn you have a choice to make, then you can learn just *how* to make it."

So the battle between the Spirit and the flesh is either won or lost, moment by moment, in the area of our willpower. In other words, our choice is where sin begins. Our choice to follow our own emotions, thoughts, and desires over what God is prompting is what quenches God's Spirit and becomes sin.

Remember Romans 14:23: "Whatever [choice] is not of faith is sin," and also, James 4:17: "To him that knoweth to do good, and doeth it not [chooses not to do it], to him it is sin."

Any choice, any unwillingness to obey God, causes the door of our hearts to slam on God—and that is sin.[15] Remember, having the original bad thought is not sinning.

We are human, and we will have ungodly thoughts until we see Jesus. The sin enters when we choose to follow what that negative thought is prompting us to do over what God is telling us to do! We sin and are separated from God,[16] when we "entertain and mull over" those thoughts rather than immediately giving them over to God. This is where the Spirit gets quenched, the sin begins, and the self life takes over.

We Can't Improve Our "Self Life"

A young woman called not too long ago who shared she was so discouraged by the seeming lack of progress in her Christian walk. She thought the longer she was a Christian, the less self-centered she would become, but, she said, it just wasn't happening that way. In other words, she thought with time she could "improve her self life."

I told her to move over, that she was just like the rest of us. I told her, "whether we have been a Christian one year or 51 years, *our self life will never improve with age*! It's still just as ugly and as self-centered now as it was the first day we believed." *We can't tame our self life, we have to kill it* (crucify it—annihilate it).

The mature Christian is simply one that recognizes his self life and makes the appropriate choices to give it over to God. "Maturity" to me is not knowing an abundance of theological facts, going to church regularly, teaching Bible studies or even writing books, but is simply making the right faith choices to cleanse ourselves of all that God shows us is sin, so that His Life can come forth from our hearts.

Hebrews 5:14 is fascinating in this light. It states, "Strong meat belongeth to them that are of full age [mature]...who by reason of use have their senses exercised to discern both good and evil."

In other words, the people who are mature are the ones who are constantly watching for and recognizing their sin. They are mature only because they know how to make faith choices ("by reason of use") to give their "self life" over to God.

We Need to Exchange Lives

As Christians we don't want to "improve," "patch up," or "fix" our self life. That's psychology! *We don't want to be a better "us" (self). We want to learn how to set that self aside so Jesus can live His Life through us.*

So the point is not that we are to "copy" or imitate Jesus' Life; rather, we are simply to *exchange lives with Him*! We give Him our life; He then gives us His.

"I am crucified with Christ: nevertheless I live; yet not I, but Christ liveth in me: and the life which I now live in the flesh I live by the faith of the Son of God, Who loved me, and gave Himself for me." (Galatians 2:20)

God's Will or Self Will: That's the Question

Being transformed into Christ's image all boils down to a continual choice. Either we allow God to will His Will through us—that which is pleasing to Him, or we will our own will—that which is pleasing to us. God's Will or self will, that's the question. Are you willing to lay down all you want, think, and feel, to do what God desires? Are you willing to choose God's Will at any cost?

Loving God with all our willpower is the *key* to our walking by the Spirit. It's binding our wills with God's and becoming one will with Him no matter what. It's saying, "I don't feel like it, I don't understand it, and I don't want to, but nevertheless, not my will, but Thine. I know I have Your authority to make this kind of contrary choice because I know I have Your Power in me to perform it in my life."

Because of the power of the indwelling Spirit, Christians are the only truly free people if they so choose to be—free from our selves, free from other's responses, free from our circumstances, and free from Satan's control! *This is what Calvary was all about!*

2 Corinthians 3:17 states, "where the Spirit of the Lord is, there is liberty [freedom]." That freedom comes in the form of a constant choice!

Endnotes:

1. "Strength" means intensely or completely or wholly.

2. Proverbs 3:5 says, "Lean not unto thine own understanding" (*biynah* or wisdom). The Old Testament saints, however, could not help but "lean on their own understanding," since they did not have the indwelling Spirit of God to give them God's supernatural Wisdom.

3. Ephesians 1:17-19; 4:23

4. Hebrews 8:10 and 10:16 (always be sure to check the Greek)

5. 1 Corinthians 7:37

6. Matthew 18:18

7. Ephesians 4: 17-18

8. See Chapter 8.

9. See Chapter 13, "Strongholds of the Enemy."

10. John 14:30

11. Romans 6:13

12. Luke 5:30

13. Romans 6:12

14. Deuteronomy 30:19-20

15. Revelation 3:7

16. See Chapter 11, "What Is Sin" and "Nothing Shall Separate Us."

Scriptural References:

Chapter 12

How Do We Become One Will With God? (Matthew 22:37)
A. *Dianoia* is the Greek word for *willpower*
    1. *Dianoia* is our will and the power to perform it
    2. *Dianoia* means channel (*dia*) of the mind (*noya*)
    3. *Dianoia* is not the mind (*nous*) itself, but only two functions of it—
        our will and the power to perform that will. Thus, I like to call *dianoia*
        our willpower, so there will be no confusion between it and our mind
        itself
B. The *Shema*
    1. God commands the Old Testament saints to love Him with all their
        heart, soul, and strength (Deuteronomy 6:5)
    2. No willpower (*dianoia*) is mentioned
    3. Yet, when Jesus quotes the *Shema* in Matthew 22:37, He adds "love
        God with all your willpower"
        a. We now have something new to love God with
        b. Something the Old Testament saints did not have—the indwelling
            power of the Holy Spirit
            . This indwelling gives us the supernatural *will and power of*
               God
            . The ability of God to choose His Will regardless of how we feel,
               what we think, or what the circumstances are
C. When we were born again, we received not only a *new* spirit and a *new*
    heart (Ezekiel 36:26), but also a *new supernatural willpower.* (See the
    Greek in Hebrews 8:10; 10:16.)
    1. Our willpower has two parts:
        a. God's supernatural Will and Power, where He shows us what His
            Will is and then gives us the supernatural Power to perform that
            Will
        b. Our own free choice, where we have authority to either choose
            God's Will and trust in His Power to perform it or choose to
            follow what we think, want, and desire
    2. What is supernatural willpower?
        a. It is God's authority and power to choose to follow God's Will, regard-
            less of how we feel or what we think (Philippians 2:13; Matthew 26:
            39; 1 Peter 4:2)
        b. It's a *contrary choice*, a choice that goes against what we naturally
            think, feel, and want to do. It's a choice to walk totally by faith, not
            sight (Mark 9:24). Jesus had the same authority (John 10:18)
    3. What is the purpose of our supernatural willpower?
        a. It determines whose life will be lived in our soul: God's or our own
            (Jeremiah 21:8; Psalm 119:109a; Deuteronomy 30:19; Proverbs 15:
            32; and, see the Greek in Romans 6:13,16; Ephesians 1:18)

      b.   The whole purpose of our supernatural willpower is for us to know God—to accept Him into our lives and to experience His Life through us (1 John 5:20; Ephesians 1:18-19)

  4.   Christians are the only ones who have supernatural willpower authority (*exousia*) (Philippians 2:23; 1 Corinthians 7:37)

      a.   *Exousia* means "it is permitted." We have the authority, or the word of the person in charge, to override our own will and do what is pleasing to God (Hebrews 13:21; Mark 9:24; John 10:17-18; Matthew 26:39; Romans 8:13; 13:1)

      b.   Christians are the only ones who have another power source within them, the Spirit of God, to perform something different from what they want, feel, and desire

      c.   Non-believers have no other choice but to follow their own self-centered thoughts, emotions, and desires (Ephesians 2:2-3; 4:17-19; Colossians 1:21; Romans 7:18)

      d.   Christians can make a *faith choice* to follow God, even though they don't understand how this kind of choice works, even if they don't feel like making it and even if they don't think it will do any good (Psalm 119:101; John 10:17-18; Luke 22:42; 1 Corinthians 7:37; Romans 7:18b)

      e.   If we are just willing, God will do the rest (Isaiah 1:19; Matthew 26:39: Philippians 2:13; John 5:30)

        .   Then He will align our feelings with our choice (Mark 9:24) in His timing

        .   He will perform that contrary choice in our lives

God Has Two Kinds of Will (*Thelo* and *Boule*)

  A.   *Thelo* is God's instinctive, emotional desires; whereas, *boule* is God's planned purposes. For God, both these kinds of will are perfect.

  B.   Because we are "created in the image of God," we also have two kinds of will or choices (*thelema* and *boulomai*) (Jeremiah 21:8; Joshua 24:15; Deuteronomy 30:15-20; 1 Kings 18:21; Romans 6:16; 7:25; 8:13; Matthew 16:19)

    1.   *Faith choices* (*boulomai*) "Not my will, but thine" (Matthew 26:39; Luke 5:5; 18:28-30; 22:42; Acts 19:21b; Philippians 2:8; Galatians 2:20; 3:11; Romans 6:6,16,18-19; 8:13) Review **Chart 5**, page 159

      a.   These are *contrary choices or non-feeling choices*

      b.   Contrary choices give the Spirit full control to "rein in" and "set aside" our own thoughts, emotions, and desires, so that God's Life can come forth (Ephesians 5:2; Galatians 5:16a; Colossians 4:5; Romans 3:22). These choices lead to intimate knowledge of God

      c.   Self-life has been "forbidden, prohibited and given over to" God, therefore God's Will becomes our will (1 John 5:14)

      d.   Single-mindedness—one life being lived

     e.   At this moment, we are freed from the power of *sin* (Romans 6:6-7; Galatians 5:24; John 14:30; 2 Corinthians 3:17)

     f.   Contrary choices bring us true freedom from self and unleashes all God's power and ability to come to our aid (Zechariah 4:6; Luke 1:45; Mark 9:23)

     g.   God then aligns our feelings with our choices (Mark 9:24)

     h.   Whatever is born of God "overcomes the world" (1 John 5:4)

2. *Emotional choices* (*thelema*) "I will" (Matthew 23:27; Luke 8:14; James 1:8; 2 Peter 2:10) Review **Chart 6**, page 161

     a.   Emotional choices give the flesh full control of our own thoughts, emotions, and desires, because they are *not* "reined in" and "set aside," but running wild. Therefore, God's Life is quenched and self life is manifested. (Joel 1:10,12; Romans 7:15,19,23) Thus, there can be no intimate knowledge of God

     b.   Self life has been "allowed and permitted," therefore, our own desires are reigning

        •   We then are hypocrites, saying one thing yet doing another (Matthew 23:24-27; Psalm 12:2; Romans 7:19)

        •   Truth of God has perished (Jeremiah 7:28)

     c.   Double-mindedness—two lives are being lived (James 1:8)

     d.   Power of sin is, at that moment, in control (Romans 7:17-21,23; Luke 11:17; John 8:34; Proverbs 5:22)

     e.   We are in bondage to self (Matthew 23:27; Romans 6:16a)

     f.   We are separated from God (Isaiah 59:2; Jeremiah 5:25; Romans 14:23; James 4:17)

Our Choice Is Where Sin Begins (Romans 14:23; James 1:14-15; 4:17)

A. Sin is a choice—a choice that *separates us from God* (Romans 6:13-14; 14:23; Isaiah 59:2)

B. The original bad thought or feeling is not sin in itself; what we choose to do about the thought determines whether we sin or not (Zechariah 8:17; Matthew 5:28)

C. Our choice to follow self over what God is prompting covers our heart and separates us from God (Psalm 17:10; Isaiah 6:10; 59:2; Acts 28:27a; Luke 8:14; Matthew 13:15; 1 Thessalonians 5:19)

D. We must continually choose to cleanse ourselves or we will not have any part of Him (John 13:8)

E. Maturity in Christ is simply knowing how to choose God's Way over our own (Hebrews 5:14; 2 Corinthians 4:10-12; Galatians 2:20)

Loving God with all our will is the *key to walking by the Spirit*. It is becoming *one will with God*, no matter how we feel, what we think, or what we desire (Deuteronomy 30:15-20) and living the rest of our lives in accord with the Will of God (1 Peter 4:2).

Chapter 13: Loving God With All Our Soul

Let's Recap

In review, loving God with all our heart is not only our born-again experience (where we become *one heart* with Him), it's also a daily experience, as we allow His Life in our heart to be the motivation for all we choose to do. Loving God with all our willpower entails making continual faith choices to obey His Will rather than our own. It's knowing we have His authority and His Power to constantly say, "Not my will, but Thine," thus allowing us to become *one will* with Him.

Loving God with all our soul encompasses an even further step. Loving God with all our soul means laying down our lives so that God's Will can be performed through them. In other words, loving God with all our soul is continually setting aside our life in action, so that God's Life—His Life from our hearts—can come forth and be manifested through us: His Love from our hearts becoming our love in our lives, His Thoughts becoming our thoughts, and His Desires, our desires. Loving God with all our soul means becoming *one Life* with Him.[1]

As we discussed in Chapter 10, our soul is essentially our conscious life—our conscious thoughts, emotions, and desires.[2] If we are born again, and if we have made the right faith choices, then our soul life will be the manifestation or the showing forth of God's Life from our hearts: God's Love, God's Thoughts, and God's Power. (Review **Chart 5**) *At this point, God will not just be a part of our lives, He will be our very Life itself!* We will have exchanged lives. We will have given Him ours; and He will have given us His.[3] At this point we can claim with Paul, "For me to live *is* Christ." (Philippians 1:21)

Faith Choices Are Not Enough

It's important not only to make the right faith choices, giving God the authority to work, but also to give Him our lives to perform those choices through. In other words, along with our faith choices, we must "present [our] bodies as a living sacrifice, holy, acceptable unto God, which is [our] reasonable service....that [we] might prove [by our life actions] what is that good, and acceptable, and perfect, will of God." (Romans 12:1-2)

How often we make the right choices in our prayer closets, giving God the authority to work, but because we feel no different when we begin to walk, act, and do what He asked, we begin to doubt that God really heard us in the first place or that any change has really occurred. Because of unbelief, we once again take our lives back into our own hands.

Example: The Hated Stepmother

My friend Amy is the "hated" stepmother in a family of five grown children who never wanted their parents' divorce. Because they adored their mom, Amy has never really been accepted. Nevertheless, several years ago, she was asked to go to a family get-together.

Having learned *The Way of Agape*, Amy was praying that it would work in her situation. As she walked up to the door where the party was to be held, Amy made those faith choices. She prayed that God would take her fear and dislike of all the kids and fill her with His Love for them. Once inside the door, however, when Amy encountered the hostile members of the family, and they began to, once again, snub her and say mean things to her, she found herself reacting and responding in the same familiar negative ways.

Unfortunately, she didn't recognize the new negative thoughts as they were coming in, so she didn't give them over to God. Instead, she allowed these new "wounds" to enter in and mingle with all the other unvented layers of hurt and rejection. As a result, the hurtful feelings once again began to consume her and motivate her actions. She became distraught and disheartened, falling into a spiral of negativity. She began to doubt that God had ever heard her prayer in the first place or that He was even there for her. Next she condemned herself as a Christian because she felt like a total failure.

When we talked, Amy wept, "See, Nancy, it just doesn't work for me. It doesn't work in my life. Something must be terribly wrong with me." The father of lies, Satan rejoices in making us feel like we're the "odd" ones; we're the only ones Christianity doesn't work for. Amy had loved God with all her willpower. She made those "contrary choices" before going to the party. She was willing to do God's Will at all costs. However, Amy never made it to loving God with all her soul. She allowed the new hurts to determine her actions rather than trust that God would perform His Life through her, *regardless of how she felt*. If Amy could have laid the new hurts at God's feet, she would see that He would be faithful to give her the Love and forgiveness she needed for these people.

Not Only a Faith Choice—a Faith Walk Also

Do you follow what I am saying? Not only must we make a "faith choice" (non-feeling choice), we must also walk a "faith walk." We must not only believe that God hears our choices, but we must also believe, by faith, that He will perform His Will in our lives regardless of how we feel, or what we think, or what we see happening.

Even in the middle of a hurtful conversation, we can choose to give God our new hurts—as they come in—rather than let them be programmed into the hidden chambers of our soul. God will then remove them from us, as the Word says, "as far as the east is from the west" (Psalm 103:12), whether we "feel" it or not. And then we can continue to stay one with Him, loving Him with all our soul, and allowing His Life to flow through us rather than our own self life.

Overload

Sometimes, however, too many hurts come in all at once and like Amy, we experience an "overload." At that moment we often find ourselves unable to speak or act without just crumbling. Psalm 118:12 explains "overload" well, "They compassed me about like bees." In such a situation, we need to excuse ourselves and go to where we can be alone with God.

Once alone with God, we need to deal with the negative thoughts and emotions that are flooding our minds. It's imperative we don't let these things accumulate. The way we deal with them is by confessing them, repenting of them, and giving them over to God. After we are cleansed, we can go back and, by faith, walk and act, knowing we are filled with God's Life.

Example: I Need to Go Be With Jesus

Sometimes in the middle of an argument with my precious Chuck, when emotions are piling up too quickly, I will stop and say, "Honey, I need to go and be with Jesus right now. If I continue to argue with you, my emotions will blow."

The first time I did this, Chuck was very offended; he didn't like my leaving at all. But now, he likes me so much better when I come back from being with Jesus that he will often say, "Yes, please go be with Jesus."

Practice this strategy with your children. When you find yourself hassled and unable to function without screaming and totally going ballistic, *stop* and confess, "Mommy is losing it right now. I need to go and be with Jesus." Give your little ones an example of how we must *all* go to Jesus to get healed, to get "cleansed," and to get just plain "nicer."

We are showing our kids that *Jesus alone is the answer to our failures,* not our spirituality, our church going, or our Bible studies. We are showing them that grownups mess up all the time and that Jesus is the *only* answer. He is the One who fixes us. He is the One who takes away our hurts and our anger. He is the One who cleanses us, refreshes us, and makes us better.

What Is Our Soul?

As we discussed in Chapter 10, the Greek word for soul (life) is psyche. *Psyche* has a very interesting twofold root meaning; it means "it shall have life" or "it shall wax cold." Our soul is either going to be Spirit filled and have life, because of the free flow of God's Life from our hearts to our souls (See **Chart 5**, page 159); or our soul will be empty and waxing cold, because God's Life in us has been quenched by wrong emotional choices (See **Chart 6**, page 161).

In other words, our soul is a neutral area that can either be filled with God's Life and moved powerfully and positively by His Spirit; or, if God's Spirit has been quenched by wrong choices, our soul will wax cold and be empty of meaning because it will be filled with self and not God at all.

As a friend once noted, "Our soul is like a spiritual playground; either it's filled and controlled by God's Spirit or it's filled and controlled by the flesh." In other words, our soul is a meeting place for two opposing forces. This, to me, is a very graphic picture.

If we are born again, then technically we are "in the Spirit."[4] By our continual choice (our willpower), however, we can either walk after the Spirit, by making faith choices and allowing God's Life to motivate our actions; or we can walk after the flesh by making emotional choices, thus allowing our self life and the power of sin to prompt our actions.

Galatians 5:25 exhorts us, "If we *live in the Spirit,* let us also *walk in the Spirit.*" (emphasis added)

Be Filled With God's Life

Our whole purpose for being called as Christians is to be filled with the fulness of God, sharing His genuine Life, His Love, and His Thoughts with others. Nothing else will bring us that joy and fulfillment we are all seeking. This is the whole meaning and purpose of our Christian walk.

Ephesians 3:19 instructs that we are "to know the love of Christ, which passeth knowledge, that ye might be filled with all the fulness of God."

Example: A Reason to Go On Living

A while ago, a woman called who has been searching for a reason to go on living. Nora has been a Christian for about 11 years, but has never experienced God's Life flowing through her. She has never felt God's Love—either for herself or for others. I believe Nora is one of thousands of Christians who have tried to live the Christian life by their own natural love and ability. She finally just got tired of the hypocrisy and quit trying.

When I questioned her, she insisted that she had laid her life down to God and committed everything to Him. However, something is very wrong because God is always faithful to His Word and He *will* do as He promises. If this dear lady truly has laid her life down and yet has never experienced God's Love, Peace, Joy, or Wisdom, something else is amiss. Because as Ephesians states, if Christ dwells in our hearts by faith (and we make those appropriate faith choices to let it flow), then, we will "know the love of Christ" and we will "be filled with all the fulness of God." (3:17, 19)

Nora has now rejected Christianity. She is out in the world, seeing an analyst and searching for happiness elsewhere. I asked her on the phone if she had found what she was looking for. She yelled at me, "Are you kidding? I am more hopeless now than I ever was before!"

Nora admits she is lonely, empty, and unfulfilled, existing without any meaning or purpose to her life. I remember feeling the same way, before God showed me His Way of Love. She avows she hates herself and cannot accept the fact that God still loves her. This precious one is like so many Christians today (and like I was for 20 years), striving and trying to be "model" Christians—doing, doing, doing—and yet never really experiencing or even knowing what God's Life is really like. Living such a life can be a devastating experience.

Unless we intimately experience for ourselves the fulness of God by *knowing His Life in place of our own*, nothing will ever bring us the meaning and purpose that we are all seeking. I have not heard what ever happened to Nora. She was unwilling to hear anything more—at that time. I know, however, God loves her far more than I ever could, so I can trust Him to do everything in His Power to bring her back to Himself.

God's Image

Our whole purpose for being called by God is to be filled with His Spirit and His Life. Then and only then can we reflect His Image in all we do. Loving God with all our soul simply means exchanging our own image—all our thoughts, emotions and desires that are contrary to God's—for the Image that we were created to bear, which is God's Image—His Love, His Thoughts, and His Power. Romans 8:29 promises, We are all predestined "to be conformed to the image of God."[5]

An image is an exact likeness of something,[6] a visible representation or repro-duction of the form of a person. As we allow God to conform us more and more into His Image and His Likeness, it will be His Image, His Life, that we will portray to the world, not our own.

Self Image

As Christians, we don't want to have a better *self image*. That's not why God has called us! He wants us to learn how to set our self aside, so we can reflect His Image, His Self, His Likeness to others.

Self image—reflecting what we think, feel, and desire—will never bring anyone to the Lord, never truly restore any relationships, nor heal any marriages. Only by reflecting and showing forth Jesus' Image (His Life) will others' lives truly be touched and changed. Jesus declares in John 5:31, "If I bear witness of Myself, my witness is not true." If Jesus says this of Himself, how much more true it is of us!

Example: You Look Just Alike!

One of my favorite stories that illustrates this concept perfectly is an incident that happened between Melody, a former neighbor of ours, and her mom.

Melody's mom had gone to the same hairdresser for years. She always had told Melody that she looked exactly like her hairdresser friend, and sometime she wanted them to meet. Finally, when Melody was home long enough on a visit and needed her hair cut, she consented to get an appointment with the hairdresser. Needless to say, Melody was anxious to see the woman who supposedly "looked exactly like her."

When Melody walked into the hair salon and was introduced to the hair-dresser, she was absolutely shocked because there was no physical resemblance between them at all. Melody is short, with a dark complexion and dark hair. She is very pretty and has rounded features. The hairdresser was tall, blond, skinny, and had angular features. There were no physical similarities between them at all.

Of course, the mom was very excited to introduce them to each other. They all talked for a few minutes, then the mom left so the two of them could talk. Melody asked the hairdresser if her mom had told her that they looked exactly alike. "Of course," the hairdresser said, "for years she has told me that. I am so surprised to meet you."

As Melody had her hair washed and cut, the two had a chance to share some details of their lives. It turned out that they both were Christians. After thinking about this for awhile, it dawned on both of them that the reason Melody's unsaved mom thought they looked alike was because she saw God in both of them. What the mother saw manifested through both of them was God's character: His Life and His Image. Physically they didn't resemble each other in the least, but spiritually they had the very same "image."

I love this story. And since hearing it, I have been told a couple of times that I look like certain people, one of whom was an author. The next time I was in a bookstore, I picked up her book and on the back cover was her picture. Again, there was no physical resemblance to me at all. And yet, I was blessed, because I knew exactly what my friends meant.

1 John 4:17 states, "As He is [Love], so [should we be] in this world." In other words, we should always reflect His Image and not our own, because this is now our true identity. This is the new "me"!

Identity and Self Image

As we love God with all our soul (**Chart 5**, page 159) and allow Him to conform us into His Image, His Image becomes more and more our true identity (who we really are), not only to others, but also to ourselves.

We covered some of this is Chapter 6, but I want to emphasize it here again. It is so important to have our identity and security built solely upon knowing God loves us, because God's Love is the only love that will never fail us or be taken away from us.

Let's clarify some terms so we don't get confused. Our identity is "who we think and feel ourselves to be." Self image is almost the same thing; however, it goes a little deeper. It's not only what we think and feel about ourselves, but our self image is also based upon what we say and do. In other words, it's our total mental self portrait.

Healthy Self Image (See Chart 5, page 159)

The only basis for building a healthy self image is:

1) Knowing and believing that *God loves us unconditionally*.[7] Knowing that God loves us no matter what we think, no matter how we feel, and no matter what we do or don't do for Him.[8]

2) If we know and accept that God loves us, *then we'll have the confidence and trust to lay down our wills and our lives to Him* and love Him in return.

3) Since we are loving Him, becoming open and cleansed vessels, *God's Life can come forth* from our hearts and be made manifest through our lives. At this point, God's Love becomes our love, His Thoughts become our thoughts, and His Will, our will—all performed in our lives by His Power. WOW! What an incredible Image! God takes my uniqueness, my temperament, and my personality and fills it with His Love, His Wisdom, and His Power. This is the "new man"—the real "me."[9]

4) Because God's Life is coming forth from us, *we will begin to like (storge) who we are*, what we say, and what we do. We will like or esteem ourselves, because it's God's Life being expressed through us. It's His Love, and we'll like being a vessel of His Love; it's His Wisdom, and we'll like being able to see things from His perspective; and it's His Power, and we'll like doing things in His strength. Healthy self esteem only occurs if Jesus' Life is shown through us.

Again, Galatians 2:20 expresses it perfectly, "I am crucified with Christ: nevertheless I live; yet not I, but Christ liveth in me: and the life which I now live in the flesh I live by the faith of the Son of God, Who loved me, and gave Himself for me."

This is who we really are now, whether we *feel* like it or not! (I would encourage you to review the *Who I am in Christ* Scriptures in the Supplemental Notes and begin to choose by faith to believe what God says about you.)

Poor Self Image (See Chart 6, page 161)

However, poor self image results when:

1) We don't really know, accept, and believe that God loves us personally and unconditionally.

2) Then we won't have the confidence and the trust to moment by moment lay down our wills and our lives to God, but instead we end up being "clogged and dirty" vessels.

3) Consequently, we will have quenched God's Life in our hearts, and therefore we won't experience His Love, His Wisdom, and His Power in our souls. Thus, the image we portray to the world will not be Jesus' Image—as it should be—but our own self image. As a result,

4) We won't *like* (esteem) who we are, what we say, and what we do because it's not God's Life through us, but our own self life. There will then be a phoniness about us and a fear of letting others *see* who we really are. We'll have no peace or joy and our frantic search for meaning and purpose will continue.

If the above things are true, then our self image will constantly be fluctuating and changing because it won't be based on God's Life through us as it should be, but on what we think of ourselves, what others think of us, and on our circumstances.

Lies and Untruths

For a lot of us, our self image has not been based upon God's Love and His Life through us as it should have been, but on the hurtful messages and downright lies that have been drummed into us by others: our parents, husbands, relatives, friends, bosses and other significant people in our lives.

For those of us in this category, we need to stop and take a good, hard look at what we have erroneously allowed to be programmed into our minds. By faith, we need to ask God to begin to expose and reveal some of this false programming, so we can choose to get rid of these messages and be reprogrammed with the truth. The truth is that God loves us and accepts us unconditionally. If we will give Him our wills and our lives, He can then fill our lives to overflowing with His very own Life! That's the truth. Now it's up to us if we choose to appropriate this or not.

Delivered Unto Death

The more we love God and allow Him to expose our sin and the junk of the past, the more we'll be able to crucify and put to death our self life. The more of God's Life we'll experience in our souls, the more we'll have that "healthy self image." And the more we have that healthy esteem, the more we will begin to like what we say, what we do, and how we do it. To me this is not "self confidence" or "self esteem" as the world calls it, but *God confidence* and *Christ esteem*. In this case, our confidence is in God and His Life in us, and not in ourselves.[10]

2 Corinthians 4:11 explains it beautifully, "For we which live are always delivered unto death [of self life] for Jesus' sake, [so] that the life also of Jesus might be made manifest in our mortal flesh."

"Always delivered over unto death" means our willingly submitting all of our "justified" hurts, pains, injustices, unforgivenesses, doubts, fears, and memories over to God, so He can free us from them. It means humbling ourselves and following God to the cross daily. Then, the Life of Jesus *can* be manifested in our bodies.

Three Areas of Our Soul

Let's explore briefly the three areas that make up our soul: our thoughts, our emotions, and our desires. If we can become more aware of the pitfalls and the dangers that quench God's Life in each of these areas, then we will be able to catch them before they occur.

Conscious Thoughts

Let's begin with our *conscious thoughts*, since they are the most important, according to Scripture. 2 Corinthians 10:5-6 says, "Casting down imaginations, and every high thing that exalteth itself against the knowledge of God, and *bringing into captivity every thought to the obedience of Christ*. And having in a readiness to revenge all disobedience, when your obedience is fulfilled." (emphasis added)

The reason our thoughts are so important to God is because our thoughts are the first area to be triggered in the "chain reaction" of our souls. Our thoughts stir up our emotions; our emotions then influence our desires; and our desires produce our actions. This is why it's so important to take every thought captive, because then we can stop the chain reaction before it even begins.

We "Think" Before We "Feel"

Thoughts produce feelings. This is why God speaks so much in Scripture about our thoughts, and so very little about our emotions. Thoughts come from audible words, silent words, written words, or from our own imaginations and reasonings. We don't have to sit down and concentrate in order to think. Thoughts are automatic, and they are formed constantly.

Everything we see and hear is immediately translated into our thoughts. Often we're not even aware of the subconscious thoughts we program into our souls, simply because of what we see and hear.

So when we hear the words of another person, either their audible words, their silent words (body language), or their penned words (as we read), these are immediately translated into our thoughts. At this point, we have a choice: either to accept these thoughts into our lives and thus allow them to stir up our emotions, our desires and eventually be manifested in our life actions, or, as Scripture instructs, to take every thought captive and deal with it the way the Lord would have us do.[11]

Four Choices to Every Action

If we could dissect our life actions, we would find that every act is made up of four choices. Now, practically speaking, it's like "splitting hairs" to do this. But if we could slow this process down, we would find we have four choices to prevent sin in every action.

1) We can choose to catch the negative, ungodly *thoughts* before they stir up our emotions; or,

2) We can choose to catch the negative, uncontrolled *emotions* before they become desires; or,

3) We can choose to catch the negative, self-centered *desires* before they become actions; or,

4) We can choose to catch the negative, un-Christlike *actions* before we act.

As God in fully human form, Jesus was able to live the perfect sinless human life. Because He was able to control His thoughts perfectly, He was able to catch every negative thought before it ever became a negative feeling.[12] In other words, His Thoughts were perfectly Spirit-controlled. While we cannot do this perfectly (only Jesus can do that), He has given us an example to follow.

When Are Thoughts Sin?

Again, we are not responsible for the original self-centered, corrupt, or bad thought when it first comes in; it's what we choose to do with that thought that produces the sin. If we choose to follow what that thought is prompting us to do—over what God is telling us to do—then we sin and end up separated from God (with that layer of grease covering our hearts and preventing God's Life from coming forth).[13]

Even if we do nothing with that bad thought, it will eventually be buried in those hidden chambers and end up quenching God's Spirit—and that, too, will be sin. If, however, we recognize that bad thought and give it over to God, we have not sinned and we are not separated from Him.[14]

God declares that it is imperative for us not even to entertain bad thoughts about others, let alone speak them. Listen to Ephesians 4:29-32: "Let no corrupt communication proceed out of your mouth, but that which is good to the use of edifying, that it may minister grace unto the hearers. And grieve not the Holy Spirit of God, whereby ye are sealed unto the day of redemption. Let all bitterness, and wrath, and anger, and clamour, and evil speaking, be put away from you, with all malice: And be ye kind one to another, tender-hearted, forgiving one another, even as God for Christ's sake hath forgiven you."

Grieve Not the Holy Spirit

Here's my translation of the above Scripture: "Let nothing come forth out of our mouth that does not edify the hearers." God has certainly called me on this one lately. Sharing our innermost thoughts, especially with our husbands or our grown children, is so easy. It's like talking to ourselves. Such sharing is so natural. But, so often our thoughts and our comments to our family are negative about someone else.

God has impressed this Scripture on my heart. He instructs that when we do share things that are not edifying to the hearer, even if they are family, then we quench His Spirit and His Life in us. In other words, when we complain out loud, or talk about another person or situation, if it doesn't "lift the hearer up" or "bring him towards God," it is an evil communication, and will quench God's Spirit in us.

When we share our ungodly thoughts with others, we not only contaminate them, but we also automatically reprogram those bad thoughts right back in us again. Thus, our emotions and desires will be stirred up all over again. It's imperative to be aware of and to catch the bad thoughts as they come in. We need to recognize them and know where they are from. Then we need to refuse them and crucify them. We are not even to think them.

This is exactly what 2 Corinthians 10:5-6 means, "...bringing into captivity every thought to the obedience of Christ; *And having in a readiness to revenge all disobedience, when your obedience is fulfilled*" (emphasis added). In other words, catching the negative thoughts as they come in and "dealing with them" immediately.[15]

Dangers of Psychology

Continually sharing and reprogramming our negative thoughts back in our hidden chambers is one of the reasons psychological counseling can be so very dangerous. In this type of counseling, we are not dealing with our sin, but analyzing, mulling over, and trying to figure out our own corrupt thinking and behavior. I don't think God intends for us to do this. When we focus on the negative things about ourselves, others, and the past, we simply reprogram those things right back into our subconscious again, thus making the strongholds even stronger.

I am convinced the Spirit of God is the one who reveals and exposes the hidden things in our souls, not us.[16] We are *not* to dwell on the bad thoughts that come in or become paralyzed by them. In our quiet times before the Lord, God will reveal the true root causes of our negative thoughts. We then can deal with them[17] by giving them over to God and allowing Him to remove them permanently. Proverbs 20:27 promises, "The spirit of man is the candle of the Lord, searching all the inward parts (*cheder*, hidden chambers)."

Thoughts: From God, Satan, or Self

How can we tell the difference between God's Thoughts, our own thoughts, and the thoughts that Satan inserts into our soul?

God's promptings come in that still, small voice. God's Spirit bears witness with our spirit that it is God's voice, and we usually have an immediate peace. God's Voice encourages us and draws us closer to Him. We should always be leery of anything that pushes us away from God and removes our peace. It's probably not from the Holy Spirit. Often, the Holy Spirit needs to reprove us and convict us of sin. But still, God's voice will always push us toward Jesus and toward being more loving, rather than away from Him.

God's voice is always in perfect agreement with His written Word. Any voice that does not corroborate what God's Word says, shelve it; don't follow it! God's voice always confirms His written Word, and then God's Spirit will bear witness that it is of God. We will always have a deep inner peace when we hear God's voice. The way I weed out a lot of spurious thoughts is by asking myself, "If Jesus was standing bodily right beside me now, is this what He would be whispering in my ear?"

Thoughts "Not From God"

Thoughts that are not from God have two other sources: the flesh and Satan. Thoughts from our flesh are sometimes harder to distinguish, because Satan often uses things of the flesh such as jealousy, bitterness, resentment, criticalness, self-defensiveness and self-consciousness to cause us to sin. If we have held on to these types of thoughts and feelings, they need to be immediately confessed, repented of and given over to God so that Satan cannot get a handle on us.

It seems thoughts that are of the flesh go away pretty quickly if we are faithful to do the before mentioned three things.

Strongholds of the Enemy

Thought processes that Satan is involved in, however, often do reappear, even after we have done the above three steps. The reason they come back is simply because they have become long-standing "strongholds" of the enemy. We have surrendered these areas to him in the past, and he is *not* going to give them up easily. This is why these kinds of strongholds often do become tough spiritual battles to overcome.

Actually, God takes our negative thoughts and emotions the moment we give them to Him; but often our feelings don't align with that choice for a while. And this is when Satan deludes us into thinking that God is not faithful and that He has not really cleansed us.

It's God's prerogative as to how long He allows us to struggle before He aligns our feelings with our choices. Again, sometimes He lets us go awhile to test us and to strengthen us. Will we keep on believing Him, even though we don't see or feel the victory?

Satan, of course, wants to use our "feelings" to destroy us. What God means for good, Satan, obviously, means for evil. God intends, however, to use Satan as His own tool to bring up some of the ungodly and self-centered thoughts we have erroneously programmed into our subconscious. Once those negative things surface—even through Satan's promptings—we have a choice: God wants us to give those buried things over to Him and be rid of them forever; Satan, of course, wants us to crumble in confusion and discouragement over them, so we'll "push" them back down again. He wants to use our wild emotions and uncontrolled desires to produce self-centered and ungodly actions.

So, if you have confessed, repented, and given the negative thoughts to God and they don't immediately go away, don't give up and cry, "Oh, this doesn't work for me!" That's just what Satan is hoping you will do. Remember, the deeper the wound, the longer it takes for your feelings to align with your choices.[18] Recognize the process as a battle. Know that you will win if you will just persevere. You are already on the winning side.[19]

In your battle, be sure to use your *"weapons of warfare"*: God's Word, His Blood, and His Name. Fast, pray, and have others pray for you. God promises us that if we do our part, He will do His! 2 Corinthians 10:3-4 promises, "For though we walk in the flesh, we do not war after the flesh: (For the weapons of our warfare are not carnal, but mightily through God to the pulling down of strong holds),"

"Submit yourselves, therefore, to God. Resist the devil (*"have a readiness to revenge all disobedience"*), and he will flee from you. Draw nigh to God, and He will draw nigh to you." (James 4:7-8)

In Chapter 14, we will learn the specific steps needed to *"resist the devil."*

Satan's Voice

Satan's voice is very different from God's Voice. Satan speaks in a loud, shrill, and demanding voice. It's an urgent, "do it now" kind of a thought. The thoughts that Satan prompts usually cause us unrest and doubt.

To make us feel like failures as Christians, Satan uses all sorts of tactics to condemn us and to make us feel guilty. Such thoughts will always push us away from God, not towards Him. Recognize thoughts like, "Oh, it doesn't work for me," "God doesn't care," "His Word is not true," "He doesn't love me," "He isn't faithful," and so on.

Satan's three main tactics come from Genesis 3 and from Matthew 4[20]: 1) "*Don't obey* God's Word; go with your own feelings and thoughts"; 2) "*Don't trust* God to do it; Trust in yourself and your own ability. Stay in control"; and lastly, 3) "Don't give your will and life to God; *follow what you want.* You are Number One."

Watch out for these temptations! Identifying Satan's tactics will help tremendously in knowing how to fight.

Our Wild Imagination

Another thing Satan revels in doing is to cause us to dwell in our past by imagining and fantasizing. He loves to prompt melancholy thoughts of dissatisfaction with today—he is a master at doing this.

A dear friend of mine who was recently reunited with her husband shared that while they were separated, Satan used her dreams to make her terribly depressed and despondent about the situation. The dreams, she said, would start out innocently enough, but would end by stirring up horrible memories and even more questions about the past, such as: "What really went on with him?" She then found herself lying there, half awake, mulling over events of the past, rather than centering in on the truth that God had already shown her.

Another recently separated woman shared with me a few weeks ago, "The thing that draws me down faster than anything else is remembering what we used to be like." She and her husband had a "storybook" marriage. They met in grammar school, went out in high school (where he was the football star and she was the head cheerleader), and married in college. They even had two adorable children and that pretty little house in the country with a white picket fence!

Thoughts of "how it used to be" and "how it could have been" pulled this woman down into the pits faster than anything else. That's our imagination working. Watch out for it! Catch those negative thoughts, and choose to deal with them rather than entertain them.

"Forgetting the Things That Are Behind"

Controlling negative thoughts is why Philippians 3:13 is so important to keep in mind: "Forgetting those things which are behind, and reaching forth unto those things which are before."

Imagination and fantasizing can simply be entertaining negative thoughts. This is not forgetting the past, but dwelling on it and trying to figure out what went wrong.

Again, here is another reason why I believe psychology is dangerous for Christians. With psychology, we are not "forgetting those things which are behind," but we are dredging them up and dwelling on them. We are not "reaching forth unto those things which are before," but we are living in the past trying to figure out our behavior with our own human understanding. I believe by doing this we are simply strengthening the strongholds of the enemy. We are not dealing with these negative things, as God would have us, by giving them to Him; we are instead reprogramming the same negative thoughts right back into our minds again. Thus, we are opening ourselves up for more "inroads" of the enemy.

Let's Get On With Our Lives

As one woman said to me recently, "I'm tired of trying to understand what I have done wrong in the past. I just want to get rid of these things and get on with my life!"

Another Christian woman, who has been in intensive therapy for six months, told me her therapist thought it would take her another two years to get rid of the things of the past. He said she must deal with her feelings by "reliving the experiences of the past." This, he felt, would take at least another couple of years.

As Christians, we don't have to figure out, reason out, or relive the experiences of the past. We don't want "excuses" as to why we acted the way we did or why others treated us as they did. Past hurts are simply the result of sin—our own and the other person's. There is absolutely nothing we can do to change or reclaim our past. We can only give our past to Jesus, allow Him to heal us by removing our hurts "as far as the East is from the West" and then change and transform our future by our present choices.[21]

We are only responsible for our own sin, not the sins of others. Their sin is the result of their own choices, and that's something they must take care of themselves for their own salvation. We can only forgive them as God would have us do,[22] and then get on with our lives.

If we are Christians, the Lord is not trying to fix us up and make us a better us.
He is trying to empty us out (show us how to set ourselves aside, relinquish ourselves),
so that He then can live His Life through us!

2 Corinthians 4:10-11 tells us, "Always bearing about in the body the dying of
the Lord Jesus, that the life also of Jesus might be made manifest in our body. For we
which live are always delivered unto death for Jesus' sake, that the life also of Jesus
might be made manifest in our mortal flesh."

Conscious Emotions and Feelings

The second area of our soul is our *conscious emotions and feelings*.

There are two very important things to remember about our emotions. First
of all, our emotions are *not* spontaneous. They are the direct result of what we have
allowed into our thought life. There is always a thought (either audible, penned, or
silent) behind each of our emotions.

Second, not all negative emotions are sin. In fact, Scripture says we can be angry,
and yet not sin. (Ephesians 4:26) Some emotions like anger, fear, and even hurt can
have a "righteous" side to them. Even though they might look at first like negative,
sinful emotions, these are some of the ones that the Bible says can be righteous, and
therefore normal, human responses with no sin involved.

Things that are sin and that *do* separate us from God,[23] however, are emotions that
are not of faith: for example, violent anger (wrath), bitterness, resentment, jealousy,
unforgiveness, coveting, envying, worry, anxiety, doubt, and the list goes on.[24] The
Bible calls these things the "works of the flesh."

These are the sinful emotions that will cause us to follow our own desires over
God's Will. *Thoughts*, it seems, are easier to capture, analyze, and be more objec-
tive about. But with *feelings*, because we become absolutely consumed with them,
it often becomes impossible to make godly choices. A perfect example of this is
depression.

Dangerous Depression

In some cases, depression has a physical cause. And, if this is the case, we need
to pray about seeking a doctor and pray about a physical remedy. But often, depression
is simply being consumed with bad thoughts or emotions that we are choosing *not* to
deal with. Depression is often an overload of negative emotions, and sometimes it
becomes overwhelming to find a way out.

Again, I believe feelings and emotions are a direct result of what we have allowed into our thought life. So the sin—the quenching of God's Spirit—arises when

we choose to hang on to, mull over, or entertain the negative thoughts that have come into our minds. Those negative thoughts will eventually stir up our emotions and thus, our desires and actions.[25]

God Is the One Who Changes Our Feelings

Remember—and this is so very important—*we are not responsible to change our negative feelings.* We can't do that! In other words, we can't change our feelings of depression. It's impossible!

Our only responsibility is to put *in charge* the Person who can change our feelings, and that's God! And, of course, we do that by confessing we own the sinful feelings, by repenting of them, and finally, by giving them over to God.

Keys to Freedom

For so many years, whenever I had an emotional problem, people would say to me, "Oh, just give it to God!" Well, that's fine, and we definitely need to do that, but first we must stand up and be counted for our part in the problem. We have made the choice to entertain, and keep those negative thoughts and feelings over what God has told us to do in His Word. Now, we might not have known that we could give those things over to God. Nevertheless, it's still our responsibility and by our retaining those negative things, we have quenched His Spirit.

When we are depressed, then, we can't simply say to God, "Please, God, take my depression away," and expect Him automatically to do it. We must first *confess* our own responsibility in the problem, which is that we have chosen to hang on to these sinful feelings over what God has told us to do with them which is to give them to Him. Then, we must *repent* or change our mind about holding on to them, and *give them to God*.

So the *choice to relinquish the negative feelings to God is ours; but the responsibility to change those feelings is God's.*[26] As we walk by faith, we'll find that God is always faithful to align our feelings with our choices, and by the time we need to do whatever it is that He has asked, we will be genuine. God promises to produce His genuine Love and all the fruit of the Spirit in us, if we are a cleansed and pure vessel.

Example: She Stood There Glaring

Here's an example of the above principles that is funny now, but certainly wasn't when it happened years ago. Right in the middle of a *Way of Agape* class, a woman who had hurt me terribly in the past, walked into the back of the classroom. She didn't say a word, but just stood there, glaring.

God has a real sense of humor because I was right in the middle of explaining how God will change our negative emotions into His positive ones if we'll only give them to Him.

I had not seen this woman in probably three years. At that time the incident happened, I had dealt with my hurt feelings and had chosen to give them to God. However, at that moment when she entered the room, God allowed (and I am sure Satan prompted) similar negative emotions to come up within me. The whole episode from three years previously flashed through my head as I saw her glowering at me.

So, right in the middle of my teaching, silently in my mind, I again confessed I was experiencing bad feelings towards her, and, by faith, I chose to give those feelings to God. I didn't let the enemy get a handle in me, nor did I let him program those hurts back down in again. I recognized those negative emotions and caught them, even in the middle of teaching a class.

God is always so faithful! By the time I finished teaching, I did experience a release and a genuine Love for this woman. Afterwards, I was able, in God's Love, to go up to her and genuinely embrace her and talk to her.

As Hebrews 10:23 states, "Let us hold fast the profession of our faith without wavering; for He is faithful That promised." In other words, know that God will be faithful and He will release us from the bondage of the negative feelings "in His perfect timing."

Conscious Desires

The last area of our soul is our own *conscious desires*. These are our own natural emotional desires (*thelema*)—things that we want, things that please us, and things that we desire.

Remember, we have the supernatural authority and power to choose to do what God desires in our lives over what we ourselves desire. That's the miracle Power of the Indwelling Spirit. We talked about this at some length in the last chapter.

[Note: Again, the Temple model (**Chart 4**, page 149) symbolizes this supernatural power and authority. We said that the two freestanding bronze pillars represent our free choice (9)—the free choice either to choose God's Will (8), as He has revealed it to us by His supernatural Counsel and then to trust His Power to perform that will in our lives (*boulomai*), or the free choice to choose our own will and desires (*thelema*), prompted by our own thoughts and emotions.

The pillars actually stood on the "upper level" of the Inner Court. I believe God is demonstrating here that we have God's supernatural authority and Power to make "faith choices" (*boulomai*), which can override our own natural and human thoughts and emotions which reside on an even lower level of our soul.[27]

This means that we have the authority and power to choose to do what God desires in our lives over what we ourselves desire. This authority and power is the most incredible gift of all. *We don't have to "feel" our choices, we don't even have to "want" to make our choices, we simply must be "willing" to make those choices.*]

"Lusts of the Flesh"

In Scripture, self-centered desires are often translated "lusts." James 1:14-15 paraphrased says we are tempted [to sin or go our own way] when we are drawn away [from the truth] by our own lusts and then enticed [captured]. And when lust has conceived [and we have chosen to follow it], it brings forth sin [separation from God] and when that is finished, death [no life].

The Greek word "lust" here is *epithumia*. *Epithumia* means "strong emotional desires." *Epithumia* comes from the "root" word *thumos* which has the root meaning, "for the purpose of revenge." Satan wants to use our uncontrolled, strong, self-centered, emotional desires for the purpose of "revenging God." Satan strikes back at God every time we choose our "own ways" over His!

Again, it's important to recognize our negative thoughts and sinful emotions before they stir up our self-centered desires and produce un-Christlike actions. Each time we make that faith choice to go God's way over our own way, we are defeating Satan and he is unable to "revenge God!"

"Desires of Our Hearts"

What is so very exciting about volitionally choosing God's Will over our own will, is that in God's perfect timing and in His perfect way, He often gives us back all the desires of our hearts anyway!

Psalm 37:4 promises, "Delight thyself in the Lord; And He shall give thee the desires of thine heart."

By choosing God's ways over our own, our will becomes one with His. God is then freed to work "all things together for good" (Romans 8:28). And often times He does give us our heart's desires.

Example: I About Fell Over Dead!

For years I dreamed of having a cleaning lady. Not necessarily every week, but just once in a while to help with the heavy housework. With four children at home, a large house, and a heavy schedule of writing and teaching, I certainly could have used some help.

Every time I had approached Chuck on this subject, however, his answer was always categorically, no! He wanted his privacy and he didn't want an "outsider" in our home. Over the years, I had tried begging, pleading, and even crying, but nothing ever made him budge on the subject.

One particular summer, I was teaching a full schedule. All four kids were home, and I found it extremely difficult to keep up with the housework and all the outside commitments. I began to talk to God about it. I knew He wanted me to teach that particular summer, so I knew He was aware of the extra load I was carrying. I also knew He would make me capable of doing what needed to be done. I left my desire at His feet and trusted that what He would do would be for my best.

A couple of weeks later, my 85-year-old mother-in-law called and said she really needed someone to help her with her housecleaning. "Do you know of anyone I could use?" she asked. As it happened, in one of my previous classes, one of my friends had told me that she was now a housekeeper and asked me if I knew anyone who needed help. I told Grandma about her and she was thrilled.

The only problem was that I now needed to ask Chuck if he would pay for my friend to come and help Grandma. God certainly tests us. After my own yearning to have someone come and help me, now I was supposed to beg Chuck on behalf of someone else. It was so neat though, because after laying my desire at the Lord's feet, I could ask Chuck for Grandma without any envy, jealousy, or hurt feelings.

Chuck immediately said, "Of course, no problem. Go ahead." As I started to leave the room, Chuck stopped me and said, "By the way, do you need any help around here?" I about fell over dead!

The end of the story is that the very next week my friend Elsie came, not only to help Grandma with her house, but also to help me with mine. God not only answered my prayer, but Grandma's and Elsie's too!

Now, it might take six minutes, six weeks, or six years for God to work that miracle in your life. That timing is God's prerogative. But I promise that He will work it out, and He will give you the "desires of your heart" if you are willing to lay them at His feet *first* and love Him.[28]

Speaking of "Feet"

Our souls, like our feet, are what constantly "get dirty" (no pun intended)! Our own thoughts, emotions, and desires must constantly be handed over to God so we might be those "cleansed vessels" that God can fill and use.

A Scripture that is provocative in this context is John 13:8, when Jesus girds Himself with a towel and begins to wash the disciples' feet. All of a sudden, Peter jumps up and says, "Lord, you shall never wash my feet!" The Lord answers him, "Peter, if I don't wash (Greek word *nipto*, which means partially wash) your feet, you will have no part of me." Peter then says, "Well, wash all of me!" Jesus responds in verse 10, "He that is washed (Greek word *louo*, which means completely washed) doesn't need to wash totally again, except for his feet!"

What I see Jesus saying here is that once we are "washed completely" (or born again), there is no need to be totally washed again. What we do need, however, is to be continually "partially washed" (or have our souls cleansed). Our souls continually get dirty and continually need to be cleansed.

Our souls are very much like our feet. When we make wrong, emotional choices, our souls get dirty, just like stepping in the mud. At that point, it's not that we need to take a complete bath again, but only to recognize our wrong choices and be cleansed from them. We do this by confessing, repenting, and giving that sin and self to God (i.e., "washing our feet").

This is the preparation, the equipping, the girding, and the "shodding of our feet" that Scripture so often talks about.[29]

Conclusion: Becoming One Life With Him

Loving God with all our soul means, moment by moment, totally giving over and relinquishing all our conscious thoughts, emotions, and desires that are contrary to God's, so that His Life can come forth in place of our own. Loving God with all our soul is becoming *One Life* with Him. It's exchanging our own image for the Image we were created to bear, which is God's Image. It's being so completely at one with Him that, for the moment, all that is seen through us is God![30]

When we love God in this way, we don't lose our own identity. Quite the contrary, we begin to experience a freedom to be the "real me," the image that God created us to be from the very beginning. We still have our personality, our talents, our capabilities, and our uniqueness, but God's Character and His Image are now pouring forth from us. We'll not only like what we see; but loving God like this will become the whole meaning and purpose of our lives.

Galatians 2:20 again says it the best, "I am crucified with Christ: nevertheless I live; yet not I, but Christ liveth in me; and the life which I now live in the flesh, I live by the faith of the Son of God, Who loved me, and gave Himself for me."

That "faith that I now live by" comes in the form of a choice; faith choices that give God the authority to work and faith choices that give Him our lives.

A true *overcomer* is one who knows how to make faith choices. *Overcoming* simply means prevailing over what our own thoughts, emotions, and desires are urging us to do, and allowing God's Spirit (His Life) in us to control us instead.

One Hundredfold

God promises us that if we are faithful to consistently relinquish our wills and lives and love Him, He will give us back "one hundredfold." He will not only give us back "in this time" all that we have chosen to lay down, but He will also give us His eternal life as well. (Mark 10:29-30)

There's the secret again. The ones that Jesus will "give back a hundredfold in this time, as well as eternal life" are those who have left all to follow Him, who totally have given themselves over to Him and, who have become one with Him.

Eighteen years ago this summer, I sat in a darkened, locked room—totally hopeless. My husband of almost 20 years had just asked me if I wanted a divorce because it was the only way he could see out of the pain and misery we were both in. My two teenage sons were rebellious and in trouble; my 18-month-old daughter, Michelle, was confined to her bed with a limp that the doctors said was permanent; I was 800 miles away from my family and my friends, with no thought of ever returning. In my eyes, my life at that point was completely hopeless.

I could have never in all my wildest dreams imagined that in just a few short years, God would not only restore our marriage; orchestrate our boys' lives so they would become productive, fabulous young men; heal Michelle totally, not only of her limp, but also of her allergies and hyperactivity; and relocate us back among our family and friends. But, most unbelievable of all, is that God would have me out teaching classes on what it means to love God; writing and speaking all over the world on what God's Love is and how we can be transformed into His Image; and most recently, doing marriage seminars on the *Way of Agape* with my precious Chuck!

If someone had told me this back then, I would have laughed in their face! Truly, "Eye hath not seen, nor ear heard, neither have entered into the heart of man, the things which God hath prepared for them that love (*agapao*) Him." (1 Corinthians 2:9)

God said it to be true, and He has performed it in my life! Let me be an example of His Love! Because if He can do these things in my life, He can certainly do them in yours, also.

Jeremiah 32:27 declares, "*Behold, I am the Lord, the God of all flesh; is there anything too hard for Me?*" (emphasis added)

Endnotes:

1.   1 John 4:17

2.   There is a subconscious part of our soul—those hidden chambers. See Chapter 10, "*Cheder*," and also *Be Ye Transformed* tape series.

3.   Galatians 2:20

4.   Romans 8:9

5.   Genesis 1:26; Galatians 1:16; 2 Corinthians 3:18

6.   Hebrews 1:3

7.   Psalm 103:17; Isaiah 43:1-4; John 15:9

8.   Jeremiah 31:3; Isaiah 49:15-16

9.   Ephesians 4:22-24; Colossians 3:9-10

10. Isaiah 43:7; 1 John 3:14a; 4:17

11. See Chapter 14, "Take Every Thought Captive."

12. Hebrews 2:18

13. See again Chapter 14, "Three Choices."

14. See Chapter 11, "What Is Sin?" and "Nothing Shall Separate Us."

15. See Chapter 14 for details.

16. See the *Be Ye Transformed* tapes.

17. See Chapter 14, "Inner Court Ritual."

18. See Chapter 12, "God Changes Our Feelings."

19. Luke 10:19

20. Review Chapter 9.

21. Be sure to listen to the *Be Ye Transformed* tapes (especially tape #6).

22. See Chapter 14, "Forgive Others."

23. See Chapter 11,"Nothing Shall Separate Us."

24. See Chapter 11, "What Is Sin?"

25. See Chapter 14, "Confess and Repent."

26. Lamentations 3:41

27. See Chapter 12, "*Exousia*."

28. See Chapter 8, "What Does It Mean to Love God?"

29. Ephesians 6:15; Matthew 25:10

30. Philippians 1:21

Scriptural References:

Chapter 13

How Do We Become One Soul With God? (Matthew 22:37)
A. Soul life is the *expression* of our conscious life (all our thoughts, emotions, and desires)
  1. It's our manifested character
  2. Emphasis is always on visibility
B. Soul life can either be:
  1. *God's Life* (Colossians 1:27): His Love, (1 John 4:8b) His Wisdom (1 John 1:1-5) and His Power (John 4:24) from our hearts or
  2. *Self life*, if we have made wrong choices and God's Life has been quenched (Galatians 5:19-20; Romans 1:21; John 5:31; Ephesians 4:17-18)
C. Therefore we must not only make right choices, we must also allow God to perform those choices in our life (soul) whether we feel like it or not. "Presenting our bodies as living sacrifices" (Romans 12:1)
  1. It's not only a faith choice, but a faith walk (Galatians 5:25)
  2. Even in the middle of a hurtful conversation, we can give God our new hurts, and God will "cast them as far as the east is from the west" (Psalm 103:12)
  3. Then, we must believe that God will perform His Will through us (Romans 4:19-21)
D. Our purpose for being called as a Christian is to show forth God's Life in our soul (1 John 4:7-8; Philippians 1:21; the new man (Colossians 3:10; Ephesians 4:24)

What Is Our Soul (*psyche*)?
A. *Psyche* means *"shall have life"* or *"shall wax cold"*
B. Our soul is like a neutral area that can be moved powerfully and positively by God's Spirit, bringing it LIFE; or, it can become empty and cold, if God's Life is quenched (Ephesians 4:18)
C. Loving God with all my soul means exchanging my own self (own image) for God's Self (His Image), the image I was created to bear (Romans 8:29; 1 John 4:17; Colossians 3:10; Matthew 10:39; Galatians 1:16a; 2 Corinthians 3:18; 4:11; Philippians 1:21)
  1. What is an image?
    a. It is an exact likeness of something (Hebrews 1:3)—a visible representation of something
    b. God wants us to reflect and glorify His Image and not our self-image (Romans 8:29; Genesis 1:26; Galatians 1:16; 2 Corinthians 3:18)
      . Self-image will never touch another's life for Jesus (John 5:31)
      . We need to reflect Jesus' Image, not our own
  2. God's Image should then become our *identity* (1 John 4:17)

     a.   Identity is the same thing as "self-image"

     b.   It's our total mental self portrait—who we think we are

3.   Healthy self-identity (image):

     a.   Only basis for building a healthy self concept knowing God loves us (Psalm 103:17; Isaiah 43:1; John 15:9b, 16; 17:26; Romans 5:5; 1 John 3:1; 4:19b)

        .   [Review *Knowing God Loves Me* Scriptures in Supplemental Notes]

        .   We must know that nothing will stop His Love from coming (Song of Solomon 8:7; Romans 8:38-39)

        .   Our self-image must be based only upon this unconditional Love, not on what we do (or don't do) for Him (Jeremiah 31:3-4; Isaiah 49:15-16)

     b.   Then we will have the confidence to lay down our wills and our lives to Him, moment by moment, and love Him, allowing Him to cleanse us of any sin (Romans 7:18)

     c.   Then, because we are cleansed vessels, His Image can come forth from our hearts and that is what will be portrayed to the world (Galatians 2:20; Ephesians 3:19; 2 Corinthians 3:18; Romans 8:29). This is the new man (Colossians 3:10; Ephesians 4:24). *The exchanged Life* (Galatians 1:16)

     d.   Because it is God's Life coming forth, we will begin to *like* (*phileo*) who we are (Galatians 2:20)

        .   This "image" is who we really are in Christ (see in Supplemental Notes *Who We Are In Christ*)

        .   This is *Christ-esteem* and *God-confidence* (Ephesians 4:13; Isaiah 43:7; 1 John 4:17; Colossians 3:3)

     e.   We will then have the freedom to take off our masks and be ourselves, yet still reflecting Christ (Jeremiah 9:23-24; John 8:32,36; Romans 8:2; 1 Peter 4:11)

4.   Poor self-image

     a.   If we don't know that God loves us personally, we are not going to have the confidence to lay down our wills and our lives and love God; He then will not be able to conform us into His Image (we are not open vessels) (Jeremiah 5:25; Isaiah 29:13; Matthew 23:25-27). So the image we portray to the world is not Christ's Image, but self (John 5:31)

        .   We then form our own image of ourselves (Ephesians 4:17-20; Romans 1:21-25)

        .   "I am no good. I can't measure up to what God wants. I am of no use to God, and so on" (Romans 7:15,18-19,24)

        .   Result: we don't like ourselves (*phileo*)

     b.   Our identity is based on what we think of ourselves and on what others say—which is constantly changing (Ezekiel 16:15a)

     c.   We then ask God, "Why have You made me like this?"

5. Only God's Love can be the foundation for a healthy self-image (Psalm 103:17), not self, others, or circumstances

6. *God is not trying to make us a "better us." He is trying to "empty us out," so that His Life can fill our souls* (2 Corinthians 4:11)

Three Areas of Our Soul

A. Conscious *Thoughts*

1. Thoughts trigger our emotions; emotions influence our desires; and our desires produce our actions (this is why it is so important to "take every thought captive") (2 Corinthians 10:5-6; 2 Samuel 11:2-4; Philippians 4:8; Hebrews 12:15)

2. We are not responsible for the original thought that comes in; it's what we choose to do with that thought that produces the sin (Ephesians 5:29-32)

3. How can we tell the difference between God's voice, Satan's voice, and our own?

    a. God's voice—a still, small voice, always in agreement with His Word (gives us "peace")

    b. Satan's voice—an urgent voice, prompting dissatisfaction and failure (Genesis 3:1,4-5; 1 Chronicles 21:1-8)

    c. Our own thoughts (James 1:13-15)

4. *Strongholds of the enemy* (imaginations, longstanding hurts) (Proverbs 5:22; John 8:34)

    a. Seem to be harder to get rid of

    b. Actually, God takes them immediately when we release them to Him, but often our feelings don't align for awhile

    c. Satan makes us think they are not gone (and that God's not faithful) (Proverbs 5:22)

    d. Recognize that it's a battle—use your "weapons of warfare" (2 Corinthians 10:3-6)

        . Pray (James 4:7-8)

        . Fast

        . Forget "things of the past" (Philippians 3:13)

        . Praise

        . "Love not (*agapao*) your life unto death" (Revelation 12:11)

    e. We have power and authority over Satan (Luke 10:19)

    f. You will win, it just might take some time (Hebrews 10:23)

B. Conscious *Emotions*

1. Cause us to follow our own desires, more than anything else

2. Feelings and emotions are not spontaneous, but are the direct result of what we have allowed in our thought life

3. God must change our feelings, we can only choose to relinquish them. Healing is a process

4. All negative feelings are not sin. "Be angry and sin not" (Ephesians 4:26)

  5. Any emotion, however, that separates us from God is sin and needs to be given over to God (depression) (1 John 5:17a)
  6. Can't just give our feelings to God, we must confess our part in holding on to those feelings (See Chapter 16) (Lamentations 3:41)

C. Conscious *Desires*
  1. Things we want, things that would please us "lust [*epithumia*] of the flesh." *Epithumia* means for the purpose of revenge (James 1:14-15)
  2. We have supernatural authority and power (because of the indwelling Spirit) to choose to do what God desires over what we ourselves desire
  3. We don't have to feel our choices, just be willing
  4. Often, after we have done God's Will, He gives us back "the desires of [our] hearts" (Psalm 37:4; Deuteronomy 6:10-11; 7:12-14; Luke 18:29-30; Matthew 6:33; Jeremiah 32:27; 1 Corinthians 2:9; Mark 10:29)

Our Souls Are Like Our Feet (John 13:8-10)
A. We must continually cleanse them (John 13:10)
B. Otherwise we will "have no part with Him" (John 13:8; Luke 12:47; Matthew 7:26)
C. This is the "shodding of our feet" (Ephesians 6:15; Matthew 25:10)

Loving God With All Our Soul Means:
A. Totally giving over and relinquishing all our thoughts, emotions, and desires that are contrary to God's (emptying ourselves) so that His Life (from our hearts) can come forth and fill our souls (Deuteronomy 30:20c; Philippians 1:21; Ephesians 3:19; 4:6; John 1:16; 12:24-26; 13:37b; 2 Corinthians 4:10-12; Mark 8:34-35; 1 Corinthians 15:31b, 36; Romans 6:11-13; Luke 9:23)
  1. It's becoming *one life* with Him (Philippians 1:21; 1 John 4:17c)
  2. It's *exchanging my image for His Image* (Deuteronomy 30:20; Galatians 3:16-19)
B. When we love Him in this way, He will give back to us all that we have relinquished (Jeremiah 32:27; Mark 10:29-30; 1 Corinthians 2:9)

"As it is written, Eye hath not seen, nor ear heard, neither have entered into the heart of man, the things which God hath prepared for them that love (agapao) Him." (1 Corinthians 2:9, emphasis added)

"Verily I say unto you, There is no man that hath left house, or brethren, or sisters, or father, or mother, or wife, or children, or lands, for My sake, and the Gospel's, But he shall receive a hundredfold now in this time, houses, and brethren, and sister, and mothers, and children, and lands, with persecutions; and in the world to come eternal life." (Mark 10:29-30)

READ: Deuteronomy 6:4-6; 10:12; 11:22; 30:20

Chapter 14: Eight Steps to Survival

David Needham, author of the book *Birthright* states, "The big task is not the finding of the truth, but the living of it!" I agree with him completely. What good are God's principles if they don't change our lives? With this in mind, let's put all we have learned so far into *practical* use. What are the steps in the moment by moment laying down of our wills and our lives to God? In other words, how do we love (*agapao*) God daily?

My Survival Kit

The following eight steps are what I call my "Survival Kit." (In the dictionary *survival* means, "keeping alive against all odds." How appropriate this definition is for these steps.) These are steps that God has laid out for us in Scripture to help us deal with our sin and once again, become open and cleansed vessels for His use. I literally go through these steps at least once a day, and sometimes as many as two and three times a day if I am dealing with something very difficult or extremely painful. These are the eight steps back to freedom of the Spirit.

The first four steps are really formalities. These are *attitudes* we need to form daily. These are not steps we have to do each time we quench God's Spirit, but simply attitudes we need to "wear" each day. We might go over these prayerfully each morning to remind ourselves to be cleansed vessels.

Inner Court Ritual

The final four steps of the Survival Kit, however, are *mandatory steps*, ones we *must* do these each time we sin and quench His Spirit. I call these four steps the "Inner Court Ritual," because they are the actual steps the priests took in the Inner Court of the Temple in order to deal with their sin.[1]

I recommend putting each of these steps, especially the last four, on 3x5 cards. Keep the cards with you at all times. When something bad occurs, take out the cards, prayerfully go through the steps, and then choose—by faith—to believe that God has reconciled you to Himself. God is faithful. If you do your part, He will do His.

Going through these steps every time we are confronted with a hurtful remark, a painful situation, pride, fear, resentment, bitterness and so on, is what enables us to be cleansed and prepared vessels for what God might call us to do next. It's imperative that we prevent the ungodly thoughts and feelings from accumulating in us. If we're *not* cleansed vessels, we will not be ready or available for God's use and we will find ourselves "contaminating" everyone we come in contact with (i.e., "making a stink" as Isaiah 3:24a says).

Paul declares in 2 Corinthians 2:15-16, "For we are unto God a sweet savour of Christ, in them that are saved, and in them that perish: To the one we are the savour of death unto death; and to the other the savour of life unto life."

Let's explore the *attitudes* that are essential to walking in God's Way of *Agape*.

Living Sacrifices

1) First, we need to have an attitude of continually *presenting our bodies [to God] as living sacrifices*. (Romans 12:1) What we are doing here is willingly giving God permission to walk through us and to expose anything that needs to be dealt with.[2]

[Notice that Romans 12:1 states, that we are to be "living sacrifices" which means (because we are living) we can get up off that altar at any time. Only by our continual choice do we choose to stay there.]

We need to be willing, on a daily basis, to offer ourselves to God and allow the Holy Spirit to expose what *He* wants in each of us. We don't have to "feel" this first step. In fact, most of these steps we will not feel at all, they simply will be "faith choices" or contrary choices.

A good prayer to pray is Psalm 19:12-13, "Cleanse Thou me from [hidden or] secret faults...Let them not have dominion over me." Also, Psalm 139:23-24, "Search me, O God, and know my heart: Try me, and know my thoughts: And see if there be any wicked way in me, And lead me in the way everlasting."

God Loves Us

As we are opening ourselves up to God, we must always remember how much He loves us and that He is always faithful to His promises. When something comes into my life that I don't understand, I often think of Job. Job said of God, "Though He slay me, yet will I trust in Him." (Job 13:15) In light of all the things the Lord allowed into his life, how on earth could Job have said that? He could say this because Job knew beyond a shadow of a doubt that God would be faithful to His promises no matter what he, himself, saw or felt.[3]

We must always keep this in mind. God will not allow anything to happen to us or allow anything in our lives that is not "Father filtered." So we can always trust Him and rely upon Him completely, knowing He is working out His purposes in our lives in His Way.

Again, if you have trouble really believing and experientially knowing in your own walk that God loves you and that He is faithful, then read Chapter 7 again. Also, go over the *Knowing God Loves Me* Scriptures in the Appendix. And, by faith, choose to believe what God says in those Scriptures.

[Remember: **Chart 6**, page 161, shows us that if we are "double-minded" (or twice souled), we will *not* be able to experience God's Love either for ourselves or for others.]

Denying Ourselves

2) The second crucially important attitude we need to *have on* each day is one of *continually denying ourselves*, denying our "justified" feelings, our rights, our frustrations, our offenses, and other hurts. This is something that we do internally (setting aside our own thoughts, emotions, and desires). As we mentioned in Chapter 8, denying ourselves on the inside is often much harder to do than denying ourselves "outwardly" (careers, positions of prominence, material things—houses, cars, clothes, etc.). Emotionally, this attitude of self denial will be very difficult because it hurts to lay ourselves down, especially when we are "justified" (by the world's standards) in feeling the way we do.

Each time we struggle with surrender, I would suggest reading Philippians 3: 8-15, where Paul says, "I count all things but loss for the excellency of the knowledge of Christ Jesus, my Lord."

We must ask ourselves, "Am I really more concerned with doing God's Will in my life then I am my own happiness?" There will be many times when we must choose to do God's Will, knowing that temporarily it will not bring us happiness.[4] But, of course, the lasting joy that will come from being in the center of His Will is something to which nothing can ever compare.

Be Willing

Luke 14:26 reminds us that we really cannot be God's disciples unless we are *willing to* (not wanting to or feeling like it, but just willing to) lay everything down (father, mother, wife, children, brothers, sisters). "Yea," He says, "even our very own lives!" Again, we don't have to *feel* willing in order to do this; we simply must be willing![5] Big difference!

I went to lunch several years ago with some dear old friends, and we began to talk about how very important it is simply to be willing to deny ourselves and follow God. One of the women said, "Nancy, I don't agree. I think some people just don't have the ability or the capability to lay everything down and do it God's way." She then gave various reasons why she was convinced they couldn't: dysfunctional families, co-dependency, poor marriages, physical abuse, emotional problems, and other environmental circumstances.

I replied, "Suzy, I really don't believe that's true! If they are Christians, then God is in them. And *He* is the One who makes them capable and gives them the ability to deny themselves. *All Christians are capable of laying themselves aside because God is in them, but not all Christians are willing to do so*! That is the bottom line!"

The people she was talking about weren't willing to lay themselves aside. And their excuses ranged from "dysfunctional families," to "my husband is not trying." I don't believe these things were the real problem because God has all the Love, Wisdom and Power they need. The real problem was that these people were simply not willing.

[Interesting to note: The same woman who made these comments to me has recently left her husband of 25 years. She is now out on her own, doing what she wants.]

Truly, *all Christians are capable, but **not** all Christians are willing!* This fact helps us to understand Matthew 24:12 a little more clearly: [in the end times] "the *Agape* of many will grow cold." In other words, all Christians have God's Love in them, but not all Christians are willing to set themselves aside, to let it flow.

When we are willing to lay everything down, God promises us in Luke 18:30 (as well as many other Scriptures) that He will return a hundredfold, in this life as well as in the world to come, all that we have chosen to give to Him.[6] It seems in my own life, the more I am willing to lay at God's feet, the more He returns a hundredfold! Read my book, *Why Should I Be the First to Change?* and see how God has restored a hundredfold my marriage, my family and my kids. The more I lay down of me, the more I get of Him. Now, I'm not any more capable than anybody else, but one thing is certain; I'm willing. And that seems to be all that's necessary! 1 Corinthians 2:9 declares, "But as it is written, Eye hath not seen, nor ear heard, neither have entered into the heart of man, the things which God hath prepared for them that love [*agapao*—totally give themselves over to] Him."[7]

So trust God completely when you lay your life down to Him; it then frees Him to perform miracles.

Get Up and Do What God Says

3) Another crucial attitude we must have is that of being willing to *obey God's Will, no matter what He tells us to do* (no matter how we feel, no matter what we think, no matter what we want). We are to get up and be willing to do exactly what God has asked us to do.

The attitude we just spoke about in step #2 (denying ourselves) concerns our *inner man* (setting aside our own thoughts, emotions and desires, so God can fill us with His Life). This next step of obeying God's Will is different; it concerns the *outer man*—our outward actions. It's getting up and *doing in action* what God has called us to do, saying, "Not as I will, but as Thou wilt" (Matthew 26:39). Or, like Peter said, "at Thy word I will" (Luke 5:5). Again, we are trusting that God will perform His Will and His Life through us.

We are emotional creatures, and God is asking us here to set aside our own emotional responses and choose to act totally out of faith. Again, we don't have to *feel* willing in order to do this; we just must *be* willing. 2 Corinthians 8:11 states, "As there was a readiness to will, so there may be a performance also."

If this is a difficult step, I would suggest reading Philippians 2:5-9. This is the passage that talks about being "obedient unto death," not only on the inside choosing to lay aside our own thoughts and emotions, but now, on the outside, getting up and actually doing in action whatever God has called us to do.

Example: "Obedient Unto Death"

Here is a wonderful example of how one of my dearest friends overcame her pride, humbled herself, and became "obedient unto death." Sarah is only five feet tall and weighs about 100 pounds soaking wet. Her husband had an affair with a woman who worked in his office. Sarah found out about it and was violently angry. The next day she marched down to her husband's office and literally beat up this woman.

A year or so later, God got hold of Sarah and really began to transform her life. One of the things God began to speak to her about was her actions to the woman at the office. He convinced Sarah that it was His Will for her to go back to the office and ask this woman's forgiveness for beating her up.

My precious friend not only chose to deny herself (she was willing to set aside her own "justified" feelings and emotions), but she also was willing to get up and *do* what God had asked her to do (go to her husband's office and ask forgiveness of this woman). Could you have done that? I'm not so sure I could have.

When the lady at the office saw Sarah coming, she understandably ran. Sarah pursued her, however, and they finally began to talk. Sarah asked the woman's forgiveness for beating her up and then told the lady she also forgave her for taking her husband away. The woman was so amazed and so bewildered that Sarah, sensing an opportunity to talk more, asked if she would like to go to lunch and she agreed.

At lunch, Sarah had a chance to share what God was doing in her own life. The woman sought to know more and more. They became friends and, to this day, are still friends. Only in God's Kingdom could something like this come about! Sarah is a real and true and precious friend of mine. I believe the miracle happened because my sweet friend was willing in action to "be obedient unto death."

Do you love God so much that you are not only willing to deny what you think, what you feel and what you desire, but also are willing to get up and *do* what God has called you to do? This is what God is asking each of us daily.

Take Every Thought Captive

4) The final attitude we must have in order to walk God's Way of *Agape* is to be willing to *take every thought captive*.

2 Corinthians 10:5-6 instructs, "Casting down imaginations and every high thing that exalteth itself against the knowledge of God, and *bringing into captivity every thought* to the obedience of Christ; and having in a *readiness to revenge all disobedience*, when your obedience is fulfilled." (emphasis added)

[Note: The next four steps (The Inner Court Ritual) are how we "revenge all disobedience."]

In the last chapter, we talked about the critical importance of catching our negative thoughts. We said our thoughts are vital because our thoughts are the first to be triggered in the chain reaction of our souls.[8] Remember, our thoughts stir up our emotions; our emotions then influence our desires; and our desires are what produce our actions. For this reason we need to go after the ungodly thoughts first and take them captive. If we can catch these negative thoughts first, then we prevent the chain reaction altogether.

When we *don't* take every thought captive and we don't put off our corrupt thoughts and we just go along with the tide of emotion, we end up confused, discouraged, and depressed. And, of course, that's just exactly what the enemy wants.

To continually recognize our negative thoughts and to renew our minds takes constant discipline and effort. Sometimes it would be a lot easier just to give in and let those wild emotions rule. But, do you know what happens when we do this? We die! *If we don't take those ungodly thoughts captive, they take us captive.*

Personal Example: Move Again?

Chuck and I have just been through several horrendous years of stretching, testing, and trial. In 1991 we lost everything through bankruptcy: our ultimate "dream home" in Big Bear, California, our cars, our insurance, and the list goes on.

We were forced to move to a smaller, rented home. The next year that rented house turned out to be on the epicenter of a 6.7 earthquake that destroyed most of our personal belongings. Actually, we were the fortunate ones. Houses on both sides of us twisted off their foundations. However, we were forced to move again.

In September of that same year we moved to Idaho, with great anticipation of finally having our own home again. When we got here, however, we found that the property we thought had been purchased for us had fallen out of escrow. Once again, we had to move since we had already moved all of our belongings into a building on the property.

That made four moves in two years, besides three total clean-up jobs after the 7.2 earthquake (15 miles away in Landers, California), the 6.7 earthquake under our home in Big Bear, and a 5.5 aftershock.

None of these moves were my choice! Moving is never easy. But moving for us now is doubly hard because we have 37 years of collectibles (really old and broken now because of extensive earthquake damage), plus all the ministry's furniture, computers, files, and office equipment.

Every time I looked at my circumstances, I would become overwhelmed, buried in my emotions, totally captive to my own negative thinking ("Why, God?"), and paralyzed in my walk.

But when I chose to obey God's Word and take those thoughts captive, whether I felt like it or not, God would always be faithful to remove my doubt, my fears, my anger, and my confusion, and fill me with His peace and strength. Once again I could go on. If, however, I didn't catch those negative thoughts, it never failed: I would sink and drown in my circumstances.[9] Truly, if we don't take those corrupt thoughts captive, they *do* take us captive!

Spirit-Controlled Thinking

Remember, we are *not* responsible for the original self-centered, negative, or bad thought when it first comes in. It's what we choose to do with that thought that produces the sin or not. If we recognize the ungodly thought and choose to give it over to God, then we have not sinned; we have not quenched His Spirit. However, if we don't do anything with that thought, and we allow it to stir up self-centered feelings, then it will be sin.

To be aware of, recognize, and then catch the ungodly thoughts as they come in is critical. We are to refuse them, crucify them, and annihilate them. We are not to even think them, let alone speak them. As Philippians 4:8 instructs, we need to fill our minds with good things. "Finally, brethren, whatsoever things are true, whatsoever things are honest, whatsoever things are just, whatsoever things are pure, whatsoever things are lovely, whatsoever things are of good report; if there be any virtue, and if there be any praise, think on these things."

Mandatory Steps

The next four steps are critical to do *each time* we recognize we have quenched God's Spirit and are separated from God. (See **Chart 6**, page 161.)

I call these four steps the *Inner Court Ritual* because, as we said, the priests of Solomon's Temple actually went through each of these steps in the Inner Court when they dealt with sin. First, the priests went to the ten Bronze Lavers to *wash their hands and feet* before worshipping, then they went to the Holocaust Altar where they *offered their sacrifices,* and lastly they *bathed totally* in the Molten Sea. (Be sure to see the *Be Ye Transformed* tapes for more details of this ceremony.)

These steps, then, are not just something I have made up or something that I found in a psychology book. The Inner Court Ritual is the actual process that the Lord has laid out in Scripture to help us deal with our sin.

So, if something has just occurred that has already caused us to make wrong emotional choices (sin), and we are already feeling hurt, angry, bitter, resentful, doubtful, prideful, fearful, and so on, then we *must* do the following four steps in order to have His Life begin to flow, once again.[10]

[Note: In the actual Inner Court Ritual, Step #5 and #6 were really only one step. But because so much goes on in this first step, for the sake of simplicity, I have made it into two separate steps.]

Recognize Self-Centered Thoughts

5) We must *recognize, acknowledge and experience the negative thoughts, emotions, and desires* (self life) that have just occurred. We must not vent these feelings nor stuff them, but learn to give them to God. We need to ask God to *expose* what is *really* going on inside of us (i.e., bring to light the real truth).

[Note: This is what the priests did at the Lavers of Bronze. The Lavers themselves were made of women's looking glasses (mirrors of polished metal).[11] As the priests bent over the lavers to wash their hands, they would see their own reflection, their own true selves in the mirrored Lavers.]

The priest's actions are symbolic of exactly what the Lord requires us to do. We are to ask God not only to bring to light what's going on in our own conscious thoughts, emotions, and desires, but also to shed light on all those things in our hidden chambers. In other words, we want the real *root causes* of our negative thoughts and emotions to be exposed. Why are we reacting so violently over what has just happened? What's really going on?

[Keep in mind the conscious, surface emotions are really just the symptoms. The real root causes are often hidden. If the root cause can be exposed and gotten rid of, then the surface emotions will not occur again.]

Get Alone With God

It is important at this point, if we can, to get alone with the Lord so we can go through these steps and deal with our sin properly. Try not to put this off. The times I have put off going through these steps, I seem to contaminate everyone I come in contact with.

As Isaiah 3:24 tells us, "Instead of [a] sweet smell there shall be [a] stink."

I stop now, whenever I find myself hurt, angry, resentful, critical, self-centered, prideful, ungrateful, anxious, afraid, confused, bitter, judgmental, or filled with any negative emotion, and I try to get alone with God and go through these steps. Jesus is the only One who can expose and cleanse our sin—and totally heal us from the inside out.

Even in the middle of an argument with Chuck, as I have said before, if I find myself getting emotional and reacting self-centeredly, I stop the conversation, and I simply tell Chuck, "I need to go and be with Jesus now or I am going to explode." The first time I did this he was offended, but now he says he likes me so much better after I come out from "being with Jesus," that he freely lets me go.

In order to respond the way God would have us, it's critical to be "cleansed." Don't ever *confront* someone or *take a stand* with someone, unless you are a clean vessel! If you're not clean, it will be self life out there and not God's Life at all. And you will sink even further into the pit than you were before.

Even if I can only go through these steps mentally at the time, I do it. By "mentally," I mean that, because I am busy, I'm not able, at that moment to pull away from the situation to be alone with God and let my feelings out. I can only go through these steps in my mind. Even if that's all I can do, I do it. Preventing sin from accumulating is essential.

Acknowledge Real Thoughts and Emotions

We are to be aware of and acknowledge the sinful feelings that are coming up. We need to recognize the fears, the insecurities and the doubts that we are experiencing. We need to call them for what they are, and "name" what we are really thinking and feeling. Being truthful and acknowledging these things is important; God knows it all anyway.

One woman asked me not too long ago if we should let our real feelings out. "Does God really want us to do that?" she asked. I told her that God has given us a perfect example in Scripture. David was called a "man after God's own heart,"[12] and yet we read how he expressed his real thoughts and feelings to God in Psalm 55:15, Psalm 109:5-20 and other Scriptures.

Remember, we must recognize our ungodly thoughts and emotions before we can hand them over to God. We can't give something to God if we don't know what it is. This is why we should try to describe what we are feeling: "I am angry; I am resentful; I feel betrayed; I am fearful." We can cry, scream, or yell if we want to. Remember, we are only doing this alone with God.

To experience our real thoughts and feelings is crucial. This will not only help us in understanding what we are really feeling, but also will help in recognizing exactly what to give to God. This is the point in God's plan where we can let our "self life" totally hang out. We're not just to say, "I am not supposed to feel this way," and then stuff our *real* emotions down in those hidden chambers. We're all human, and we are to acknowledge our real feelings.

This acknowledgment is part of dealing with our sin and part of the healing process. Often times, I will go through these steps and either because of time pressures or a lack of opportunity, forget to really let my feelings out. After a day or so, I wonder why my peace has not returned. More often than not, it's because I have forgotten to really experience my negative feelings. They are still bottled up within me. Therefore, I have to go back once again through these steps. Acknowledging how I feel, I believe, is part of the restoration process.

Example: "This Message Is Impossible"

Emily, a dear friend of mine shared with me that she knew she had years of emotional walls that she had never released and given over to God. All these things old thoughts and feelings were coming to the surface because Emily's husband had just recently left her after 35 years of marriage.

Emily had always known there was *something* preventing her from intimately knowing Jesus, but she could never figure out exactly what it was. She received the *Be Ye Transformed* tapes and immediately gave God permission to expose whatever He wanted in her.

Two days later, she called me up and said, "Nan, this message is absolutely impossible. Ever since I listened to these tapes, I've been an emotional basket case! I started two days ago to try to live this message, and today I feel I am worse off than when I started. I am consumed with jealousy, bitterness, and anger! I am such a failure as a Christian and I feel horrible!" Of course the enemy was right there on her shoulder, whispering his lies.

I asked Emily if she had given God permission to expose what He wanted in her. She avowed, "Certainly, that's the first thing I did." Then I replied, "Praise Him and thank Him. He is just answering your prayer! God is showing you all your real thoughts and emotions. Don't worry, you are right on course."

We Must "See" Our Sin

I told Emily to simply recognize what God was bringing up and then experience those feelings. I told her to name the emotions and the thoughts as they came up; get them out any way she could; and then, go through the steps we are now learning and get rid of those thoughts and feelings for good.

What Emily forgot was that God must expose our negative, ungodly thoughts and emotions *before* we are able to hand them over to Him. Being human, my friend needed to see what she was feeling before she could choose to give it to God. *We can't give things over to God if we don't know what they are!* Because of ignorance, Emily was allowing the hurtful feelings to push her into depression and discouragement.

Scripture never says we won't have negative, bad, and self-centered thoughts, emotions, and desires.[13] We're all still human and we'll have these thoughts and feelings until the day we see Jesus. The Bible does say, however, that we can have victory over the "desires of the flesh,"[14] if we constantly make faith choices to give these negative things over to God—not allowing them to motivate our actions.

Galatians 5:16 tells us that if we choose to "walk in the Spirit," then we won't carry out the desires of the flesh.

Three Choices

The question becomes, "What do we do with our constant negative thoughts and emotions?" We have three choices: We can *vent them to others,* we can *stuff them down in the hidden chambers*, or we can *give them to God and be rid of them forever.* We do this last choice by learning the Inner Court Ritual.

It's important to understand that we can't hold on to negative thoughts and feelings without eventually acting out of them. Even if we try to keep them buried, they still become the motivation for all our actions, whether we are aware of it or not. Burying our hurts, memories, fears, and so on, does not get rid of them. The only thing that gets rid of them, is allowing God to expose them and then our giving them over to Him.

Example: Twenty Years of Buried Hurt

A woman wrote to me several years ago after she had attended a retreat where I had spoken. She shared how much she hated the "Inner Court Ritual" part of the *Be Ye Transformed* message. She said she had such a hard time with these principles, but she wasn't really sure why. Even after she left the retreat, she just couldn't get the study off her mind. Finally, she decided to ask God to expose why she was so upset. "Let's see if this really works," she sarcastically thought to herself. Then she went through these steps.

God answered her prayer and exposed exactly why she was so upset. He showed her that she still had tremendous resentment and bitterness towards her first husband, who had left her some 20 years before. God showed her that she was reacting to these principles out of those hurts—she never wanted to have to think about that man again.

This dear woman thought she had dealt with all those hurt feelings years ago. In reality, all she had done was bury those negative emotions and for twenty years she had carried them around with her. After wrestling with God for some time, she decided to go through these steps all over again. Only this time, she wanted to deal with her hurts the proper way. So she asked God to bring up all that was buried down in her soul.

She said she experienced such a freedom that day that even her new husband commented that evening, "What's going on! You look so happy!" Even our physical countenance will be changed when we learn to really love God and are freed from something we have carried around for years. She sat right down and wrote me a sixteen page letter about what the Lord had shown her.

After I had written her back, I got another ten page letter from her, telling me of the most exciting miracle of all. Five years previously, she had suffered a major heart attack during an operation. Since then she had been in constant pain and on a heavy dosage of heart medication. When she made the choice to let go of the horrible feelings of hate for her first husband, God supernaturally healed her heart condition. She wrote me that she has no more pain and has taken no heart medication since. The doctor, who has confirmed her healing, is totally baffled. I don't believe we realize how closely tied our spiritual and psychological well-being is with our physical bodies. Healing in one area often does affect the other.

In order to be truly free of our past and be able to act out of God's Love, we must get rid of our ungodly thoughts and feelings the proper way: by allowing God to expose them, by looking squarely at them and calling them what they are, and then by choosing to give these things back over to God and be rid of them forever. (Psalm 103:12)

Confess and Repent

6) Along with step #5 (recognizing and experiencing our feelings), we must now *confess and repent of all that the Holy Spirit has shown us*. In addition we must, by faith, *unconditionally forgive anyone who has wronged us*, just as God has unconditionally forgiven us. (Lavers of Bronze)

[Note: If we have caught the negative, ungodly thought and we have not entertained it or mulled it over, then we can skip this step of confession and repentance because there is no sin or disobedience involved. We can just unconditionally forgive the other person involved and go on to the next step.

If, however, we know we have held on to these unrighteous thoughts and feelings for a while and mulled them over or entertained them, then we need to confess them as sin. They have already separated us from God and we need to repent of them (change our mind about holding onto them), and choose to go God's Way.]

This step of confession and repentance is *our* responsibility. As 1 John 1:9 says, "If *we confess* our sins, [then] *He is faithful and just to forgive* us our sins." (emphasis added)

To acknowledge that what we have done has quenched God's Spirit in us is critical.[15] So we need to confess *ownership* of our negative thoughts and emotions and then simply choose to *turn around* from following them.

Example: "I Confess I Am Depressed"

For example, if we are depressed (I am assuming that the depression is emotional and mental, and not physiologically caused), and we have been following this emotional way of thinking for some time, we can't just say to the Lord, "Help me with my depression," and expect Him to take our sad and brooding thoughts away.

We must say, "Father, I *confess* I am depressed (I *own* these emotions). I confess I have chosen to entertain and follow these morose feelings over what You would have me do (i.e., give them to You), and it has quenched Your Spirit in me. That is sin. I now choose to turn around (I *repent)* from following what these things are telling me to do and choose instead to follow You."

Remember, we are not responsible to change our own feelings. We can't do that. We are only responsible to put in charge the Person who *can* change our feelings, and that Person is God. And we do that by confessing we *own* the feelings and then repenting of them. God, then, is free to begin to change our feelings and align them with our faith choice.

Forgive Others

In this sixth step, we are not only to confess and repent of our own sins, but we are also unconditionally to *forgive others* of theirs. God is hindered (we've quenched His Spirit) from working on us and also the other party until we have released them.[16] And we release them by unconditionally forgiving them, whether they ask for it or not![17]

So, we choose to forgive because we are commanded to by Jesus: "And when ye stand praying, forgive, if ye have anything against any, that your Father also, who is in heaven, may forgive you your trespasses. But if ye do not forgive, neither will your Father, who is in heaven, forgive your trespasses."[18] (Mark 11:25-26) In other words, we forgive, because He has forgiven us.

Jesus gave us His own example: In Luke 23:34, as they were crucifying Him, He said, "Lord, forgive them; for they know not what they do."

Sometimes, it's difficult to forgive others in our own strength. This is just another place that we can give God our own hurt feelings and trust Him for His *unconditional* Love. Through Jesus, we can extend that unconditional forgiveness—because of what He has done for us. In other words, if we love Him, He will enable us, strengthen us, and give us the grace to forgive others. 2 Corinthians 2:10 tells us the way we can unconditionally forgive them is "in the person of Jesus Christ." [19]

That we receive (by faith) God's forgiveness for whatever sin we may have committed is imperative. 1 John 1:9 again says, "If we confess our sins, *He is faithful and just to forgive us [all] of our sins*." (emphasis added)

If you have trouble believing and receiving His forgiveness, read Chapter 7 again. Make a list of all the Scriptures on forgiveness and read them over and over again. By faith, make those contrary choices to believe those Scriptures as truth. (Remember, it's not by *feelings*, but by *faith*.) God then, in His perfect timing, will align your feelings to match what you have chosen to believe by faith.[20]

If we are at fault in a situation, sometimes (but not always) God will have us go back and ask forgiveness from the other person involved. If we have offended them, God will often require us to go and reconcile with them. Remember, however, each situation is different. Sometimes we can just seek God's forgiveness in our minds and that will be enough. At other times, however, God will have us physically go and ask the other person for forgiveness. In each instance, we must pray and seek God's Will as to what He would specifically have us do. God is so wonderful. He will not only tell us what to do, but He will also give us the strength to be able to do it.

Give All to God

7) Once God has shown us not only our conscious negative thoughts and emotions but also their root causes, and we have confessed them as sin and repented of them, then it's imperative that we *give all these things over to God*. God will not violate our free will by forcibly taking these things from us; we must willingly choose to give them or cast them over to Him. (This step is symbolic of the priests *sacrificing* their offerings for sin on the Holocaust or Brazen Altar.)

In like manner, God wants us to give Him—to sacrifice to Him—not only all of our conscious negative thoughts and emotions, but also their subconscious root causes in those hidden chambers. In other words, He wants to purge all of our sins by His Blood.[21] As we give these things over to Him, He then is able to purge them from us, "as far as the east is from the west." (Psalm 103:12)

A Miracle

So often we take for granted the miracle that God really does take our sins away "as far as the east is from the west," when we confess and repent of them. Do we realize what this really means? It means that we are allowed to begin each day with a clean slate—a fresh start. Chuck and I were talking last night what an incredible gift this is. It allows us to blow it badly with each other; and yet, if we confess and repent of those things and forgive each other, God *does* totally cleanse us—even with the memory of that sin wiped away. What a miracle this is!

As Christians we take this so for granted. Just think of it. If you were a nonbeliever, all your fights with loved ones, all your guilt, your failures, mistakes, ungodliness, errors, wrongs, immorality, and every sin you commit would always be with you. You would bury them in the "hidden chambers" but they would always be there to motivate your actions. You could never get away from them or have a fresh, new start. No wonder so many relationships without Christ are doomed to failure. I weep at the thought, because that miracle is there for the asking. But many simply refuse to take it.[22]

Give As "Love Gifts"

Luke 11:39-41 states: "And the Lord said unto him, Now do ye Pharisees make clean the outside of the cup and the platter; but your inward part is full of ravening and wickedness. Ye fools, did not He that made that which is without make that which is within also? But rather give alms [give as "love gifts"] of such things as ye have [within]; and, behold [then] all things are clean unto you [without]."

Alms in the New Testament were *love gifts* "with no strings attached." I think of giving our sins over to God as "alms." It's just like giving Him "love gifts (or offerings) with no strings attached." As we sacrifice or offer up to God our alms—all that is not of faith—He then cleanses us (and makes all things clean for us) from the inside out.

Do Something Physical

Doing something "physical" with the things that we give over to God is important, in order to truly experience getting rid of them. A dear friend of mine writes down on a scrap of paper all her hurts, wounds, memories—whatever God has shown her. Then she literally wraps these pieces of paper up in packages and presents them to God as "love gifts."

Personally, I like to burn them! I write down everything I give to God and then burn that scrap of paper. I like to watch it being consumed. It's a graphic picture to me that those things are gone forever.

Most of the things that God shows us are "of the flesh," and will usually go away immediately or at least within a few days if we are faithful to go through these cleansing steps.

Recognize the Battles

Some of the things that will come up however, are longstanding strongholds of the enemy. These often become spiritual battles in order to get rid of.[23] So, if certain things seem to stick around for awhile, don't give up and say, "Oh, this just doesn't work for me!" That's exactly what the enemy wants you to do. Recognize it's a battle. Know you will win if you will just persevere. God is already the Victor. Luke 10: 19 assures us that we have authority over all the power of the enemy. Recognize, however, that it might take some time before you can *see* that victory.

[Please review Chapter 13, "Strongholds of the Enemy" about the critical importance of our thoughts. More details of this spiritual battle are covered there.]

Read God's Word

8) After we have given over to God our negative thoughts, emotions, and desires, the last step in dealing with our sins is that we must *read God's Word.* We must replace the lies with the truth. God is the only One who, by His Word, can *cleanse, sanctify and heal our souls* completely.

[Remember, it was at the Molten Sea that the priests actually immersed themselves bodily, in order to receive total cleansing. They had become splattered with blood at the Brazen or Holocaust altar and now needed a complete bathing.]

Reading God's Word after sacrificing is a very critical step. After we have confessed, repented, and given all to God, we are still *bloody* and in desperate need of God's complete healing power. Only God's Word can totally restore us. God is the One who washes us "with the washing of water by the Word." (Ephesians 5:26) At this point, as I read God's Word, I literally picture myself being bathed in God's Love. One of my favorite Scriptures to read at this moment is Psalm 18:

"...In my distress I called upon the Lord...He heard my voice out of His temple...He bowed the heavens, and came down...." (verses 6 and 9)

Another suggestion: Memorize appropriate Scriptures. Often, we must go through these cleansing steps when we are away from home and don't have our Bible at hand. If we have memorized Scriptures, then we can bathe in His Word anyway.

Many have asked me what Scriptures I memorize. My answer is always, "Check the outlines at the end of each chapter, or the 'Survival Kit Prayer' at the end of this chapter. See which Scriptures minister to you and use those."[24] Most importantly, remember *truth must be put back in where the lies have been removed,* so that more lies don't return. Be sure to read Luke 11:24-26.

Now step out in faith, knowing that God will be faithful to perform His Will through you and to align your feelings with your choices.

Praise Him

A very important thing to do after we have finished the Inner Court Ritual is to fill our thoughts and minds with praise. Again this is what the priests did after they finished in the Outer Court. They returned to the Holy Place where they changed their clothes and began to sing and praise God.

After we have read God's Word, we, too, can change our clothes. We have "put off" the old and "put on" the new, and now we can worship the Lord. We can praise Him for who He is (that He has everything under control) and that He "will work all things together" for our best, since we do love (*agapao*) Him.[25] See Romans 8:28.

This Scripture, by the way, doesn't speak to those who *storge* or *phileo* God, but only to those who *agapao* Him. To those who totally give themselves over to Him, God can then maneuver the circumstances according to His perfect Will.

Example: Jilted At the Altar

I received a letter from Barbara, a dear friend of mine who had just gone through a very traumatic experience. The man she was in love with and engaged to marry fell in love with someone else. He didn't tell Barbara until he broke off the engagement and announced that he was going to marry this other woman.

Of course, Barbara, was devastated. She wrote me of the tremendous struggle she went through those first few nights after she learned the truth. She said the hurtful thoughts and emotions kept wanting to crush her, but she was determined to give them to God and not to crumble.

Barbara said she kept choosing to hand her hurts over to God, reading His Word, and praising Him. She praised Him because she knew He loved her and that He would not withhold any "good thing" from her. By faith, and by making those continual contrary choices, Barbara said she persevered and broke through. By the next day, she had the victory. Her thoughts and feelings were aligned with what she had chosen, and she had peace.[26]

Example: Putting It All Together

One woman came up to me after a recent seminar and said: "Okay, Nan, this is great material. I love the class. But I need one last practical and simple example of how all these steps work together. Can you please tell me an example that points out all the steps?"

Here, then, is a hypothetical story which shows all these steps in action:

Your unsaved mother-in-law comes over for dinner. You are sitting across from her at the table when all of a sudden, in front of everyone, she makes some very derogatory comments about your dinner, your house, your kids and so on.

At first you get flustered, then humiliated, then hurt, and then just plain angry. At this point what would you do? Do you continue to sit there and hypocritically smile at her when you would really like to sock her and tell her off?

Remember, we are not responsible for the original ungodly thoughts when they first come in; it's what we choose to do with them that produces the sin or not. And as we mentioned before, if you don't do anything with those negative thoughts, they will automatically stir up your bitterness and resentment, which will definitely affect your choices, and eventually, all your actions towards her.

If I were in this sensitive situation, I'd deal with my angry thoughts right then. I'd excuse myself from the table and I would go to wherever I could be alone with the Lord (my bedroom, the bathroom, my car, wherever). I'd want to catch those hurts and negative thoughts before they are programmed in and before I act out of them!

The first step then, is to *recognize and acknowledge the negative (unloving) thoughts and feelings* I am experiencing, so I can deal with them. I can't deal with them unless I know what they are.

In the "prayer closet," wherever that might be, I'd tell God that my mother-in-law's remark really hurt. "It is humiliating and embarrassing every time she puts me down in front of everyone." I'd go on and express and name all my genuine feelings about her. I'd even cry if I needed to. In other words, I would *experience my real emotions*.

At the same time, I would also ask God if there are any "root causes" for why I'm reacting this way. Perhaps my mother-in-law has behaved this same way numerous times over the years, but I have never really dealt with it before. Perhaps before, I simply buried my feelings. I'd ask God to expose everything He wants to from my *hidden chambers* regarding this situation.

If God shows me that I have felt this way for years over my mother-in-law's insults, but I have never properly dealt with these things before, then I would obviously need to *confess* that I "owned" these unrighteous thoughts and feelings.

Even though I wasn't aware that I could give my hurts to God, I still chose to follow my own ways over God's ways. Therefore, it has quenched His Spirit in me, and it has become sin. At this point then, I would need to change my mind, turn around, and *repent* from following these bad thoughts and emotions even if they might be justified by the world's standards.

Also at this point, I would need to *unconditionally forgive* my mother-in-law so that God could be released to work in her life as well as my own.

I would then *give all the hurts, bitterness, resentment and anger, "justified or not,"* and anything else that God has shown me over to God and ask Him to purge these things from me.

Finally, I would *get into His Word* and read a few of my favorite passages, so that His soothing truth could go back into the hidden chambers where the lies have been. Then I would praise Him for being my God and for doing all these things for me.

Even though I might not *feel* any different at that moment, I would know by faith that I am a cleansed vessel; therefore, God's Life has been freed to flow through me once again. At this point I would go back to the table, expecting God to love my mother-in-law through me.

Hebrews 10:22 states, "Let us draw near with a true heart in full assurance of faith, having our hearts sprinkled from an evil conscience, and our bodies washed with pure water."

This is how the Inner Court Ritual works. It might seem like a lot to remember now because it's all so new. But, I promise you, if you are faithful to continue to confess, repent, and give all (anything that is not of faith) to God these steps will become first nature to you, because, as you will soon see, there really is no other choice!

"Just Give It to God"

For years, whenever I had a problem, I've heard, "Well, just give it to God." But I have never understood exactly what it really meant... *until now*! Daily I go through these steps (and sometimes two or three times a day if I am dealing with a particularly hard situation). This is how I *keep alive against all odds*.

In the back of this chapter I have enclosed my own daily prayer, my *"Survival Kit Prayer."* I wrote this prayer when I first started to practice these steps years ago. I found I really needed something to lead me to the feet of Jesus and to help me go through the Inner Court Ritual. The prayer was a guide to help me capture my wild and frantic thoughts and feelings after I have had a painful experience. It's just a rote prayer and it's long, but it does work.

Some of the ladies have taken the basic content of my prayer, shortened it, made it personal to them and written it on 3x5 cards. This is a great idea! So if this prayer doesn't suit your needs, write your own. Keep it with you at all times—believe me, you will need it.

[A couple of women suggested that I make a word game out of the four steps. One named them 1) See it; 2) Say it; 3) Send it; and, 4) Supplant it. The other called them 1) Recognize it; 2) Repent of it; 3) Rocket it up; and, 4) Replace it. If these suggestions help, by all means, use them.]

At those moments when we are dealing with doubt, hurt, fear, pride, bitterness, resentment, anger, and other negative feelings, we often are too emotional to take every thought captive to the obedience of Christ. And we need something to help us along.[27] Having those steps or this prayer handy, will help you through many tough times and assure you victory.

Be An Example

Be open and frank with your children when you use these steps. Give them an example and a model to follow. They, too, have hurts and fears and insecurities just as we do. God wants them healed also. (I have been praying about writing a *Way of Agape* book for youth. Please join me in that prayer. God's timing will be perfect.)

Keeping a notebook or journal of your adventure with God is also very important. Date the entries, especially when you give something over to God. That way when Satan tries to counterfeit feelings and thoughts that have already been dealt with, you can point to the entry and say, "That has already been handled!" (I might not feel it yet, but by faith I believe it.[28])

In Conclusion: "For Me to Live Is Christ"

Loving God *practically* means moment-by-moment relinquishing our wills and our lives to Him. It means laying down all our thoughts, emotions, and desires that are contrary to His so that His Life, from our hearts, can come forth. Loving God is becoming *one heart, one will and one Life with Him*. It means exchanging our own image for the Image we were created to bear, which is His Image: His Thoughts, His Love, and His Power. Loving God is being so completely at one with Him that all that's seen through us is Jesus! And we can say like Paul, "For me to live is Christ." (Philippians 1:21) Christ, at this point, is not just *in* our life, *He is our life!*

This is the faithful marriage relationship that God desires for each of us, and He expresses it so beautifully in Hosea 2:19-20:

> "I will betroth thee unto Me for ever; yea, I will betroth thee unto Me in righteousness, and in judgment and in lovingkindness, and in mercies. I will even betroth thee unto Me in faithfulness: and [then] thou shalt know the Lord."

Endnotes:

1. See the Be Ye Transformed tapes.

2. Genesis 15:17

3. Job 19:25-26

4. See Chapter 8, "Do You Love God?"

5. 2 Corinthians 8:11-12

6. See Chapter 13, "One Hundredfold."

7. Job 42:10b

8. See Chapter 13, "Conscious Thoughts."

9. The end of this story is in Chapter 7, "Lost Everything."

10. This is the "putting off" and the "putting on" that Colossians 3:8-14 talks about. This is also how we "resist the devil" as James 4:7 and 1 Peter 5:8 exhort us. Finally, this is also how we "renew our minds" (Romans 12:2).

11. Exodus 38:8

12. Acts 13:22

13. Romans 7:15,19

14. Romans 7:25

15. Again, see Chapter 11, "Nothing Shall Separate Us."

16. John 20:23 says there is a supernatural "bond" that occurs between the one who committed the trespass and the one who will not forgive it. God is hindered from working until unconditional forgiveness releases that bond. Satan, in the mean time, works havoc. (2 Corinthians 2:10-11)

17. Mark 11:26; Matthew 18:35; and especially John 20:23

18. Matthew 18:32-22; Ephesians 4:32; Colossians 3:13

19.   2 Corinthians 2:10

20.   Ecclesiastes 3:11a

21.   Hebrews 9:14

22.   Proverbs 28:13

23.   See Chapter 13, "Strongholds of the Enemy."

24.   Proverbs 24:4

25.   Romans 8:28

26.   Isaiah 26:3

27.   Psalm 40:12b

28.   Every step of "giving ourselves over to God" (the Inner Court Ritual) is covered in great detail in the eight tape series—and in a future book called Be Ye Transformed.

SURVIVAL KIT PRAYER

PRAISE HIM: Psalms 8, 9, 19, 33, 34, 47, 48, 66, 89, 93, 96, 98, 100, 101-105, 107, 111-113, 115, 118, 134-136, 138, 144-150.

I love you, Lord God, with all my heart, all my will, and all my soul. I pray my actions today will show and prove my love for You. *I praise you, Father,* for who You are and thank You for this (situation, circumstance, feeling, opportunity, etc.) because I know You have allowed it for my learning and my growth, so I might come to intimately know You better and be more conformed into Your image. (Matthew 22:37; Hebrews 13:15; 1 Thessalonians 5:18; Deuteronomy 8:16c)

I choose to *present [my body] as a living sacrifice.* I choose to set aside my own thoughts, emotions, and desires and to listen to and follow only Your Voice (Your Word), no matter what You tell me to do because I know You love me and I am precious in your sight. (Romans 12:1-2; Philippians 3:8-15; Psalm 91; Psalm 18; 2 Corinthians 3:5; 10:5; Proverbs 23:4b; Isaiah 43:2-5; 54:10; 55:8-9; Jeremiah 31:3)

I know, Father, that You will never leave me nor forsake me. So *I choose to do Your Will,* Your pleasure, above my own at all costs. For You are my life. (Philippians 2:5-9; Matthew 26:39; Philippians 1:21; Galatians 2.20; Deuteronomy 30:19-20; Hebrews 13:5)

Inner Court Ritual

I choose, Father, to allow You to search my heart and my soul, and *expose any sin* (grease, fat), any barriers that have quenched Your Spirit and separated me from You. Show me my "self" (my hurts, my doubts, my fears, my pride, my anger, my insecurities, my unforgiveness, my criticalness, my bitternesses), any self-centeredness that has prevented me from being filled with Your Life to give to others. Shine your Holy Spirit light on any *root causes* for these things, so that I might be rid of them forever. (Isaiah 1:15; 59:2; Psalm 26:2; 51:10; 139:23-24; Nehemiah 4:10)

I *confess*, Father, that I am separated from You. I know that whatever is not of faith is sin, and I have sinned by letting my own self-centered thoughts and uncontrolled feelings consume me and motivate me. I have chosen to hang on to these things and follow them rather than follow what You want. I confess also that I have tried in my own ability and strength to work things out. I have not relied upon You. I have not obeyed and trusted You, and that is sin. (Romans 14:23; Psalm 51:1-4; Proverbs 28: 13; Isaiah 1:16; Psalm 141:8)

I *repent* of these things. I desire to turn around from following my own thoughts and feelings. I know if I don't release them to You, I will continue to act out of them. And I don't want to do that. I ask You, dearest Father, to forgive me for my sin, as I choose to *forgive* those who have hurt me and let me down. (1 John 1:9; Matthew 6: 14-15; 18:21-22,35; Isaiah 1:18b) **(Ten Bronze Lavers)**

Father, I choose to sacrifice and *give all these things* that You have shown me over to You and I ask you to purge them from me "as far as the east is from the west." (Psalm 103:12; Philippians 3:8; 2 Timothy 2:21; Isaiah 1:25) **(Holocaust or Brazen Altar)**

I trust You, by faith, to *cleanse, sanctify, and heal* me by the "washing of the water of Your Word." I receive, by faith, Your forgiveness of my sins, Your renewing of my mind and Your healing of my soul. I trust You, Father, to now change my feelings and my emotions to align with the choices I have made and to make me genuine. (Romans 12:2; Ephesians 5:26; Hebrews 10:22; Psalm 103:2-5; Psalm 119) **(Molten Sea)**

* * * * *

I know, by faith, that Your Life has now been freed to come forth from my heart and fill my soul. (Colossians 3:8,10; Ephesians 3:17-19; 4:22-24; 5:1-2; Romans 6: 13; 13:14; John 4:14; Philippians 1:21; Zechariah 3:4; Isaiah 52:1)

Also, by faith, I believe You will now openly hear and answer my prayers, because they are according to Your Will and not my own. (1 John 5:14-15)

By faith, I have done all that You have asked, so I can now stand firm against the enemy. Even if my feelings and my circumstances seem like nothing at all has changed, I will keep on choosing to walk by faith knowing that *You will do what You promise.* (Romans 4:21; Ephesians 6:10-18; Isaiah 40:29-31; James 1:12; 2 Corinthians 10:3-6)

My faith is in Your faithfulness, Father. I love You. (Isaiah 26:3-4; 1 John 5: 4b; 3:22)

Scriptural References:

Chapter 14

My "Survival Kit" (John 12:24-25; 2 Corinthians 4:11)

A. *Attitudes*
1. "Present [our] bodies as a living sacrifice" (Romans 12:1; Psalm 19:12-13; 139:23-24; Job 13:15; 2 Corinthians 7:1; 2 Timothy 2:21)
   a. Open ourselves up to God's inspection (Genesis 15:17)
   b. Remember how much He loves us (Psalm 118:6; Job 13:15)
2. (Inside) *Deny ourselves* (our "justified" feelings, own rights, frustrations, offences, etc.) (Philippians 3:8-15; John 12:24; Colossians 3:5, 8-10)
   a. Be willing to *lay everything down* (Luke 9:23; Ephesians 4:31; Matthew 10:39; Acts 20:24; Hebrews 12:1)
   b. Don't have to "feel willing," just be willing (Luke 14:26-33; 2 Corinthians 8:11-12)
   c. All Christians are capable of laying things down, but all are not willing to do so
   d. God will return hundredfold all we choose to lay down (Luke 18:29-30; Mark 10:29-30; 1 Corinthians 2:9)
3. (Outside) Get up and do what God has asked (Philippians 2:5-9; Ephesians 6:6; Psalm 40:8; Isaiah 1:19)
   a. "Not my will, but Thine" (Matthew 26:39; Luke 5:5; 1 Peter 4:2)
   b. Again, we don't have to "feel willing" (2 Corinthians 8:11)
4. "Take every thought captive" (2 Corinthians 10:5-6)
   a. If we don't take them captive, they will take us captive (James 1:14-15)
   b. Don't share negative things with others (Ephesians 4:29-32)
   c. Think only on good things (Philippians 4:8; Isaiah 43:18)

B. *Mandatory steps* (Inner Court Ritual) (2 Corinthians 10:5-6; James 4:7; 1 Peter 5:8-9) See *Be Ye Transformed* Series for more details
1. *Recognize the negative thoughts and emotions* as they come in (2 Corinthians 10:5)
   a. Get alone with God
   b. Acknowledge and experience negative feelings (2 Corinthians 13:5)
   c. Ask God to expose root causes from hidden chambers (Proverbs 20:27; Psalm 119:9-11; Job 12:22; 1 Corinthians 4:5; 2 Corinthians 13:5)
   . Why are we "reacting" this way?
   . We must "see" our own sin, before we can give it over (Psalm 139:23-24)

2. *Confess them as sin and repent of them* (Proverbs 1:23; 28:13: Isaiah
    1:16; Ezekiel 18:30b; James 4:8-10; 1 John 1:9; Acts 8:22a; Colossians
    3:13; John 20:23) (Lavers of Bronze)
    a.   We also must unconditionally forgive anyone who has wronged
         us (Matthew 6:14-15; 18:32-35; Colossians 3:13; 2 Corinthians
         2:10-11; Luke 23:34; Mark 11:25-26; John 13:14; Ephesians 4:32)
    b.   We must also know that God has forgiven us (1 John 1:9; Mat-
         thew 6:14)
3. *Give over to God* all that He has exposed (even the "justified" hurts
    and injustices) (Luke 11:39-40; Colossians 3:5,8; 1 Peter 5:7; Galatians
    5:24; Romans 6:11-13; 2 Timothy 2:21; Ephesians 5:2; 1 John 1:7)
    (Holocaust Altar)
    a.   Ask God to purge these things "as far as the east is from the west"
         (Psalm 103:12; Isaiah 6:1-7)
    b.   By faith believe God has done so
    c.   Ask God to change our feelings to match our choice (1 John 3:21)
4. *Get into the Word* and reprogram the truth back into where the lies
    have been (Luke 11:24-26; Ephesians 5:26; John 15:3; 17:17; James
    1:21; 2 Peter 1:4; Psalm 19:7-8) (Molten Sea)
    a.   God will heal our souls (Psalm 18, 51:7; 107:20; 119:9; Philippians
         3:13)
    b.   God will restore us back to His Image (Hebrews 10:22)

Now walk by faith (1 Corinthians 2:5; 2 Corinthians 5:7) *and know that God has
cleansed us and has transformed us back into His Image* (Hosea 2:19-20; Philippians
1:21; Romans 8:1; Hebrews 8:12; 10:22; 1 Peter 1:22a)

Section Six

Chapter 15: Loving Others As Ourselves

Summary So Far (See **Chart 5**, page 159)

In review, to love (*agapao*) God with all our Heart means binding our hearts with His and becoming one Heart with Him. This is our born again experience. Loving God with all our heart also means—moment by moment—letting His Life in our hearts be the *motivation* for all we think, say, and do.

To love (*agapao*) God with all our willpower means binding our will with His and becoming one Will with Him. Loving God with all our will is knowing we have His authority and His Power to continually say, "Not my will, but Thine," no matter how we feel, what we think, or what we desire. Loving God with all our will means letting His Will, moment by moment, determine the *direction* or the course of our lives.

Finally, to love (*agapao*) God with all our soul means binding our lives with His and becoming one Life with Him, exchanging our image—our own thoughts, emotions, and desires—for the image we were created to bear, which is His Image—His Love, His Thoughts, and then His Power to perform these in our lives. Loving God with all our soul means letting our soul be the *expression* of God's Life from our hearts.

Where Do We Go From Here?

1 Peter 1:22 perfectly sums up these three steps of loving God, as well as instructing us on what we are to do now: "Seeing ye have purified your souls in obeying the truth through the Spirit unto unfeigned love [*Agape*] of the brethren, [now] *see that ye love* [*agapao*] *one another with* [from] *a pure heart fervently."* (emphasis added)

Until this point, genuinely loving others has been impossible. There is no way we can totally give ourselves over to loving others, unless we have first totally given ourselves over to loving God. God is the only One who can make loving others genuinely possible. However, once we have loved (*agapao*) God, we can't stop there. We must go on and be those open channels of God's Love to others. In other words, we must love others as God would have us to do—putting their will and desires before our own.

First and Second Commandments

The First and Second Commandments must go hand in hand, and they must operate in the order they were given. In other words, we really can't love others as ourselves until we have *first* learned to love God.

Matthew 22:36-40 states we are to "Love God with all our heart, willpower, and soul," and then we are to "love our neighbor as ourselves."

1 John 4:21 repeats this admonition, "And this commandment have we from Him, that he who loveth God [must also] love his brother."

Why Is Loving Others a "New" Commandment?

In John 13:34 and elsewhere,[1] Jesus calls this Second Commandment "loving our neighbors as ourselves" a *new* commandment. What is new about this commandment? In the Old Testament (Leviticus 19:18) we are told to "love our neighbor as ourselves." Why does Jesus now in the New Testament call this a new commandment? The explanation is that only since God gave us the indwelling Power of the Spirit at our new birth, have we had the authority and the power within us to truly set our will and our lives aside and love (*agapao*) our neighbor as ourselves.

Remember in Chapter 8 we learned that to *agapao* something means to totally give ourselves over to it; to bind ourselves to it. To *agapao* something is what we give our will and our life over to, what we are consumed with, and what we put first in our lives. Setting ourselves aside and genuinely loving (*agapao*) others before or instead of ourselves would not have been possible before the power of the Holy Spirit became ours.

The Old Testament saints lacked this supernatural ability. In the Old Testament, the "common" believer, with the exception of the supernaturally anointed saints like Moses, David, etc., did not have the indwelling Spirit of God. The Spirit came alongside them, He helped them and He guided them, but He never permanently indwelt them as He does us.[2] Therefore, this kind of supernatural Love for others—which comes only from the indwelling Spirit—was an impossibility for them.

Even today, without God, this kind of supernatural Love for others is equally impossible. In general, people are functioning only on the natural and human loves (*storge, phileo*, and certainly, *eros* love).[3] And even with Christians who are unwilling to lay down their wills and their lives, who are not willing to love God first, and who are not willing to be open vessels, this kind of unconditional Love for others is also an impossibility. They, too, are still functioning on erratic and unpredictable *storge, phileo*, and *eros* love. (See **Chart 6**, page 161)

It's only because Jesus died for us that God's *Agape* Love could be manifested and given to us. And it's only when we die to our self life that God's unconditional Love can be manifested and given to others through us. (See **Chart 5**, page 159)

Love As Jesus Loved

Throughout the New Testament, Jesus commands us to love as He did. In John 13:34, Jesus says, "A new commandment I give unto you, that ye love one another; *as I have loved you*, that ye also love one another." (emphasis added)

How did Jesus love us? He died for us! He gave up everything for us. He gave up His rights, His Will, His Desires, His Life—everything. This is God's model for each of us to follow.

Are you willing to choose to relinquish your life, to die to yourself, so that God's Love can be released through you to those He has called you to love? Are you willing to choose to love others before or instead of yourself?

What Does the Second Commandment Really Say?

This is really what the Second Commandment says: Not that we are to love ourselves first, but that if we are loving (*agapao*) God first,[4] *He then will enable us to love others before or instead of ourselves*. In other words, we'll be given the supernatural ability to unconditionally give ourselves over to and be genuinely consumed with another's will and desires before our own. By loving God first, we'll become those "open channels" through which He can freely pour His Love and Life to others.

"Greater love [*Agape*] hath no man than this, that a man lay down his life for his friends." (John 15:13)

As Christians, we have the supernatural authority and power to be able to love like this. All we need to do is be willing. Again, Jesus is our example. He freely and willingly surrendered His Life so He could be God's open vessel, full of God's Love and Life, to give to us. And since "we are to be in this world, as He is" (1 John 4:17), becoming that open and cleansed channel is our mission and our purpose also. We are to freely lay down our lives, so that we can be full of *His* Love to give to others. In other words, we are to love them before or instead of ourselves.

This, to me, is what the Second Commandment really says. Not that we are to love (*agapao*) ourselves first, but that if we love (*agapao*) God first, He will enable us to love others *before* or *instead of* ourselves.

Loving Others First Is "Naturally" Impossible

This kind of genuine, self-sacrificing Love for others is naturally and humanly impossible because instinctively and automatically, even as Christians, we love (*agapao*) ourselves first. Let me explain:

Intuitively, we give ourselves over to our own will and desires before others, even after we have become believers. It's not that we have to be *taught* to love (*agapao*) ourselves first as some people espouse today; I believe we do this naturally. (Review **Chart 6**, page 161). To me, this is really the root problem to begin with and what God is so desperately trying to change in all of us.

Ephesians 5:29 states, "No man ever yet hated his own flesh; but nourisheth it and cherisheth it." And Philippians 2:21, "For all seek their own, not the things which are Jesus Christ's."

Even as Christians, we are naturally self-centered. We are naturally consumed with our own thoughts, our own feelings, and our own desires before those of others. Some of us do this in a prideful, boastful, and arrogant way, and obviously we can see that this is wrong. Others of us, however, are just as much consumed with ourselves through self-hate, self-pity, and self-abasement.

Both ways of thinking are wrong because in both cases we are consumed with— and totally given over to—our own thoughts, emotions, and desires *before* God and *before* others! Therefore, if we are doing either one of these, we are not loving God first as we are supposed to, but we are loving (*agapao*) ourselves first!

Jesus wants to now reverse this natural order of things. And by our loving God first, totally giving ourselves over to Him, and becoming one heart, one will, and one soul with Him, He then can fill us with His Love and enable us to love others before or instead of ourselves.

Are We Ever to Love Ourselves?

"Well, Nancy," you might ask, "aren't we ever to love (*agapao*) ourselves? The world and so many Christians are now teaching that in order to love God and others, we must first learn to love ourselves."

My answer to this is that Jesus is our example and there are absolutely no Scriptures that say, or even hint at Jesus' loving Himself. The Bible tells us that He had emotions such as we experience, but He *always* chose to set Himself aside and do as His Father desired. What Scripture reveals to us is that the Father loved Jesus with *Agape* Love; Jesus accepted that Love of the Father into His Life; He set aside His own emotions and desires, and then became a vessel to pass that Love on to others. This, I'm convinced, is the exact pattern that God wants for our lives.

Likewise, we must accept that Jesus loves us. This Love is what gives us the confidence and the trust to lay our wills and our lives down before Him and become that open conduit. Then, we can be assured that it will be God's Life and His Love coming forth through us and not our own, supernaturally loving others before or instead of ourselves.

The truth is that the source of real Love is not in ourselves, but in the Father. And only to the extent that we accept the Father's Love into our lives, and become filled with that Love, are we ever going to be able to love others as God desires. So there's no need to ever love (*agapao*) ourselves—God has already done that. We are only to love (*agapao*) God and others.

Example: "It Only Hampers the Whole Process"

A woman at one of my seminars a few years ago had been going to one of those Christian "self-love" courses which teach that you need to love yourself before you can love God or others.

This dear sister said she had been waiting years to "feel" good enough about herself so she could go on and love others, particularly her boss at work. She said she had waited and waited, but "it just never happened." She told us she was so frustrated, because no matter how much she tried to love herself, she still didn't have the love she needed to give to her boss.

As this precious sister began to learn the principles of God's Way of *Agape*, it all began to fit together for her. "Nan," she said, "my problem isn't that I don't love myself. The problem is I must learn that God loves me unconditionally and that I can unreservedly love (lay my life down to) Him in return. Until I do this, I won't be able to genuinely love others. Loving myself has nothing at all to do with it. In fact," she said, "it only hampers the whole process!" I agree with her 100 percent. Just as she said, loving (*agapao*) herself only compounds the original problem of self-centered-ness, making it worse!

Confusion Over "Loving Ourselves"

I believe the confusion over loving (*agapao*) ourselves happens for two reasons: First, the confusion is, no doubt, fueled by the enemy. When we are not having victory in our Christian walk, the enemy comes along and taunts, "Your problem is that you don't really love yourself, and that's why you can't love others. You have to learn to love yourself more, then you will be able to love others." Of course, what happens as a result of this way of thinking is that we again reinforce what the "root problem" is all along—more self-centeredness. We become more consumed with ourselves than ever before and, of course, Satan rejoices.

A second reason for the confusion over loving ourselves is that most of us don't know the difference between the natural, human, feeling loves (*storge* and *phileo*) and *agapao*, the commitment love. Again, this is critical!

Poor Self-Esteem

The basic problem in each of us is *not* that we don't love (*agapao*) ourselves—remember we do that naturally. The problem is that many of us don't *like* (*storge*) ourselves.[5] We don't like who we are; we don't like what we say; and we don't like what we do.

The reason most of us don't like, value or esteem ourselves is fourfold: 1) We really don't know experientially that God loves us. 2) Thus, we don't have the confidence and the trust to continually lay our wills and our lives down before Him and become that open vessel. 3) Therefore, it's not God's Life coming forth through us, but our own self life (Review **Chart 6**, page 161). And, 4) The result of this is that we don't "like" what we say, what we do, or how we do it. And no wonder—it's not God's Life coming forth, but our own.

So the problem is not that we don't *love* (totally give ourselves over to) ourselves at this point—we really do—it's simply that we don't *like* or have affection for ourselves. And according to Scripture, there's a world of difference between these two words.

Healthy Self-Esteem

The only thing that will bring us that healthy self-esteem for ourselves is when we become those open vessels, so God's Life can freely flow through us. (Review **Chart 5**, page 159.) Then we will begin to like what we say, what we do, and how we do it because God's Life is coming forth and not our own. This, to me, is not self confidence or self esteem as the world likes to call it, but *God-confidence and Christ-esteem*. God's Life and His Character are now freely coming forth through us and *this* is what we like about ourselves.

Proverbs 3:26 proclaims, "For the Lord shall be thy confidence."[6]

True confidence and proper self-esteem of ourselves come only from being what God meant us to be from the beginning. He wants us to be open vessels, receiving His Love for ourselves and then passing that Love on to others, loving them rather than ourselves.

In conclusion, we are *never* to *agapao* self; we are to *agapao* God and others. What we do want, however, is to be able to "like" (*storge*) ourselves, and that occurs only if God's Life is coming forth through us. The truth is that we have *not* loved ourselves first in order to do this, but *we have loved God first* in order to do this. We have been "conformed into His Image" and this is now the basis of our self-liking and our self-esteem.

1 John 4:17 teaches, "Herein is our love made perfect [complete, fulfilled], that we may have boldness in the day of judgment; *because as He is* [Love], *so are we in this world* [open and cleansed vessels passing His Love on to others]." (emphasis added)

The question we always come back to is: "Are you willing? Are you willing to surrender your life to God so that He can initiate His Love through you to those He has called you to love?"

Extensions of God's Love

God's Love is passed on through us. God's Love doesn't just fall down upon us from heaven. We are His "arms and legs" of Love in this world. *We are extensions of His Love* if we so choose to be. He just requires a cleansed life and body to work through.

John 12:25 tells us that, "He that hangs on to his life [in this world], shall lose it; but he that is willing to lay his life down [in this world] and love God, he shall bear much fruit." (Nancy's translation)

Being extensions of God's Love doesn't really sound too complicated and too hard. Why, then, is there not more of God's Love being extended in the Christian body? If Jesus is in us and we have His Love in our hearts, why are we having such a hard time loving others as God would have us to do?

Where Is God's Love Today?

If so many people today are Spirit filled, as they claim to be, then why don't our churches, our homes, our marriages, and our relationships reflect this? *Where is God's Love?* Why are there more split churches, more divorces, and more ruined relationships in the Christian body than ever before? *How can we be "Spirit filled" and not love filled?* I thought they were one and the same thing! To me, *love is simply the measure by which we can tell how "Spirit filled" a person is.*

Where is God's Love among His people today? Matthew 24:12 gives us the answer. "...because iniquity shall abound, *the Love [Agape] of many shall wax cold.*" (emphasis added)

This "waxing cold" is exactly what's happening. We have allowed our prideful thoughts, our hurt emotions, and our self-centered desires to cover over and quench God's Love in our hearts and it has "waxed cold." (Interestingly, "shall wax cold" here in Matthew 24:12 is the same root meaning as our psyche [soul] without God's Life. [See Chapter 13, "What is our Soul?"])

The Cross has been forgotten in many of our Christian homes and churches. We are again preferring our own happiness over God's Will. Many of us don't really know what it means to love God—to deny ourselves, pick up our crosses, and follow God. We *talk* a lot about doing these things, but how many of us are really *living them*?

Example: Everything Except Love

A woman named Nancy shared with me not too long ago how she had been part of a team of American Christians who recently smuggled Bibles across the Burmese border.

She said that the Burmese Christians had nothing materially at all, no Bibles or any Christian materials whatsoever. They each had torn out pages of one old Bible that they all shared. Each of them cherished their own pages and had every word memorized. Even though the Burmese Christians were lacking in material things, Nancy said, "The Love they displayed for each other and for us was overwhelming."

The American Christians who accompanied Nancy had everything materially you could want. Each of them had brought their own "personal" Bibles (sometimes a Greek or a Hebrew Bible besides); they each had their own concordances, different commentaries, and so on, everything materially one would desire as a Christian. What was conspicuously missing, however, among these American Christians was God's Love. God's Love was absent from these Christian brothers and sisters. Nancy described them as continually backbiting and quarreling.

When the Burmese Christians left their group, the whole mission fell apart. There was no "glue" (none of God's Love) left to hold the rest of the body together.

1 John 2:10 admonishes us, "He that saith he is in the light, and hateth his brother, is in darkness even until now. He that loveth his brother abideth in the light, and there is none occasion of stumbling in him."

And 1 John 4:20, "If a man say, 'I love God,' and [yet still] hateth his brother, he is a liar; for he that loveth not his brother whom he hath seen, how can he love God Whom he hath not seen?"

Practical Things We Can Do to Love One Another

If we are willing to love others before, or instead of, ourselves as the Second Commandment says, the following are some practical things we can do.

Love in Action

As Christians, it's so very important for us to *love in action*, not just with our words. A hypocrite is one whose words and deeds don't match. Scripture teaches us that we need to put our actions where our mouths are in order for it to be the truth.

1 John 3:18, "My little children, let us not love in word, neither in tongue; but in deed and in truth."

Example: Bumper Sticker Christian

One Sunday night a few years ago, I flew back to California from a seminar in Washington State. Tired and hungry, I still had to face a one hour drive home from the airport.

Trying to check out of the airport parking lot, I found at least 30 cars in the line ahead of me, moving very slowly. After I had been sitting in the line for over 25 minutes, 10 or 15 cars from the back of the line pulled out and went around the whole long line of waiting cars trying to butt their way into the front of the line from the side aisles of the parking lot.

One big magenta truck jammed its way in front of me. I yelled out the window, "Please, you need to wait in line just like the rest of us." He just laughed at me and pushed his big truck in front of me all the more. His kids were in the truck with him and they, too, were laughing as he pushed and maneuvered and finally crashed the line.

After he bullied his way in front of me, to my disbelief, he stopped the whole line of cars behind him and let the 10 cars that had followed him get in the line in front of him, adding another 10 to 15 minute wait for the rest of us.

I was appalled that someone would be that self-centered and rude. As we got closer to lights and the check-out place, I could see, plastered clearly on the back of this magenta truck, a big Christian *Ichthus* (fish). I regret now that I didn't get out of my car and go over to his window and say, "So this is how a Christian acts!"

"Let us not love in word, neither in tongue [or signs], but in deed and in truth."

Deeds of Love

Deeds of real love (deeds of righteousness as Scripture calls them) are ones that God motivates in our hearts. Then out of obedience, we trust and allow Him to perform them in our lives.

These are not deeds that we do out of duty to earn the other person's love, but simply deeds that we do out of the natural outflow of God's Life within our soul. They are not actions that are contrived, worked at, or planned; they are actions that are a result of loving God, of being in fellowship with Him, and of being that open vessel.

Begin with your spouses. Show them you love them from a pure heart—fervently—by doing those little things you know mean so much to them. Do those deeds "unto the Lord," in spite of how you feel.

Example: "It's a Man's Job!"

A friend of mine, Jeanne, whom I dearly love, knows that her husband simply adores having her mow the lawn. Now, Jeanne hates to mow the lawn. She has always felt mowing the lawn was a "man's job." For years, she objected to doing it, and it caused a lot of tension between them.

Recently, however, the Lord has shown my friend that she is to "love her husband as herself." In other words, she is to do things for him that she knows will please him. She knows mowing the lawn will please him. So now Jeanne gets her heart right with God first.[7] She asks God to enable her to do the job without bitterness, then she puts on her Walkman and does the job joyfully "unto the Lord."

Do whatever you know pleases your spouse: cooking his favorite meal, going shopping with him, cleaning his office, jogging with him, skiing with him , doing errands, or whatever it is that will make him happy. (Remember, I even learned to scuba dive at forty-five to please my Chuck. If I can do that, God can make you capable of anything too!)

But again, it is critical that you do these things genuinely from a pure heart, and simply, as a result of being that open vessel of God's Love. Don't do these things from a clogged or covered heart.[8] (See **Chart 6**, page 161). In other words, don't do it with self-centered motivations, or in order to "earn your spouse's love." Believe me, he or she will know the difference. Love in deed, not just with words.

Comfort the Fainthearted

Another thing we can do to love each other before or instead of ourselves is to *comfort and encourage the fainthearted.* We love each other by *sharing each other's burdens.* We are not to carry other's burdens all by ourselves. We are to roll those burdens over onto Jesus, who is our "burden bearer," and we are to leave them there with Him.

We are to comfort and encourage each other by praying and listening to one another. We have a lot of talkers in the Body of Christ. What we really need is more listeners.

It's important to understand that we don't need to have all the answers in order to be a good listener. If we have not gone through something similar to what the other person is sharing, then we must just listen. We really don't know what he or she is feeling, and we don't want to be like Job's friends! We just need to love this person—by holding him, praying with him, and being a burden bearer to him.

Be Genuine and Real

Another crucial thing in loving others is to be real and genuine with each other. *If we are being transparent to God on the inside, then He will enable us to be real and genuine with others on the outside.*

Sharing our own experiences of being downcast and hurt is important, and how God touched us and stood us back on our feet. We need to keep the conversation personal and on what God has done for us. We need to be brave enough to be vulnerable. I know being vulnerable is scary, but God commands us to love—and anytime we love, we become vulnerable.

The neat part about loving God's way, however, is that each time we give ourselves over to another, we put on the armour of God (Ephesians 6:11-18) and then God Himself protects us. Isaiah 59:19 proclaims, "When the enemy shall come in like a flood, the Spirit of the Lord shall lift up a standard [banner of Love] against him."

Perfect People Are Not "Touchable" People

Now being genuine and real does *not* mean being *perfect*. Far from it! Perfect people are not touchable people because no one can really identify with them. As Christians, we are not to strive to be self righteously perfect, but to be real and genuine, pointing others to the only One who is perfect. And that is Jesus.

This point was brought home to me recently when someone shared, "One of the things I can't stand about 'church people' is that they put on such an air of being perfect and faultless." He then went on to declare, "I just can't relate to that."

I, too, remember as a young Christian, seeing some of the speakers at our church just "float in" in their long white robes. Somehow I never could identify with them, or get close to them because they appeared to have it "all together." They just seemed so unreal.

This is one of the reasons why I love David of the Old Testament so much. I can identify with him. He blew it, just as I do. Yet God called him "a man after His own heart."[9] David experienced things that I am experiencing. He went through all the temptations that I go through. And if God called him, "a man after His own heart," then there's hope for me. David comforts me in his Psalms "by the comfort he received from God" when he was going through his hard times.

2 Corinthians 1:3 declares, "Blessed be God, even the Father of our Lord Jesus Christ, the Father of Mercies, and the God of all comfort; Who comforteth us in all our tribulation, that we may be able to comfort them which are in any trouble, by the comfort wherewith we ourselves are comforted of God."

This is my desire also. To comfort others "by the comfort I've received from God" when I have gone through trials. I do this not to make people think I'm perfect, but to lead them to Christ and His perfection.

Sharing Our Failures As Well As Our Victories

One of the most common remarks I hear from those who listen to or read *The Way of Agape* is that they could really identify with me. The feeling of identification is *not* because I am perfect—far from it—but because I am honest and real in sharing my failures, as well as my victories in Christ.

We all need to be honest with each other in the sharing of our deficiencies as well as our victories. Nothing will cause the masks of others to come down faster than being real, honest, and touchable, pointing others to Christ. As one young woman said to me recently, "Nancy, *being transparent is contagious*!"

Example: "I Don't Need to Be Best Friends With Everyone"

I have a sweet friend named Patty who used to live across the street from her best friend, Lyn. Both Christians, Patty and Lyn, had grown up together in the Lord. About five years ago, for no apparent reason, Lyn became very distant. She pulled her kids out of Christian school, and one day she just quit speaking to Patty. When the two saw each other, it was awkward because of the "phony smiles" and the "surfacy" chit chat!

Patty's daughter, who used to be inseparable from Lyn's children, also decided to quit the Christian school and go to the public school. Once enrolled, however, Lyn's children totally ignored her. They wouldn't sit with her on the bus, walk with her at school, or let any of their new friends be around her. Now this made Patty absolutely furious. The situation went on for over a year, progressively getting worse and worse.

One night, Patty saw some teens toilet papering her house. The next day she found out it had been Lyn's kids, and she again was furious. "Why?" Patty asked herself, "What have we done to her?" Patty told me on the phone one day that she felt like bashing Lyn's teeth down her throat, or jumping on her back and choking her.

How could two grown adults who love the Lord and who had been such close friends for many years wind up being so full of anger and resentment towards each other?

After listening to the *Be Ye Transformed* tapes, the Lord revealed to Patty that it was her continual choice to hang onto her bitterness and resentment towards Lyn or to give those things over to Him. God promised Patty that if she would relinquish herself to Him, He would enable her to unconditionally love Lyn.

Patty decided to make those *contrary choices* to love God, choosing to give Him all of her hurts. She sat down and wrote Lyn a long letter and in total honesty told her how she felt about their estrangement. She told Lyn how hurt she was and how desperately she wanted to reconcile with her. She even asked if Lyn would please come over and talk.

Two days later, Patty was in her front yard and saw Lyn drive by in her car. She knew Lyn saw her, but Lyn never acknowledged it. Patty was sure that by that time, Lyn had received her letter. Again, she had a choice. She could pray and choose to unconditionally forgive Lyn, or she could hold on to her "justified" hurts and block God's working. She chose to love God.

While reading her Bible the next morning, Patty came across, "You will have victory today because of confessing your sins." One hour later, Lyn called saying she would like to come over and talk. When she walked in she had dark glasses on, and for the entire time she never took them off. She denied that anything was wrong, saying to Patty, "I don't have to be best friends with everyone I meet!"

Again, Patty had a choice. Pride would have her say, "Okay, forget it. I don't need this! I've got other friends. I don't need her; let her go home." But had Patty done that, nothing at all would have been accomplished. She finally looked at Lyn and began to cry. "I am so sick and tired of putting up a facade," she said. "You have hurt me so much and I have obviously hurt you. I am sick of acting strong when I'm really not. Will you please forgive me for whatever it is that I have done to offend you?"

Taking off her glasses, Lyn, too, began to cry. She reached over and hugged Patty and, sobbing, began to share the real reasons behind her actions. Some years previously, she and her husband had gone through some terrible financial reversals. Too embarrassed and too proud to tell the truth to anyone, the "lie" just got bigger and bigger. She said she felt threatened and intimidated by Patty and her obvious financial success. She didn't want to behave the way she had been, but she said she couldn't stop her emotional responses! Things had just gotten totally out of hand.

They shared together for hours. After confessing the truth to each other and asking each other's forgiveness, they were once again beautifully reconciled in the Lord. Once again, they are now "better" best friends.[10]

Plastic Masks

Many Christians are walking around today hiding behind plastic masks and facades just as Lyn was. These people have pasted smiles on the outside that say, "Praise the Lord; everything is great." And yet, on the inside, their hearts are bleeding.

I know this to be true because I used to be a plastic Christian. During the years of Chuck's and my marital trials, we held Bible studies in our home every week. People would come up to me and say, "Nan, how are things going?" And, of course, I would answer with a big smile, "Oh great, the Lord is blessing us; He is doing this... and He is doing that...!" In reality, my life behind closed doors was falling apart.

There were two reasons I was afraid to let anyone see the truth. And perhaps these are some of the reasons why so many are wearing masks today.

First, I felt it was "my" responsibility to carry God's reputation. After all, Chuck was a well-known Bible teacher, teaching others the Truth; how could I let anyone see that the Christian life wasn't working in our own home?

God has since shown me that He doesn't need me to carry His reputation. That is not my responsibility! My responsibility is only to "love Him" and then to allow Him to "love others" through me. Had I had been doing both of these things, there would never have been the need for masks or coverups! So we don't need to worry about God's reputation. If we are doing our part, we can be assured God will do His.

[Note: *Self life wants to hide the truth, whereas God's Life wants to expose it!*]

The second reason I wore a mask was pride. I wanted everyone to think that I had it all together. I wanted everyone to believe that I was really a *mature* Christian (after all I had been a Christian for 20 years at this point!). The truth was that I was just a *babe* in the Lord because I didn't even know what it meant to *love Him*.

Need to Be Humble

Only a truly humble person can admit his need and admit that he can't do live the Christian life on his own. *Humble* simply means a willingness to lay down our life so God can live His Life through us. Humility is knowing and admitting the truth about ourselves. Oh, how desperately we need humble and willing Christians today. We all need to be humble enough to admit when we fail and when we really blow it. If our *security* is in Jesus and in His Love for us, we'll be able to do this more and more.

A mature Christian will be able to admit that *self* is inadequate and often fails because this person's identity and security is in Jesus and His Love, and not in himself. This mature person will not be devastated when he falls down and blows it badly, because he knew he would *in the flesh* anyway.

Romans 7:18 states, "For I know that in me [that is, in my flesh,] dwelleth no good thing."

If, however, our security and our identity is based upon ourselves (in our own actions and performance), then admitting failures and mistakes becomes impossible. That admission is too painful because our whole self-esteem is based upon how we see ourselves, upon the things we say and do, and upon the love we receive from others, not upon Jesus' Life through us—the way it should be. Thus it becomes extremely difficult for us to humble ourselves and say we are wrong, because then we crack the only secure foundation that our life is built upon—ourselves.

Example: "When I Am Weak"

The Apostle Paul was obviously one of the most mature and Spirit filled Christians in the entire Bible. Yet, he admits in 2 Corinthians 1:8 that he had such huge problems that he despaired even of life itself. The way Paul handled these problems, however, was not to cover them up or pretend they didn't exist, but he "boasted in his infirmities" and in his human frailties. He knew that God loved him no matter what.

He knew that as he would give these frailties over to God, God would work all things together for good.[11]

Listen to what Paul says in 2 Corinthians 12:9-10: "... Most gladly therefore will I rather glory in my infirmities [weaknesses, failures], [so] that the power of Christ may rest upon me. Therefore, I take pleasure in infirmities, in reproaches, in necessities, in persecutions, in distresses for Christ's sake: *For when I am weak* [willing to lay my life down—admitting that self is inadequate], *then I am strong.*" (emphasis added)

Paul could say this because his complete identity, his total security, his whole life was *not* based upon himself. Instead, it was wrapped up in Jesus Christ and upon what Christ continued to do through him. Paul claims as much in Philippians 1:21, "For to me to live is Christ." And this is what we must remind ourselves of daily. *It's not I, but Christ.*

Be Careful

Now we are not to go around to everyone we meet and admit and boast of our failures and weaknesses. Not everyone would understand. But God has given each of us certain intimate friends whom we can trust—friends who don't talk and who don't gossip. These are the ones to whom we should be able to freely share our failures, as well as victories. *Transparency with God will allow us to be real and honest with others.* Nothing has brought Lisa, Michelle, and me closer recently than our being able to be honest with each other and admit our failures and weaknesses, because along with our failures comes God's forgiveness and His provision.

So it doesn't matter whether we have been a Christian one year, or six years, or 26 years; we need to be able to admit to weariness and failures. Paul, at the point he made the above statement in 2 Corinthians 12:9, had been with the Lord many, many years.

God does not want us to be hypocrites. Remember, the "leaven of the Pharisees" was hypocrisy (Luke 11:42-44). We are not lesser Christians if we are real and genuine and admit when things are tough.

My mom was so cute. Years ago she worried so about me because she knew that I am very open and honest when sharing in my classes. And it troubled her. She used to say to me, "How can you stand up there and share all your dirty linen?" (Doesn't that sound like a mom?)

My answer to her was always the same, "Mom, I'm free now. I'm free to be who God really created me to be, and I don't have to hide anything anymore. If I have prayed about it and God leads me to share the truth of the past, He must know that somehow, someone will be touched and helped, and He will be glorified through it." "Most gladly therefore will I glory in my infirmities, that the power of Christ may rest upon me."[12]

God wants His Body united. And there's no faster way to unite us than to be real and honest with each other, confessing our sins one to another (James 5:16) as well as our victories.

Example: Transparency Is Contagious

In one seminar a few years ago, many people came up to me privately and shared how they had tremendous anger and resentment towards others in the body there. There seemed to be so many hurts and divisions in that church.

At the end of the three-day seminar, we gathered together to share what we had learned personally. God prompted one sister in the front row to stand up and publicly ask forgiveness from a woman in the back row of the auditorium. The first lady said she had been holding resentment and bitterness towards the other woman for years. The woman in the back row was so overcome by God's Love that she, too, stood and asked forgiveness. She was crying as she, too, admitted to being consumed in bitterness.

Then all over the audience, women began to stand and share their hurts and ask for Love. One person in leadership who looked like the most gregarious of them all, shared how it was all an act and how really scared and lonely she was. She humbled herself and asked for love from all of us.

After the class was over, we stayed for three hours sharing and praying and hugging and loving. It was the most rewarding of all the seminars I've given. God broke down those prideful walls and the truth was able to come forth. Those women were set free.

Luke 4:18 states, "The Spirit of the Lord is upon me, because He hath anointed me to preach the gospel to the poor; He hath sent me to heal the brokenhearted, to preach deliverance to the captives, and the recovering of sight to the blind, to set at liberty them that are bruised."

God wants us one in Him, our self life separates us. If we *get rid of our self life, you watch our churches become united in the Spirit and one in Love*!

Be Supersensitive to Each Other

Another practical way we can love others is to *be supersensitive to each other's needs*. Even at the retreats I go to, I encourage the women to disband their cliques, get out of their habits, and to sit and eat with someone new.

We are creatures of habit, and I know it's so much easier to stick with those we know rather than to venture off trying to make new friendships. Often, however, when we're so busy and consumed with our own friends, we miss what God is trying to teach us personally, and we also miss what He is trying to tell us about others around us.

You Initiate God's Love

I remember one woman at a Christian fellowship meeting, who came up to me and complained, "None of my own friends are here, and no one else comes up to talk with me." In response to her statement I asked her, "Well, Honey, do you go up to the others and initiate talking with them?" "No, of course not. I don't know them," she replied, very surprised that I had even asked her that question. This woman would not go up to another person and begin a conversation because "she didn't know them," and yet, she expected the other women to come up to her and initiate a conversation, even though they didn't know her.

What would happen if we all felt that way. No one would ever reach out. That's not God's Love! Remember, God's Love is initiating Love. This means that God's Love takes the first step. God's Love reaches out first.

I understand that wounded people do want to stay within themselves, and they don't want to reach out. I understand it's hard to reach out, especially when you are going through a rough trial, as was the case in point. (I really understand because I have been there myself.) However, hurting or not, if we are Christians, we have God's Love within us. And, if we want to, each of us can choose to set that hurt, that pain aside for the moment and allow God's Love to flow through us to someone else who is also in need. We will be blessed, not only because of our obedience, but because of God's presence.

Clearly, God wants each of us to be humble enough, sensitive enough, listening enough, and mature enough that when He prompts us, we can initiate His Love to someone whom He knows desperately needs it.

Example: Backslidden For Three Years

Years ago in one of my seminars, there was a severely overweight, twenty-one year old, who always sat in the back row, almost out of sight. She never spoke to anyone and no one ever spoke to her. She never smiled. Her pretty face was always sullen and withdrawn.

God laid this girl so heavily on my heart that after one of the sessions, I went up to her and said, "Hey, let's go and have lunch together." Surprised that I was talking to her, she turned around as if I meant someone else behind her. You could see on her face that she was convinced I certainly didn't mean her. "No," I said, "*You* and I!" I took her by the hand and led her to the coffee shop.

At first it was very difficult to get her to talk, but once I got her started, I couldn't stop her. I could tell that it had been a long, long time since she had felt God's Love through anyone. What do you think this young girl's self-image was built upon? Do you think it was built upon God's Love and what He thought of her? No way! Her self-image was totally built upon what she thought of herself and upon what *she thought* others thought of her.

I know this young woman experienced God's Love that day because at the very next session there she was, sitting in the front row wearing a great big smile. That night we had an "afterglow" meeting, and this precious girl recommitted her life to Christ. She told us later that she had been backslidden for three years because she had not experienced Love from anyone. God, however, opened her up that day and loved this precious child right back to Himself.

I am convinced that *God's Love comes through us,* His body. *Each of us is God's arms and legs in this world!* We are *extensions of His Love.*

Personal Example: "We'll Be Right Over"

In 1991, Chuck went through probably the hardest year of his life. His business failed; we were about to lose our "dream house"; we owed the I.R.S. over two million dollars; and many of our oldest and dearest "friends" had turned their backs on us. It was an incredibly tough time.

One afternoon, Chuck was particularly depressed. I suggested that he take his Bible and go out into the woods and pray. He finally did go for a long walk, but I was very concerned about his despondency.

I picked up the phone and called our dear friend Hal Lindsey. I simply wanted him to pray for Chuck. After I shared briefly about what was happening, Hal said, "We'll be right over!" (Hal and Kim lived four hours away from us!) "No, Hal," I said, "I'm just calling for prayer for Chuck!" "I know," Hal said, "we'll be right over."

He and Kim cancelled a birthday party they had planned that night, driving for four hours to "hold Chuck." That Love made the difference for Chuck! (This was the night he decided to go into full-time ministry.) We will never forget Kim and Hal's "extension of God's Love" to us.

Sensitive to Others' Needs

It's so critical to be supersensitive to God's Spirit. When God lays someone special on our hearts, we obviously need to pray for them. But, if we can, we need to do even more. We need to call them or write them or visit them, if possible. Whatever God leads us to do, we need to be obedient.

We must not only be *hearers of God's Word,* but we must also be *doers of His Word.* When God brings someone to your mind, be sure to follow through with what He tells you to do in that person's life.

Example: "We're Going to Get a Divorce"

A friend of ours, whom we had not seen for least ten years, came to California on a business trip, looked Chuck up, and took us both out to dinner. During the dinner, I inquired about his wife Lucy because the four of us had been very good friends at one time. "Oh Nan," he said, "it's really been bad between us. I think we are definitely going to get a divorce."

I was so grieved and saddened for my friends. The news really broke my heart. For a couple of weeks after that dinner, I just couldn't get them off my mind. Finally, I recognized it must be the Lord's prompting, and I decided to write a letter to Lucy. All I did in my letter was share the miracles that God had done in our own marriage, how bad it had been between us, what God had done, and what was going on now.

I had no idea where this couple was in their relationship with God. Ten years ago, they were not believers. When I sent the letter, I was concerned as to how Lucy might receive it because I had given God all the credit for saving our marriage. I just prayed God would use the letter and that she would somehow see His Love.

A few days later, Lucy called. She was so excited. She told me she had become a believer about five years previously and had been earnestly seeking God as to His Will in the matter of her marriage. The day the letter had arrived was the actual day she and her husband were to sign the final papers for the divorce. After reading the letter, she was convinced that God speaking to her and telling her to wait, as she was the one initiating the divorce.

That little letter, where I simply was honest and transparent as to what God had done in Chuck's and my life, changed the course of Lucy's life. I wish I could say that things miraculously worked out and that they reconciled and lived happily ever after. But life isn't always that way.

God did do a miraculous work in her life; He taught her to "love Him with all her heart, will, and soul." Then He showed her how to "love her husband as herself."

The miracle, remember, is not necessarily that the marriage is healed and miraculously goes back together. The miracle may be what God is allowed to do in the individual lives that are involved; the miracle here is that she was conformed back into God's Image, and began to love as she was created to love.[13] Now it's up to God and Lucy's choices as to how this story is going to end!

God wants us to be His open vessels carrying His *Agape* Love to those who desperately need Him. If we don't obey His Spirit's leading, because of our own hang ups or our own insecurities, we're blocking and stopping God from showing that other person just how much He loves them.

Love One Another—Don't Judge

One important thing for us not to do when we are "loving others," is *not to judge by another's words or deeds what is going on in their hearts.* God is the only One who can see our hearts; therefore, He is the only rightful One to judge.

Isaiah 11:3-4 declares, "...And He shall not judge after the sight of His eyes, neither reprove after the hearing of His ears: But with righteousness shall He judge the poor, and reprove with equity for the meek of the earth."

Classic Example: "Nancy Missler, You Are Not to Judge"

A woman came to one of my early seminars, sat right in the middle of the front row, and after five minutes of the study promptly fell asleep. After several weeks of this behavior, I found myself getting quite angry at her. "Why does she even come if she is going to fall asleep? And if she wants to sleep, why does she have to sit right in the middle of the front row?"

As I was still quite new at teaching, and therefore insecure, I found her to be a distraction. When I would look out into the audience, trying to make a particular point, there she would be—sound asleep in the front row. I would totally lose my train of thought and think to myself, "Is what I am saying so boring?"

Finally, after about the fourth time this happened, I went to the women in charge and "subtly" asked them about her. "Oh," they said, "Nan, don't worry about her. She needs this study more than anyone else, and she is loving it! *She has a physical impairment of the eyes which prevents her from looking into bright lights, but she hasn't missed a thing that you have said!*"

God said to me that day, "*Nancy Missler, you are **not** to judge what I am doing in someone else's heart by what you see, or by what you think.*" He showed me that had I prayed about her and not complained about her, He would have assured me of His purpose for her.

Don't Judge Appearances

When I go to churches to speak now, and the people *appear* cold or unfriendly or unloving, I don't question God anymore as to *why* He sent me. I can almost hear His answer, "It's none of your business why I sent you here, just do what I have called you to do and I will handle the rest!" This is so true. God has called us simply to love Him and be that "open channel" for His Love. If we do our part, He will assuredly do His.

So when we look at people who *appear* to be spiritual, or *appear* not to be spiritual, we are not to judge them! We can only test their fruit.

Luke 16:15 tells us, "That which is highly esteemed among men is an abomination in the sight of God." And I've seen this to be true.

Fruit, by the way, is something we can "see." Fruit is not just the words, nor is it how many people a person has led to Christ. The fruit that the Lord talks about in Scripture is how loving these people are in all their relationships. This is the fruit that God looks for and that we can see!

"By This All Men Will Know You Are My Disciples"

When we love in the way God wants us to by loving others as (or instead of) ourselves, then all men are going to know, not by what we say but by how we live and how we love that we are Christians.

I have learned over the past 18 years, since I have been walking in God's *Way of Agape*, that whether I am relating to someone on a casual basis, responding to a hurtful remark someone has just made, or taking a stand with someone over a major issue, if I don't respond in God's Love by His Wisdom, nothing at all will be accomplished. Furthermore, the relationship will often deteriorate.

Only loving God first and then loving others as myself will free me to respond the way God wants me to. When we love like this, others will come to know and see the real Jesus!

John 13:35 supports this, "*By* [only] *this shall all men know that ye are My disciples, if ye have love one to another.*" (emphasis added)

So the only way others are going to know whether or not we are real Christians is by our Love. Not only our love for God—they can't always see that, but by our love for one another. That is always visible.

"Herein is our love made perfect, that we may have boldness in the day of judgment, *because as He is, so are we in this world.*"[14] (emphasis added) And that is Love!

Endnotes:

1. 1 John 2:7-8 and 2 John 5

2. Psalm 51:11

3. See Chapter 5, "Three Natural Loves."

4. See Chapter 8, "Key Discovery."

5. See Chapter 5 (*storge* is our natural, human affection love). See also Chapter 13, "Poor Self-Image."

6. Proverbs 14:26

7. See Chapter 14, "Inner Court Ritual."

8. See Chapter 11, "Four Types of Hearts." (Review **Chart 6**)

9. Acts 13:22

10. 2 Corinthians 5:18

11. Romans 8:28

12. 2 Corinthians 12:9

13. See Chapter 3, "Are You Willing to Love?"

14. 1 John 4:17

Scriptural References:

Chapter 15

What Does It Mean to "Love Our Neighbor As Ourselves?" (Matthew 22:39)

A. To love (*agapao*) means to totally give ourselves over to something; to bind ourselves to it. It's what we put first in our lives, and what we give our will and our life to

    1. We are not only to love (*agapao*) God, but we are also to love (*agapao*) our neighbor (1 Peter 1:22; 1 John 4:21)

        a. Nourish and cherish them

        b. Put them first—protect them from hurt

        c. Promote their welfare (1 Samuel 18:1-4)

    2. This is only possible if we are first loving God (Matthew 22:37; 2 Corinthians 8:5b,c)

B. Jesus calls "loving our neighbor as ourselves" a *new* commandment (John 13:34; 1 John 2:8-11; 3:11). Why? In Leviticus 19:18,34 we are told to "love our neighbor." Why does Jesus now call this new?

    1. It's a new commandment because:

        a. It's only since Jesus gave us the power of the indwelling Spirit that we can begin to keep the Second Commandment as God intended (Roman 5:5; 1 John 2:8-11)

           . Old Testament saints did not have this supernatural ability

           . In the world today, this type of Love is also impossible

           . Even with Christians who don't lay their will and their lives down, this kind of Love is impossible (Matthew 24:12; 1 John 4:20)

        b. Only when we die to our self, can this kind of Love be manifested (John 12:24; 15:13; 2 Corinthians 4:11-12; Philippians 2:5-9)

    2. It was only because Jesus died for us, that His Love was given to us and it's only as we, by the Holy Spirit, become an open vessel, that God's Love can be passed on to others (Matthew 22:37-39; 1 Peter 1:22)

C. To love others means:

    1. Not that we are to love (*agapao*) ourselves first (we already do that naturally), but if we are loving God first, then he will enable us to love others *before or instead of* ourselves (Ephesians 5:29; Philippians 2:21; 2 Timothy 3:2,4) (Galatians 5:13c; 2 Corinthians 4:11-12; 8:5; 1 John 4:12)

        a. Put others first in our lives (1 John 4:12; Philippians 2:3; 1 Corinthians 10:24; Ephesians 5:33; Romans 9:2-3)

        b. Be consumed with their will and desires, before our own (Romans 13:8; 1 Corinthians 10:24,33)

2.   Jesus is our example and we are to love as He loved (John 10:15,17; 13:15-17,34; 15:12-13,17; 17:26; Philippians 2:5-9; 1 Peter 2:21-23; 1 John 3:16; Matthew 20:28)
   a.   He died in order to give us His Love (John 15:13; 1 John 4:19)
   b.   Only as we die to ourselves can we become open vessels so God's Love can be manifested through us to others (John 12:24; 15:13-14; Luke 14:26; Ephesians 5:2; Revelation 12:11c; 1 John 3:16; 4:12; 2 Corinthians 12:15)
      .   Then we can love with God's supernatural Love (1 Corinthians 13:1-8; 1 John 4:12,19-21)
      .   Then we can *"be in this world as He is"* (1 John 4:17)
      .   Then His Love is "perfected" (completed) through us (1 John 4:12)
   c.   Unfortunately, most of the world (and many Christians) are still functioning on human love and thus unable to love like this (Matthew 6:19-20; Haggai 1:6)

Loving Others Is "Naturally" Impossible

A.   Naturally, even as Christians, we love (*agapao*) ourselves first (Ephesians 5:29; 2 Timothy 3:2,4; Isaiah 47:8)
   1.   We are naturally consumed with our own will and desires before others
   2.   Some do this in a *prideful* way and we recognize this as wrong. Others are totally given over to themselves in a *self-pity* or self-abasement way and this, too, is wrong. Both these attitudes are self-centered and not God-centered.
B.   Loving ourselves first is the root problem to begin with and what God is trying to change in all of us (Isaiah 47:8; Philippians 2:21)
C.   By our loving God first (Isaiah 46:9), He can fill us with His Love and enable us to love others before or instead of ourselves (1 Corinthians 10:24)

Are We Ever to Love (*agapao*) Ourselves?

A.   Jesus is our example. There are NO Scriptures that say He ever loved (*agapao*) Himself
B.   What happened was:
   1.   The Father loved (*agapao*) Jesus (John 15:9)
   2.   Jesus accepted the Love of the Father into His Life
   3.   Because He was an open and cleansed vessel, Jesus was able to pass that Love of the Father on to us (John 15:9; 17:26; 2 Corinthians 8:9)
   4.   This is exactly what God desires from us, only as we love Him, will we ever be able to love others (Galatians 5:6,13-14; 1 Peter 4:8)
C.   So, we never love ourselves (it's a lie of the enemy) (Isaiah 47:8; Ezekiel 16:15; 28:17)
   1.   Because God has already done that (loved us) (1 John 3:16; John 15:9, 12; 17:26)

2. We just need to accept that Love of God into our lives
3. Then become an open vessel to pass that Love on to others (John 15:13)
4. Then we will "not love our own lives" (Revelation 12:11c; Luke 14:26; John 12:25; Acts 20:24), but our neighbor as or instead of ourselves

D. We are to *agapao* God and we are to *agapao* others, never ourselves

Confusion Over "Loving Others"

A. Confusion occurs because we don't know the difference between human love (*phileo, storge*) and the kind of love God desires (*agapao*)
1. The problem is NOT that we don't *agapao* ourselves; we do that naturally, but we often *don't like* or have affection for (*storge*) ourselves
   a. We don't like what we say
   b. We don't like what we do
2. This occurs because:
   a. We don't know God loves us
   b. Therefore, we don't have the confidence to lay down our wills and our lives and become open vessels
   c. It is not God's Life coming forth through us, but our own self-life
3. The only thing that will bring us that "healthy self-liking" is when we are open and cleansed vessels showing forth God's Life
   a. Then we will like what we say and do
   b. This is not self-confidence, but God-confidence (John 5:30)
   c. This is not self-esteem, but *Christ-esteem* (Isaiah 30:15c; Proverbs 3:26; 14:26a; Psalm 65:5b 118:8a; Galatians 6:14; Colossians 1:8-11; Philippians 1:21; 4:13; 2 Corinthians 3:5; 4:6-7; 12:9-10; 1 John 4:17) My life is now "hid in Christ" (Colossians 3:3)

B. So, true confidence and proper self liking come only from being what God meant us to be: *open vessels receiving His Love for ourselves and then passing it on to others.* Loving them rather than ourselves (1 John 4:17)

Practical Things We Can Do to Love Others

A. Don't just love with our words only, but *love in action* (1 John 3:18; Luke 10:30-37).
1. Truth is where our words and our deeds match and become one (Psalm 33:9)
2. Deeds of real Love are ones that are done not out of duty, but actions God has motivated in our hearts (Proverbs 12:12b)
3. We are to wash one another's feet (unconditionally love and forgive each other) (John 13:14-15)
4. Only by Love can we serve one another (Galatians 5:13)

B. *Comfort and encourage the fainthearted* (2 Corinthians 1:3-4; Acts 14:22a; Hebrews 12:3)

1. Listen to them; pray with them; share what God has done for us (James 5:16b; 1 Thessalonians 1:2) We don't need to have all the answers (Proverbs 17:27-28)
2. Share their burdens (Matthew 11:28-30) as Jesus does for us (1 Thessalonians 2:8)
3. Be genuine and real (2 Corinthians 1:4)
   a. Transparency to God will allow us to be real with each other
   b. Dare to be vulnerable (touchable). This is scary to do, but any time we love we are vulnerable (Matthew 22:37-39)
   c. We can be vulnerable: God will protect us (Isaiah 59:19)
   d. He puts His shield and His banner over us (Song of Solomon 2:4)
   e. Share what God has done for us. Be an example (1 Timothy 4:12)
      . Be genuine
      . You don't have to be perfect; Only Jesus is
      . Point others to Him
      . Transparency is contagious (James 5:16)
   f. Confess our sins one to another (James 5:16). Only expose "inner self" to intimate friends
      . Don't gossip (Proverbs 6:16-19; 18:8; James 1:26)
      . Don't be a hypocrite (wear a mask) (Luke 11:42)
4. Only a person loving (*agapao*) God can truly be transparent and admit failures about himself
   a. Only then can we "boast in our weaknesses" (Jeremiah 9:24; Galatians 6:14; Romans 7:18a; 2 Corinthians 1:8; 11:30; 12:9-10; 1 Corinthians 1:31) because we know that God is our strength
   b. Others can then identify with us
   c. Then God will be glorified in all we do
5. God wants His body united and there is no faster way than to be real and transparent (Philippians 1:27; 2:2; Acts 2:46; Ephesians 4:3-4; 1 Corinthians 1:10; 12:25)
   a. *Self-life wants to hide the truth* (causes us to wear masks), *whereas God's Life wants to expose the truth.*
      . God's Life sets us free (Luke 4:18)
      . It allows us to be humble and put others first
   b. God has given us the ministry of reconciliation (2 Corinthians 5:18)

C. *Be super-sensitive to each other's needs*
   1. Initiate God's Love to someone new today
   2. Call, write, or visit them (deny self)
   3. Minister to them (Acts 4:20; 5:20)
      a. God's Love comes through us (1 John 4:12)
      b. We are extensions of His Love (1 John 4:17)
D. *Don't judge* what is going on in another's heart by their words or actions (Isaiah 11:3-4; Jeremiah 1:17-19; Luke 16:15c; Romans 14:13a; John 7:24)
   1. God is the only one to judge our hearts (1 Samuel 16:7)
   2. Only by Christ's Love will others know we are Christians (John 13:35)

Chapter 16: Loving in Our Marriages

"Above All Things Have Love for One Another"

How does loving one another before or instead of ourselves apply to our marriages?

God's Will for our lives as husbands and wives, no matter how we feel, what we think, or what we desire, is for us to unconditionally love our spouses. I know this is a very radical statement, but I believe no matter what the circumstances are, no matter if we are married, separated, or divorced, we are to love (*agapao*) that other person "as ourselves."

Now I didn't say that our marriages should be perfect and working harmoniously in order for us to love our spouses as ourselves. Some circumstances and situations are totally out of our control. Nonetheless, God's Will for each of us is that we unconditionally love our spouses as ourselves, and they don't even need to be in the home for this to apply.

1 Peter 4:8 declares, "And above all things have fervent charity [*Agape*] among yourselves; for [*Agape*] shall cover the multitude of sins."

If we are *not* loving our spouses as ourselves, something is wrong with our fellowship with God—and we are not loving Him as we should. Evidently, something is still preventing us from being those open channels whereby we *can* genuinely put our spouse's desires before our own.

1 John 4:7-8 instructs us, "Beloved, let us love one another: for love is of God; and everyone that loveth is born of God, and knoweth God. He that loveth not knoweth not God; for God is Love."

And also, 1 John 4:20-21: "If a man say, 'I love God,' and hateth his brother, he is a liar: for he that loveth not his brother whom he hath seen, how can he love God Whom he hath not seen?"

Why Should I Be the First to Change?

Ephesians 5:22 tells us about our role as husbands and wives. "Wives, *submit* yourselves unto your own husbands, as unto the Lord." And verse 25, "Husbands, *love* [*agapao*] your wives, even as Christ also loved the church, and gave Himself for it." (emphasis added)

Many of us wives balk at this "submission bit." I did for years. We say, "It's not fair. Why should I submit, revere, and respect him, when he doesn't even love me? He's not submitting to the Lord, so why should I submit to him? *Why should I be the first to change?*"[1]

Well, after wrestling with God over this issue for a long time, God finally said to me, "Nancy, if you have a problem with Ephesians 5, then simply apply the Second Commandment *before* Ephesians 5. "Thou shalt love [totally give yourself over to] thy neighbour as thyself." God said to me, "Doesn't Chuck apply as your neighbor?" I had to admit, "Of course he does."

Love (*Agapao*) Our Neighbors

The Second Commandment tells us that we are to love our spouses unconditionally, whether or not they are believers and whether or not they are returning our love. Our "neighbors" may be believers or they may not. Our neighbors may return our love or they may not. God says it doesn't matter—we are still to love (*agapao*) them.

Why is it easier sometimes to love our neighbors as ourselves, than it is to love our own spouses? The reason is that our spouses really know us. We can't get away with any phoniness with them. We can't pretend God's Love with them. They know when love is real and they know when it's not.

God is saying here in this Second Commandment that we are to love our spouses with His Love *not* only when things are going smoothly, but also we are to love them with unconditional Love even when things are not going well.

Love Our Enemies

If we still have a hard time with loving our husbands (or our wives) as ourselves (i.e., putting the Second Commandment before Ephesians 5), God goes even further and in Luke 6:27-28 He states that, *we are to love our enemies with this same kind of unconditional Love.* The word for love here is still *agapao*. We are to totally give ourselves over to our enemies! (God said it, I didn't!)

Maybe, at certain times, some of our spouses fit into this *enemy* category. Nevertheless, God says we are still to love (*agapao*) them.

Romans 12:20-21 says, "If thine enemy hunger, feed him; if he thirst, give him drink: for in so doing thou shalt heap coals of fire on his head." In other words, we are not to be "overcome by evil, but [we are to] overcome evil with good."

Live Christ's Life

People often ask me, "What is the best thing I can do for my unbelieving spouse and my wayward kids," or "my wayward spouse and my unbelieving kids?" "What book should I get?" "What tapes should I listen to?" "What class would you recommend?" The answer is simple. *Live Christ's Life! Live His Love!* Show that it works for you in the bad times, as well as the good times.

I found a Scripture recently that is very appropriate here. We are exhorted in Isaiah 24:15 to "Glorify the Lord in the fires." In other words, at all times we are to reflect and manifest Him. God's Will for our lives as husbands and wives is to unconditionally love our spouses.

[Note: Many husbands in the past have been fearful to have their wives take *The Way of Agape* class. They thought it would be just another marriage class where "they" would be the ones required to change. However, after seeing the changed lives of their wives and experiencing the new love that their wives had for them, many of them have written me. One man wrote, "I just couldn't stay away from her any longer." Another guy said, "I thought she had an affair, she was so changed." And my favorite is, "Can she stay in this class for the rest of our marriage?"]

It's Not Sloppy *Agape*

Now, unconditionally loving our spouses does not mean "sloppy *Agape*," or unbalanced Love. *Love without God's Wisdom* (or the Mind of Christ alongside) *is not God's Love at all.* In Chapter 3, we mentioned the importance of God's Love and the Mind of Christ always going hand in hand. This is the perfect balance that God desires for each of us.[2]

When we become open and pure channels of God's Love, that Love will always be accompanied by—and inseparable from—God's supernatural Wisdom. God's Love, with His Wisdom and Power alongside, is the total character of God. God is Love (1 John 4:8); He is the Word, i.e., Wisdom (John 1:1); and He is Spirit, i.e., Power (John 4:24). He is the triune God: Father, Son, and Holy Spirit. He is one God in three persons, and He lives in us. When we become cleansed vessels, the Life that will be manifested through us is the total character of God.

God's Wisdom is what will teach us how to walk in God's Love wisely. Only God has the Wisdom and that right answer for each of our situations. And only God has the Power to enable us to walk in that Way.

How do we Walk in Love Wisely?

How do we walk in God's Love wisely? This is what God has been teaching me these past ten years. He taught me about His Love back in the 1970s, but I didn't know or understand anything about the Mind of Christ (or the Wisdom and Power of God). Therefore, I didn't realize the incredible capabilities that I possess as a Christian. I didn't know that it's only through the Mind of Christ that we can love wisely in each situation.

As we mentioned in Chapter 3, God's Love in the Old Testament is called *chesed* in the Hebrew. *Chesed* Love has two facets or two sides to it. One facet is a longsuffering and merciful Love; the other side of *chesed* Love is a discipline or severe Love. This Love manifests itself in strictness, or sternness, as the occasion demands.[3] *Agape*, therefore, can manifest itself mercifully in our lives, or it can manifest itself in strictness and firmness, when needed.

The question then becomes, which type of Love do we use for our particular situation—God's longsuffering and merciful Love, or His severe and disciplinary Love? Both are God's Love, but in our own unique situation, which kind of Love do we use? We desperately need God's Mind (His Wisdom) on this. Only *He* can tell us how to personally love wisely. Every person and every situation is different and what works for one situation or one person will not necessarily work for the next.

We Need God's Wisdom

One woman came up to me not too long ago and asked, "How would God have me love my husband who is constantly leaving me, then changing his mind, repenting, and coming home?" (No other woman was involved.) This precious wife went on to say, "He is always apologizing for his actions, but then he goes out and does the very same thing all over again. She said, "I love this man, but when am I to be strict and disciplinary in loving him? And when am I to be merciful and longsuffering and take him back?"

Another woman asked me, "How would God have me love my teenage daughter, who at times is absolutely wonderful and adorable, but then abruptly changes and becomes intolerably rebellious? When should I be lovingly firm with her? And when should I be compassionate and say 'it's okay?'"

Are we to continue to be merciful and compassionate to these people who keep on doing the same thing over and over again? When are we to be strict and stand firm? And when are we to cover over and forgive their sin?

We desperately need God's supernatural Wisdom in order to answer these questions. God's Wisdom in our lives is what will balance out the "sloppy *Agape*" message. Sloppy *Agape* preaches only one side of God's total loving nature—His Mercy. It's God's Wisdom that will teach us and instruct us when to love in mercy and compassion and when to love in strictness and firmness. Each situation, each circumstance, and each person is totally different. Only God has the answer we need, because only He has the Love, the Wisdom, and the Power to perform that answer in our lives. The following is a perfect example:

Example: I Want Out!

Janice and Roger are a Christian couple who, at the time of this story, had been married about 20 years. They had two young children whom they adored. Janice had been very proud of her marriage to Roger. She knew the marriage had some problems, but essentially she thought it was built on a pretty solid foundation.

One day, Roger came home from the office and out of the blue announced to Janice that he wanted a divorce. He told her that he no longer loved her, that he had a girlfriend, and that he wanted out! Of course, Janice was devastated. She had never suspected a thing, so his announcement came as a total shock.

However, Janice handled it well. Rather than fall apart right then, she decided to go away for the weekend and seek God as to what He wanted her to do. She spent the entire weekend crying, confessing, and giving God all her devastation, pain, anger and bitterness. Continually she asked God to cleanse her and give her His supernatural Love and His forgiveness for Roger. She also pleaded with God to let her know what she was supposed to do next.

God not only answered Janice's prayer for unconditional Love for her husband, but He also showed her specifically how she was to proceed. Roger was to move out of the house and seek professional help (besides infidelity, he had an alcohol problem).

When Janice came home she did exactly as God had told her. She asked Roger to leave immediately and to seek medical help. Roger begged to stay; he wasn't ready to go just yet. Janice, however, insisted and so he moved out and sought counseling from their church. A month or so later, the counselor called Janice in for a meeting and he told her, "I think this is a hopeless situation. Roger is never going to change. You might as well throw in the towel, Janice."

Hearing the counselor's advice was a shock, but in her heart Janice didn't have peace about what he had said. God had not told her to quit yet. And until God did, she felt that all things were still possible.[4] She urged Roger to quit going to that counselor and to find another one. He did so. The new counselor was great, immediately diagnosing Roger as a manic depressive and an alcoholic. He put Roger on strong medication to control the mood swings and advised abstinence from all alcoholic beverages.

Things began to get better between Roger and Janice. However, just when they began to think of a possible reconciliation, the girlfriend came back into the picture. After seeing her again, Roger told Janice he was still in love with her, and he really wanted to file for an immediate divorce.

Janice loved Roger and would have done anything to have the marriage reconciled. Their relationship had been going so smoothly for about six months, but now it was all over—everything was shattered. Up until now, Janice felt as if she had the upper hand in the situation—she was the one "in control." But now, that feeling was gone, and she no longer wanted to live. At this point, she was totally devastated.

Again, Janice didn't do the "natural thing" and fall apart. As she had done before, she chose to go away and seek God and His Wisdom. That weekend she had a glorious time with the Lord. She chose to lay her will and her life down at His feet and be open for all that He had for her. And, of course, God was faithful to meet her. He led her to Philippians 4:4-7 which says: "Rejoice in the Lord always... in everything, by prayer and supplication with thanksgiving, let your requests be made known unto God. And the peace of God, which passeth all understanding, shall keep your hearts and minds through Christ Jesus."

Janice began to sleep with her Bible. Everywhere she went, she took it with her, continually making her requests known unto the Lord. That Bible literally became her lifeline as God kept answering her and giving her specific promises.

[It's too bad that many of us have to learn this lesson the hard way. *The Bible is our lifeline* not only in the deepest of trials but also in our ordinary everyday lives. Avoid learning this lesson the hard way, like Janice did.]

Meanwhile, Roger stopped seeing Janice. He stopped supporting the kids and began spending full time with his girlfriend. The court became involved in the case because of the children, and it ruled, incredulously, that the children must spend the weekends with their father, who was now living in an adulterous relationship.

Again, Janice kept making those faith choices to forgive and to love Roger. You know she didn't *feel* those choices. They were strictly contrary choices.[5] She kept telling the kids, "We can hate what Daddy is doing, but we must continue, with God's help, to love him." The kids even learned to pray for the other woman.

Janice was able to keep her focus on the overall picture: Roger's reconciliation to God. She knew that the battle was not hers alone, but God's. More than anything else, she wanted the restoration of the marriage, but that was still secondary to Roger's salvation.

Because of Janice's prayers and her attitude towards the whole situation, the kids adopted the same outlook. Sometimes on the weekends when they had to go with their Dad, they would read the Bible to him the whole time. Often, they would say, "Daddy, show us in the Bible where it says what you are doing is okay with God." Roger, angry and completely flustered, would immediately bring the kids home.

Because Janice stayed that open and cleansed vessel, loving God first and unconditionally forgiving Roger, God was freed to work mightily—not only in her own life, but also in Roger's life.

[John 20:23 tells us that if we don't unconditionally forgive that other person, we will be spiritually bound to them. If this is the case, God cannot work in our own life because of sin, nor can he work in the other person's life because there's a supernatural bondage. Only our unconditional forgiveness will release that tie.]

God saw to it that Roger went down in a big way. He lost his business, his health deteriorated, and his car was totaled. (In other words, God loved Roger with a severe and disciplinary Love.)

Finally one afternoon, Roger was so violently ill that he came to the point where he couldn't *feel* God's presence anymore. He said it was as if God was not there anymore, and it scared him to death. He decided right then and there to get right with the Lord. He left his girlfriend and moved in with his pastor's family, and over the next year, as he repented, God began slowly to cleanse and transform him. After a year or so, Roger began seeing Janice again. They dated for almost a year, under the watchful eye of the pastor. Finally, Roger asked Janice if he could come home.

Janice's friends, her counselor, her Bible study teacher, and even her parents said, "You are crazy if you take him back. How can you ever trust him again after what he has done to you?" God, however, convinced Janice that it was His Will for her to take Roger back. God convinced her that she could trust Him for the Love and the security that she needed. And He promised her that He would take care of her and that He would "never leave her or forsake her."

The Scripture God gave Janice that convinced her to allow Roger to come home was 2 Corinthians 2:5-11. It is an incredibly specific passage for Janice's situation:

"Remember the man I wrote about, who caused all the trouble... I don't want to be harder on him than I should. He has been punished enough by your united disapproval. Now it is the time to forgive him and comfort him. Otherwise, he may become so bitter and discouraged that he won't be able to recover. Please show him now that you still do love him very much. I wrote to you as I did so that I could find out how far you would go in obeying me. When you forgive anyone, I do too...A further reason for forgiveness is to keep from being outsmarted by Satan; for we know what he is trying to do." (The Living Bible)

Janice and Roger were reconciled. Their marriage healed and they both began to help other marriages in similar situations. I love this story because it proves that, if we are willing to give Him ourselves as cleansed vessels, God can accomplish His Will in our lives against all odds and teach us to love wisely.

Tough Love

Several years ago, we all were introduced to the term *tough love*. Many counselors and psychologists were promoting the idea that if your loved one was doing something ungodly or unscriptural, then you were advised to put up your own guidelines, restrictions, and stipulations by which the other person had to abide. And if he or she didn't, then certain consequences would occur.

For awhile it seemed the *right thing* to do and in many situations, these concepts were applied. I noticed, however, in many of my friends' homes where these principles were implemented, their spouses or their children were often pushed farther and farther away from them and also from God. And in a few cases the relationships broke apart altogether. Is this *Agape* Love?

Colossians 3:14 urges, "Above all these things put on [*Agape*], which is the bond of perfectness [or, *perfect bond of union*]." In other words, *Agape* is the glue that pulls us together, not pushes us apart.

When we take a stand in *Agape* Love, even though God's Love often exposes the sin of the other person, the end result is usually that the people involved are brought closer to each other and closer to God.[6] Now, this does not mean to say that categorically the marriage or the relationship will be completely healed (remember Bill's example in Chapter 3), but God promises us that His *Agape* Love will never fail.

How, then, do *Agape* Love and tough love differ?

When we are in the flesh, tough love is very easy—it seems like the natural and right thing to do. Putting up our own guidelines, boundaries, and consequences for our loved ones is so much easier than relinquishing ourselves and giving ourselves completely over to God, so that *He* can love them "wisely" through us.

A dear friend of mine couldn't wait for God's timing and His perfect way of dealing with her wayward husband. So she devised her own list of things that her husband could and couldn't do (i.e., he could only see the children on certain days; he could have no meals at home; he couldn't call, etc.). One by one, God knocked down all my friend's guidelines and told her, "My ways are not your ways. Leave your husband to Me; you just love him. Be that open conduit for My Love and I will not only teach you *how* to love him wisely, but I will actually love him for you."

We must each constantly check ourselves to be sure we are truly loving with God's Love and not with our own human self-serving love. If our loving is *not* done when we are truly being led by the Spirit (see **Chart 5**, page 159), then it won't be *Agape* at all, but our own natural, human love (see **Chart 6**, page 161). And, of course, this latter type of love is destined to fail, no matter how many boundaries we put up.

So, in order for it to be genuinely *Agape* Love—with the Mind of Christ alongside—we must first be that yielded and cleansed vessel, having confessed all our own sins. Then, and only then, will it be the real *Agape* "strict and disciplinary" Love.

The Easy Way Out

Every one of us wants the easy way. We want to get our direction from someone we can see and hear *now*. That's why we run to our ministers, to our counselors, to books and classes, etc. I know, I did it for 20 years! But, that's the easy way. Now, I'm not saying we shouldn't seek these avenues for advice—by all means do. I am just saying we shouldn't substitute the answers we get from these sources for the answer only God can give us.

Seeking God's answers and His Wisdom takes time. Most of us are in too much of a hurry to sit at God's feet waiting for His answer. God will use ministers, counselors, books, and classes along the way, but the final decision—and the peace that comes only from it—must come from God alone. I encourage you not to move until you have that.[7]

Example: "I Am the Cause of My Son's Tragedy"

On Thursday, February 23, 1984, the *Los Angeles Times* printed an article describing the horrible ordeal John Hinkley, Jr.'s parents have suffered since their son shot the President of the United States, Ronald Reagan.

The article stated that one week before the shooting, the senior Hinkley's had kicked their son out of the house, telling him to do something with his life and to be a man (tough love). One week later, John Hinkley, Jr. fired a bullet into the chest of the President.

Mr. Hinkley, Sr. said at his son's trial, "I am the cause of my son's tragedy...I am sure it was the greatest mistake of my life." He and Mrs. Hinkley are now crusading around the country trying to raise money for research and public education on mental illness. Mr. Hinkley says, "For heaven's sake, don't kick somebody out of the house when they can't cope. But," he goes on to say, "I had never heard of that before, and kicking John out of the house at that time seemed to me to make a lot of sense."

Proverbs 14:12 warns, "There is a way which seemeth right unto a man [in our own wisdom and understanding], but the end thereof are the ways of death."

At that time, the Hinkley's were paying a doctor, a specialist, to tell them what to do. As Mr. Hinkley said, "kicking John out seemed to make sense" (human, tough love). However, now he says, "*It was the biggest mistake of my life.*"

I can really identify with the senior Hinkley's. They, too, love the Lord. They were simply trusting someone whom they thought would have all the answers as to how they were supposed to love their troubled son. So often we depend upon our doctors and specialists and neglect God's advice.

And what often happens is that our doctors tell us one way to love, our ministers tell us another way, and our counselors, yet even another way. Which way is right for us? I believe God allows these various answers to baffle and confuse us so that we will seek our *ultimate* answer only from Him!

Only God knows the right way for us to love in each situation—only He knows the heart of the one being loved. Only God can tell us *how* to walk wisely in Love; only God can show us *which* type of love is required; and only God can produce that Love in our lives.

As 1 Corinthians 2:16 states, each of us has the Mind of Christ for our individual situations. If we seek His Mind—His Thoughts, His Wisdom, and His Discernment—each time, He promises He will show us and counsel us *how* to love with that perfect balance. Remember Janice? I believe if more of us ran to God for *His* answers and His Will with each situation as she did, we wouldn't need the massive counseling industry we have today!

Psalm 32:8 promises us, "I will instruct thee and teach thee in the way which thou shalt go: I will guide thee with mine eye." (*Eye* in the Old Testament often referred to God's Mind, His Spirit, and the way God would lead them.)

Loving Others Does Not Mean "Overlooking Sin"

Loving others wisely with *Agape* Love does *not* mean overlooking the sin they are involved in or pretending that the sin does not exist, nor does it mean taking responsibility for that sin by pointing it out and trying to fix it ourselves. When we love someone with *Agape* Love, we still see the sin in their lives, but we don't take it upon ourselves to point it out. We give our feelings about the sin to God and then we trust God to do something about it. In other words, we just get out of God's way as Janice did.

Janice didn't close her eyes to Roger's infractions, she didn't continually point them out to him, nor did she take responsibility to fix the sin herself. She knew it wasn't her responsibility to fix the sin, but simply to trust God to reveal the awfulness of the sin to Roger, which God did. She also trusted God to bring Roger to repentance and wholeness, which He did.

Don't Need to "Trust" Our Spouses

We don't need to trust our spouses completely in order to love (agapao) them. I know this is a radical statement, but the Bible says we need only to trust God completely in order to love our spouses. An example is Sarah in the Old Testament. In Genesis 12:11-20, Abraham persuades Sarah to tell the Egyptians that she is his sister, not his wife. Sarah was beautiful, and Abraham was afraid that they would kill him if they knew she was his wife.

How did Sarah handle this proposed deception? In 1 Peter 3:5-6 it says that *Sarah obeyed Abraham* (she did what he wanted), but it also says that *she trusted God.* This is exactly what the Lord wants for each of us.

As it turns out, the Egyptians did think Sarah was beautiful, and they did take her to Pharaoh's house. But the Lord, as He promised, watched out for her and protected her. God plagued Pharaoh with sickness and calamities, until he finally figured out for himself what was going on. Pharaoh then released her.

God works in the same way with us today. We don't need to trust our spouses completely in order to love (*agapao*) them. What we do need to do is to trust God completely in order to love (*agapao*) them, just exactly like Sarah did.[8] However, if we are only functioning on *storge* love (human affection love),[9] we'll have a desperate need to trust our spouses. In other words, "I'll love you, only if I can trust you." And when we find in certain circumstances (like Janice's and Sarah's) that we can't trust them, the whole relationship will crumble and fall apart.

[Note: I am speaking here of normal husband-wife relationships; I am not talking about extreme circumstances like adultery, or child abuse, or wife beating. If this is the case, then our obedience to God must supersede our loyalty to our spouse.[10] We need to take steps to remedy the situation: seek competent counsel, temporarily separate if God leads you to, and use the time to seek God and His Will. Please, however, don't be in a hurry to divorce. God is in the miracle-making business. And He can perform a miracle in your life, just like He did in Janice's and Sara's, if you or your hurt feelings don't get in the way.]

Remember, God's Love is the only Love that "trusts all things, endures all things, bears all things." (1 Corinthians 13) Our biggest job as spouses is to love: to totally give ourselves over to God first (love Him), so He then can enable us to love the people He has put in our lives, before or instead of ourselves.

Don't Be Holy Spirit "Naggers"

Remember something else—and this is critical—it's *not* our responsibility to point out all of our spouse's faults. It is not our role to be a "Holy Spirit nagger!" (I tried that route for 20 years, and nearly "sunk the ship!")

1 Peter 3:1 instructs, "Likewise, ye wives, be in subjection to your own husbands; that, if any obey not the word, they also may *without a word* be won by the conversation [quiet behavior] of the wives." (emphasis added)

Janice wrote me that during that whole year and a half that Roger was gone, the one thing God kept saying to her was simply, "Don't nag him, just trust and obey Me." I believe we need to obey God by giving Him all our hurts, our fears, our hatred, our devastations, our unforgivenesses, our resentments, our bitternesses, and so on, just as Janice did. Then we can be that open channel and trust that God will, in His timing and in His way, show our spouses their own faults.

Who Fulfills Our Two Basic Needs?

Janice's story also exemplifies that *we can be loved, and we can love, regardless of our circumstances, regardless of how we feel, and regardless of how others are treating us*! It doesn't matter where we are—married, separated, divorced, single, or widowed—for these two basic needs of ours to be fulfilled. These two needs—our need to be loved and to love—cannot be fulfilled by anyone, or anything else, but God Himself. *He is the only One who can meet our needs for love, security, meaning, and purpose.*

When my daughter Lisa and I went to lunch a few years ago, she kept talking about how hard it is to be single. She said, "Mom, when I get married, my husband and I will be best friends...we will do everything together...and he'll love me...and I will finally feel whole and complete." In other words, this "knight in shining armor riding on a white horse" was going to be the *one* to "meet all her needs."

I replied, "Honey, I don't want to be the one to burst your bubble, but I love you and so I am going to tell you the truth. No matter if you are single, married (happily or unhappily), separated, widowed, or divorced—no matter where you are—you must look to God first to meet all your needs. He is the only One who will make you whole and complete, not your husband!

"Once that vertical relationship is working, then you can have that 'dream relationship' you desire with your husband, because your basic needs will already have been met by Jesus. Then the love you receive back from your husband will just be the frosting on the cake."

Philippians 4:19 declares, "My God shall supply all [not "some" or "most," but *all*] your need according to His riches in glory by Christ Jesus." (emphasis added)

We must quit using our circumstances, our situations and our status in life as excuses for not having our needs met: "Well, if only I were married, then I would feel secure and loved." "If only I had a loving husband, then I could love the way God wants me to." "If only I had children, then I would feel complete...If only....."

The if only's must stop! Because we *can* be loved and we *can* love now, regardless of where we are walking or our present situation. Our two basic needs are not fulfilled by anyone or anything else but God Himself!

God is the only One who can meet our needs for love, security, meaning, and purpose! If we have a spouse who loves us and children who adore us, that's icing on the cake; and, praise God, we are very blessed and fortunate, indeed. But, even so, our two basic needs—our need to be loved so we can know who we are and our need to love so we can have meaning and purpose in life—can still only be filled by God and His Love.

Sometimes, for those who have a secure home life, looking to God in all situations and for all provisions is difficult. It's so much easier to look to this wonderful family God has given us to meet our needs. Be careful of this! God is still the only One who can meet our basic needs. And this is true whether we are happily married with ten kids, or whether we are going through a separation and a divorce like Janice.

As husbands and wives, our jobs are simply to love. We're to love God first, so that then we can love our spouses and our families "as" (before or instead of) ourselves.

Satan is on an all-out attack on the Christian marriage, family, and home. He will do everything he can to destroy our marriages and homes, even to the sending of "angels of light" that masquerade as our friends and our lovers. Satan does this expressly to stop and to quench God's Love from spreading. God's Love starts in our homes and this is why Satan is bent on destroying our marriages and our families.

Vow of Marriage

In God's eyes, marriage means to fit, join, cleave (like glue), and bind ourselves to another, no matter what happens, how we feel, what we think, or what we desire. God wants us to cleave and become one with our spouse, not only in our bodies but also in our souls (in our thoughts, emotions and desires). Marriage is an unconditional commitment—a vow before the Lord, for better or worse, in sickness and in health, with very few Scriptural exceptions.

One of my mom's dearest friends got polio shortly after her children were born. As a result, she became totally incapacitated. Her precious husband nursed and loved her for over 30 years until she finally passed away. To me, this is commitment love—unconditionally laying down our life for another, no matter what the cost and no matter what the price, unconditionally loving that other person before or instead of ourselves.

Webster's dictionary says that a vow is "when a person binds himself to an act," no matter what happens. Scripture says it even more strongly: "When thou shalt vow a vow unto the Lord thy God, thou shalt not be slack to pay it; for the Lord thy God will surely require it of thee; and it would be sin in thee [if you didn't pay it]." (Deuteronomy 23:21)

I am not trying to frighten anyone, but only to make us realize that making a vow before the Lord, like most of us have done in our marriages, is a serious matter to the Lord and not to be thrown aside easily.

I had no idea what my vow of marriage meant 17 years ago when I was going to leave Chuck. All I knew was that I was so miserable that I couldn't stand it any longer. I hurt so much that I just had to leave. I had to run away! All I could think about was *my* happiness, *my* feelings, *my* well-being and *my* future—my, my, my. I don't think I even bothered to ask God what His Will was in the matter.

Many books have been written espousing the position that if you are not happy in a relationship, then leave. "If there is too much stress in your life and no peace, then get out." "You have your own life to live." "You have a right to live in peace and harmony." "You have a right to fulfill yourself, to find yourself, and so on."

Joy Dawson is a wonderful Bible teacher who rebuts these statements. She asserts that as Christians, we have only two rights: 1) The right to know our Lord's Will,[11] and 2) The right to have the Power to carry it out.

If we are Christians, the Bible is our only reference and our only guideline. Scripture is very specific in outlining our reasons for leaving our marriages. Stress, incompatibility, unhappiness, hurts, and dissatisfaction are *not* among the list, quite the opposite. Read the book of Hosea.

I'm not saying don't ever leave your spouse or separate under any circumstances. Again, if there is an adulterous situation or circumstances that are dangerous or abusive to you or your children, then take immediate steps to remedy the situation: seek competent counsel, temporarily separate if God leads you to and use the time to seek God and His Will. Get counsel only from one who is living the *Way of Agape*. This counselor doesn't have to be perfect; none of us are, but at least he should be walking in the same direction as you are.

Seek Only Christian Counsel

Many people turn to secular counselors in times of need. We must remember, however, that no matter how wonderful and how helpful these counselors are, if they don't know the Lord, the direction we'll receive from them will usually be totally opposite from what God would have us to do. It's worldly counsel and not Godly counsel. So be careful. "Blessed is the man that walketh not in the counsel of the ungodly...." (Psalm 1:1)

Isaiah 30:1 states, "Woe to the rebellious children, saith the Lord, that take counsel, but not of Me; and that cover with a covering, but not of My Spirit, that they may add sin to sin."

If God says that you are to leave your spouse and your Christian counselor agrees, then by all means go. Just make sure, however, that you are following God's Will and *not* your own emotions. Again, please don't be in a hurry to divorce. There are not just *two* choices in a failing marriage—to stay together or to divorce. There's a third option and often this is the best one to make. And that's to temporarily separate, specifically to seek God and His Will. Remember Janice temporarily separated and God rewarded her for her patience and longsuffering.

God is in the miracle-making business. Even more than you, He wants to put your marriage back together. And even if you don't want that marriage put back together, if you are just willing to do what God wants, He then will change your heart and your feelings to align with His Will.[12]

When God Restores a Marriage

There is something else to keep in mind. When God restores a marriage, I assure you, it won't be the same as it was before. Many people are afraid of getting back together because they think their relationship will be exactly the same. This is not true.

Even if only one partner is willing to love the way God desires and she becomes the open vessel by which God's Love is initiated back into the marriage, that relationship will change. Because when *Agape* becomes the foundation of a marriage, then the natural loves that have died *can* become the blessings[13] that God designed them to be from the beginning. And, it is to be hoped, the other spouse will notice and be drawn to God. That marriage, I assure you, will be completely changed.

While *Agape* cannot create a marriage without any of the other natural loves working, I do believe it can carry and sustain a marriage until the human loves are rekindled. So even if all three of the natural, human loves have died in a marriage, if only one partner is willing to be that open channel for God's Love, that marriage has a good chance of being restored and becoming all that God intends it to be. (Ours was, and still is.) However, if all three natural, human loves have ceased in a marriage, and neither party is willing to initiate God's Love (it's buried under a ton of rubble in each heart), then that marriage is probably doomed to failure.

God's Love through us is the only thing that will close the gap between us and open a way for God to begin to work miracles in our lives.

No "Doormat Feelings"

Let me also emphasize that when we love with God's Love, *we won't feel like doormats*! So many spouses are petrified of being taken advantage of, of being stepped on, or walked all over if they love like I am suggesting. I would like to put an end to that myth.

Since God has directed us to love like this (and we know He has with our mates), then we must know that He will not allow us be taken advantage of because what we are doing is exactly what He has commanded us to do. It's not out of duress that we have chosen to love this other person, but we have freely chosen to do God's Will—which is to love. God, then, assures us that He will be our armor, our protection, our discernment, and our wisdom. He promises us that if we love Him first, He will give us the Wisdom and the Power to love wisely.

Again, *if we do our part, God will always be faithful to do His!* He will see to it that we will not be taken advantage of. Isaiah 59:19 declares, "When the enemy shall come in like a flood, the Spirit of the Lord shall lift up a standard against him."[14]

Feel Like Powerhouses

When we are filled with God's Love and His Wisdom, we won't feel like door-mats, but more like *powerhouses* because we've become what we were designed to be from the beginning: cleansed, pure, and open vessels not only experiencing God's Life for ourselves, but also passing His Life on to others.

God's Love is electric, and when we allow Him to love through us, we also become *radiant*. Psalm 34:5 says, "They looked unto Him and were radiant." This in-filling experience is the whole meaning and purpose of our lives. Ephesians 3:17-19 confirms this, "That Christ may dwell in your hearts by faith; that ye, being rooted and grounded in love, May be able to comprehend with all the saints what is the breadth, and length, and depth, and height; And to know the love of Christ, which passeth knowledge, that ye might be filled with all the fulness of God."

To me, this is strength, not weakness![15]

Jesus was the most powerful being on earth, and yet He chose out of His own free will to relinquish His Life so the Father could pour forth His Love through Him. "For though He was crucified through weakness (yieldedness), yet He lived by the power of God." (2 Corinthians 13:4) This yieldedness is God's plan for each of us—to be those open, cleansed vessels where God can pour His Love through us to our loved ones.

"To Them That Perish, It's Foolishness"

I had a woman tell me not too long ago, "Nancy, you are crazy. This teaching is totally opposite to everything I have ever been taught!" My friend was a Christian, but at that time she was getting her master's degree in psychology. She said to me, "It's all total foolishness."

She is right. This is a foolish way of loving to the world, because it is *not* natural! It's certainly not our normal, human reaction. In fact, this way of acting and re-acting is completely opposite to our instinctive, self-centered ways of thinking and responding. But God Himself tells us that "the preaching of the cross is to them that perish foolish-ness;[16] but unto us which are saved it is the power of God." (1 Corinthians 1:18-19)

It's the same paradox with His Love. To them who don't know His supernatural Love, loving like this is foolishness. But to them who see God work out "impossible miracles," when they are willing to lay down their wills and their lives, it's not only the power of God working, but it also becomes the whole reason and purpose for living.

God's Love through us is the only thing that will bring our husbands, our children, our relatives, and our friends back to God. Only God's lovingkindness—in spite of the circumstances, in spite of how we feel, and in spite of what we think—is going to draw them.[17] God's Love drew Roger back, and it will draw your loved ones back also!

However, we'll only be able to mirror and reflect on the outside the Love we are intimately and genuinely experiencing on the inside. In other words, if we are not experiencing God's Love for ourselves—either because we don't believe, or because we have blocked His Love off by a wall of hurts, bitternesses, or insecurities—then we certainly are not going to be able to pass that Love on to others.

Marriage in God's Eyes

I believe the reason marriage is so sacred to the Lord is because He designed marriage as a prophetic picture of our relationship with Him. He wanted us to have an earthly picture, something we could see and relate to, of how wonderful a loving relationship could be—how two people could become one! He was giving us a fore-taste or a foreshadow of how our relationship with Him could be.

Listen to Ephesians 5:31-32: "For this cause shall a man leave his father and mother, and shall be joined unto his wife, and they two shall be one flesh. This is a great mystery: but I speak concerning Christ and the church."

How grieved God must be as He looks down and sees what we have done with His earthly example.

Our Responsibility

What are our responsibilities in loving our spouses as ourselves? There are only three:

First, we need to *accept that God loves us personally* and intimately expe-rience His Love for ourselves.

Then, we need to *love (agapao) God with all our heart, willpower, and soul*—continually denying ourselves and giving Him our will and our lives to work through.

Lastly, if we have done the above two things, God's Love will be released through us and we'll be able to *love (agapao) our spouses before, or instead of, ourselves.* We'll be able to put their will and their desires above our own.

God's Responsibility

If we are doing the above three things, what then are God's responsibilities in our marriages? Again there are three:

First, the Holy Spirit will show us, moment by moment, *how to love our spouses wisely.* And God will let us know His guidelines for our particular situation.

Second, if we do our part, God will then be free—because we are out of His way—*to change and transform our spouses in His perfect timing and in His perfect way.*

Finally, *God will work out His perfect Will in our spouses' lives* in the way only He knows is best.

There is such *freedom* in this; I am not responsible for how Chuck thinks, feels, or how he acts anymore. I'm totally aware of the areas that need changing and can continue to pray earnestly about them, but my *only* responsibility is to be that open vessel so that God can love Chuck through me.

Focus Only On Jesus

When we stay that open vessel for God's Love and we keep our eyes squarely focused on Jesus to meet our desperate need for love, three important things happen:

First, we'll be able to *stop strangleholding and suffocating our spouses to meet our basic needs.* (We'll know that only God can meet our needs for love, meaning, and purpose.)

Second, we'll be able to *stop trying to conform our spouses into our desired image for a mate*, what we *feel* we need. We'll be able to accept our spouses as they are, and genuinely love the "whole package" (faults and all).

Lastly, and most importantly, we will be able to *trust God to fix what He wants fixed in our spouses*, in His timing and in His way. God always does a much better job of changing and transforming someone than we ever could.

However, the minute we stop being open channels and stop looking to the Lord, watch out. It never fails, we will grab hold of our spouses, and once again we'll both sink.

Willing to Love Unconditionally

We need to be willing to love with God's Love, even if our circumstances and our situations never change.[18] Our motivation is wrong if we are loving only to have the circumstances or the other person change. That's conditional human love and not God's Love at all. Even if what we see happening as a result of our loving is totally opposite from what we would like to see happen, as long as we keep loving God's way, He promises us that His Love will never fail![19]

I have another friend who is a widow of ten years, and she told me to tell you something. "Tell them, Nancy, to look at their spouses as *gifts* from God and don't reject or give up on what God has given you as a gift." She said, "You don't appreciate God's gift until you don't have it anymore."

Now you might be saying to yourself, "Well, that's easy for her to say, she doesn't know my spouse and she doesn't know my situation!" You're right. My friend doesn't know your spouse and she doesn't know your situation and neither do I. But God does, and He is the only one who counts because He is the only one who can do something about your situation.

Your Choice

The question becomes: Will you give God your will and your life to work through to reach your spouse? Are you willing to lay your life down so that God can pour His *Agape* through you to them?

God desires us all to have His abundant, love-filled Life right where we are walking now. John 10:10 declares, "I am come that *they might have life, and that they might have it more abundantly.*" (emphasis added)

Jesus is not talking about *heavenly* life, but life right here on earth—right where we are walking now! *Abundant Life is simply experiencing God's Life in place of our own.* God wants us to have this kind of life, even in the midst of our terrible trials and circumstances.

That's the miracle God is after. To me, a changed "Love-filled" life is so much more dramatic and so much more of a testimony to others than all the "signs and wonders" in the world. *Joy, Peace, and Love come not with the absence of trials, but only with the presence of God.*[20]

The questions we always come back to are: Are you willing to allow God to perform a miracle through you? Are you willing to relinquish yourself so that God's Love can be released through you to others?[21]

In closing, John 13:34-35 instructs, "A new commandment I give unto you, That ye love one another; as I have loved you, that ye also love one another. By this shall all men know that ye are My disciples, if ye have love one to another." (emphasis added)

Endnotes:

1. The title of my book, *Why Should I Be the First to Change?*

2. Be sure to get the *Be Ye Transformed* tape series on the "Mind of Christ" (soon to be a book).

3. See Chapter 3, "*Chesed* Love."

4. Luke 1:37

5. See Chapter 12, "Contrary Choices."

6. See Chapter 3, "God's Love Exposes Sin."

7. See Chapter 11, "When in a Hurry."

8. John 2:24, 2 Corinthians 1:9-10; 1 Timothy 4:10

9. See Chapter 5, "Three Natural Loves."

10. Exodus 1:17, Daniel 3 and 6; Acts 5:29

11. See Chapter 11, "How Do We Know God's Will?"

12. See Chapter 12, "God Changes Our Feelings."

13. See Chapter 5, "Can Become a Blessing."

14. Isaiah 54:17

15. 2 Corinthians 12:9-10

16. 1 Corinthians 1:20b and 2:14

17. Jeremiah 31:3

18. See Chapter 3, "Example: Justified Wrongs."

19. 1 Corinthians 13:8

20. Psalm 16:11

21. Luke 10:25-28

Scriptural References:

Chapter 16

Love For One another

A. Above everything else, we are to have love for one another; whether we are married, separated, divorced, single, or widowed (1 Peter 4:8; Philippians 1:9) "*He that loveth not, knoweth not God*" (1 John 4:7-8,20-21; 2:10-11; 3: 17-18)

    1. I believe, if we are not loving our spouses as ourselves, something is wrong with our fellowship with God; we are not loving Him as He desires (1 John 3:14-16; 4:7-8,20-21). Our spouses do not even have to be in the home to have this apply

    2. When we love (*agapao*) God first, then we can obey, cleave to, and love our husbands as God intends (Ephesians 5:1-2,28; 2 Corinthians 8:5)

        a. We can then become one with them (Genesis 2:24; Matthew 19:5-6; John 17:22; Mark 10:7; Philippians 2:2; Ephesians 5:31)

           . One Love (1 Peter 1:22; 3:8c; Philippians 2:2)

           . One mind (1 Corinthians 1:10; Philippians 1:27; 1 Peter 3:8a)

           . One soul (Galatians 2:20; 1 John 3:16)

        b. Then our marriage becomes complete and the way that God de signed it to be from the beginning

B. We can then submit to one another (Ephesians 5:21-32)

Why Should I Be the First to Change?

A. We wives don't like having to submit to our spouses (Ephesians 5:22; 1 Peter 3:1)

    1. If this is a problem in your marriage, apply the Second Commandment *before* Ephesians 5:22, "You shall love (*agapao*) your spouse before or instead of yourself" (Matthew 22:39)

        a. Whether or not he is a believer

        b. Whether or not he is returning that love

        c. Whether or not he is at home

    2. If we still have a problem with this, apply Luke 6:27-38 *before* Matthew 22:39. "Love your enemies" (Matthew 5:44-48; Proverbs 25:21-22; Romans 12:14,19-21)

        a. Jesus is our example

        b. He loved us when we were still enemies of the cross (Matthew 9:12-13; John 3:16; Romans 5:8)

        c. He loves us with an everlasting Love and by it has drawn us to Himself (Jeremiah 31:3)

B. We are to love as He did (1 John 4:12,17)

Live Christ's Life
A. At all times we are to reflect and show forth God's Life
   1. Only if we are loving God will we be able to do this (Matthew 22:37-39; Galatians 5:13)
   2. This does not mean sloppy *Agape* or unbalanced love. God will give us His thoughts as to how to love wisely. God's Love and His Wisdom always work together (Ephesians 3:17-18; 4:15a; Philippians 1:9) *Mercy and truth* are always together in the Old Testament (Psalms 85:10; 86:15; 98:14; Proverbs 16:6)
   3. God will show us how to love wisely (Job 37:13; Psalm 32:8; Romans 11:22; Matthew 10:16). We constantly need the Mind of Christ (1 Corinthians 2:16; James 1:5-6; Matthew 10:16)
      a. We don't overlook sin, nor do we point it out, nor do we take responsibility for it (Colossians 3:12-13)
      b. We just trust God and His Love to expose the sin and bring about their repentance in His timing and in His way (1 Corinthians 13:7; Ephesians 5:13; John 8:3-12; Romans 2:4b; 1 Peter 3:1-2; 2 Samuel 7:14; Psalm 89:14; Hebrews 12:5-7)
        . Sarah obeyed Abraham (Genesis 12:11-20)
        . But she trusted God (1 Peter 3:5-6)
        . By staying open and cleansed vessels, unconditionally forgiving others, we will not be "bound" to any (John 20:23)
        . Don't look to our spouses to meet our two basic needs. Only God can meet those needs (Philippians 4:19)
        . Our job as spouses is to love our other half before or instead of ourselves
B. We are to trust God and love our spouses (Proverbs 3:5-6; 1 John 4:7-8)

What Is Our Responsibility in Loving Our Spouses?
A. First, accept that God loves us and learn to intimately know His Love for ourselves
B. Love (*agapao*) God with all our heart, will, and soul (Matthew 22:37; 2 Corinthians 8:5) no matter how our mates respond and no matter what the circumstance
   1. God must be preeminent in our heart before our mates can be preeminent in our lives (1 John 3:18; Ephesians 5:22-23)
   2. Become *one heart, one will, and one life* with God (Philippians 1:21a)
   3. This releases God's Love within us to give to others (1 John 4:17)
C. Then we will be able to love our spouses "as or instead of" ourselves, whether or not they are returning that love and no matter what the circumstances are (Matthew 19:5-6; 22:39; Hosea 1-3; Psalm 91:14; Ephesians 5:31; John 13:34; 15:12-15; Romans 13:8; Hebrews 6:10-15; Galatians 5:13c; 1 Peter 4:8)
   1. Putting their will and desires above our own (assuming they are godly desires)
   2. If they are not, we are to obey a higher authority (Exodus 1:17; Daniel 3 and 6; Acts 5:29)

3. Stay that open channel for God's Love
    a. Stop strangleholding our spouse to meet our needs
    b. Stop trying to conform them to "our desired mate"
    c. Let God fix in them what He wants to and in His timing
    d. Things to recognize in marriage trials
        .   God has allowed the trial for His purposes
        .   God is in us to carry us through on His power and ability
        .   If God wants the marriage to work out, He will heal it; if not, He will let us know when to leave
        .   We must not harden our hearts (Matthew 19:8; Mark 10:5)

What Is God's Responsibility in Our Marriages?

A. If we are doing the above three things, God then will show us how to love our spouses wisely (1 Corinthians 13:4-8; James 1:5; Ephesians 4:15a) God will "guide us with [His] eye [His Mind]" (Psalm 32:8b)
B. God is then free to change and transform our spouses in His timing and in His way (Romans 8:28)
C. Finally, it is God's responsibility to work out His perfect Will in our mate's life (Isaiah 55:8-9)
    1. We are aware of the areas that "need changing," but continue to only pray about them
    2. We just "love the whole package"

Marriage in God's Eyes

A. Marriage means:
    1. To fit, join, cleave together, unconditionally loving one another (Ephesians 5:31)
    2. To become one (Genesis 2:23-24; 1 Peter 3:8; Philippians 1:27; 2:2; 1 Corinthians 1:10; Matthew 19:5-6; Mark 10:7; Ephesians 5:28)
    3. A commitment, an unconditional vow before the Lord (Deuteronomy 23: 21; Ecclesiastes 5:4)
        a. Take counsel from God first
        b. Be careful of "worldly counsel" (Isaiah 30:1)
        c. Don't be in a hurry to divorce (Matthew 19:3-9; 1 Corinthians 7:12-17)
        d. It is better to forgive and accept spouse back in love (Hosea 1-3; Malachi 2:13-16)
    4. *Marriage is supposed to be a prophetic picture of our relationship with God*—that oneness (Hosea 2:20; Ephesians 5:31-32). How grieved God must be
B. The *Cross has been forgotten* in our marriages and homes (Matthew 19:21; Colossians 3:3; 2 Corinthians 4:10a; Galatians 2:20; 5:24)

1. We don't love unconditionally with forgiveness (Colossians 3:12-13; Ephesians 4:1-3,31-32)
2. Our own negative thoughts and emotions have taken over and caused a separation not only between God and us, but also between others and ourselves

We Must Be Willing to Love Unconditionally

A. God's Love through us is what will bring our estranged spouses, our children, our relatives, and our friends to God (Jeremiah 31:3; Hosea 1-3; 11:4a; 1 John 4:19; Romans 2:4b; John 13:35) *"Love covers a multitude of sins"* (1 Peter 4:8; Proverbs 10:12b)

B. We need to be willing to love with His Love, even if our situations never change (1 Corinthians 13:4-8; Acts 20:24; Romans 5:3-5; 1 John 4:7-8, 20-21; Luke 6:27-28)

C. God desires us to have His abundant Life right where we are walking now (John 10:10; 1 John 5:20)
   1. Enjoying abundant Life here and now is the miracle God is after
   2. Joy, peace, and Love come, not with the absence of trials, but with the presence of Jesus (Psalm 16:11; 1 John 4:7-8)

D. The meaning of life lies in our relationships—our relationship with God first and then our relationship with others (Luke 10:25,27-28)
   1. *Loving God with all our heart, will, and soul* (Matthew 22:37)
   2. *Loving others as, or instead of, ourselves* (Matthew 22:39)

"Herein is our love made perfect...as He is, so are we in this world." (1 John 4: 17, emphasis added) *"God is Love"* (1 John 4:8)

Section Seven

The More Excellent Way

In conclusion, *Agape is summed up in Jesus Christ;* He is God's Love personified.

"In this was manifested the Love of God toward us, because that God sent His only begotten Son into the world, that we might live through Him." (1 John 4:9)

Jesus is the mediator and the vessel of God's Love to us. He died expressly so that God's Love might be released to us.[1] Jesus' whole purpose and ministry in life was to willingly lay down His Life for us, so that we might receive the Father's Love.

Jesus instructs us in John 15:9, "As the Father hath loved Me, so have I loved you: continue ye in My Love."

This intimacy is the difference between Christianity and all the other religions of the world. Our God is tangible, touchable, and reachable, because He lives in us. His dwelling place is in our hearts. If our hearts are open and pure, then we can experience His Love surrounding us, His Wisdom and discernment enlightening us, and His Power strengthening and carrying us.

Our God is not up in heaven, totally out of reach and untouchable. Jesus has brought God and His Love into our very beings, our hearts, and our souls. God's purpose is that we, too, might pass that Love and that Life on. "Hereby perceive we the Love of God, because He laid down His Life for us: and we ought to lay down our lives for our brethren." (1 John 3:16)

When He walked the earth, Jesus was a true representation of God's Love. He not only loved His own, but He also loved His enemies.[2] Jesus knew that perfect balance between God's merciful and longsuffering Love and His strict and disciplinary Love. He was and is our perfect example of *Agape* Love. And as we lay down our wills and our lives to Him, He can pour His perfect Love through us to a very needy, and dying world.

Your Turn

Have you experienced God's Love? Has Jesus kept reaching out to you and kept on loving you and drawing you to Himself, even when you didn't answer? Has He wooed you as a lover would and pursued you with His Love, showering it upon you, even when you didn't feel worthy or deserving of it?[3]

Have you responded to His Love? Have you said, "Yes, God, I want Your Love. I need Your Love. I need Your forgiveness. I want You to come into my heart and be my Love and my life."

Accepting that Love of God into our hearts and knowing that He loves us unconditionally is the foundation or the building pad that our whole spiritual house is going to be built upon. "For God so loved the world, that He gave His only begotten Son, that whosoever *believeth* in Him should not perish, but have everlasting life" (John 3:16, emphasis added).[4] And 1 John 4:15, "Whosoever shall *confess* that Jesus is the Son of God, God dwelleth in him, and he in God." (emphasis added)

God's Love for us doesn't come with conditions! His Love for us is *not* based upon *what we do* or *what we don't do* but simply upon who we are in Christ Jesus. The incredible news is that God not only loves us but that He loves us just the way we are.

We can't go further in *God's Way of Agape* until we first know that we belong to Him, that we have received His Love, and that He has the central place in our hearts. We must know that Jesus loves us *before* we can have the confidence and the trust to lay down our wills and our lives to Him and love Him in return. Once we know that, then we can go on and "love others as ourselves" as God would have us do.

"These things have I written unto you that believe on the name of the Son of God; that ye may *know* [and experience] that ye have eternal life, and that ye may believe on the name of the Son of God." (1 John 5:13, emphasis added)

The meaning of life lies in our relationships: first our relationship with God, then our relationship with others. By first loving God with all our heart, will, and soul, we not only will experience His Love for ourselves, but we'll also be able to pass His Love on to others.

This is truly the King's "*HIGH*" Way: *GOD'S WAY OF AGAPE*

1 John 4:17 declares the way our love is made perfect, completed, or finished, is that we might become in this world as He is...and that is *LOVE*!

Endnotes:

1. Romans 8:32 and 1 John 4:10

2. Romans 12:20; Matthew 5:44-48; Luke 6:27,32,35

3. Hosea 2:14-16

4. 1 John 5:12

An Engineer's View

You have had a chance to review Nan's discoveries from a woman's point of view. It is absolutely fascinating to me to see all of this from the point of view of a computer systems engineer. You will find the many parallels to modern system design surprising.

The Frustration of Psychology

We all try very hard to understand *ourselves*. Some of us resort to the literature of the behavioral sciences and psychology in our pursuit of meaningful insights on how we are put together. While often eloquently presented, this introspection for most of us invariably leads to frustration and little practical benefit.

We live in an age which is obsessed with idioms from the field of psychology, and yet practitioners in this field actually understand very little about how we are organized and why we behave the way we do. Current articles on psychology and its related fields are now beginning to cast increasing doubts about the real effectiveness resulting from the many decades of behavioral science research.

Likewise, research in neurophysiology and related fields also yield little insight on how we are really put together from a system architectural point of view. Yet, we need to understand our internal system design if we are to ever understand our behavior.

Computer Systems

Having spent over 30 years in the computer industry in both hardware and software, I have noted some instructive parallels from the field of computer systems engineering. It was interesting to observe how many of the Biblical perspectives which Nan uncovered are actually parallel to architectural insights familiar to those in the system sciences.

Since most of us these days have had some exposure to personal computers, I thought that some of these insights and parallels might prove instructive. However, we have left this discussion to the back of this book to avoid intimidating the non-technical reader.

Computer Systems Architecture

From a hardware standpoint, most computers can be summarized as shown in Figure 1 on the next page.

The main elements include some way of storing information in memory, a collection of circuits to retrieve, combine, and store information, and a large repository, usually a disk drive, for storing larger files.

In addition, a collection of circuits is required to communicate with the external world, typically called "Input/Output" paths for the keyboard, monitor, printers, etc.

While we can easily get absorbed and distracted with the amazing details of the current state of the art, it is instructive to realize that all the knowledge of the hardware—the circuits, the devices—*is of no use in trying to predict the system's behavior.* You can know everything there is to know about every circuit, every hardware element, every wire in the entire system, and still not be able to predict what its actions and responses will be to any particular stimuli, situation, etc.

The *behavior* of the system is, of course, *a software issue entirely.*

The hardware is simply an elegant residence of the software. There are some instructive insights from the development of computer software, however, that may help us in understanding *ourselves.*

Software Development Process

A little historical background will also be useful. As the early computers emerged in the late 40s and early 50s, it was necessary to write the programs for them in machine language: the specific machine-readable codes that would indicate "add," "multiply," or other functions. This was a tedious, error-prone, and expensive procedure.

Eventually, programmers developed computer programs to assist this process, programs that would manage the memory, link sub-portions of the programs, and so on. For certain esoteric reasons, these programs were called *assemblers.* These dramatically reduced the effort to write programs.

The big breakthroughs came in the 1950s with the development of *problem-oriented* languages that allowed super-programs called *compilers* to translate expressions natural for certain types of problems into the machine-executable codes that actually ran on the computer. Examples of these were ALGOL and FORTRAN for engineers and mathematicians, COBOL for business programmers, etc. There are over a hundred specialized *languages* that are presently in use in various fields of computer-oriented endeavor.

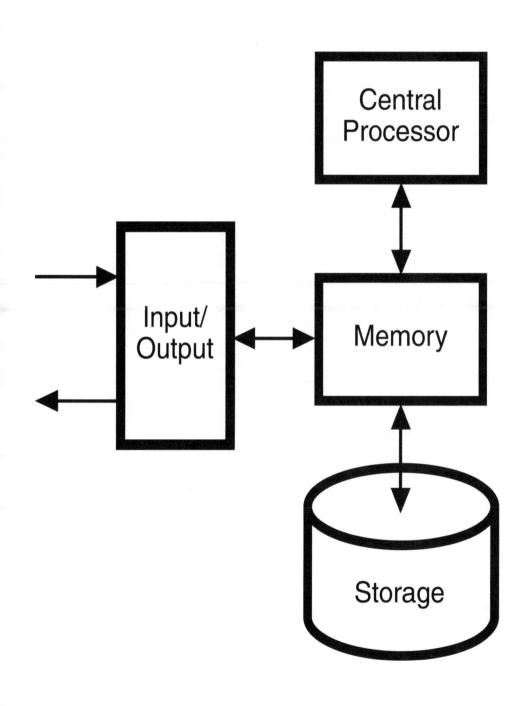

The emergence of compilers reduced the costs of programming by over 100:1 and made the resulting programs *independent of any particular computer hardware.* Thus began the explosion of the entire software industry, quite separate from any particular hardware manufacturer.

As the industry progressed to even higher level techniques, there developed application generators, heuristic programs, programs that learn and explore alternatives on their own, and such esoteric pursuits as artificial intelligence, pattern recognition, virtual reality, and other increasingly sophisticated levels of programming.

A summary map of the evolution of programming languages and the software development process is highlighted on the following page.

The Key Insight

One of the things that makes the software industry possible is the difficulty of going *backwards:* the flow in figure 2 is from the general expressions toward the specific executable instructions; from *source code* toward *object code.*

A sophisticated computer program is self-modifying. It is what a mathematician would classify as an *infinite state machine.* That implies that it is *impossible to infer* the *source code* by examining the *object code.* You cannot backtrack *uphill* in figure 2.

That is why you can go to a computer store and purchase a proprietary software package and still not be able to change the *design* of the package. You can run the program on your computer, but you do not have access to its design. You can't modify or change it. Generally, you cannot discover the hidden internal design of the software from its external behavior.

This nonlinear aspect also applies to ourselves, and this is why the field of psychology is doomed to frustration as it tries to infer our software design by observing our external behavior. This is also why it is of little use to become expert on neural nets or brain physiology in pursuit of the soul, the spirit, or these other aspects of our internal design.[1]

But there is even more we can glean from a perspective of computer software.

Software Process

Conceptual Environment

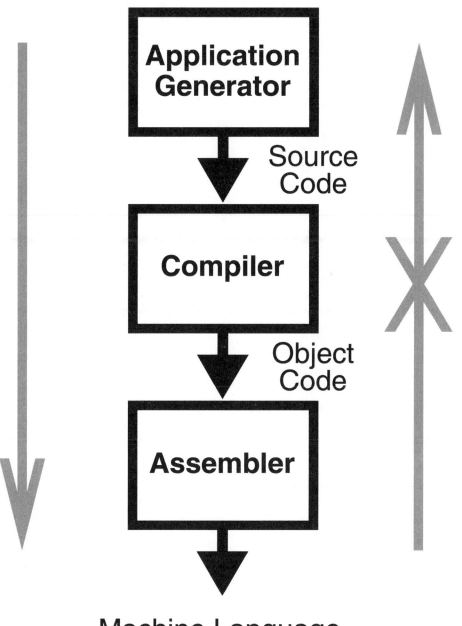

Machine Language

Software Architecture

Most of us are probably not aware of how computer software is organized. The key element of any proprietary software package, usually called the *kernel*, is the central core that is based on the principal formulas, algorithms, and insights that make the package useful. This kernel draws upon a library of *system resources* to accomplish the various tasks such as managing files, sorting lists, processing graphics, and so on. (See Figure 3 on the next page.)

This body of software is then *wrapped* in an *applications interface* that causes the program to behave in a style consistent with the intended community that it is designed for. Examples might include a word processor for writers, a spreadsheet program for accountants, or a mathematics package for engineers, etc.

On most computers today, one may use many different applications programs that are usually collectively embedded in a *user interface*, the most common one being the familiar Graphic User Interface found on a Macintosh, or Windows on a personal computer ("PC").

And all of this is embedded in a hardware environment such as a Macintosh or an IBM-compatible computer.

What's the Point?

From an understanding of the technology, it becomes clear why it is virtually impossible to *discern the architecture* of the system from its external behavior alone. If one is to really understand the inner workings and behavior of a system, one needs to consult the Designer's Manual. This will lay out the complete system architecture and detail how the various elements work together to determine the actual behavior of the system.

So it is with ourselves. It's surprising that so many still look to the writings of Sigmund Freud for their primary vocabulary and insights concerning our behavior, rather than explore the Designer's Manual—the design guide from the Creator Him-self—the Word of God!

Our Software Architecture

The only way to get a perspective of our own *software architecture* is to consult our own Designer's Manual.

It is interesting that the New Testament declares *seven times* that "ye are the Temple of God."[2] Even Jesus referred to His own body as the Temple.[3] It is this architectural insight that has been the foundation for many of the insights in this book. A comparison of the generalized software architecture of Figure 3 with the Temple architecture of Chapter 10 is striking. But there's more.

Software Architecture

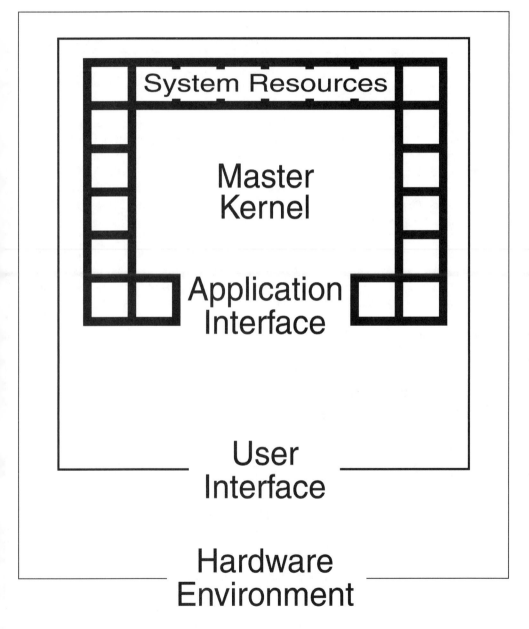

A Lesson From Physics

In modern physics we now discover that time is a *physical* property, that it varies with mass, acceleration, and gravity. We live in a four-dimensional space in which time itself is one of the physical dimensions.

A time measurement device in a weaker gravitational field runs faster than one in a stronger field. Near the surface of the earth the frequency increases about one part in 10^{16} per meter, so a clock 100 meters higher than a second clock will have a frequency higher by one part in 10^{14}.

Acceleration also affects time. Clocks carried eastward around the world on an airplane will differ very slightly from a clock at rest on the earth or one carried westward, since they are in rotation at different speeds about the center of the earth and there is a difference in gravitational potential. In 1971, in experiments with atomic clocks sent around the world on aircrafts by the U. S. Naval Observatory, the eastward flying clock *lost* 0.06 microsecond and the westward one *gained* 0.27 microsecond, confirming the predicted relativistic effects.

Most textbooks on Einstein's Theory of Relativity will also use the illustration of the two imaginary twin astronauts. One remains on the earth; the other, for example, undertakes a space mission in which the vehicle attains a speed of half the velocity of light, enroute to and from the nearest star, Alpha Centari, about four light years away. When the traveler returns to the earth, he would be more than *two years younger* than his twin brother.

Time varies with respect to mass, acceleration, and gravity, that which has no mass has no time.

The Geometry of Eternity

We assume that time is linear and absolute. When we were in school, we drew *time lines*. The left end of a line was the beginning of something: a nation, or a person's life. The right end of the line was the termination of that something.

Thus, when we encounter the concept of *eternity*, we tend to visualize a line that begins at infinity on the left and extends to infinity on the right. We visualize God as someone "who has lots of time."

But that's an error of physics. Does God have "mass?" Is He subject to gravity? Hardly.

God is not someone who has lots of time; He is someone who is *beyond* the domain of time altogether. That's what Isaiah means when he says it is He who "inhabiteth eternity." (57:15.)

Since God has the technology to create us, He certainly has the technology to get a message to us. But how does He *authenticate* it? How does He let us know it is really from Him? By demonstrating that the source of the message is from *outside* the domain of time. He alone knows "the end from the beginning." (Isaiah 46:10)

The Bible consists of 66 books written by 40 authors over thousands of years, yet we now discover that it is an integrated message that describes history in advance. We call that *prophecy.*

The Eternal You

Software has no mass. A blank computer diskette weighs about 0.7 of an ounce. If you load it with over a million bytes of software, costing hundreds of dollars, it still weighs 0.7 of an ounce. It can even be transported over the air waves or a communication line because it has no mass of its own. Therefore, it has no time dimension of its own.

The real *you* has no mass. It is like software. Call it the *soul*, the *spirit*, or whatever you will, it has no mass. It temporarily inhabits this body for a while, but it has no mass of its own. It therefore has no time dimension. It is eternal. The real you—the part of you that is not limited to physical mass—will exist throughout eternity.

That's the problem. You will spend eternity either *in* the presence of God, or forever *banished from* His Presence. God's inherent nature includes righteousness and requires the banishment of imperfection from His Presence. We call our imperfection *sin*. It is a genetic defect which we inherited from Adam.

Fortunately, God has anticipated this barrier and has provided a remedy. His remedy is the result of a love story—a love story written in blood on a wooden cross in Judea almost 2,000 years ago. Jesus substituted *His eligibility* on our behalf, and His eligibility is available simply for the asking.

Most of us assume that *eternity* is in the future. The past is but a memory. The future is an ephemeral hope. It may come as a surprise to realize that our connection with eternity is *now.*

The Geometry of Eternity

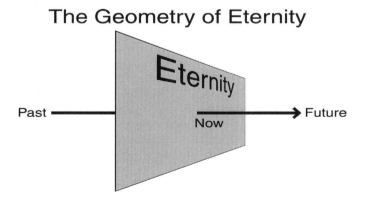

Your connection with eternity is right now. Are you really in Christ? Are you certain of your position in eternity? You can determine your eternal destiny—right now—in the privacy of your own will, by just asking Jesus Christ to apply His eligibility to you, and take over.

That commitment will launch you on the Grandest Adventure of all. That commitment is the very reason you are here reading this, right now.

Endnotes:

1. This is the import of Hebrews 4:12: only as revealed by the Word of God.

2. 1 Corinthians 3:9-16; 6:19; 2 Corinthians 6:16; Ephesians 2:20, 21; Hebrews 3:6; 1 Peter 4:17; 2:5

3. Mark 14:58; John 2:19

Supplemental Study Notes

I. What Is *Agape*?

(In the following Scriptures, we have used the word *Agape* wherever the word "love" appears in the original.)

God is Agape. (1 John 4:8b, 16b)

Herein is Agape, not that we loved God, but that He loved us, and sent His Son to be the propitiation for our sins. (1 John 4:10)

God is Agape. In this was manifested the Agape of God towards us, because that God sent His only begotten Son into the world, that we might live through Him. (1 John 4:8-9)

But God, Who is rich in mercy, for His great Agape wherewith He loved us. (Ephesians 2:4)

But God commendeth His Agape toward us in that, while we were yet sinners, Christ died for us. (Romans 5:8)

Nothing will separate us from the Agape of God. (Romans 8:35,39 paraphrase)

Agape never faileth. (1 Corinthians 13:8a)

Agape is the fulfilling of the law. (Romans 13:10)

Behold, what manner of Agape the Father hath bestowed upon us, that we should be called the sons of God. (1 John 3:1)

The Agape wherewith Thou (the Father) hast loved Me (Jesus), may be in them, and I in them. (John 17:26)

And above all these things put on Agape, which is the bond of perfectness. (Colossians 3:14)

Hereby perceive we the Agape of God, because He laid down His life for us: and we ought to lay down our lives for the brethren. (1 John 3:16)

[We are] to walk in Agape, as Christ also has loved us, and hath given Himself for us an offering and a sacrifice to God for a sweet-smelling savour. (Ephesians 5:2)

II. Our Responsibility

   A. Accept God loves us (see "Knowing God Loves Me" Scriptures).

   B. Keep His Commandments.

> *For this is the Agape of God, that we keep His commandment.* (1 John 5:3)

> *And this is Agape, that we walk after His Commandments.* (2 John 6)

> *Whoso keepeth His word, in him verily is the Agape of God perfected.* (1 John 2:5)

> *If ye keep My commandments, ye shall abide in My Agape, even as I have kept My Father's commandments and abide in His love.* (John 15:10)

     1. Which Commandments?

        a. *Thou shalt love the Lord, thy God, with all thy heart, and with all thy soul, and with all thy mind [dianoia].* (Matthew 22:37)

> *We love Him, because He first loved us.* (1 John 4:19)

> *As the Father hath loved Me, so I have loved you; continue ye in My Agape.* (John 15:9)

> *God is Love and He that dwelleth in Agape dwelleth in God, and God in him.* (1 John 4:16)

        b. *Love thy neighbor as thyself.* (Matthew 22:39)

> *And this commandment have we from Him, that he who loveth God love his brother also.* (1 John 4:21)

> *Let us love one another: for Agape is of God and every one that loveth is born of God, and knoweth God.* (1 John 4:7)

> *No man hath seen God at any time, If we love one another, God dwelleth in us, and His Agape is perfected in us.* (1 John 4:12)

> *A new commandment I give unto you, that ye love one another, as I have loved you.* (John 13:34)

> *By this shall all men know that ye are my disciples, if ye have Agape one for another.* (John 13:35)

Hereby perceive we the Agape of God, because He laid down His life for us: and we ought to lay down our lives for the brethren. (1 John 3:16)

Greater Agape hath no man than this, that a man lay down his life for his friends. (John 15:13)

By Agape, serve one another. (Galatians 5:13)

III. Walk in Agape (Ephesians 5:2)
(Following Scriptures paraphrased with emphasis added)

PUT ON Agape, which is the bond of perfectness. (Colossians 3:14)

FOLLOW AFTER Agape. (1 Timothy 6:11)

PUT ON breastplate of faith and Agape. (1 Thessalonians 5:8)

BE ROOTED AND GROUNDED in Agape. (Ephesians 3:17)

KNOW the Agape of Christ which passeth knowledge. (Ephesians 3:19)

ABOUND in Agape. (Philippians 1:9)

SPEAK the truth in Agape. (Ephesians 4:15)

GIVE all diligence to...Agape. (2 Peter 1:5-7)

HAVE the same Agape, being of one accord and one mind. (Philippians 2:2)

BE KNIT together in Agape. (Colossians 2:2)

LET ALL THINGS BE DONE in Agape. (1 Corinthians 16:14)

Finally brethren, BE PERFECT...and the God of Agape shall be with you. (2 Corinthians 13:11)

A. Faith is the Key

Keep yourselves in the Agape of God, look for the mercy of our Lord Jesus unto Eternal Life. (Jude 21)

Abound in faith and utterance and knowledge and in all diligence and in your Agape to us... to prove the sincerity of your Agape. (2 Corinthians 8:7-8)

We have heard of your faith in Christ Jesus, and of the Agape which ye have to all the Saints. (Colossians 1:4)

For in Jesus Christ, nothing means anything but faith which worketh by Agape. (Galatians 5:6)

Agape with faith (Ephesians 6:23)

Work of faith, labor of Agape (1 Thessalonians 1:3)

Your faith groweth and the Agape of everyone of you aboundeth. (2 Thessalonians 1:3)

For the Agape of Christ constraineth us. (2 Corinthians 5:14)

Christ may dwell in your hearts by faith, that ye being rooted and grounded in Agape, may be able to know the Agape of Christ which passeth knowledge, that ye might be able to be filled with all the fulness of God. (Ephesians 3: 17-19)

B.   Be an example one to another

Above all these things, have Agape among yourselves. (1 Peter 4:8)

Provoke one another unto Agape and good deeds. (Hebrews 10:24)

Confirm your Agape towards him [one another]. (2 Corinthians 2:8)

We have great joy in thy Agape. (Philemon 7)

Forebear with one another in Agape. (Ephesians 4:2)

Whole body [church] fitly joined together...in Agape. (Ephesians 4:16)

Esteem [our ministers] very highly in Agape. (1 Thessalonians 5:13)

Be an example of the believers, in word, in deed, in Agape, in spirit, and in faith. (1 Timothy 4:12)

IV. Warnings

*Though I speak with the tongues of men and of angels, and have not Agape, **I am become as a sounding brass, or a tinkling symbol**. And though I have the gift of prophecy, and understand all mysteries, and all knowledge; and though I have all faith, so that I could remove mountains, and have not Agape, **I am nothing**. And* *though I bestow all my goods to feed the poor, and though I give my body to be burned, and have not Agape, **it profiteth me nothing**.* (1 Corinthians 13:1-3)

Love not the world, neither things that are in the world, or the Agape of the Father is not in you. (1 John 2:15)

Don't let your Agape wax [grow] cold. (Matthew 24:12)

Ones who receiveth not the Agape of the truth, perished. (2 Thessalonians 2:10)

We don't have the Agape of God in ourselves. (John 5:42)

Don't destroy, through petty grievances, your walking in Agape. (Romans 14:15)

If a man says I love God, but hates his brother, he is a liar, for he that loveth not his brother, whom he hath seen, how can he love God, whom he hath not seen? (1 John 4:20)

He that loveth not, knoweth not God: for God is Agape. (1 John 4:8)

Whoso hath this world's goods and seeth a brother in need, and shutteth up his bowels of compassion from him, how dwelleth the Agape of God in him? (1 John 3:17)

My children, let us not love in word, neither in tongue, but in deeds and in truth. (1 John 3:18)

V. **Agape - Miscellaneous Scriptures**

There is no fear in Agape, but perfect Agape casteth out fear; he that feareth, is not *made perfect in Agape.* (1 John 4:18)

The Lord directs our hearts into the Agape of God. (2 Thessalonians 3:5)

Hope maketh not ashamed, because the Agape of God is shed abroad in our hearts by the Holy Spirit, which is given to us. (Romans 5:5)

The fruit of the Spirit is Agape...against such, there is no law. (Galatians 5:22-23)

Beloved, let us love one another, for Agape is of God; and everyone that loveth is born of God and knows God. (1 John 4:7-8)

Agape edifies. (1 Corinthians 8:1)

Agape, a spirit of meekness (1 Corinthians 4:21)

Agape covers a multitude of sins. (1 Peter 4:8)

Let Agape be without dissimulation [hypocrisy]. (Romans 12:9)

Herein is our Agape made perfect...because as He is, so are we in this world. (1 John 4:17)

Greater Agape hath no man, than a man lay his life down for his friends. (John 15:13)

For God hath not given us the spirit of fear, but of power, and of Agape and of a sound mind. (2 Timothy 1:7)

Four More Attributes of God's Love

Let us look a little more closely at some further attributes of God's Love. *Attributes* simply mean peculiar qualities that distinguish God's Love from other loves. What distinctions do God's Love have that the other natural loves do not have?

Agape Love has four prominent attributes which make it totally unique and completely different from any other love. God's Love is *electing* Love, *initiating* Love, *identifying* Love, and *maintaining* Love.

1) What is ***electing*** Love? With electing Love the "lover" selects or chooses its object to love. We didn't choose God. He chose us.[1] Ephesians 1:4-5 confirms this, "According as He hath chosen us in Him before the foundation of the world, that we should be holy and without blame before Him in love: Having predestinated us unto the adoption of children by Jesus Christ to Himself." God chose us before the foundation of the world to be His *treasured possessions* and His Love objects.

Just as God called the Israelites to be His chosen and beloved people, He has done the very same thing with us. Just as He elected to send the Israelites His Love, He has done the very same thing with us. God's pure and unconditional Love was the sole motivation for His choosing and selecting the Jewish people to be His children. Even when they rejected Him over and over again, He still remained faithful to His promises and His Word. In like manner, God unconditionally chooses and selects us to love and then remains faithful to His Word concerning us.

The meaning for the word *charity* is love with *no strings attached.* (See 1 Corinthians 13.) In other words, charity is love freely given to the poor and the needy. We certainly are poor and needy. All of us are in desperate need of God's charity, His *Agape* Love. God knows this and He unconditionally chose to send us His Love—with no strings attached. Regardless of what we've done or *not* done for Him, God has freely elected to love us.

2) God's Love is also ***initiating*** Love. Initiating Love means that the lover is the first one to act. He is the first one to begin the loving process. God is the Lover and He is the One who has chosen to begin that circle of Love.

God's Love is a one-sided and a one-way Love! Remember, 1 John 4:19 which tells us that, "We love Him [only], because He first loved us" (emphasis added). In other words, God first initiated His Love towards us by choosing to send us His Son.

"In this was manifested the love of God towards us, because that God sent His only begotten Son into the world, that we might live through Him. Herein is love, not that we loved God, but that He loved us and sent His Son to be the propitiation for our sins." (1 John 4:9-10)

Another one of my favorite Scriptures is Jeremiah 31:3, which promises, "Yea, I have loved thee with an everlasting love: therefore with lovingkindness have I drawn thee."

It's only God's Love that will draw us to Him. He is the Lover and we are His chosen objects of Love. God is loving and courting us, just waiting to see what our response will be. Will we open ourselves up to Him for His merciful and righteous Love? Or will we close ourselves off from His Love and miss all He so desperately wants to give us?

Initiating Love always prompts a response from the one being loved. For example, just as God instigated a response from the Israelites[2] by lovingly sending them Moses to watch over them, the commandments to guide them, and prophets to show them the future, He does the very same thing with us. God has not only *chosen and elected* us to be His Bride, but He has also initiated His unfathomable Love to us, prompting a response.

Will we believe in Him? Will we accept Him? Will we receive Him? Or will we reject Him, just as the Israelites did? By His Love, we are prompted to choose one way or the other.[3]

"For God so loved the world, that He gave His only begotten Son, that whosoever believeth in Him should not perish, but have everlasting life." (John 3:16)

If our response is "yes, I need your Love," God then pours His supernatural electing, initiating, and identifying Love into our hearts through Jesus Christ and consummates our marriage with Him. The union between us is then sealed by His Holy Spirit.

The groom has finally become *one* with His Bride. (Galatians 2:20) They have both *totally given themselves over to each other* and have become one. This is called "Covenant Love." It's a marriage or a bonding together by God's "cords of Love."[4] "I will betroth thee unto Me for ever." (Hosea 2:19)

3) The next attribute of God's Love, and perhaps the most unfathomable of all to me, is that God's Love is ***identifying*** Love. Identifying Love is Love that *puts itself in the other's place*, and becomes "totally one with him."

That the Creator of the Universe would love us so much that He would involve and identify Himself with us by becoming a *created* being, take our sins upon Himself, and die to save us, is astounding and absolutely incredible. Jesus *put Himself in our place* on that cross, so that we could live![5] That, to me, is *ultimate Love*!

Hebrews 2:17-18 says it all, "Wherefore in all things it behoved Him to be made like unto His brethren, that He might be a merciful and faithful High Priest in things pertaining to God, to make reconciliation for the sins of the people. For in that He

Himself hath suffered being tempted, He is able to succour [identify with] them that are tempted."

4) The last attribute of God's *Agape* Love, and perhaps the most wonderful, is that God's Love is ***faithful and maintaining*** Love. In other words, it's a Love that simply keeps on coming no matter what the object of that Love does and no matter how he responds. Faithful Love is being trustworthy, loyal, steadfast, and loving no matter what the consequences.

God faithfully loves us no matter how we respond because His actions are always consistent with His Word. "I will even betroth thee unto Me in faithfulness: and thou shalt know the Lord." (Hosea 2:20)

God will always remain faithful and maintain His Love in our relationship, no matter how we feel, what we think, or what we do. God's Love maintains the relationship, we don't.

"For thou art a holy People unto the Lord thy God: the Lord thy God hath chosen thee to be a special People unto Himself, above all people that are upon the face of the earth. The Lord did not set his love upon you, nor choose you, because ye were more in number than any people; for ye were the fewest of all people: But because *the Lord loved you.*" (Deuteronomy 7:6-8 emphasis added)

In review, God *elects* and chooses whom He will love. Next, He *initiates* His Love to that loved one causing that loved one to respond. He then *identifies* with the object of His Love by becoming one with it. And finally, because God's Love is a *maintaining* Love, a faithful and loyal relationship is established.

Endnotes:

1. John 15:16

2. Deuteronomy 30:15-20

3. See Chapter 16, "Tough Love."

4. Hosea 11:4

5. Isaiah 63:9; 1 John 2:2; and especially 1 John 4:10

KNOWING GOD LOVES ME

(The following Scriptures are paraphrased with emphasis added)

*Herein is Love, not that we loved God, but that **He loved us** and sent His Son to be the propitiation [substitute offering] for our sins.* (1 John 4:10)

He bowed the heavens also, and came down. (Psalm 18:9)

He sent from above, He took me, He drew me out of many waters. (Psalm 18:16)

The Lord appeared unto me saying, 'Yea, I have loved thee with an everlasting Love.' (Jeremiah 31:3)

I have engraved thee upon the palms of my hand. (Isaiah 49:16)

I will never leave thee or forsake thee. (Hebrews 13:5)

For the mountains shall depart and the hills be removed; but my Lovingkindness [chesed] shall not depart from thee, neither shall my covenant of peace [rest] be removed, saith the Lord that hath mercy on thee. (Isaiah 54:10)

As the heaven is high above the earth, so great is His Mercy [lovingkindness] towards them that fear Him. (Psalm 103:11)

Many are the afflictions of the righteous. But the Lord delivers them out of them all. He keepeth all his bones; not a one of them is broken. (Psalm 34:19-20)

*When you pass through the waters [trouble] I will be with you; and through the rivers, they won't overflow you; when you walk through the fire, you won't be burned; neither shall the flame kindle upon thee. For I am the Lord...You are precious in My sight and **I love you**.* (Isaiah 43:2-4)

God commendeth His Love toward us in that, while we were yet sinners, Christ died for us. (Romans 5:8)

For God so loved the world, that He gave His only begotten Son. (John 3:16)

Greater Love hath no man than this, that a man lay down his life for his friends. (John 15:13)

Behold, what manner of Love the Father hath bestowed upon us, that we should be called the sons of God. (1 John 3:1)

...having loved His own which were in the world, He loved them unto the end. (John 13:1)

What shall separate us from the Love of Christ? Shall tribulation, or distress, or perse-cution, or famine, or nakedness, or peril, or sword?...I am persuaded that neither death, nor life, nor angels, nor principalities, nor powers, nor things present, nor things to come, nor height, nor depth, nor any other creature shall be able to separate us from the Love of God which is in Christ Jesus, our Lord. (Romans 8:35, 38-39)

WHO I AM IN CHRIST

The Word of God states that if I am *born again* I am:

Reconciled to God (2 Corinthians 5:18)

A son of God (1 John 3:1)

A new creature (2 Corinthians 5:17)

Called of God (2 Timothy 1:9)

Chosen (1 Thessalonians 1:4; Ephesians 1:4; 1 Peter 2:9)

The temple of the Holy Spirit (1 Corinthians 6:19)

Holy and without blame before Him in Love (Ephesians 1:4)

A partaker of His divine nature (2 Peter 1:4)

In Christ Jesus by His doing (1 Corinthians 1:30)

Accepted in the Beloved (Ephesians 1:6)

Beloved of God (Colossians 3:12; Romans 1:7; 1 Thessalonians 1:4)

Complete in Him (Colossians 2:10)

Alive with Christ (Ephesians 2:5)

The apple of my Father's eye (Deuteronomy 32:10; Psalm 17:8)

Forgiven of all my sins and washed in His Blood (Ephesians 1:7; Hebrews 9:14; Colossians 1:14; 1 John 1:9; 2:12)

Healed by the stripes of JESUS (1 Peter 2:24; Isaiah 53:5)

Delivered from the power of darkness and translated into God's kingdom (Colossians 1:13)

Set free (John 8:31-33)

Kept by God and the evil one does not touch me (1 John 5:18)

Free from condemnation (Romans 8:1)

Dead to sin (Romans 6:2,11; 1 Peter 2:24)

God's workmanship created in Christ Jesus for good works (Ephesians 2:10)

Being changed into His Image (2 Corinthians 3:18; Philippians 1:6)

Victorious (Revelation 21:7)

Strong in the Lord (Ephesians 6:10)

More than a conqueror (Romans 8:37)

The righteousness of God in Him (2 Corinthians 5:21)

The light of the world (Matthew 5:14)

An ambassador for Christ (2 Corinthians 5:20)

The salt of the earth (Matthew 5:13)

Sealed with the Holy Spirit of promise (Ephesians 1:13)

Joint heirs with Christ (Romans 8:17)

Raised up with Christ (Ephesians 2:6)

Partakers of His inheritance (Colossians 1:12)

Established to the end (1 Corinthians 1:8)

Firmly rooted, built up, established in the faith and abounding with thanksgiving (Colossians 2:7)

In this world as He is (1 John 4:17)

THE MARRIAGE RELATIONSHIP

The *mystical relationship* of Christ to His Church (His Bride) is parallel to the union of the husband to his wife. (Ephesians 5:28-32)

1) Christ is the *head* of the Church (as the husband is to his wife).

    Head over all things (Ephesians 1:22)

    In Love, we may grow up into Him who is the head. (Ephesians 4:15)

    Christ is the head of the Church and He is the Savior of the body. (Ephesians 5: 23)

    In all things, He should have preeminence. (Colossians 1:18)

    The head from which all the body having nourishment ministered and knit together increaseth with the increase of God. (Colossians 2:19)

2) Church is *precious* to Christ (as the wife should be to her husband).

    Kept as the apple of His eye (Deuteronomy 32:10)

    Will be a crown of glory, a royal diadem in His hand (Isaiah 62:3)

    Fitted as stones of His crown and lifted up as an ensign upon His land (Zechariah 9:16)

    We shall be His and He shall spare us. (Malachi 3:17)

3) Christ *loves* His Church (as husband is to love his wife).

    Christ loved the Church and gave Himself for it. (Ephesians 5:25)

    His dearly beloved and longed for (Philippians 4:1)

4) The Church was *divinely instituted* (as marriage is).

    Upon Christ shall the Church be built. (Matthew 16:18)

    Christ is the cornerstone. (Ephesians 2:20)

5) The Church is like a *bride*.

   The bridegroom rejoices over his bride. (Isaiah 62:5)

   Espoused to one husband (2 Corinthians 11:2)

   Prepared as a bride, adorned for her husband (Revelation 21:2)

6) *Union* with Christ (bride united with husband)

   God says He is married to us. (Jeremiah 3:14)

   Betrothed forever with lovingkindness and mercies (Hosea 2:19)

   Love Him with all our heart, mind and soul (Deuteronomy 6:5)

   Married to one another, even unto Him, that we should bring forth fruit unto God. (Romans 7:4)

   Kingdom of Heaven like unto a marriage (Matthew 22:2)

   Ten Virgins; only five were ready for the groom. (Matthew 25:10)

   Marriage of the Lamb; Bride is ready. (Revelation 19:7)

7) *Duty* of the bride

   Give honour to her husband. (Esther 1:20)

   Look well to the ways of her household and not be idle (Proverbs 31:27)

   Submit to her husband, as unto the Lord (Ephesians 5:22)

   Faithful in all things (1 Timothy 3:11)

   Be in subjection, so that if husband obeys not, they may be won without a word, by our behavior. (1 Peter 3:1)

   Let not the wife depart. (1 Corinthians 7:10)

8) *Abiding* in Christ (Marriage Relationship)

   Abide in Him (John 15:4)

   If we abide in Him, our prayers will be answered. (John 15:7)

If we keep His commandments, we shall abide in His Love. (John 15:10)

If we say we abide in Him, we ought to walk even as He walked. (1 John 2:6)

If we abide in Him, we will have confidence when He comes. (1 John 2:28)

We will abide in Him, if we don't sin. (1 John 3:6)

Those that abide in doctrine of Christ, have both the Father and the Son. (2 John 9)

"For this cause shall a man leave father and mother, and shall cleave to his wife: and they twain shall be one flesh. Wherefore they are no more twain, but one flesh. What therefore God hath joined together, let not man put asunder." (Mark 10:7-9)

Bibliography

Bible:

The Companion Bible, King James Version, Kregel Publications, Grand Rapids, 1990.

The Companion Bible, King James Version, Zondervan, Grand Rapids, 1974.

The Interlinear Bible, Hebrew, Greek, English, Associated Publishers and Authors, Wilmington, Delaware, 1976.

The Septuagint Version: Greek and English, Sir Lancelot C.L. Brenton, Zondervan, Grand Rapids, Michigan, 1970.

The Thompson Chain Reference Bible, B.B. Kirkbride Bible Co., Indianapolis, Indiana, 1988.

The Zondervan Parallel New Testament, Greek and English, Zondervan Publishing Co., Grand Rapids, Michigan.

Technical:

Botterweck, G. Johannes & Helmer Ringgren, *Theological Dictionary of the Old Testament*, Vol.1-3, Eerdmans, Grand Rapids, 1974.

Bromiley, Geoffrey, *Theological Dictionary of the New Testament* (abridged), Eerdmans, Grand Rapids, 1985.

Brown, Colin, *New International Dictionary of New Testament Theology*, Vol.1-3, Zondervan, Grand Rapids, 1978.

Chafer, Lewis Sperry, *Systematic Theology*, 'Pneumatology,' Vol.4 of 8, Dallas Seminary Press, Dallas, 1947.

Encyclopedia Judaica, (16 vols), Keter Publishing House, Jerusalem, Israel.

Jamieson, Fausset and Brown, *Critical and Experimental Commentary*, (6 vols), Eerdmans, Grand Rapids, 1948.

Keil, C.F. and Delitzsch, F., *Commentary on the Old Testament*, Eerdmans, Grand Rapids, 1977.

Murray, John, *The New International Commentary on the New Testament*, The Epistle to the Romans, Eerdmans, Grand Rapids.

Strong, James H., *Strong's Exhaustive Concordance*, Baker Book House, Grand Rapids, 1985.

The International Standard Bible Encyclopedia (old and new), Vol.1-4, Eerdmans, Grand Rapids, 1939, 1979.

The Pulpit Commentary, Eerdmans, Grand Rapids, 1963.

Theological Dictionary of the New Testament, Vol.1-10, Eerdmans, Grand Rapids, 1976.

Theological Wordbook of the Old Testament, Vol.I and II, Moody Press, Chicago, Illinois.

The Zondervan Pictorial Encyclopedia of the Bible, Zondervan, Grand Rapids, 1975.

Vine, W.E., *An Expository Dictionary*, Revell Company, Old Tappan, New Jersey, 1966.

Vine, W.E., *The Expanded Vines*, Bethany House, Minneapolis, Minnesota, 1984.

Wilson, William, *Old Testament Word Studies*, Kregel Publications, Grand Rapids, 1978.

Zodhiates, Spiros, *Lexicon to the Old and New Testaments*, AMG Publishers.

General:

Barks, Herbert, *Prime Time*, T. Nelson, Nashville, 1978.

Bible Reading Plan: *Victory Bible Reading Plan*, Omega Publications, Medford, Oregon.

Billheimer, Paul E., *Don't Waste Your Sorrows*, Christian Literature Crusade, Fort Washington, Pennsylvania, 1977.

Bonhoeffer, Dietrich, *The Cost of Discipleship*, MacMillian Publishing Co., N.Y., N.Y., 1979.

Brownback, Paul, *The Danger of Self Love*, Moody Press, Chicago, 1982.

Crabb, Lawrence J., *Basic Principles of Biblical Counseling*, Zondervan, Grand Rapids, Michigan.

Crabb, Lawrence J., *Effective Biblical Counseling*, Zondervan, Grand Rapids, Michigan.

Denk, Dan, "Can we love ourselves too much?", *Moody Monthly*, June 1982.

Edman, V. Raymond, *They Found the Secret*, Clarion Classics, Zondervan, Grand Rapids, Michigan, 1984.

Finney, Charles, *Love is not a Special Way of Feeling*, Dimension Books, Minneapolis, Minnesota.

Gordon, A. J., *Ministry of the Spirit*, Bethany House, Minneapolis, 1985.

Harper, Michael, *The Love Affair*, Eerdmans, Grand Rapids, Michigan, 1982.

Hayford, Jack, *Prayer is Invading the Impossible*, Logos International, Plainfield, N.J., 1977.

Hession, Roy, *Be Filled Now.*

Hession, Roy, *The Calvary Road*, Christian Literature Crusade, Fort Washington, Pennsylvania, 1977.

Hession, Roy, *We Would See Jesus.*

Hoekema, Anthony A., *Created in God's Image*, Eerdmans, Grand Rapids, Michigan.

Howard, J. Grant, *The Trauma of Transparency*, Multnomah Press, Portland, 1979.

Jackson, Edgar, *Understanding Loneliness*, 1st Fortress Press, Philadelphia, 1980.

Katz, Arthur, *Ben Israel,* Logos International, Plainfield, New Jersey, 1970.

Law, William, *Wholly for God*, Andrew Murray, Dimension Books, Minneapolis, Minnesota, 1976.

Lewis, C.S., *The Four Loves*, Harcourt Brace Jovanovich, N.Y., N.Y., 1960.

McDowell, Josh, *His Image, My Image*, Here's Life Publishing, Inc., San Bernardino, California, 1984.

Missler, Chuck, *Architecture of Man,* Koinonia House.

Missler, Chuck, *The Coming Temple,* Koinonia House.

Missler, Nancy & Chuck, *A More Excellent Way,* Koinonia House.

Missler, Nancy, *Why Should I Be the First to Change,* The King's High Way Ministries, Inc.

Missler, Nancy, *Be Ye Transformed,* The King's High Way Ministries, Inc.

Murray, Andrew, *Absolute Surrender,* Moody Press, Chicago, Illinois.

Murray, Andrew, *Not My Will*, Zondervan, Grand Rapids, Michigan, 1977.

Needham, David, *Birthright*, Multnomah Press, Portland, 1979.

Packer, J.I., *Knowing God*, Intervarsity Press, Downers Grove, Il., 1993.

Rankin, Peg, *Yet Will I Trust*, Regel Books, Glendale, Ca., 1983.

Scofield, C.I., *New Life in Christ Jesus*, The Gospel Hour, Greenville, South Carolina, 1915.

Smith, Hannah Whithall, *The Christian's Secret of a Happy Life*, Revell, Westwood, N.J., 1952.

Solomon, Charles, *Handbook to Happiness*, Tyndale House Publishers, Wheaton, Il., 1989.

Solomon, Charles, *The Ins and Outs of Rejection.*

Solomon, Charles, *The Rejection Syndrome*, Tyndale House, Wheaton, Illinois.

Sparks, Austin, *What is Man?* Pratt Printing Company, Indianapolis, Indiana.

Swindoll, Charles, *Three Steps Forward, Two Steps Back*, Nelson, Nashville, Tn. 1980.

Webber, Robert, *God Still Speaks*, Thomas Nelson Publishers, Nashville, Tennessee, 1980.

White, John, *The Fight.*

Glossary

The purpose of this glossary is to present briefly the thoughts that lie behind important words found in this book. Many people use these same words and phrases differently. This glossary is to help clarify how I have used these words in this text. No attempt is made to be exhaustive. More information may be gathered by consulting the Outlines at the end of each chapter and the Index.

ABUNDANT LIFE. Intimately experiencing God's Life flowing through us to others. Firsthand knowledge of God's Love, Wisdom, and Power.

AGAPAO. To totally give ourselves over to something. To become one with it. To yield our wills and our lives to something.

AGAPE. God's supernatural Love that is *not* dependent upon how we feel, what we think, or what we want; upon others' reactions; or upon our circumstances. God's Love is an unconditional, one-sided, freeing, and other-centered Love. It is always a *gift of Love* i.e., a present with no strings attached.

AGAPE **OF MANY IS GROWING COLD.** God's Love is quenched and blocked off in the hearts of these Christians because they insist upon holding on to hurts, resentments, bitternesses, etc., that quench God's Love.

ALIGNING OUR FEELINGS. God is the one who brings our feelings in line with our choices. He is the one who makes us *feel* genuine after we have made a faith choice or a contrary choice.

AS HE IS, SO ARE WE IN THIS WORLD. Because we are cleansed and open vessels through which God's Life can flow, we are "witnesses of Christ" in our own worlds. We are extensions of His Love.

BIND. To prohibit or forbid self (own thoughts, emotions, and desires that are contrary to God's) from reigning.

BLOCKING GOD'S LIFE. God's Spirit is quenched and His Life prevented from coming forth from our hearts.

BODY. The *vehicle* or the carrier for the expression (showing forth) of our life.

CARNAL CHRISTIAN. A Christian living two lives. One who has Christ's Life in his heart and yet, because of sin, is showing forth self life in his soul. Double-mindedness.

CHESED **LOVE**. Old Testament word for God's merciful (longsuffering) and yet strict (disciplinary) Love. Only God knows the perfect balance between these two aspects of His Love.

CHRIST ESTEEM. Liking (*storge*) what God does through us. When it's God's Love and His Wisdom that comes forth through us, we will have affection for ourselves.

CHRIST IN US. This is God's Life in our hearts (His Love, Wisdom, and Power), our hope of glory. This is the hidden man of the heart and why God says we, as Christians, have a new heart.

CLEANSED HEART. A heart that is cleansed of sin. Christ's Life in this person's heart is now free to flow out into his life, because there is nothing blocking or quenching it. This person has made faith choices to follow what God desires over his own will.

CLEANSED VESSEL. An open channel through which God can pour His Life to others.

CONFESS. To admit our own responsibility for sin and for being separated from God.

CONTRARY CHOICES. A choice that goes against what we think, feel, and want to do. A choice to walk by faith and not feelings. By our supernatural willpower, we have God's authority and power to make this kind of a choice. God then *aligns our feelings* with that choice.
These are simply choices to follow what God wants us to do, over what our own flesh is telling us to do.

CORDS OF SIN. Things from our hidden chambers (subconscious) that Satan uses to bind us and hold us in his power.

COVERED HEART (grease). A sin-laden heart. God's Life is quenched in this person's heart because of his emotional choices to follow his own will over God's. Thus, his heart is covered and God's Life is unable to come forth into his soul.

DENY SELF. Choosing to *set aside* what we want, feel, and desire and instead doing what God wants. Setting aside our own thoughts, emotions, and desires that are contrary to God's so God's Life from our hearts can come forth. Barring *ourselves* from following our self life.

DIE TO SELF. Choosing to set aside and relinquish ourselves to God (becoming a cleansed vessel), so that His Life can come forth from our hearts.

DOUBLE-MINDED. Living two lives. Twice souled. God's Life is in our hearts (if we are Christians), but self life is being shown forth in our souls.

DOUBT. Not believing what God says and not trusting Him to perform His Will in our lives. Not seeing or feeling His Presence; therefore, we take back our lives and do what we feel and what we think is right.

EMOTIONAL CHOICES. Choices to follow our own will over God's, prompted by our own self-centered thoughts and desires.

EXCHANGING LIVES. We are not to copy Jesus' Life, we are to trade lives with Him. We surrender, yield, and give our self life to Him, He then gives us His supernatural Life. And we can say, like Paul, "for me to live is Christ."

EXPERIENTIAL KNOWLEDGE OF GOD. Firsthand experience of God's Life flowing through us—His Love, Wisdom, and Power.

EXPERIENCING OUR REAL THOUGHTS AND EMOTIONS. Honestly talking to God about what we are thinking and feeling so we will know exactly what to confess and give over to Him. Identifying our feelings so we can name what is really going on within us.

EXTENSION OF GOD'S LOVE. Cleansed and open channels or vessels through which God's Love can flow.

FAITH. The choice to obey and trust God no matter how we feel, what we see, or what we think. Being fully persuaded that God is real and that He will do what His Word says.

FAITH CHOICES. Non-feeling choices to obey God's Will, regardless of our own thoughts, emotions, and desires.

FLESH. The part of our old human nature (soul and body) that has not been regenerated yet. The residue (remainder, left-over garbage, dross) that still remains in our soul from the "old man."

FOLLOWING GOD. Worshipping and serving God only. Becoming *one* with Him—one heart, one will, and one soul. Not only being willing to suffer and be rejected as He was, but also willing to die (to self) as He did.

FORGIVENESS. Unconditionally releasing anyone who has wronged us.

FREE CHOICE. (*Exousia* in the Greek) The freedom to either follow what God has counseled us and trust in His ability to perform it, or to follow what we think and feel. *Exousia* means *it is permitted*. We have God's authority and power to make this kind of choice. Born-again believers are the only ones who have a free choice, because they are the only ones who have another power source within them to perform something different than what they think, feel and want to do.

FREEING LOVE. Only God's Love frees the "lover" from expectations and presumptions. And only His Love frees the "one being loved" to respond from his heart and not his defenses.

FULNESS OF GOD. Filled with God's Life. God's Love and Wisdom flowing through our souls to others.

GIVE OVER TO GOD. Relinquish or *sacrifice* to God anything that is not of faith. (Inner Court Ritual).

GOD CONFIDENCE. When we love God (and are cleansed vessels), it will be God's Life flowing through us. Then we will have the assurance that what we do will be in His power and in accordance with His Will.

GOD'S IMAGE. God's supernatural Life (His Love and His Wisdom) coming forth through us—the Image we were created to bear.

GOD'S LIFE. His supernatural Agape Love, His Wisdom, and His Power.

GOD'S LOVE COVERS SIN. This is God's supernatural Love (1 Corinthians 13) that doesn't stop when it gets hurt, but keeps on loving no matter what. God's Love doesn't notice when others do it wrong and it will always draw them back to God.

GOD'S LOVE NEVER FAILS. God's *Agape* Love never stops coming.

GOD'S WILL. God has two types of will. They are *thelo*, His instinctive, emotional desires—things that please Him, and *boule*, His planned purposes—the resolve of His Mind.

HEART. (*Kardia* in the Greek) The origin of life. The place where life is started, created, or begun. The inward *motivation* of our lives (souls).

HEART LIFE. As Christians, the life that now resides in our hearts is Christ's Life: His Love, His Thoughts, and His Power. An analogy would be the *root life* of plants. No one can see this life—it's hidden. Just as God is the only One who knows our hearts.

HIDDEN CHAMBERS (*cheder*). Innermost part. The subconscious part of our soul. The place where we hide and bury all of our painful memories, experiences, hurts, fears, and so on, thinking no one will see; no one will know.

HUMAN LOVE. Affection love (*storge*), sexual love (*eros*) and friendship love (*phileo*) are three natural loves that we are born with. All are dependent upon what we think, feel and want to do, upon others' reactions, and upon our own circumstances. Human loves are always going to be conditional, two-sided (reciprocal), bondage, and self-centered loves. They are always *need loves*—i.e., "you need to love me back."

HUMBLE OURSELVES. Willingness to set aside what we want, think, and feel and become *obedient unto death* doing what God wants.

HYPOCRITE. A person whose words and deeds *do not* match. They are not living the truth, but are two-faced.

IDENTITY AND SECURITY. Knowing who we are and that we are loved. This assurance comes only from knowing that *God loves us* personally and experientially, and that His Love will never leave us or forsake us, no matter what we do. Love and identity have become synonymous.

IMAGE. An exact likeness of something or somebody.

IN THE SPIRIT. If we are believers, then we are always in the Spirit (God's Spirit is in us); however, it's our continual choice to *walk by the Spirit* or not.

INTELLECTUAL KNOWLEDGE OF GOD. Knowing *about* God from books we read and from what we hear others say, but not knowing Him intimately in our daily walk. Knowing Him only in our heads, not in our lives. Not experiencing His Life through us.

INITIATING LOVE. Only God's Love prompts the *lover* to be the first one to extend kindness, gentleness, compassion, goodness, etc.

INNER COURT RITUAL. These are the four steps we must do each time we sin and find ourselves separated from God. They are: recognizing our self life, confessing and repenting of it, giving it over to God, and then, reading God's Word. Doing these four steps daily is what it means to love God—totally giving ourselves over to Him. This is called the Inner Court Ritual because it's what the Priests did in the Inner Court of the Temple in order to deal with sin.

"JESUS IS MY LIFE." God's Life is freely flowing from this person's heart out into his soul. He has yielded and relinquished his self life to God and God has given him His own Life in exchange.

KNOWING GOD LOVES ME. Experiencing firsthand in our daily walk God's Love filling us, His Wisdom guiding us, and His power strengthening us. Now we can love Him in return.

LAY OUR LIFE DOWN. Choosing to yield, surrender and relinquish our self life to God (becoming a cleansed vessel), so His Life can flow from our hearts.

LOOSE. To permit or allow self to reign (own thoughts, emotions, and desires that are contrary to God's).

LOSE SELF. To choose to abandon or deny our selves (self life) so that God's Life can come forth.

LOVE (*agapao*) GOD. To totally give ourselves over to God. To confess, repent of and give over to God anything that has separated us from Him. To deny ourselves, pick up our cross, and follow Him (Matthew 16:24). To obey His Word, trust His Spirit to perform His Word, and worship and serve Him only. To become an open and cleansed vessel where He can pour His Life through us to others. To become *one* with Him—one heart, one will, and one life. *To love God is to lose self.*

LOVE *(agapao)* OTHERS. To totally give ourselves over to others (before or instead of ourselves). To put their will and desires before our own.

MATURE CHRISTIAN. This is a person who continually recognizes his self life and makes the appropriate choices to give that self over to God. One who is walking God's Way of Agape.

MEANING AND PURPOSE. This fulfillment in our lives can only come from loving the way God intended—first loving Him and then loving others.

MIND. (*Nous* in the Greek) Mind is a whole process of thinking—from the conception of an idea to its fulfillment in action.

NEW HEART. This is the brand-new heart (totally new nature) that God gives us when we are born again. This is Christ in us, the Hope of Glory. This new heart is filled with God's supernatural Love, Wisdom and Power.

NEW MAN. This is Christ's Life from our hearts that we are to, moment by moment, *put on* in our lives—thus making us a *new man* (*Chart 5*).

OBEYING GOD. Choosing to obey God's Word (His Will) in our lives, rather than what we think, feel or want to do. This is the response that shows God we love Him.

OLD HEART. This is our old human heart, filled with our old human thoughts, emotions, and desires. It's the *old man* (evil and corrupt from birth) that is crucified and done away with at our new birth.

OLD MAN. This is the old, unconverted self (the old human heart), strong in deeds of sin. This is the part of our old human nature that was destroyed at our new birth and replaced with a totally new heart (Christ in us, our hope of glory).

ONE-SIDED LOVE. Only God's Love can enable the lover to be the first one to initiate Love, forgiveness, kindness, and so on. It's unilateral Love.

OPEN VESSEL. A cleansed channel through which God can pour His Love to others.

OTHER-CENTERED LOVE. Only God's Love can unconditionally put the other's interests before its own.

OUR WILL. Like God, we have two types of will. However, they are not *perfect* like God's. In the Greek, they are *thelema*—our own natural and emotional desires (things we take pleasure in) and *boulomai*—our disciplined willing (choices we make free of emotion).

OVERCOMER. A Christian who continues to make faith choices that prevail over his own self-centered thoughts, emotions, and desires (self life). A person walking by the Spirit.

PICKING UP OUR CROSS. Getting up and doing in action what God has asked, regardless of how we feel or what we think.

POWER OF SIN. An energy force that dwells in our unredeemed bodies, whose whole intent and purpose is to cause us to *veer off course* and *miss the mark*. The mark or the goal of our lives is to *be conformed into the Image of Christ*. Satan uses the power of sin as his tool to stop this process and to revenge (or get back at) God.

PRIDE. Choosing to follow what we think and feel over what God is prompting us to do. Pride is choosing our own way over God's. It's loving self, not God.

PUTTING OFF THE OLD MAN. This is the old heart life that we put off when we were born again. Putting off the old man is two-fold: positionally (in our hearts) at our conversion and experientially (in our souls) in the gradual process of sanctification.

PUTTING ON THE NEW MAN. This is the putting on of Christ in our lives (souls). This new man is Christ's Life in our hearts that we are to daily *put on in our souls*.

REPENT. Change our mind about holding on to that *thing* that has quenched God's Spirit and separated us from God. It's choosing to turn around and follow God.

SANCTIFICATION. The process by which we learn how to "set aside" our own thoughts, emotions, and desires so that God's Life can come forth from our hearts.

SELF-ESTEEM. Liking what we say, what we do, and how we do it.

SELF-IMAGE. Our total mental self-portrait, based on what we feel about ourselves, what others tell us about ourselves and on our circumstances.

SELF LIFE. Our own human thoughts, emotions, and desires that are contrary to God's.

SERVING GOD. Something we do *on the outside*. Presenting our bodies as living sacrifices and getting up and doing what God has called us to do—being actual extensions of His Love. Being open channels, ready and willing to do His Will.

SINGLE-MINDED. Living one life (one soul). God's Life in our hearts is flowing freely into our souls. It's God's Life that others see in our souls.

SIN. Any choice that is not of faith quenches God's Spirit and covers our hearts with a layer of grease (Psalm 119:70). This then puts a barrier between God and ourselves—thus causing us to be separated from Him. The concordance defines sin as *missing the mark* (being conformed into the image of Christ).

SOUL (*psyche*). The *expression*, the outflowing, or the manifestation of our life. Our soul is a neutral area that is either going to be filled with God's Life (if we have made faith choices), or self life (if we have made emotional choices).

SOUL LIFE. The life others see, hear, and feel coming forth from us. This life can be God's Life, if we have made the appropriate choices, or our self life, if we have quenched God's Spirit in us.

SPIRIT. (*Pneuma* in the Greek) Our spirit is the energy source or power source of our lives. It's the generator or engine of our souls. As Christians, our spirit is united with God's Spirit giving us a *new spirit*.

SPIRIT-CONTROLLED THINKING. The ability to catch the negative thoughts before they stir up our emotions, desires and actions.

SPIRIT FILLED. Our soul is filled with God's Life from our hearts. We have chosen to set aside our own self life and God's Life has freely come forth. It is a moment-by-moment decision to be filled with God's Spirit.

SPIRIT GRIEVED OR QUENCHED. God's Life in our hearts is blocked from coming forth into our lives by sin. This is a sin-laden (or grease covered) heart.

STRONGHOLDS. Things (hurts, memories, guilt, fears, bitterness, etc.) we have pushed down and stuffed in our *hidden chambers* (subconscious) that Satan uses as his "cords of sin" to bind and hold us.

SURVIVAL KIT. Eight steps back to freedom of Spirit, including the four Inner Court Ritual steps. A process by which we watch out for, are aware of, and deal with our sin, so we can stay open and cleansed vessels—loving God.

"THERE WAS NOT A 'ME' THERE." Having set aside our self life so that God's Life can come forth—exchanging lives with Him. Experiencing His Love in place of our own; His Wisdom in place of our own; and His Power in place of our own.

TOUGH LOVE. This is a worldly term but it could easily refer to God's chesed Love—His strict, disciplinary Love administered by His Wisdom. In this case, the person being loved will be drawn to the one loving, his sins exposed and the gap between them narrowed. The only way God can love like this through us is when we have become an *open and cleansed vessel* with our self life set aside. If, however, we are *not* a cleansed vessel, it will simply be human love putting up guidelines, restrictions and consequences. The end result of this will be further separation and more hurt.

TRUSTING GOD. Relying upon God's Spirit to perform His Word in our lives, rather than our own ability and power. Cleaving to God with unreserved confidence and being fully persuaded that He will do what He says.

TRUTH. Where the *word* and the *deed* match and become one.

UNCONDITIONAL. No conditions. Loving, regardless of what we feel or think, how the other person responds, or what our circumstances are.

WALKING AFTER THE FLESH. This is emotionally choosing to follow what we think and feel over what God is prompting us to do, so that our bodies reflect and show forth self life rather than God's Life. The flesh is a combination of our unredeemed souls and bodies.

WALKING AFTER THE SPIRIT. This is choosing by faith to follow God's leading no matter what. It's following His prompting over our own will and desires so that our bodies reflect and shine forth God's Life.

WEAPONS OF WARFARE. Scripture tells us that our spiritual instruments for fighting are God's Word, His Blood, and His Name. Ephesians 6 tells us the only way we can stand against the wiles of the enemy is to put on our armor and use these weapons.

WILLING HEART. This is a believer who, like David, is willing to do all that God wills. This is a person who has an open and pure heart, allowing God's Life to flow freely.

WILLPOWER. (*Dianoia* in the Greek). Willpower is our will and the power to perform it. As Christians, we have God's supernatural authority to choose His Will over our own and the supernatural power to perform it. Our willpower is the *key* to our Christian walk because it determines whose life will be lived in our souls.

WORSHIPPING GOD. Something that we do *on the inside*. Laying aside our self life, so God's Life can come forth. Prostrating ourselves before God. Praising Him for who He is.

YIELDING OUR MEMBERS. A person who has yielded his members is one who has chosen to lay down his life and *his body*, so that God might use *his* body to perform His Will.

YIELD SELF. Surrender, relinquish and give over to God our self life (our selves), so that God's Life can pour forth from our hearts.

Topical Index

How Do We Love God?

1) Recognize, acknowledge and experience the negative thoughts, emotions, and desires that have just occurred. Don't vent these feelings and don't stuff them. Get alone with God and experience your emotions. Name how you are feeling. Ask Him to expose the real root cause of your ungodly thoughts and feelings.

2) Confess and repent of any negative thoughts and emotions you have held on to for awhile; these are sins that have separated you from God. Choose to follow what He is felling you to do instead. **Unconditionally forgive others** involved. God will then forgive you.

3) Give over to God all that He has shown you, not only the conscious negative thoughts and emotions, but also their root causes. He will then purge your sin and reconcile you to Himself.

4) Read God's Word. Be sure to replace the lies with the Truth. He will then cleanse and heal your soul with "the washing of the water of the Word."

At this point, by faith (whether you feel like it or not) you have been emptied of self life and filled with God's Life. And then you can say, like Paul, "For me to live is Christ." (Philippians 1:21)

How Do We Love God?

1) Recognize, acknowledge and experience the negative thoughts, emotions, and desires that have just occurred. Don't vent these feelings and don't stuff them. Get alone with God and experience your emotions. Name how you are feeling. Ask Him to expose the real root cause of your ungodly thoughts and feelings.

2) Confess and repent of any negative thoughts and emotions you have held on to for awhile; these are sins that have separated you from God. Choose to follow what He is felling you to do instead. **Unconditionally forgive others** involved. God will then forgive you.

3) Give over to God all that He has shown you, not only the conscious negative thoughts and emotions, but also their root causes. He will then purge your sin and reconcile you to Himself.

4) Read God's Word. Be sure to replace the lies with the Truth. He will then cleanse and heal your soul with "the washing of the water of the Word."

At this point, by faith (whether you feel like it or not) you have been emptied of self life and filled with God's Life. And then you can say, like Paul, "For me to live is Christ." (Philippians 1:21)

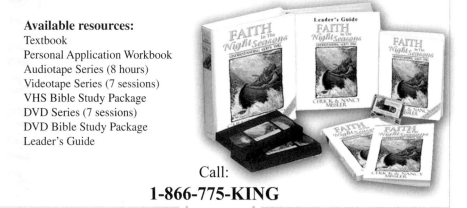

Plain & Simple Series

The Key
HOW TO LET GO AND LET GOD

This book teaches us the moment-by-moment steps to letting go of ourselves, our circumstances and others and *putting on Christ.* It gives us a practical guide to giving our problems to God and leaving them there. One of our most popular books.

Why Should I be the First to Change?
THE KEY TO A LOVING MARRIAGE

This is the story of the amazing "turnaround" of Chuck and Nancy's 20-year Christian marriage which reveals the dynamic secret that releases the power of God's Love already resident in every believer. Riveting, yet easy reading.

Tomorrow May Be Too Late
DISCOVERING OUR DESTINY

A simple, non-threatening and easy to read book that chronicles God's whole plan for mankind. In just a little over a hundred pages, it relates man's spiritual journey from the beginning of time to the very end, showing how God has been personally and intimately involved all along. Perfect for non-believers.

The Choice
HYPOCRISY OR REAL CHRISTIANITY

As Christians, we are faced with a constant choice: either to live our Christian life in our own power and ability, or to set ourselves aside and let Christ live His Life out through us. Written especially for youth.

Against the Tide
GETTING BEYOND OURSELVES

This little book gives the practical tools we need to implement "faith choices" in our lives. These are choices that set aside our natural thoughts and emotions, and allow us to love and be loved as God desires. Great for understanding emotions.

Coming Soon - *Never Give Up,* The Fruit of Longsuffering

What is The King's High Way?

The King's *High* Way is a ministry dedicated to encouraging and teaching Christians how to walk out their faith, i.e., focusing on the practical application of Biblical principles. Our passion is to help believers learn how to love as Jesus loved; how to renew their minds so their lives can be transformed; and, how to have unshakeable faith in their night seasons. Isaiah 62:10 is our commission: helping believers walk on the King's *High* Way by gathering out the stumbling blocks and lifting up the banner of Jesus.

For more information, please write to:

The King's *High* Way Ministries, Inc.
P.O. Box 3111
Coeur d' Alene, Idaho 83816

or call:
1-866-775-KING

On the Internet:
http://www.kingshighway.org